CROSSING BORDERS,
DRAWING BOUNDARIES

CROSSING BORDERS, DRAWING BOUNDARIES

The Rhetoric of Lines across America

Edited by
BARBARA COUTURE
PATTI WOJAHN

UTAH STATE UNIVERSITY PRESS
Logan

© 2016 by the University Press of Colorado

Published by Utah State University Press
An imprint of University Press of Colorado
5589 Arapahoe Avenue, Suite 206C
Boulder, Colorado 80303

All rights reserved

 The University Press of Colorado is a proud member of
The Association of American University Presses.

The University Press of Colorado is a cooperative publishing enterprise supported, in part, by Adams State University, Colorado State University, Fort Lewis College, Metropolitan State University of Denver, Regis University, University of Colorado, University of Northern Colorado, Utah State University, and Western State Colorado University.

ISBN: 978-1-60732-402-7 (paperback)
ISBN: 978-1-60732-403-4 (ebook)

Library of Congress Cataloging-in-Publication Data

Names: Couture, Barbara, editor. | Wojahn, Patti, editor.
Title: Crossing borders, drawing boundaries : the rhetoric of lines across America / edited by Barbara Couture, Patti Wojahn.
Description: Logan : Utah State University Press, [2016] | Includes bibliographical references and index.
Identifiers: LCCN 2015050083 | ISBN 9781607324027 (pbk.) | ISBN 9781607324034 (ebook)
Subjects: LCSH: Communication in politics—United States. | Rhetoric—Political aspects—United States. | Rhetoric—Social aspects—United States. | Democracy—United States.
Classification: LCC JA85.2.U6 C76 2014 | DDC 320.97301/4—dc23
LC record available at http://lccn.loc.gov/2015050083

Cover illustration: "Mending Fences" © Jessica Wesolek (www.cre8it.com), all rights reserved.

For Paul Couture and Pat Morandi

CONTENTS

Foreword: Crossing the Threshold
Nancy Welch   ix

Acknowledgments   xiii

1 Democratic Discourse and Lines across America
   Barbara Couture and Patti Wojahn   3

   PART I   IMAGINING BOUNDARIES: RHETORIC RESISTING/DEFINING SYMBOLIC BORDERS

2 Metonymic Borders and Our Sense of Nation
   Victor Villanueva   29

3 Continuity and Contact in a Cosmopolitan World: Code-Switching and Its Effects on Community Identity
   Christopher Schroeder   43

4 Humor's Role in Political Discourse: Examining Border Patrol in Colbert Nation
   Jonathan P. Rossing   60

5 Employing Ethos to Cross the Borders of Difference: Teaching Civil Discourse
   Karen P. Peirce   76

6 Crossing Linguistic Borders in the Classroom: Moving beyond English Only to Tap Rich Linguistic Resources
   Anita C. Hernández, José A. Montelongo, and Roberta J. Herter   93

7 Traversing Rhetorical Borders of Spirituality in Academic Settings
   Susan A. Schiller   *111*

8 Difference as Rhetorical Stance: Developing Meaningful Interactions and Identification across Racial and Ethnic Lines
   Mónica Torres and Kathryn Valentine   *129*

PART II   LIVING BORDERS: RHETORIC CONFRONTING/ERASING PHYSICAL BOUNDARIES

9 "I Am the 99 Percent": Identification and Division in the Rhetorics of the Occupy Wall Street Protests
   Randolph Cauthen   *151*

10 American Rhetorics of Disappearance: Translocal Feminist Problem-Solving Rhetorics
   Tricia Serviss   *171*

11 "A Melting Pot That's Constantly Being Stirred": Rhetorics of Race and Tolerance at a Regional Museum
   Cori Brewster   *192*

12 *De pie sobre la valla y mirando por la ventana*: Border Realities of the Immigrant Experience
   Vanessa Cozza   *209*

13 Fostering Inclusive Dialogue in Emergent University-Community Partnerships: Setting the Stage for Intercultural Inquiry
   Elenore Long, Jennifer Clifton, Andrea Alden, and Judy Holiday   *227*

14 Rhetorical Education at the City's Edge: The Challenge of Public Rhetoric in Suburban America
   Robert Brooke   *254*

15 In Sum and Review: The Rhetoric of Lines across Us
   Barbara Couture and Patti Wojahn   *270*

   About the Authors   *285*
   Index   *289*

FOREWORD
Crossing the Threshold

Nancy Welch

> *Because white men can't police their imaginations, black men are dying.*
> —Claudia Rankine (2014)

Sitting down to write this foreword, just days after grand-jury failures to indict police officers for the killings of Michael Brown and Eric Garner, I pause for news of the previous night's protests. In the Bay Area, NPR reports, the message of Black Lives Matter activists "got muddled" when they carried their protest into a Berkeley lecture hall where high-tech start-up guru Peter Thiel was promoting his new book. Although the reporter briefly explains why the marchers crossed such a threshold—"Thiel, protestors said, is linked to the national security apparatus" (Gonzales 2014)—his tone signals his skepticism of any sensible connection between racist policing and a Berkeley lecture-hall speaker. He does not mention that the tie between national security agencies and Thiel's Palantir Industries, which peddles web-surveillance and data-mining technologies, is more than a matter of "protestors said" opinion. He does not connect dots between this protest inside what Piya Chatterjee and Sunaina Maira call the "imperial university" and the recently revealed Department of Defense program to militarize local police (Chatterjee and Maira 2014). Concluding with the observation that protestors then "wound their way" to Oakland where they "prompted the temporary closure of two transit stations," the reporter also omits mention of the route's significance: an Oakland transit station is where police shot and killed another unarmed African American, twenty-two-year-old Oscar Grant.

In their introduction to *Crossing Borders, Drawing Boundaries: The Rhetoric of Lines across America,* Barbara Couture and Patti Wojahn extend Donald Davidson's conception of "charity" as a necessary ingredient for public democratic exchange: such exchange is dependent on "the fundamental assumption that to converse, one must be willing to try to understand the other participants in the conversation," mutual charity involving an expansive act of listening that includes "a willingness to try to understand not only *what*, but also *how* others are communicating" (emphasis added). The NPR reporter's failure of charity—his inability, his unwillingness to imagine that these activists intended to make sense, that this protest path had direction, logic, meaning—is, I admit, unsurprising. The clichéd theme of protestors without a purpose, Randolph Cauthen points out in this volume, was prominent in Occupy Wall Street coverage as well. Numbingly commonplace, too, is the storyline of protestors breaching civil boundaries and thereby squandering sympathy. When Vermont healthcare activists disrupted the inauguration of a three-term governor who had just reneged on his perennial campaign promise of single-payer support, media coverage focused almost exclusively on how "the disruptions in the Statehouse worked against the protestors" (Dobbs 2015). (Naturally, no news outlet acknowledged that they'd given no coverage at all to the civil and mannerly press release these protestors had issued days earlier.) To be charitable, I can also recall from my own long-ago days as a news reporter the attractions of an instant template—protestors forfeiting sympathy, protestors failing to make any sense—for cranking out a two-minute story on deadline.

So given how routine such stories are, why does this instance—the failure to hear the arguments of Black Lives Matter—so arrest me? One reason can be found in what's particular about this case of a mass appeal discounted and ignored: Black Lives Matter, Ferguson Action, the Black Youth Project, and other burgeoning grassroots formations would bring to national attention the systematic and routinized ways in which (borrowing from Couture and Wojahn's introduction) black and brown Americans "are so discounted," they are denied "having rights basic to human survival or well-being, let alone the 'American Dream.'" Because it has become customary to hear with the day's news the report of yet another African American shot by police or killed in police custody and because lethal force against some populations is taken so much as a matter of course that no agency even tracks the numbers (Robinson 2014), such protests must necessarily disrupt. "Shut it down" is both the method and message as activists shut down transit stations and shopping malls, as they interrupt the annual MLA convention, a Manhattan brunch, or the flow of fans into a major league football stadium—no business as usual so long as the killing of black boys and men continues.

I have paused so long, then, over this single NPR news report because it not only reinscribes that familiar theme of nonsensical protest, it reinforces the lines of exclusion and denial allowing what Michelle Alexander (2012) terms America's New Jim Crow to flourish, its death toll to grow. And I have paused, too, because of what hits me as a clear—yet unmarked, unremarked upon—connection to the report that NPR airs next: about the psychological defenses a group erects against recognizing the organized harm it carries out against others (Vedantam 2014). American progress, American exceptionalism, abiding investment in the American Dream ethos that Couture and Wojahn flag in their introduction: Such are the psychological defenses marshaled to enlist us in a set of beliefs (that wealth is earned, that Americans enjoy the best health care in the world, that racism is a thing of the past) and erect a bulwark against recognizing even significant numbers of dissenters.

The essays in *Crossing Borders, Drawing Boundaries* explore how borders are socially, historically, and linguistically constructed—and thus how they can be rhetorically examined and contested. Importantly, contributors undertake this exploration without ever losing sight that borders, social and historical constructs they may be, are also zealously policed. A border, observes Victor Villanueva, may be "a fiction within the fiction of a nation," but it is nonetheless a fiction with a purpose as it "*serves racism in an era that no longer admits to racism*" (my emphasis). Together these essays draw attention to a dialectical interplay between figurative and physical realms— between, for instance, the fiction of a boundary demarcating one nation and its citizens from another *and* the material histories of *English only* exclusion and *Papers, please* repression that the fiction creates and is reinforced by.

I might say that the aim of this volume is—appropriately—humble: contributors cognizant that rhetorical consciousness-raising alone will not bring an end to divisions that deny, degrade, and deport. But, especially when I consider the effort it takes to discern the naturalized boundaries and exclusions of just one news story from an ostensibly liberal news outlet and when I consider what is at stake in learning to hear that story's subtext, I can think of no collection more important to read and to teach right now. "Limits," argues Ann Berthoff (1981, 77), "make choice possible and thus free the imagination." Limits can operate in such freeing fashion, however, only when we become aware of them (and what forces may be amassed to secure them) as such. By attending to taken-for-granted boundaries, writes Jonathan Rossing in this volume, we and our students learn how "supposedly rigid borders can be confused and muddied." Though it will take more than a classroom rhetorical education to, as members of the Black Youth Project proclaim in their uptake of the Civil Rights freedom song, "chant down

Babylon," such a border-conscious, border-blurring education can equip students to question the lines of division and defense that would dismiss a protest message as "muddled." Such an education might even equip students—and their teachers with them—to consider the thresholds they, too, might be willing to cross.

References

Alexander, Michelle. 2012. *The New Jim Crow: Mass Incarceration in the Age of Colorblindness.* New York: The New Press.

Berthoff, Ann. 1981. *The Making of Meaning: Metaphors, Models, and Maxims for Writing Teachers.* Portsmouth, NH: Heinemann.

Chatterjee, Piya, and Sunaina Maira. 2014. *The Imperial University: Academic Repression and Scholarly Dissent.* Minneapolis: University of Minnesota Press.

Dobbs, Taylor. 2015. "Single Payer Advocates Protest at Shumlin's Inaugural." Vermont Public Radio, January 8.

Gonzales, Richard. 2014. "First the Protests, Then the Storm: Bay Area's 5 Straight Night of Clashes." National Public Radio, December 11.

Rankine, Claudia. 2014. *Citizen: An American Lyric.* Minneapolis: Graywolf Press.

Robinson, Eugene. 2014. "What America's Police Departments Don't Want You to Know." *The Washington Post,* December 1.

Vedantam, Shankar. 2014. "What Is Torture? Our Beliefs Depend in Part on Who's Doing It." National Public Radio, December 11.

ACKNOWLEDGMENTS

We have many to thank for all the venues and discussions that inspired this book. In part, the collection grew out of conversations held at the 2010 Western States Rhetoric and Literacy Conference, "Transforming Rhetoric: Discovery and Change," which honored Richard E. Young, Alton L. Becker, and Kenneth L. Pike's call in *Rhetoric: Discovery and Change*, a text connecting rhetoric with inquiry, particularly through an expanded notion of the rhetor's analysis. In order to connect with an audience, Young, Becker and Pike posited a process that encouraged rhetors to examine problems from several dimensions—the expansive view that we advocate here—acknowledging all points of view, an approach to rhetorical inquiry which welcomes change.

In exploring these dimensions of inquiry, we found particularly compelling the conference work that brought together studies of border rhetorics, rhetorics of difference, and rhetorics that cross boundaries that prevent: the promise of change through discussion and communication; the promise of eliminating boundaries that divide, exclude, or separate us; and, in the civic sphere, the promise of a democracy that welcomes full participation. For laying the ground for such conversations to occur, we are grateful to Richard E. Young and his colleagues. For the Western States Rhetoric and Literacy Conference, always a small but rich venue, we thank its founders, Peter Goggin and Maureen Mathison.

In approaching scholars to contribute to this volume, we went beyond the boundaries of the conference that inspired it, inviting colleagues, long in as well as new to the field, to explore the meaning of borders and boundaries as they affect discourse exchange. Many wonderful colleagues, friends, and relatives offered their support for this work. We wish to thank in particular Loel Kim, Maureen Daly Goggin, Elenore Long, Barb and Rich Bullock, Peter Goggin, Maureen Mathison, Stephen A. Bernhardt, David Fleming, Chris Burnham, Mónica Torres, Kathryn Valentine, Barbara Pearlman, and Joyce Baskins for years—decades—of academic collaboration and, more so, friendships enriched by shared concerns about ways that rhetoric can assure and deny inclusive participation.

We also wish to thank the editors and technical team at the Utah State University and University of Colorado Presses, including USU Press Editor Michael Spooner, and editors Karli Fish, Laura Furney, and from the University Press of Colorado, Darrin Pratt. Also, our appreciation goes to Linda Gregonis, who prepared the index; to Kami Day, our copyeditor; and to Jessica Wesolek, the artist whose work appears on our cover.

For their unfailingly wise recommendations and assistance in reviewing the chapters we co-authored, we thank Jane Detweiler and Maggie Laware, brought together with Patti through Cheryl Geisler's Career Retreat for Associate Professors launched at a Rhetoric Society of America conference. We are grateful, too, to the Career Retreat endeavor that also brought incisive advice from the career retreat group's mentor Thomas P. Miller.

For general support of our work, our thanks go to New Mexico State University, especially the various entities that supported the 2010 conference, including the Department of English, the College of Arts and Sciences, and the Office of Research Development.

And, finally, for their constant support, we thank our spouses, Paul Couture and Patrick Morandi, whose patience, laughter, and love enrich our lives beyond bounds.

CROSSING BORDERS, DRAWING BOUNDARIES

1
DEMOCRATIC DISCOURSE AND LINES ACROSS AMERICA

Barbara Couture and Patti Wojahn

Those of us who graduated from American high schools or colleges and were introduced to the "classic" exemplars of literature that define the American experience will have read or seen Thornton Wilder's (2003) *Our Town*—the bittersweet life story of an American girl in a small town that is her whole world, though the world she dreams she is in is so much larger.[1] And, if you have seen or read the play, you cannot fail to remember the strangely addressed letter Rebecca tells her brother George about: a minister had sent a letter to Rebecca's friend, Jane Crofut, and Rebecca tells George, "It said: Jane Crofut; The Crofut Farm; Grover's Corners; Sutton County; New Hampshire; United States of America." George, in turns, says, "What's funny about that?" And Rebecca goes on, "But listen, it's not finished: the United States of America, Continent of North America, Western Hemisphere; the Earth; the Solar System; the Universe; the Mind of God—that's what it said on the envelope." "What do you know!" replies George (Wilder 2003, 46).

What do you know, indeed! The expansiveness of this address and its endpoint in a single unity presumed to contain everything that came before it could not fail to capture our imagination. To consider that our personal experience is circumscribed somehow in the mind of God, with several other earthly entities defining one's place in that mind along the way, is both liberating and binding. After telling George about this strange address, Rebecca quips, "And the postman brought it just the same" (Wilder 2003, 46). Despite enormous possibilities for loss and limitation carried across enormous distances, one person manages to connect with another across villages, counties, countries, continents and so on by way of the postman.

Our Town touches us because of its power to display both the joy and the tragedy associated with our attempts to connect to one another and

DOI: 10.7330/9781607324034.c001

make life meaningful for ourselves by defining a place where we belong. That struggle is bound by the way we locate and describe ourselves and by how others locate, describe, and choose to communicate with us. And it is this phenomenon of connecting and communicating across borders as experienced in the United States that our volume *Crossing Borders, Drawing Boundaries* attempts to explore. In the United States, citizens all share the title American, but not all who live within its boundaries and are subject to its laws are perceived to be equally worthy of that title.

In presenting this diverse set of essays exploring the ways groups of Americans experience "American-ness" in our country as they try to communicate with others about their lives and needs, we explore both the power and perversity of framing identity by places—real or imagined—that are defined by borders and boundaries. And we are reminded, too, that in our very presentation of these essays, we are drawing borders and boundaries around their meaning as well. In particular, we are staking a claim about the function of lines across America—real or imagined—in the sphere of another bordered universe: democratic discourse. To defend—as far as we can in a brief introduction—this leveling of sorts, we offer here some reasons it is important to think about democratic discourse in America and reasons lines, borders, and boundaries are important elements that dictate or diffuse the success of democratic discourse among those who choose to pursue it.

A few caveats before we begin: our purpose in introducing the topic of borders and boundaries in America from a rhetorical perspective is not to assume or defend a particular political or juridical perspective on borders and boundaries, nor to assume a definitive stance on what comprises America or American-ness. Rather, it is to offer a perspective drawn from themes that define our expectations for rhetorical interaction as identified by theorists (including ourselves) and from general expectations about American-ness that underlie perceptions of this quality as a popular ethos in the United States—an ethos that presents some challenges for creating a fair space for public discourse in our democratic society.

In short, our objective is to inspire thinking about elements of interaction that contribute to or exacerbate fair exchange in a variety of rhetorical situations here in the United States. In presenting this illustrative sample of discourse situations that inspire thinking about borders and boundaries, we have loosely arranged our collection into two sections. We consider in part 1, "Imagining Boundaries," what we perceive as more figurative border divisions. Here our authors theorize about specific categories of difference that have consequence for how individuals interact when striving to learn in the classroom, understand key issues in a national context, or get their needs met in local communities—categories defined by language, academic context, or definition. In part 2, "Living Borders," our contributors examine more specifically the communication experiences of individuals confronting physical boundaries—be they national, community based, or self-selected. Our authors explore how these boundaries—crossed or drawn—have implications for rhetorical scholarship, language teaching, and valuing difference here in the United States. In the sections below, we introduce these works, framing them within the rhetorical context of democratic discourse. Admittedly, we are creating a very loose division here, for as the reader will see when delving into these essays, metaphorical, linguistic, and rhetorical boundaries and borders often are related to physical, geographical, and societal borders and boundaries. We leave it to the reader to tease out these relationships within the contexts of the situations each of the essays explores. At the end of this volume, we offer our reflection on the whole, along with some suggestions for future research and teaching practice.

We shall open our discussion of democratic discourse by calling out the terminological assumptions we are making in discussing democratic discourse in "America." And we shall start with what popularly is assumed about democracy and about the United States—that it is a place where all can pursue the American Dream. What is that dream exactly? Perhaps the most simply put description appears in an apt popular reference: *Wikipedia*. The openly editable and free encyclopedia claims the "American Dream is a national ethos of the United States, a set of ideals in which freedom includes the opportunity for prosperity and success, and an upward social mobility achieved through hard work" (*Wikipedia* 2014). The encyclopedia entry continues: "The idea of the American Dream is rooted in the United States Declaration of Independence which proclaims that 'all men are created equal' and that they are 'endowed by their Creator with certain inalienable Rights' including 'Life, Liberty and the pursuit of Happiness.'" In short, this dream assumes an environment in which all boundaries can be overcome in its quest since all have equal opportunity to pursue it. Underlying this dream of equal opportunity, we argue, is a staunch faith in democracy as the vehicle through which equal opportunity is protected. In the United States, where the American Dream is espoused, it is common knowledge that democracy is perceived as a good; in fact, the many attempts that the US government has made to spread democracy across the world—regardless of their success or failure—have been overtly justified as trying to do good. Philosophers and political scientists have taken a less biased stance toward democracy as an ultimate good, defining the accepted "objective" meaning of *democracy*, labeling criteria for achieving a true democracy, and also evaluating whether democracy once achieved is universally accepted as a flat-out good.

Let's explore for a moment the values democracy as a good assumes, values that gird the ethos of the American Dream. The *Stanford Encyclopedia of Philosophy* (SEP) offers a handy summary of "normative democratic theory" that addresses the reasons democracy might or might not be "morally desirable," beginning first with a common definition of democracy and moving on to analyze the arguments made that this form of government is morally defensible (Christiano 2008, 2). *Democracy*, as defined in our *SEP* reference, "refers very generally to a method of group decision making characterized by a kind of equality among the participants at an essential stage of the collective decision making" (Christiano 2008, 2). The entry's author talks about the viability of a system in which all participants are considered equal and up to the task of decision making and also discusses whether there is essential merit in collective decision making in the first place—an important point affecting individuals' decisions to participate and their effectiveness in doing so. In short, the author aims to describe what democracy is and how we know it when we see it rather than to demonstrate its essential merit or value as a moral good.

If we were to poll the authors whose essays we present in our volume about the value of democracy and its signature of collective decision making, we would likely hear them answer resoundingly that yes, collective decision making that values all voices is a moral good. In fact, several of our authors raise concerns about what they identify as communities and circumstances in which boundaries or limits have been put on how decisions or actions are collectively determined.

Collectively, this volume and its authors argue that when the discourses of some are ignored due to slighting others, intentionally or not, communities do not function to preserve or to honor the ability of all to participate in group decision making, nor do they protect the freedom of all to participate. Nonetheless, freedom is a touted American value, a very cornerstone, if you will, of the American Dream. Going back to the *SEP* entry on *democracy*, its author supports the essential nature of this value, noting that, for many, freedom or liberty is the foundation of democracy: "Democracy [say some] extends the idea that each ought to be master of his or her life to the domain of collective decision making" (Christiano 2008, 6).

In the United States, when citizens pledge allegiance to our nation, they promise to preserve "liberty and justice for all." This pledge does not acknowledge that there is a problematic connection between freedom and collective decision making, a point elaborated in the *SEP* entry. On the one hand, if all are free to participate, the quality of collective decision making is at risk, not only because of the possibility of irresolvable dissension but also because not all can be equally qualified to make decisions that will best serve the whole (see Christiano 2008, 5). On the other hand, if all are not allowed to participate in democratic deliberation, then individual freedom to participate is curtailed. Yet holding this position is questionable as well because to assure freedom for each individual "each person must freely choose the outcomes that bind him or her," and if they do not so freely choose, "then those who oppose the decision are not self-governing" and, therefore, not "free." In short, "they live in an environment imposed by others" (Christiano 2008, 7). Given this essential contradiction inherent in the very idea of a democracy, what good does discussion do to preserve individual freedom when it aids deliberation leading to a collective decision? We will come back to this dilemma when we discuss the second term within our definition of *democratic discourse*. For the present, let's assume for discussion's sake that for democracy to function effectively, it must honor both individual freedom and collective decision making, and let's take up briefly what is required to preserve a democracy that works this way.

Scholars have identified a few environmental criteria requisite for democracy to function. In his wonderfully compact treatise *On Democracy*, Robert A. Dahl, for example, presents an excellent list of criteria that must be in place for democracy to be sustained: "effective participation," "voting equality," "enlightened understanding," "control of the agenda," and "inclusion of adults" (Dahl 2000, 37–38). Three of these criteria are especially pertinent to our focus on democratic discourse. The first of these is "effective participation," which, Dahl says, requires that "all . . . members must have equal and effective opportunities for making their views known to the other members as to what the policy should be" (37). Clearly, in a discourse exchange, if some are kept from participating, the discourse cannot be democratic. The second is "enlightened understanding," or the opportunity for all participants to have "equal and effective opportunities for learning about the relevant alternative policies and their likely consequences" (37). We will come back to this one, which has resonance for academics: beneath "enlightened understanding" is the scientific approach to knowledge seeking presumed to be the foundation of democracy, that is, reasoning from facts—the legacy of the Age of Enlightenment. And, finally, for democracy to be preserved, individuals must have opportunity to take "control of the agenda," that is, must be given "the exclusive opportunity to decide how and, if they choose, what matters are to be placed on the agenda" (38–39).

We shall take effective participation as a first requirement for democratic discourse and then look to rhetorical and critical theory to help us define elemental factors allowing for effective participation in a system or situation that involves collective decision making. We wish to posit a set of three guidelines that must be in place in order for effective participation in such situations to take place: first, a charitable perspective in which speakers assume that all others intend to make sense; second, a generous acknowledgment of bodily difference that averts dismissing the ways, needs, and speech of others; and finally, unreserved openness to others that goes beyond mere tolerance of those who share our societal space. Along the way, we will introduce the reader to essays in this collection that highlight these elements and raise awareness of their importance to fair exchange in rhetorical situations.

In explaining the first condition for fair exchange in collective decision making, it is instructive to consider assumptions that render a speaker eligible to participate in any exchange or conversation. A first assumption is accepting that another has something to contribute, a conversational condition Donald Davidson (1984) defines as "charity." Not to be confused with love or affection, charity here is the fundamental assumption that to converse, one must be willing to try to understand the other participants in the conversation. Davidson makes no attempt at a moral theory of behavior here; rather, he attempts to define what is essential for effective communication, and basically, it is essential for each speaker involved to assume the other speakers are trying to make sense and that all involved have a workable theory about what can be said to be "true"; this condition of mutual charity with regard to assumptions about a speaker's intentions is basic to communication. Yet this condition, as our contributors to this volume show, is not always what prevails in public-discourse situations.

For instance, in "American Rhetorics of Disappearance: Translocal Feminist Problem-Solving Rhetorics," Tricia Serviss addresses how even in the field of rhetoric, we could do more to extend a willingness to try to understand not only what but also how others are communicating. Using the case of feminist activists in Juarez, Serviss calls on theorists and researchers to work more diligently to recognize the nature, sources, and layers of the activists' rhetorical practices. In short, she argues that dismissing such layers prevents us from increasing our understanding of the true meaning and effect of these discursive strategies—strategies that, at once, work and are recognized across national boundaries and contexts yet convey specific meanings that are embedded locally.

To bring us back to what Davidson tells us, making a choice to assume there is value in what others are contributing is essential to the process of viewing others' discourse with charity: "Charity is forced on us; whether we like it or not, if we want to understand others, we must count them right in most matters. If we can produce a theory that reconciles charity and the formal conditions for a theory, we have done all that could be done to ensure communication. Nothing more is possible, and nothing more is needed" (1984, 197). Without the assumption of charity, conversation cannot occur, that is, conversation that involves the true interchange of ideas. And prior to the assumption of charity, we would add, are even more basic assumptions about the inherent worth of the speaker, worth determined all too often, we argue, on the basis of established borders between those similar to one's self and those different from one's self.

If a speaker is not considered to have the same qualities that give value to one's own self, then one's openness to the idea that another is making sense when speaking is almost irrelevant. Jacques Derrida (1997) explores the hazards of our very human tendency to treat others as lacking the personal worth we ascribe to ourselves in his treatise *Politics of Friendship*. Politics, including political systems such as democracies, are based on the ancient conceptualization of friendship, which makes of some individuals friends and of others enemies. Derrida made overt claims about friendship and democracy in a discussion at a conference at the University of Sussex. When interviewed, he said, "As you read the canonical texts in political theory starting with Plato or Aristotle you discover that friendship plays an organising role in the definition of justice, of democracy even" (quoted in Bennington 1997, n.p.).

Our current national difficulty in reaching consensus about any number of issues affecting the future prosperity of Americans is rooted in broad-based characterizations of those who disagree with us as enemies, that is, as individuals who are against "American" values—against our Constitution, against traditional families, or against the deity our forefathers invoked to bless us. Derrida claims there is a clannish blindness to notions of right and wrong underlying the kind of affiliation that values only friends. Friends protect friends—whether the bonds that tie friends together be personal, ethnic, geographical, or national—and they do so regardless of the objective consequences of their actions or behavior. And this is where a moral danger lies.

As we write, a recent illustration of blind fealty to friends comes to mind in the action taken by roommates of Dzhokar Tsarnaev, suspected perpetrator of the 2014 Boston Marathon bombings, in tossing his backpack, loaded with material to make explosives, in a landfill to keep authorities away from his trail. In a land where one's friends, whether defined by religion, neighborhood, or some other affiliation, are always more important than the others—the *not friends* who share the same place—safety and personal freedom cannot be assured for all.

In the United States, we continue to face contexts in which individuals can be said to fall into groups we consider friends and those we do not. A pressing issue dividing the United States now, what to do about the twelve million Mexican immigrants who are in the country without documentation, presents a poignant illustration of the consequences of such labeling. By persistently describing some immigrants' experience and lives as "illegal," for instance, we define them as enemies before an unbiased conversation about their actual circumstances or fate can even begin. And, of course, such exclusionary tactics have been employed to define as enemies certain subgroups of our "legal" citizens as well. Yet for some, the boundaries that include them are as significant—albeit in different ways—as those that others use to shun them. For instance, as another author in this volume, Vanessa Cozza, notes, geographical, cultural, legal, and psychological borders all set recent "legal" immigrants apart from other US citizens. In "De pie sobre la valla y mirando por la ventana:[2] Border Realities of the Immigrant Experience," she argues for opening dialogue about personal and public experience in our classrooms (and beyond) to include valuable perspectives and narratives of immigrants who have experienced these barriers. Such openness can lead us, she contends, toward a broader sense of community, interpersonal understanding, and collective decision making. We extend this call to other subgroups who are defined by some as certainly not friends, including those labeled pejoratively as gay, black, Hispanic, female, senior, and so on.

But to truly enter a discourse exchange in the spirit of charity presumes that, regardless of differences between them, speakers acknowledge and recognize each other as having basic rights, a perspective that requires us to honor fully the bodily differences of others—our second requirement for effective participatory exchange. It is shocking to recall that within the span of a few centuries, bodily differences have led some to dismiss others as not having even basic human needs. Such an erasure occurs when individuals are so discounted they are not even worthy of being named or having rights basic to human survival or well-being, let alone the American Dream. Roslyn Diprose (2002), a scholar of the philosophical perspectives of such luminaries as Derrida, Nietzsche, and Levinas, explores the physical and psychological effect of being in a group not even recognized, let alone categorized, in her thoughtful argument for "corporeal generosity." By this she means quite literally accepting with generosity the bodily differences of others. She illustrates the horrific consequences of not doing so by describing the erasure of indigenous peoples and their rights that took place when Europeans inhabited Australia.

Citing Nietzsche, Diprose (2002) explains the power of naming and how our ability to name something can disguise the truth about something or deliberately establish a lie as truth. This happened, she claims, when early Europeans described Australia as "terra nullius," or a land belonging to no one. Seeing no established buildings or dwellings recognizable in European terms as homes, the early settlers there assumed the inhabitants had no ownership of the land, and the settlers therefore felt no compulsion to honor any rights to that property. In short, the Europeans' named conception of home simply had no equivalent in Australia—there was nothing there they recognized as belonging to anyone. What was lacking in the Europeans' callous dismissal of the peoples who did, in fact, inhabit Australia was "corporeal generosity," or an opening of oneself bodily to the bodily experience of another. In developing this concept, Diprose distinguishes the kind of thinking about inclusion that dominates current politics from a new "politics of generosity," which is based in a conceptualization of generosity toward all. To our minds, Diprose's "politics of generosity" extends the basic requirement for conversation that Davidson calls "charity" to another specific requirement for true democratic discourse: "corporeal generosity." In short, bodily recognition of everyone—that is, recognition of everything they are rather than of how they are spoken about—must characterize political conversation about the common interests of our society if collective decision making is to effectively take place.

This important point is acknowledged by several of our authors whose examinations of both current and historical representation of certain groups reveal how these representations fail to truly recognize the humanity or individuality of such groups. Specifically, in "Metonymic Borders and Our Sense of Nation," Victor Villanueva takes up and takes on nationalist narratives, calling into question the notion of nation as a fixed entity by using the case of Puerto Rico to show the absurdities of what can be seen as our current border hysteria. Calling for us to move beyond intolerance of different Others, Villanueva explores the racism beneath exclusionary tactics, racism increasingly evident, for instance, in the enactment of Arizona's SB 1070 and Alabama's HB 56 anti-immigration laws.

Legislation like this, we argue, can lead some people to unilaterally and unreflectively suspect those who are nonwhite or those of "ethnic" heritage, limiting from the get go marginalized people's right to participate in discussions or decisions that should serve to protect democratic processes for all. In other instances, such legislation and the historical precedents behind it allow others to treat those not having English as their first language as ineligible for basic rights, such as the right to an effective education, as a number of our authors show. In "Crossing Linguistic Borders in the Classroom: Moving beyond English Only to Tap Rich Linguistic Resources," Anita C. Hernández, José A. Montelongo, and Roberta J. Herter address this injustice, taking on the issue of English-only instruction in our public schools and its ramifications. Practices such as this, they show, can close paths to the types of exchange and understanding critical for democratic discourse to thrive through building a discursive environment in which all participants are valued equally.

Similarly, in "Continuity and Contact in a Cosmopolitan World: Code-switching and Its Effects on Community Identity," Christopher Schroeder argues for theorists and teachers to discover and explore the expanded understanding gained when language barriers are crossed. Through evaluating a newspaper column in an award-winning Chicago ethnic newspaper, he shows that the moves made in code-switching or mixing languages can work toward expanding individuals' social identities, helping them overcome the challenges of cultural differences, and even complicating, instructively, nationalist narratives—thus opening up possibilities for greater participation. In our view, Schroeder shows how language use can encourage "corporeal generosity"—as Diprose calls it—and empower those who appear outside recognized groups to take charge of their own lives and circumstance and thereby thrive within a shared community.

Critical to expressing corporeal generosity toward all in a community is a commitment to acknowledge bodily difference while all learn together in the given, present environment. Diprose (2002) establishes the importance of bodily recognition (i.e., corporeal generosity) of varied identities occupying the same community by drawing a contrast between notions of community characterized by Nietzsche as opposed to Levinas. As Diprose tells us, Nietzsche's conception of community is "a sociohistorical formation built by truth, by language, which, through the mnemotechniques of pain, through the discipline of a body-memory, constitutes our experience in common" (167). In explanation of this claim, she says, "By concepts we share, those of us who belong to the one social body will see the same leaf and share an understanding of its nature, we will build bridges together and understand their purpose, and we will look at each other with recognition of the passions and reasons that drive us" (167). For Levinas, however, what builds community is not the recognition of shared experience but rather the "generosity" that individuals have in recognizing "alterity." Putting this in terms of language use, the community Nietzsche envisions is based on the "said," or what has already been written or historically established as given about various identities. The community of Levinas is based on "saying," or what we are learning together about each other through talking in the present. As Diprose summarizes, "Beneath the community of commonness grounded in the said of language is the community of the saying, of exposure to alterity" (168). Inherent in the "said of language" is the construction of "social imaginaries," or preconceptualizations about difference that limit and stifle the possibility of building true community.

In our volume, Cori Brewster presents a compelling illustration of the importance of learning together about each other through talking in the present rather than referencing our past perceptions. In "'A Melting Pot That's Constantly Being Stirred': Rhetorics of Race and Tolerance at a Regional Museum," Brewster addresses how even in a site (a regional museum) designed to display openness to diversity and the stories of immigrants, the efforts of its designers nonetheless overlook discourses (such as those of indigenous people) outside of the dominant community narrative focused on "progress," failing to even acknowledge the existence of some groups (specifically, Chinese and African Americans) important to the history of the region. Whether this omission is the result of benign neglect or insidious prejudice is secondary to the fact that we have tendencies to dismiss those who appear to not conform to a history a certain community may espouse or presume to share.

A sea change in perspective may be required to overcome the societal tendency to repeat reference to only what is commonly shared by some. Diprose identifies this sea change as a shift in attention to the "politics of generosity": "Attending to the politics of generosity is a matter of attending to the source of any potential transformation of social imaginaries that . . . continue to do the damage to difference" (Diprose 2002, 171–72). As many of our volume authors would contend, "damage to difference" allows individuals and groups to dismiss differences as barriers simply standing in the way of creating more meaningful relationships between them, differences that, if acknowledged, would allow for more generous interpretations of true societal opportunity for economic success, or effective education, or even personal safety.

But making this shift does not forego a certain amount of discomfort, as others of our authors show. In "Difference as Rhetorical Stance: Developing Meaningful Interactions and Identification across Racial and Ethnic Lines," Mónica Torres and Kathryn Valentine contrast a situation that exposes the threat of violence underlying one kind of engagement across racial lines with a situation in which engaged participants display reluctance to acknowledge differences, even when doing so would warrant productive discussion. Presenting both situations as problematic, Torres and Valentine employ rhetorical and cultural theory to construct a framework for productively analyzing the complications and potentials of these types of cross-racial interactions. Along with them, we believe that building identification with ethnically or racially different others without ignoring or "even fully bridging [such] differences" can be an important move toward building understanding, or, in Diprose's terms, toward acknowledging and accepting bodily difference.

From Diprose's point of view, preconceptualizations about bodies and relations between bodies are at the heart of modern politics and, for her, if political activity has any hope of improving society, it must transform to allow for relations that recognize all bodily difference. In short, modern politics must recognize "intercorporeality." As Diprose states, "My argument . . . is that . . . the generosity of intercorporeality is where politics (the organization of society for the improvement of human survival) takes place" (173).

Our discourse conventions in themselves can at times lead us to dismiss the needs and desires of others and avert a commitment to the "generosity of intercorporeality," as Diprose puts it. In public settings, we often are committed to listening to a particular way of speaking while dismissing speech that falls outside of that realm. For instance, in considering or making a reasoned argument, speakers and listeners may dismiss language that does not conform to discourse conventions common to argument, not only finding such expression inappropriate but also, in some cases, not crediting its connection to real experience. Yet to ensure the continuation of a true democracy and the freedom of all to enjoy effective participation, public discourse must allow for disruption, for the possibility that conversation, writing, or discussion may not fall within conventions common to a particular setting or may make us uncomfortable, confused, and even angry. In fact, the very goal to reach consensus or agreement through reasoned argument in the interest of collective decision making may fall gravely short of meeting the needs and experiences of those sharing in this conversation. Contemporary critical theorists, including Diprose, have argued that public discourse must create a space where expectations for discourse performance do not negate the open possibility of entertaining a new perspective. And we agree.

We argue, in fact, that public discourse must make room for new perspectives required for the construction of knowledge. In *The Postmodern Condition: A Report on Knowledge,* Jean-Francois Lyotard (1989) characterizes the necessary conditions for building knowledge, defending a tension between form and disruption as key to achieving new perspectives. In an afterword to the essay entitled "Answering the Question: What Is Postmodernism?" he defines this tension as the linguistic expression of postmodernism, examining its historical and philosophical precedents in modernism. The project of modernism, he claims, is one of capturing reality, and in doing so, aiming for the best possible expression of what the majority perceive to be real—an expression that removes all doubt of our understanding of the situation described. Lyotard equates such "realism," or the relentless insistence upon expressing the real, with political power and with the suppression of art, which disrupts our perceptions of what reality may truly be. In Lyotard's words, here's how political power uses language's relationship to "reality" to retain control:

> When power assumes the name of a party, realism and its neoclassical complement triumph over the experimental avant-garde by slandering and banning it—that is, provided the "correct" images, the "correct" narratives, the "correct" forms which the party requests, selects, and propagates can find a public to desire them as the appropriate remedy for the anxiety and depression that [the] public experiences. (Lyotard 1989, 75)

In short, the existence of political parties itself is a threat to expression that may not conform to a consensual perception of what is real. For example, political parties and movements can create a vision of life as it is "supposed to be" that dismisses the realities of life for one or another segment of the population not adhering to their vision, thus making the parties' or movements' followers comfortable with dismissing these same realities.

Again, more than one of our volume authors demonstrate how the situation described by Lyotard is experienced in American society when "correct" visions of what we should value are presented by a party or some other segment of society while disruptive perspectives are dismissed. A danger to democracy lies, we argue, in accepting the power of these visions to effectively dismiss the vision and expression of other realities. In "'I Am the 99 Percent': Identification and Division in the Rhetorics of the Occupy Wall Street Protests," Randolph Cauthen, another of our authors, highlights how those affiliated with the Occupy Wall Street movement were dismissed, denied, or derided for their visions that some saw as outside the norm. Invoking a Burkean lens, Cauthen focuses on unconventional rhetorical practices of the Occupy Wall Street movement, such as foregoing leadership hierarchy and direction to create more room for diverse voices. He demonstrates how, ironically, the rhetorical moves of the 99%, in themselves, though designed to foster inclusion, stood in contrast to many people's perceptions of a correct vision for discourse in a democracy where life is as it is "supposed to be." And, of course, the very presence of the Occupy protestors in Zuccotti Park drew a physical boundary between them and those who espouse other values as well.

In addition to political powers using language practices to shape what "ought to be," thereby threatening others' visions of life as it is experienced by them personally, there is also another threat to the interpretation of reality as it is truly experienced. Lyotard labels this threat "techno-science," or the domination of technology and its power to produce and influence well-formed conceptualizations of reality—a power that leads the technologist to value performance over true substance.

Just as art and literature can be subordinated to political power and the power of the popular public market, so too can science be subordinated to the technologies that allow us to produce information and results perfectly and immediately. Lyotard concludes that the current trend to value this technical performance over inquiry is a threat to artistic or disruptive expression and ultimately to our intellectual perception of reality.

> There is no denying the dominant existence today of techno-science, that is, the massive subordination of cognitive statements to the finality of the best possible performance, which is the technological criterion.... The objects and the thoughts which originate in scientific knowledge and the capitalist economy convey with them one of the rules which supports their possibility: the rule that there is no reality unless testified by a consensus between partners over a certain knowledge and certain commitments. (Lyotard 1989, 76–77)

As a demonstration of this claim, Lyotard draws a comparison between "knowledge," which is dominated by technical expression, and "taste," which is dominated by our perception of an art object as it conforms "in principle" to a concept and contrasts this with the Kantian notion of the sublime, which is the effect of having an idea of what something is but not being able to express it, a condition of tension that combines the sensations of pleasure and pain. The experience of the "sublime," Lyotard tells us, is like this: "We can conceive the infinitely great, the infinitely powerful, but every presentation of an object destined to 'make visible' this absolute greatness or power appears to us painfully inadequate" (78). The beautiful exists somewhere here, in the space that prevents what Lyotard calls the "stabilization of taste." The truly artistic experience goes beyond "taste" and is fully within that space where reality can be conceived of but not presented.

Two authors in this volume specifically introduce ways of speaking that, like artistic expression, disrupt the "stabilization of taste," provoking new or different perceptions of a good—or one might say beautiful—society, a possibility not adequately expressed in our current ways of talking about it. Susan A. Schiller, for example, explores ways we reject certain kinds of language as inappropriate for expressing a studied view in "Traversing Rhetorical Borders of Spirituality in Academic Settings." Here she acknowledges that academic discomfort with the term *spirituality* as a perspective on living and learning all too often closes down the possibility for exchange in academic settings. She goes on to propose introducing spirituality into the writing classroom as a secular means toward achieving an enriched inner life, an invitation toward creativity and inspiration, and a path beyond cultural borders and limitations she sees as restrictively imposed by the academy.

And in yet another argument for expanding our notion of acceptable discourse for serious discussion, Jonathan P. Rossing, in "Humor's Role in Political Discourse: Examining Border Patrol in Colbert Nation," calls for more acceptance of alternative discourse strategies, showing how comedy and humor can participate vitally in public discourse on sociopolitical issues such as immigration. As a case in point, Rossing explores the rhetorical critique performed by political satirist Stephen Colbert, host of the now past, faux-conservative news program *The Colbert Report*, in calling popular positions on immigration into question. He shows how Colbert challenges the limits of expressible discourse in public settings—crossing boundaries that for some should never be crossed, such as that between serious debate and farce, and provocatively introducing issues that have remained buried in more formal settings, such as courtrooms and legislative hearings.

Rossing's argument that humor and comedy can disrupt the borders of serious public discourse in productive ways echoes, we believe, Lyotard's defense of preserving the conditions in which "inexpressible" expression survives. For Lyotard, preserving the possibility of disruption that is "postmodernism"—and ultimately, we could extrapolate, preserving the diversity of ideas and perceptions that creates a healthy democracy—is a tantamount safety mechanism for society. Lyotard hints that our increasing quest for unity, for seeking the "illusion" that reality should conform to our "pre-vision" of it, has terrible consequences. A relentless pursuit of conformance to a political ideal, a religious ideal, a racial ideal has fomented abroad, and now in the United States, a return to "terror."

> The nineteenth and twentieth centuries have given us as much terror as we can take. We have paid a high enough price for the nostalgia of the whole and the one, for the reconciliation of the concept and the sensible, of the transparent and the communicable experience. Under the general demand for slackening and for appeasement, we can hear the mutterings of the desire for a return of terror, for the realization of the fantasy to seize reality. The answer is: Let us wage a war on totality; let us be witnesses to the unpresentable; let us activate the differences and save the honor of the name. (Lyotard 1989, 81–82)

Although Lyotard's argument is primarily one that speaks to the importance of disruption in artistic expression, it also speaks to what is lost when expression conforms to what is known or expected. Not only do we cater to taste rather than engage with art in doing so, or cater to performance rather than attend to science in doing so, but we risk creating a world where difference, not being heard, demands to be heard in ways frighteningly disruptive, in ways that spawn nothing less than terror.

But what, in the long run, does this theorizing—and the discussions raised in this volume—have to do in practical terms with the survival of democracy, and by association, democratic discourse? Quite simply, the way we choose to talk about and treat different Others and their reality—for instance, choosing to treat them as if they live and communicate inside or outside of our own borders of acceptability—can be a serious threat to democracy. In short, the borders we choose to draw or invent can threaten the underlayment of effective participation that girds democracy in action. In some ways, in fact, even continuously demanding consensus, as opposed to advocating argument, can be a threat to democracy—primarily because demands for consensus that force concession of one party or another can also threaten the charitable relationship between parties that must abide for democracy to flourish.

And this problem underlying an unyielding commitment to consensus leads us to our third requirement for public discourse in the service of effective participation, or *democratic discourse* as we are calling it. In order for public discourse to assure effective participation, there must be room for dissent that is not dismissed or merely tolerated. In ending arguments that for whatever reason cannot be resolved we often hear the phrase *let's agree to disagree*. Underlying this statement is a tacit assumption of tolerance—we agree to tolerate the existence of an argument that does not conform to our own, and at the same time we do not let that argument deter us from continuing our own perception. The theorist Giovanna Borradori provides a provocative discussion of the virtues and faults of advocating tolerance in her interpretation of her dialogues with Jürgen Habermas and Jacques Derrida. For Habermas, dialogue that emerges from effective communication leads to the possibility of consensus; Borradori tells us, "His crucial argument is that every time we communicate with one another, we automatically commit to the possibility of a freely achieved dialogic agreement in which the better argument will win" (Borradori 2005, 60). This leaves the loser of the argument in the position of tolerating the other when all is said and done. Derrida complicates this notion of tolerance in the face of difference, citing its origins in religious depictions of certain sects' agreements to tolerate the presence of other beliefs. He notes that in our current difficulties with terrorism and its association with Islam, we often separate the actions of terrorists from those who are Muslims but not terrorists by making "official declarations of tolerance" (quoted in Borradori 2005, 127). The problem with the discourse of tolerance, Derrida explains, is not only that it reflects "religious roots" but also "that it is most often used on the side of those with power, always as a kind of condescending concession" (127). In short, Derrida prefers a different conceptualization for the recognition of difference, and he calls it "hospitality."

Hospitality assumes an openness to difference and to communication that does not necessarily conform to norms that are known or expected—a difference crucial to the survival of a healthy democracy. Tolerance, though charitable, always draws a line between those who are tolerating, who have bounded a space—whether real or imaginary—as their own and those who are the subjects of tolerance and who are, consequently, marked as outside that boundary or intruding within it. Hospitality, in contrast, is the open-armed acceptance of whatever guest comes our way. Hospitality presumes a willingness to meet the unknown unafraid, to be welcoming, even in the face of potential danger.

> But pure or unconditional hospitality does not consist in such an invitation ("I invite you, I welcome you into my home, on the condition that you adapt to the laws and norms of my territory, according to my language, tradition, memory, and so on"). Pure and unconditional hospitality, hospitality itself, opens or is in advance open to someone who is neither

> expected nor invited, to whomever arrives as an absolutely foreign visitor, as a new arrival, nonidentifiable and unforeseeable, in short, wholly other. I would call this a hospitality of visitation rather than invitation. The visit might actually be very dangerous, and we must not ignore this fact, but would a hospitality without risk, a hospitality backed by certain assurances, a hospitality protected by an immune system against the wholly other, be true hospitality? (Derrida quoted in Borradori 2005, 128–29)

Derrida goes on to acknowledge that a society or state cannot fully realize unconditional hospitality given legal and safety concerns; nonetheless, for it to truly represent the interests of all, it must have an ethical intention of unconditional hospitality—a physical and political parallel, perhaps, to the basic requirement of charity, which Davidson has told us must abide for any hope of communication to occur. And, if we are to remain true to our desire to uphold a democracy that ensures effective participation, as we defined it earlier, a hospitable openness to differences, whatever their source in our society, would seem requisite to that purpose.

A number of authors in this volume describe enacting this hospitable openness to differences. Elenore Long, Jennifer Clifton, Andrea Alden, and Judy Holiday address practices of the academy that have the potential to shut down rather than open up true exchange and dialogue with the outside public and communities where academics work. In "Fostering Inclusive Dialogue in Emergent University-Community Partnerships: Setting the Stage for Intercultural Inquiry," these authors offer new, more hospitable ways to cross university-community borders and to enhance open dialogue across diversity. Also addressing the public turn, Robert Brooke examines how community involvement is advanced or not advanced by public rhetorics within the boundaries of suburbia, a space apart that can be isolated from diverse social interactions—as well as from the natural and cultural landscapes of both urban and rural locations. In "Rhetorical Education at the City's Edge: The Challenge of Public Rhetoric in Suburban America," he argues that this isolation from engaging with contrasting and more diverse environments "makes it hard to engage in the full work of democratic [and participatory] citizenship" that welcomes all. And, finally, Karen P. Peirce, in "Employing Ethos to Cross the Borders of Difference: Teaching Civil Discourse," asks how we can alter the landscape of rhetorical education so that resolutely arguing for one's own point of view is no longer taught as the sole and ultimate aim of argumentative discourse, as we often teach when covering argument in writing classes; she asks that we also teach a hospitable openness, if you will, to alternate points of view and ways to express them in our discourse.

To conclude, in drawing together the perspectives we have shared throughout this chapter, we can form a definition of democratic discourse that realizes the intent of democracy to foster governance "by the people" and "for the people," to assure freedom of expression, and to guarantee inclusion of all within its realm through ensuring their effective participation in collective decision making. Democratic discourse, so defined, would demand conditions for conversation, dialogue, and policy making that

- *recognize all individuals within its bounds* without prejudice, that is, without defining some individuals outside the bounded circle of friends, and by adopting the charitable assumption that all are trying to make sense; that
- *recognize deeply corporeal differences* that, in order to be acknowledged, demand that we give all individuals the freedom to speak their minds in the manner suited to and comfortable for them, that is, without necessarily conforming to some preconceptions that may be held about what constitutes a well-formed performance; and that, given this recognition,
- *accept all with hospitality unreservedly* insofar as we are able to preserve the safety and security of others, that is, without the presumption of mere tolerance of some within the discourse sphere that keeps the tolerated perpetually under the thumb of those who are tolerating.

This is a tall order for conversation, dialogue, and discussion within a democracy where boundaries are drawn every day, defining rights of some and not others, providing quality education for some and not others, and offering equal opportunity to earn a living for some but not others. Some would have us define our democracy as healthy and secure within boundaries like these. But can we truly realize the American democratic promise in doing so? We argue that we cannot.

Along with Derrida, we agree that a society cannot practice democracy by curtailing the participation of some within it, offering them the protection of mere tolerance, and we support his dream of a democracy in which equal rights truly are granted to all.

> Within a democratic community whose citizens reciprocally grant one another equal rights, no room is left for an authority allowed to one-sidedly determine the boundaries of what is to be tolerated. On the basis of the citizens' equal rights and reciprocal respect for each other, nobody possesses the privilege of setting the boundaries of tolerance from the viewpoint of their own preferences and value orientations. (Derrida quoted in Borradori 2005, 73)

But beyond this, we believe practicing democracy within a space that merely tolerates difference is a threat to democracy itself. When individuals or groups are excluded or at best merely tolerated, their ability to participate is blocked and consequently so are the benefits of the society that such inclusion would accrue to them. A society that blocks expression, refuses to recognize difference, or at best merely tolerates it is a society ripe for terror.

Borradori (2005) contrasts two societal conditions that potentially create an environment for terror, referring to the work of Habermas and Derrida. For Habermas, terror is the result of a clash of systems across which dialogue cannot take place because the opening has not been found; in short, there is no communication channel to allow communicative interaction to take place in a reasoned way across opposing viewpoints. Such a condition exists, for example, when language expressing the religious conviction of fundamentalist spirituality is thrown up against language expressing the secular consumerism of Western democracies—here never the twain shall meet, as the expression goes. The solution, according to Habermas, is to build trust across this divide, and trust begins by dissolving the inequalities that have allowed such polarization in characterizing the societies with opposing perspectives to grow.

But for Derrida, terror is not as easily limited to clashes between secular and religious systems or between ethnic clans or even between nation-states and the language barriers that define them. Terror can be exacted across the boundaries of clan, system, and state without reference to any bounded group. Terror is fostered anywhere where barriers make it impossible to recognize alterity, let alone include it and support it. For Derrida, modern democracies are at risk not because they do not have the mechanisms to build trust, carry on reasoned discourse, or develop inclusive policy but rather because these mechanisms of the modern democratic state cannot deal with something wholly other and not definable even within these structures. The stubborn blockage that such systems create against the Other exacts, for Derrida, a formula for terror.

At the same time, a willingness to risk admittance of the Other, that is, an acceptance of the fact that the danger of terror exists when difference confronts established systems, is absolutely essential to democracy. The old conception of democracy, Derrida tells us, is one based on a community of friends—outside of this circle of friends, be they defined by race, ethnicity, state, party, or nation, lies the enemy. A future in which true democracy can thrive would define democracy as a never-finished project, one in which we live democracy as an ever becoming project.

In the concluding pages of *Politics of Friendship*, Derrida (1997) imagines this future democracy—one that looks into the face of terror and recognizes that fomenting terror can be the "price" of maintaining a democracy based in the exclusivity of "friendship"; he says,

> Is it possible to think and to implement democracy, that which would keep the old name "democracy," while uprooting from it all these figures of friendship (philosophical and religious) which prescribe fraternity: the family and the androcentric ethnic group? Is it possible, in assuming a certain faithful member of democratic reason and reason *tout court*... not to found, where it is no longer a matter of *founding* but to open out to the future, or rather, to the "come," of a certain democracy? (306)

This vision of democracy requires not an abandonment of reason but a realization that reason, our Enlightenment legacy, also can keep us from seeing or hearing all that needs to be known. In the end, Derrida wistfully pines for this future approach to democratic governance, saying, "When will we be ready for an experience of freedom and equality that is capable of respectfully experiencing that friendship, which would at last be just, just beyond the law, and measured up against its measuredness? / O my democratic friends . . ." (306).

When? We cannot predict, but we can say there is merit in studying the processes of democracy as they are reflected in conversations with and across the boundaries that separate individuals into friends and enemies, citizens and "illegals," Americans and non-Americans, the documented and the nondocumented, the Anglos and the Hispanics, the liberals and the Tea Partiers. Each of the essays in this volume explores how actual public discourse at the site of such borders and boundaries represents or confounds effective participation. The settings are various, from vast public spaces such as cities and the spaces within them to the rhetorical spaces of history books, museum displays, newspapers, and media outlets to the intimate settings for public conversation in classrooms. At the end of each essay, our authors discuss implications for teaching about discourse that encourages effective participation and for research on how discourse functions to do so. At the end of our volume, we come back to these suggestions, adding some of our own and proposing some new directions to explore in our quest to understand the effects of borders and boundaries on public discourse.

Finally, to bring this discussion full circle, let us return for a moment to Thornton Wilder's fictional town of Grover's Corners, USA, and set it beside Gabriel Garcia Marquez's (2006) mythical South American town of Macondo in his masterwork *One Hundred Years of Solitude*. Wilder's simple depiction of the solitary pain of individual lives and families in a community where love and connection are fleeting moments erased by death and neglect resonates with Marquez's complex depiction of a community wrapped in isolation—solitude—where all that is written and all that is remembered about the rich history of its founding family, the Buendias, becomes forgotten. Both Wilder's and Marquez's depictions invite us to reflect on how community perceptions and histories both connect and isolate those within them. After recording pages and pages of the fantastic lives of seven generations of family members who thrived and perished in one town, Marquez seems to conclude there is no truth to such history; it is subject to too many different interpretations. As one of his protagonists concludes of the villagers of Macondo, they must concede that "the past was a lie, that memory has no return, that every spring gone by could never be recovered, and that the wildest and most tenacious love was an ephemeral truth in the end" (403). Marquez claims at the end of his saga that this inability to recover a truth from the past is the fate of "races condemned to one hundred years of solitude," to the isolated truth of memory and myth; they "do not have a second opportunity on earth." And neither does Wilder's Emily Webb, who, tragically dead in childbirth, has no business remembering the living.

But our story, unlike that of plays and novels, goes on beyond the tale's end, beyond what was written and remembered. Perhaps, in fact, we—of the American Dream—can have that second opportunity to thrive across generations by bolstering within our public discourse democracy's promise of fair participation and assuring that our conversations do not neglect or forget anyone's depiction of their experience. We can choose to isolate ourselves and our views, protecting them from knowledge about those whom we do not know, or we can find ways to talk about and negotiate individual experience in the societies we share that allow these settings ever to be created anew.

We do believe that through study and analysis of the interactions at borders and boundaries, as undertaken by each of the authors in this volume, we can discover how language use creates the conditions for establishing identity and admitting difference in ways that help us create ever anew a thriving American democracy—one in which we both honor the known traditions that bind us and release those bounds to include what we cannot now know. This American democracy would be filled with hope, like the world of Rebecca in *Our Town* that ever expands its boundaries to adjust for inclusion, becoming as diverse, wonderful, and unfathomable as the mind of God.

Notes

1. In this chapter, we treat the term *American* in reference to those living in the United States. Other chapters treat the term more inclusively to reference people from across all the Americas.
2. Standing on the fence and looking out the window.

References

Bennington, Geoff. 1997. "Politics and Friendship: A Discussion with Jacques Derrida." Living Philosophy. http://www.livingphilosophy.org/Derrida-politics-friendship.htm.

Borradori, Giovanna. 2005. *Philosophy in a Time of Terror: Dialogues with Jürgen Habermas and Jacques Derrida.* Chicago: University of Chicago Press.

Christiano, Tom. 2008. "Democracy." In *The Stanford Encyclopedia of Philosophy* edited by Edward N. Zalta. http://plato.stanford.edu/archives/fall2008/entries/democracy.

Dahl, Robert A. (1998) 2000. *On Democracy.* New Haven, CT: Yale University Press.

Davidson, Donald. 1984. *Inquiries into Truth and Interpretation.* New York: Oxford University Press.

Derrida, Jacques. 1997. *Politics of Friendship.* Translated by George Collins. New York: Verso.

Diprose, Rosalyn. 2002. *Corporeal Generosity: On Giving with Nietzsche, Merleau-Ponty, and Levinas.* Albany: SUNY Press.

Lyotard, Jean-Francois. 1989. *The Postmodern Condition: A Report on Knowledge.* Translated by Geoff Bennington and Brian Massumi. Theory and History of Literature, vol. 10. Minneapolis: University of Minnesota Press.

Marquez, Gabriel Garcia. (1970) 2006. *One Hundred Years of Solitude.* New York: Harper Perennial Modern Classics.

Wikipedia: The Free Encyclopedia. 2014. "American Dream." En.wikipedia.org/wiki/American Dream.

Wilder, Thornton. (1938) 2003. *Our Town: A Play in Three Acts.* New York: Harper.

PART I

Imagining Boundaries

Rhetoric Resisting/Defining Symbolic Borders

2
METONYMIC BORDERS AND OUR SENSE OF NATION

Victor Villanueva

HEURISTICS (OR STORIES AND RUMINATIONS)

Of my four daughters, she was the one who most looked like some stereotypical notion of the Latina. The others learned of racialized representations in their travels: the blonde, presumed to have blue eyes because of her fair skin and natural blonde hair. Her eyes are actually brown. Stereotypes affect vision.

> "Ah," they say of 'Looks Latina,' "she has dark eyes like you." But the dark eyes come from her mother, eyes so dark one can't see the pupils. We don't really know her mother's ancestry; she is an orphan.
> My eyes are not dark; they are hazel.
> "Wow, do you know your eyes turn green in the sun?" They don't. Their color just becomes unignorable in direct sunlight.

"Blonde" discovered racialized representations abroad, in Chile, when folks in her presence spoke of the German woman, not knowing she's an American, fluent in Spanish (more than I am, really, having had a formal education in Spanish). The others discovered the representations in travels through the East Coast, where more fluid perceptions of the Latino are likely, given long exposure to Cubans and Puerto Ricans.

> West Side Story: A Cautionary Tale on Miscegenation. On Broadway 1957. But everyone got to see it in 1961, in the movies (IMDb n.d.). This was the time when "ethnicity" was morphing as a term to "race" (in scare quotes), the ethnic not quite a race but subject to racism, reflected in Glazer and Moynihan's (1963) book—and the book's title—Beyond the Melting Pot. The movie played with Puerto Rican-ness: the almost white Maria, "colored" by her bad accent (nothing close to a Puerto Rican's accented English, the accent itself a stereotype), the olive Bernardo (played by George Chakiris, a second-generation Greek), the mulata Anita (Rita Moreno, whose stage name translates to "brown pearl," though her birth name was Rosa Dolores Alverío), the Asian-like Chino (José DeVega), the Asian-like Francisca (played by Japanese-American Joanne Miya), and the indigenous-like Indio

DOI: 10.7330/9781607324034.c002

(another Greek, Gus Trikonis). All but one of Puerto Rico's "colors"—Black—is represented in the movie. No Black because that wasn't really an ethnicity but an established "race"; no need to muddy the racializing waters.

"Looks Latina" had been active in theater: from grip to director and, recently, playwriting, working in a moderate-sized city in the Pacific Northwest. Her script concerned the subtle ways racism presents itself. Rejected. Then there was the script based on Rudolfo Anaya's *Bless Me, Ultima*. Nope. And then there was the acting, trying out for role after role, succeeding only at playing the Hot Latina Chilipepper or Maria-the-Housemaid. Then came the time she was advised to change her stage name because it sounded too much like Maria. Her name is AnaSofía, Ana among the family, but never Sofía.

Stereotypes also affect hearing, apparently.

After nearly fourteen years in theater, she has decided to go back to school, American ethnic studies, to try to figure some of this out beyond what she's experienced and heard from her parents.

AN INTERLUDE (OR DISCIPLINARY AND METHODOLOGICAL CONSIDERATIONS)

When composition studies was in its era of invention and heuristics—clustering, brainstorming, freewriting, tagmemics—it was also a time in which composition studies was enjoying its attachment to rhetoric (Moberg 1990). In that revival of rhetoric, scholars like Ross Winterowd (see Kinneavy 1998) and William Irmscher (1979) turned to Kenneth Burke's pentad (see Burke 1969a) to add to the list of methods of invention. This was a reasonable move given the relation between Burke's "five key terms of dramatism" and the heuristic developed, perhaps, by the rhetorician Hermagoras of Temnos but surely espoused by the Medieval philosopher Boethius—and, more important, commonly known to students: *quis, quid, cur, quo modo, quando, quibus auxiliis* or who, what, why, how, where, when, with what (Robertson 1946). Burke's version—act, scene, agent, agency, purpose—is, says Burke, the key to all human motivation, the key to ideology. Pretty powerful, though Burke himself stated that its intended use was as a tool for literary criticism, to analyze product more than to engage in writing processes (Babin and Harrison 1999, 157). To make the heuristic work as more than just the 5Ws+H using dramatic terms, Burke said we needed to set the pentad into ten ratios and "circumference," an understanding of the possibilities and the limitations of the scene (Lauer 2004, 87). This is complicated, much more than a quick method for jotting down ideas to be developed in the writing. At the same time it was incorporated as part of writing processes, though as much as scholars like Ross Winterowd tried to argue that Burke's conceptual framework would be non-Aristotelian (see Lauer 2004), Burke himself was an extension of Aristotle, neo-Aristotelian, perhaps, but not non-Aristotelian. Using the pentad as a heuristic was not the same as using it as *pre*writing; it was a formulation prior to writing, potentially contrary to writing as a process of discovery. Besides, five terms, ten ratios, with expanding notions of what comprises scene—it's cumbersome. That is why, I imagine, we seem to have settled on freewriting. It is writing. It is thoroughly uncomplicated. But what's most interesting to me in what follows is that in *A Grammar of Motives* (1969a), the same book in which Burke lays out the pentad, he also reprints an essay he had published some years prior in the *Kenyon Review*. "The Four Master Tropes" (Burke 1941). Just as Burke claims that the pentad will uncover motives, ideologies, his four master tropes also play a role "in the discovery and description of 'the truth,'" the scare quotes pointing to a relative understanding of truth, a world-view, an ideology (Burke 1941, 421). Compared to five terms, rendered as ten pairs with a protean half of the pairs, scene, the four tropes seem a lot less cumbersome for the purposes of rhetorical analyses. And, too, the four tropes seem no less comprehensive insofar as they can be rendered as matters of perspective (metaphor), representation (synecdoche), a reduction (metonymy), and the dialectic (irony) (421). The four master tropes are inherently powerful heuristics.

For Burke, the most masterful of the four tropes is irony because, of the four, irony alone is dialectical, he says. This is a reflection of the importance of the dialectic in rhetorical, cultural, and political economic history (the areas that permeate all of Burke's writings). But I see all four as engaging dialectic interplay: the metaphor is point to some representation's counterpoint, synecdoche and metonymy cause us to engage with the matters they represent, symbolic dialectical play. Insofar as language is inherently "symbolic action," with rhetoric as the "symbolic means of inducing cooperation" (Burke 1969b, 50), language and its rhetorical manifestations are always representational (Hall 1997). Symbols engage dialectically with symbols as well as the things and ideas represented by the symbols.

In terms of this chapter, the trope with which I am most concerned is metonymy, a reduction with grand representational possibilities. Whereas a synecdoche is a part that represents a whole, like Homer's masts to represent ships, the metonymic is not organic to that which it represents, not a part of, but something that represents something larger or greater. To refer to a man as *a suit* is to represent male authority, whether as a businessman or a bureaucrat or even a law enforcement plain-clothes officer. The concept is large, represented metonymically as a few items of clothing. Terms like *nation* and *border* represent huge hegemonic matters, at least one matter of which I will explore in what follows.

WAXING CLASSICAL (TO MAKE A MINOR POINT)

Both in China and in the Mediterranean at about the same time, the fifteenth or fourteenth century BCE, a new architectural phenomenon arose as a response to the beginnings of larger-scale imperial expansion—the walled city (Iakovidis 1983; Needham 1971). Before the Golden Age of Athens, the grand citadels and internal castles were to be found in the cities of the Mycenaeans, especially the city of Agamemnon, Mycenae itself. They were designed to protect and to exclude. Our best example in classical lore is, of course, the city of Troy and the clever way Agamemnon's troops gain access. Over time, the walled city grew to the Great Wall or Hadrian's Wall or Operation Gatekeeper, the name of the initiative in California that included California's portion of the Mexico-United States barrier wall (Nevins 2002). As empires grew, so did their walls. And whenever war was eminent, the walls were manned, the gates barricaded, the drawbridge drawn.

The United States is a grand empire, at war with so many. As Niall Ferguson (2003) noted a few years ago in the *Chronicle of Higher Education*, Americans would rather not see themselves as imperialists: "The reality is that the United States has—whether it admits it or not—taken up some kind of global burden [as the British empire had]. It considers itself responsible not just for waging a war against terrorism and rogue states, but also for spreading the benefits of capitalism and democracy overseas. And just like the British empire before it, the American empire unfailingly acts in the name of liberty, even when its own self-interest is manifestly uppermost. . . . It is an empire, in short, that dare not speak its name. It is an empire in denial" (B7).

Once its Destiny had been Manifest and metamanifested in its global reach, large bodies of water offered some of the boundaries, walls built along an imaginary line, vigilance at the drawbridges of El Paso and Detroit, and the rhetorical handling of the Other of the south (and the socialist tendencies of the Not Quite Other of the north). Bridges, walls, and even gates. The United States is symbolically a walled city.

OF BORDERS AND BIGOTRIES (OR NATIONS AND NONSENSE)

It has been such a commonplace that citation isn't even necessary: anti-immigration laws are not about racism but about national and economic security. Then there's Arizona's passing of SB 1070, essentially a pass law, in which anyone looking somehow like an immigrant falls under "reasonable-suspicion" laws. This law was quickly followed by the decision to end ethnic-studies courses, particularly Raza studies, in Tucson high schools (a matter that has since been overturned) and the state's monitoring of teachers who spoke with "foreign accents" (which has been modified to be district monitored—see Kossan, *Arizona Republic*, September 12, 2011).

But perhaps the most telling travesty on the law books is the passage of even more stringent anti-immigrant laws in Alabama, where foreign-born Alabamians comprise 3.4 percent of the population, with Latinos or Latinas comprising 4.1 percent of the state population as opposed to 16.9 percent nationally or 30.2 percent in Arizona (US Census Bureau n.d.). A story from Alabama, reported by the Southern Poverty Law Center (2012):

> When Carmen Vélez tried to renew her car tag in Athens, Ala., she was told she needed to show her birth certificate.
> She had not brought it because she didn't think it was necessary. She returned later with two copies—an older copy and a newer one. The attendant refused to accept them, saying she needed a US birth certificate.
> Carmen was at a loss. She was born in Puerto Rico, which is, of course, an unincorporated territory of the United States. Its residents have been US citizens for nearly a century.
> "I thought they were joking with me," said Carmen, 44. "I couldn't believe it. I never thought they wouldn't know that Puerto Rico was part of the U.S."
> Her ordeal is an example of how HB 56 [known as Alabama's Taxpayer and Citizen Protection Act] complicates the most mundane tasks for many Latinos, even those with legal status. She never had this problem before the law took effect.
> Carmen tried to explain that Puerto Rico is part of the United States, but it seemed futile. She became upset. Finally, the attendant asked for another form of identification. She took Carmen's driver's license and told her to wait.
> She waited for two hours with her 5-year-old son. "Everyone was looking at me like I had two heads."
> Finally, the attendant appeared after speaking with another official.
> "She called me back up and said we'll take a copy of your birth certificate, but next year when you come in you'll have to have a birth certificate from the U.S."

> Though she was able to renew her tag, she left wondering what will happen next year. How do you prove your citizenship when officials don't believe your birth certificate is from the United States?
>
> "It's like they've passed the law but they haven't taught people how to implement it and they don't know what they're doing," Carmen said. "They've just created confusion. Now I'm afraid to go to any government office." (23–24)

During the time I lived in Alabama, I traveled with my birth certificate in my glove box. It says "Brooklyn, Kings County, New York." Might be another incursion from the North (the phrase I tended to hear in reference to the Civil War), but can't deny it's the United States.

At a furniture store, I was asked if my surname was German (and a colleague was with me, a witness, needed because this seems so preposterous). That's how great the immigrant threat is in Alabama. Don't even know a Spanish name when they see one. But the state's security was still evidently at risk.

The border is a metonymy, a fiction within the fiction of a nation, a trope that serves racism in an era that no longer admits to racism. In the words of Harvard political scientist Samuel P. Huntington, "One of the greatest achievements, perhaps the greatest achievement, of America is the extent to which it has eliminated the racial and ethnic components that historically were central to its identity and has become a multiethnic, multicultural society in which individuals are to be judged on their merits" (Huntington 1998, xxvii). Who doesn't, as this quote does, invoke Martin Luther King Jr.—the dream deferred, the ways in which the dream means denial of the dream? In her blog *The Answer Sheet* for the *Washington Post*, posted on February 10, 2010, Valerie Strauss includes Tom Horne's "Open Letter to the Citizens of Tucson," in which he makes the case for ending ethnic studies, notes that he marched on Washington in 1963, invokes MLK, states that he "believe[s] people are individuals, not exemplars of racial groups. What is important about people is what they know, what they can do, their ability to appreciate beauty, their character, and not what race into which they are born." And therein lies the nonracist argument for a racist move—the censorship of those who would speak and teach of their ancestry, as if it is somehow substantively different from learning of British trans-Atlantic expansion, the history of a people more than individuals.

Underlying such perceptions is a belief in the nation, the United States, sovereign, given to equal opportunity if not quite equality (thereby placing the blame for the inequality on individuals mainly, their lack of resourcefulness or initiative or ambition). The inherent contradictions can be dismissed or ignored because the community is after all, as Benedict Anderson reminds us, an imaginary construct—"an imagined political community—and imagined as both inherently limited and sovereign" (Anderson 2006, 6).

> It is imagined because the members of even the smallest nation will never know most of their fellow members, or even hear of them, yet in the minds of each lives the image of their communion....
>
> The nation is imagined as *limited* because even the largest of them, encompassing perhaps a billion living human beings, has finite, if elastic, boundaries, beyond which lie other nations. No nation imagines itself coterminous with mankind. The most messianic nationalists do not dream of a day when all members of the human race will join their nation in the way that in certain epochs, for, say, Christians [dreamt] of a wholly Christian planet....
>
> Finally, it is imagined as a community, because, regardless of the actual inequality and exploitation that may prevail in each, the nation is always conceived as a deep, horizontal comradeship. Ultimately it is this fraternity that makes it possible, over the past two centuries, for so many millions of people, not so much to kill, as willingly to die for such limited imaginings. (6–7)

It is this imagined overarching entity of "nation" that allowed for the oxymoronic proposition that some of its people could be separate but equal. But let me take this a step into the imaginary further with a bit of the history of Puerto Rico, both nation and not, both a part of the United States and not, insofar as the rendering of Puerto Rico's status becomes itself an indication of the "elasticity" of imagined boundaries/borders, the degree to which borders become representations of larger things, metonymic renderings of nation and of Othering.

'TIS AND 'TAIN'T (OR PUERTO RICO AS NATION?)

On February 15, 1898, the United States was attacked by Spaniards—or Cubans—off the coast of Havana by way of the explosion of the USS Maine—the ship itself a metonymy of a nation, explicitly so (though as it turns out, that explosion was likely an accident, a fire and explosion caused by coal dust [see Wegner 2001]). And so began the Spanish-American War, and that led to the acquisition of Puerto Rico. The rhetoric attached to the war in the US press told of freeing Cuba from tyranny, but the rationale for the war was the maintenance of US naval superiority in the Caribbean, the Atlantic gateway to the United States, a water border. The islands of Puerto Rico and Cuba were critical, as was the creation of a Panama Canal and the establishment of Pacific naval bases on Hawaii and the Philippines. Military exigency was sold as America the Liberator, the now-familiar trope.

Thanks to some Spanish artillery fire from la Fortaleza de San Cristóbal in San Juan, Puerto Rico, the USS Yosemite and other battleships could lob a few rounds back to the island for a day or two in May 1898 and declare Puerto Rico's involvement in the war. US land troops arrived on the island in July, but before making their way into San Juan, the war was over, 13 August 1898, a four-month war. Puerto Rico becomes a possession of the United States, ratified by the Treaty of Paris of 10 December 1898.

The island's peasantry, the majority of the island, hailed the entry of the United States on the assumption that the liberal ideals of liberty and equality that had been touted would apply to them. Given the rhetorics of nationalism, they failed to see that if the one did not apply, liberty (as in being a possession of the United States), neither would the other. Nor could they know that the United States would soon impose Jim Crow laws on its own land while maintaining the banner of "liberty and justice for all"—just not all occupying the same space.

US military and economic interests needed to be protected, which gave rise to a number of Supreme Court decisions concerning the newly obtained islands—the Insular Cases. The most notable case was the 1901 *Downes v. Bidwell* decision. The same US Supreme Court that had decided five years earlier that black Americans would be separate but equal in *Plessy v. Ferguson* determined in 1901 that Puerto Rico would be an "unincorporated territory" of the United States. The impetus for the decision was a suit by Downes and Co. against the collector of import taxes at the Port of New York. Downes sought to recover taxes levied against the company's shipment of oranges to the port on the grounds that the shipment had moved between two US ports and was thereby subject to the constitutional mandate that all taxes within the country would be uniform. Downes lost the decision through a rhetoric of definition that would make Aristotle's head spin were it not for the precedent set by *Plessy*. The court held that Puerto Rico was both a part of and separate from the United States—a ghostlike border. In the assenting opinion, Justice Edward Douglas White stated that "whilst in an international sense Porto [sic] Rico was not a foreign country, since it was subject to the sovereignty of and was owned by the United States, it was foreign to the United States in a domestic sense, because the island had not been incorporated into the United States, but was merely appurtenant thereto as a possession" (quoted in Kaplan 2002, 2). 'Tis and 'tain't.

In terms of taxes, Puerto Rico was foreign, but in terms of sovereignty, it was domestic. "Our foreigner" but the world's "our domestic," not foreign in a foreign sense because Puerto Rico was disallowed international trade without the expressed consent of Congress. More important, Puerto Ricans themselves would be "foreign in a domestic sense," with Justice White declaring that its people are "alien and hostile" and Justice Henry Billings Brown (the writer of the majority decision in *Plessy*) declaring that though "the annexation of distant possessions [might be] desirable," there remains the need to remember that those possessions are "inhabited by alien races, differing from us in religion, customs, laws, methods of taxation, and modes of thought" (quoted in Kaplan 2002, 6). The language and sensibility—the rhetoric—that has been recently used in the promotion of English-only laws and anti-immigrant hostility has been a part of American discourse since the US empire extended beyond Manifest Destiny.

In economic terms, Puerto Rico's value, apart from sugar and some tobacco, was less important than its military value (see Grosfoguel 1997). The United States, in fact, poured money into the island, declaring that the people of the island were incapable of self-rule both politically and economically. Accordingly, the United States invested in the education of the island's citizenry, including the imposition of mandatory English instruction in primary schools. Rampant illiteracy remained the norm, however, since little was done to improve access to schools from rural areas (Negrón-Muntaner 1997, 258–59). Even the 1917 Jones-Shafroth Act, which granted Puerto Ricans citizenship, was military in its passage. Two months after the 1917 Jones Act, the US Congress passed the Selective Service Act of 1917. Eighteen thousand Puerto Ricans were immediately pressed into service for World War I (Global Security 2011). Puerto Rico served a much greater military need than economic from 1898 through the end of World War II.

In 1951, Puerto Rico was granted permission to elect its own government. The United States made Puerto Rico a model for third-world industrialization through an effort called *Operation Bootstrap*. But when the United States "saved" Puerto Rico from its agrarian economy by installing an industrial one, the number of jobs available to the farm workers dwindled. One of the effects of Operation Bootstrap was that finding the work with which to pull oneself up meant leaving the island. Over five hundred thousand Puerto Ricans emigrated from the island from 1948 through the 1950s, mainly to New York City. And so the new group that "no speak English," the no-speaks, quickly became spics. Although the racialization of Puerto Ricans had begun with the Supreme Court's determination that the island was "inhabited by alien races," it was the mass migration of Puerto Ricans that fostered a new meaning for the word *ethnic*. Whereas the word once specified a group's commonality in ways that resemble a nation-state, in the 1950s especially, the term came to substitute for race when physiognomy was insufficient. Race, in that physical sense, could not apply to Puerto Ricans, who claim three heritages—*las tres razas*—European (tending to mean "Spaniard," though contained within that are the Basque, Italians, French, Arabic, and Jews, reflected in common Puerto Rican surnames like Irizarry, Cotto, Betancourt, Abad, or Pérez), African, and indigenous (tending to mean Taíno); there also were the Chinese who ended up in Puerto Rico as part of the nineteenth-century coolie trade as well as those who chose Puerto Rico when denied entry to the United States under the Chinese Exclusion Act of 1882. There is no Hispanic or Latino race. There is only the exclusion that comes from being domestic in an international sense and foreign in a domestic sense. Imaginary indeed.

RAZA AND THE ETHNO-NATION

When Arizona's superintendent of public instruction wrote against Tucson's Raza studies in his "Open Letter to the Citizens of Tucson," stating that "the very name 'Raza' is translated as 'the race,'" (*The Answer Sheet*) he missed that "the race" is comprised in the Latino imaginary as the coming together of three races—equal not separate (though Latinos have our own racialized hierarchies). In like manner, Puerto Ricans cannot be reduced to any single race. But there remains racism. It is no wonder, then, that Romeo and Juliet got reshaped as a warning against a kind of ethnic miscegenation with *West Side Story*.

Once racialized, complete assimilation becomes unattainable. The result is that once colored as black, Latino, or ethnic, Puerto Ricans by and large hold on to the island, even when the island is a nearly mythic homeland for those who have never known it or who are removed from its stateside Puerto Rican communities. In a similar manner, Mexican Americans hold on to mythic Aztlán and the name of the Chican-Ostionoid, who are also ancestors to Puerto Rico's indigenous Taíno peoples (Rouse 1992). Puerto Ricans thereby form, to extend a term coined by Grosfoguel, Negrón-Muntaner, and Georas (1997), an *ethno-nation* (though the authors use the term to account for the island's inhabitants' sense of the island as a nation even as it is not). As the United States' imaginary boundaries and imaginary unity disallow full entry to Latinos and Latinas, the Latinos and Latinas form their own national identities, as do Chicanos and Puerto Ricans and Dominicans and the like, and as do Latinos, Latinas, and in certain parts of the US Southwest, Hispanics.

It is reasonable that once articulated as Other, the Other would rearticulate as its own Same, as is the case with American Indians who claim a unity where once they warred; as is the case with African Americans, who claim a commonality—Africa—where they were and are from many nations and tongues within a large African continent.

And it is the rigidity of this sense of the southern US border that makes holding on to a sense of an ethno-nation imperative, a response to the national imaginary. Invoking the concept of the nation and its border, Samuel Huntington argues that this nation, the United States, is under an immigration threat, noting,

> The central issue will remain the degree to which Hispanics are assimilated into American society as previous immigrant groups have been. . . . Mexicans walk across a border or wade across a river. This plus the increasing ease of transportation and communication enables them to maintain close contacts and identity with their communities. Second, Mexican immigrants are concentrated in the southwestern United States and form part of continuous Mexican society stretching from Yucatan to Colorado. Third, . . . resistance to assimilation. . . . Fourth, the area settled by Mexican migrants was annexed by the United States after it defeated Mexico in the nineteenth century. . . . In due course, the results of American military expansion in the nineteenth century could be threatened and possibly reversed by Mexican demographic expansion in the twenty-first century. (Huntington 1998, 205–06)

In *Who Are We? The Challenges to America's National Identity*, Huntington revives the stereotypes that have long characterized the Latino, arguing for the solidification of the border, claiming that America's "national identity" will be altered by a people whose values contain a "lack of ambition" (thereby circumventing the contradiction of being lazy and doing the work no one else will do; they do the work because they lack ambition) and taken over by a people for whom the "acceptance of poverty as a virtue [is] necessary for entry into Heaven" (Huntington 2004, 36). The only way the interlopers will not ruin America's national identity is for them to embrace the Anglo-Protestant ethos, its American Dream— to be able to "share in that dream and in that society only if they dream in English" (36).

Failing to see the nation as imaginary, itself a trope, Huntington and others call to solidify the border, even when that border doesn't exist, as is the case with Puerto Rico. The nation as trope, as an imaginary, is rendered as Anglo-American (and Protestant), allowing for a conception of the enemy at the gate, the invading horde. My brother-in-law can say to me that he is "white, last of a dying breed" (to which I say, yep, only 84 percent of the population). The nation as trope allows us to accept the metonymic gates, to render those who have always been among "us" (since I am the rendered and the "us," of this nation born, a protector of the state, once with my very body in foreign soil, and then—and now—as a guardian of its *de facto* national language). The nation as trope allows for the forgetting that the national identity is fluid, changing character, adapting language, not nearly as unified as is imagined. *Kindergarten* becomes an English word; a corporation with a Scottish name sells a product named after a German city: millions of McDonald's Hamburgers are consumed every day; and Americans eat "a slice," synonymous with the American pizza (itself derived from Arab flat bread—the pita). And even as Taco Bell once told us to "run for the border," the taco has become thoroughly a part of the national identity. The only conclusion one can draw is that in a nation-state that has yet to break from its structural racism, racism's expression finds new tropes, not necessarily pointing to a people as racialized (even as that's the case) but pointing to structures, the border, a metonym. It is that imagining that allowed Republicans during the 2012 presidential election, for example, to be surprised at the power of the Latino and Latina voter—even though Latinos and Latinas have been a part of the United States from its inception, insofar as Spain had declared the territory it called *la Florida* from contemporary Florida to Delaware and west to Texas as its own before the thirteen colonies (see Forever Changed 2013), insofar as Hernándo de Soto had encountered "Indians" who already knew Spanish when he landed in the land we think of as Georgia in 1540 (Smith and Gottlob 1978), insofar as Manifest Destiny meant incorporating the former citizens of Mexico and New Spain. Latinos have always been a part of the United States, yet we were imagined to be Others, the ones who live across some water—the Rio Grande, the Caribbean Sea. This is how the imaginary functions: the Same and the Others. There is, of course, the nation, with agreed-upon lines, serving economic interests, the things of World Banks and International Monetary Funds, and dollars and euros and pesos and yen, and even ancient notions of territory, symbolically played out in sports like football or soccer or hockey—strategized incursions and conquests.

Money, territory, empire—abstract, even symbolic, but very real in consequences. There is little that we—that is, the public in general, which certainly includes us, the rhetoricians—can do about such things in the short term, apparently, even as we, or some of us, shout "not in our name." But whatever our limits in affecting the goings on of stateswomen and statesmen, we—the public in general and rhetoricians specifically—are not wholly without power. That is why we are all being told stories and are being wooed, why we, the public, is led to fear imaginary incursions into "our way of life" rendered as an assumed monolith even as we know our way of life is fluid. We, the public, must consent to incursions and exclusions. Hegemony demands our consent. We, the rhetoricians, can instead accept that part of what we must do (as language folk) is both to see and to publicize the rhetoric at play and then to work to demystify and demythify the ideological. We as rhetoricians have important work to do in helping the public see the need to withdraw consent when the myth of border, the trope of border, endangers the least powerful among us.

References

Anderson, Benedict. 2006. *Imagined Communities: Reflections on the Origin and Spread of Nationalism.* New York: Verso.
Babin, Edith, and Kimberly Harrison. 1999. *Contemporary Composition Studies: A Guide to Theorists and Terms.* Westport, CT: Greenwood.
Burke, Kenneth. 1941. "Four Master Tropes." *Kenyon Review* 3 (4): 421–38.
Burke, Kenneth. 1969a. *A Grammar of Motives.* Berkeley: University of California Press.
Burke, Kenneth. 1969b. *A Rhetoric of Motives.* Berkeley: University of California Press.
Ferguson, Niall. 2003. "America: An Empire in Denial." *Chronicle of Higher Education* 49 (29): B7. http://chronicle.com/article/America-an-Empire-in-Denial/29867.
Forever Changed: La Florida 1513–1821. 2013. http://www.museumoffloridahistory.com/exhibits/permanent/foreverchanged/foreverChangedPowerpoint.pdf.
Glazer, Nathan, and Daniel Patrick Moynihan. 1963. *Beyond the Melting Pot: The Negros, Puerto Ricans, Jews, Italians and Irish of New York City.* Cambridge, MA: MIT Press.
GlobalSecurity.org. 2011. "Puerto Rico National Guard." GlobalSecurity.org. http://www.globalsecurity.org/military/agency/army/arng-pr.htm.
Grosfoguel, Ramón. 1997. "The Divorce of Nationalist Discourses from the Puerto Rican People: A Sociohistorical Perspective." In *Puerto Rican Jam: Rethinking Colonialism and Nationalism,* edited by Frances Negrón-Muntaner and Ramón Grosfoguel, 57–76. Minneapolis: University of Minnesota Press.
Grosfoguel, Ramón, Frances Negrón-Muntaner, and Chloé S. Georas. 1997. "Beyond Nationalist and Colonialist Discourses: The Jaiba Politics of the Puerto Rican Ethno-Nation." In *Puerto Rican Jam: Rethinking Colonialism and Nationalism,* edited by Frances Negrón-Muntaner and Ramón Grosfoguel, 1–36. Minneapolis: University of Minnesota Press.
Hall, Stuart. 1997. "The Work of Representation." In *Representation: Cultural Representations and Signifying Practices,* edited by Stuart Hall, 13–74. London: Sage.
Huntington, Samuel P. 1998. *The Clash of Civilizations and the Remaking of World Order.* New York: Simon and Schuster.
Huntington, Samuel P. 2004. *Who Are We? The Challenges to America's National Identity.* New York: Simon and Schuster.
Iakovidis, Spyros E. 1983. *Late Helladic Citadels on Mainland Greece.* Leiden, the Netherlands: E. J. Brill.
IMDb (Internet Movie Database). "West Side Story: Full Cast and Crew" n.d. IMDb.com. www.imdb.com/title/tt0055614/fullcredits.
Irmscher, William F., ed. 1979. *The Holt Guide to English: A Contemporary Handbook of Rhetoric, Language, and Literature.* New York: Holt.

Kaplan, Amy. 2002. *The Anarchy of Empire in the Making of U.S. Culture.* Cambridge, MA: Harvard University Press.
Kinneavy, James. 1998. "Winterowd: Rhetorical Pioneer and Warrior." *JAC* 18 (3): 413–26.
Lauer, Janice M. 2004. *Invention in Rhetoric and Composition.* West Lafayette, IN: Parlor.
Moberg, Göran (George). 1990. "The Renewal of Rhetoric: A Bibliographic Essay." *Journal of Basic Writing* 9 (2): 66–82.
Needham, Joseph. 1971. *Science and Civilisation in China.* Vol. 4: *Physics and Physical Technology,* Part 3: *Civil Engineering and Nautics.* Cambridge: Cambridge University Press.
Negrón-Muntaner, Frances. 1997. "English Only Jamás but Spanish Only Cuidado: Language and Nationalism in Contemporary Puerto Rico." In *Puerto Rican Jam: Rethinking Colonialism and Nationalism,* edited by Frances Negrón-Muntaner and Ramón Grosfoguel, 257–86. Minneapolis: University of Minnesota Press.
Nevins, Joseph. 2002. *Operation Gatekeeper: The War on "Illegals" and the Remaking of the U.S.-Mexico Boundary.* New York: Routledge.
Robertson, D. W. Jr. 1946. "A Note on the Classical Origin of 'Circumstances' in the Medieval Confessional." *Studies in Philology* 43 (1): 6–14.
Rouse, Irving. 1992. *The Tainos: Rise and Decline of the People Who Greeted Columbus.* New Haven, CT: Yale University Press.
Smith, Hale G., and Marc Gottlob. 1978. "Spanish-Indian Relationships: Synoptic History and Archaeological Evidence, 1500–1763." In *Tacachale: Essays on the Indians of Florida and Southeastern Georgia during the Historic Period,* edited by Jerald Milanich and Samuel Proctor, 1–18. Gainesville: University Presses of Florida.
Southern Poverty Law Center. 2012. "Puerto Rican Birth Certificate Causes Confusion." Alabama's Shame: HB 56 and the War on Immigrants, 23–24. http://www.splcenter.org/alabamas-shame-hb56-and-the-war-on-immigrants/puerto-rican-birth-certificate-causes-confusion.
US Census Bureau. n.d. "State and County QuickFacts." http://quickfacts.census.gov/qfd/states/01000.html.
Wegner, Dana. 2001. "New Interpretations of How the USS Maine Was Lost." In *Theodore Roosevelt, the U.S. Navy, and the Spanish-American War,* edited by Edward J. Marolda, 7–18. New York: Palgrave.

3
CONTINUITY AND CONTACT IN A COSMOPOLITAN WORLD
Code-Switching and Its Effects on Community Identity

Christopher Schroeder

In our efforts to achieve a more perfect union, we have been challenged, as Barack Obama suggested when he was still a presidential candidate, by the gap between our political principles and social practices. We profess a profound belief in political equality, yet we seem uneasy around cultural diversity. For example, those who live in diverse communities, according to Robert Putnam (2007) of *Bowling Alone* fame, tend to participate less in community projects and contribute less to charities, have less confidence in local leaders and local news programs, and have fewer friends and more television time. In fact, Americans, concludes Putnam after testing for other possible explanations, are uncomfortable, in both attitude and behavior, with diversity.

This gap between principles and practices is reflected in the tensions between contact and continuity. On the one hand, our American origins emerge from widespread cultural contact, which sometimes results in gaping inequalities. On the other, our own identity comes from the cultural continuity of this widespread cultural contact and other foundational values, which function as defining features of who we are. For example, we have enshrined a recognition of differences in the role of individual states in relation to the federal government even as we often understand proficiency in English, despite widespread linguistic varieties, as a transcendent feature of who we are. Moreover, the tensions between the reality of our diversity and "American" cultural values still surface in ongoing debates over identity politics, as suggested by the recent US Supreme Court decision to allow individual states to ban race-based public university admissions (see, e.g., Schmidt 2014).

DOI: 10.7330/9781607324034.c003

Tensions related to cultural diversity can challenge our foundational equality, and this cultural contact is complicated by efforts of diverse peoples to maintain cultural continuity, which can create conflicts over identity politics. These latter conflicts, according to political scientist Ronald Schmidt (2000), typically involve both the relations of self-identities to group identities or selves to other selves as well as the disputes over distribution of social goods, both of which surface in ongoing culture wars involving racialized ethnicities and social inequalities (47–56, 83). And these conflicts in turn often involve assumptions about identity and language. Many believe, for example, that "good" (US) Americans speak English and that public schools should provide instruction in American patriotism (e.g., Baron 1990, 154–56).

One response to these tensions between contact and continuity has historically occurred in print media generally and the periodical press specifically. In part, this response represents what Benedict Anderson (2006) has called "imagined communities," with the print media allowing individuals to imagine themselves as holding shared values and identities. At the same time, this response reflects other factors, such as postal subsidies on newspapers and the social emergence of the penny press. In general, by the end of the American Revolution, the press was seen as a means of preserving liberty by providing information for citizens who participated in government and held it accountable. Although the press could not be considered a source of national identity at that point, by 1840, the United States had 1,404 newspapers that ranged anywhere from 4 in South Carolina and Iowa to 245 in New York (Tucker 2010, 390–404), hence extending its reach as a tool to solidify national sentiment.

The periodical press was especially important to ethnic minorities in the United States, although the process of influence was perhaps more complicated than expected. For example, German immigrants who lacked the shared political, religious, and linguistic centers of their European relations struggled to maintain a German-language press and a shared German identity in the United States at least until the mid-nineteenth century (Roeber 2010). By late in the nineteenth century, almost 800 different ethnic newspapers were being published in the United States; the number peaked at 1,300 in 1917 before decreasing, in part the result of 1924 immigration restrictions, to 1,000 or more in thirty-eight languages by 1940 (Miller 2009, 301, 310).

Throughout this period, the European ethnic press in the United States served several functions for the communities that sponsored these publications, including communicating with others within these groups, maintaining connections with home, explaining politics and institutions in primary languages, and facilitating assimilation into new identities (Miller 2009, 299). Although immigrants after 1880 were less likely to read due to limited educational opportunities before coming to the United States, they still encountered an ethnic press, even if orally, that provided news from their former and current homes as well as information about cultural events and current issues. These immigrants and others largely came from places that were only starting to form national identities and traditions. Many used diverse dialects that were synthesized—stabilized and standardized—by the ethnic press, which in so doing structured their communities and organized their lives, a function that was only strengthened as a result of developments in transportation and technologies, even as challenges to retaining identity remained (301–2).

The successful establishment of immigrant populations and their identities was nonetheless challenged by ongoing questions related to cultural continuity and contact, which were often negotiated in debates about language. For example, the ethnic press was restricted by the federal government as a result of World War I when immigrants were expected to demonstrate their loyalty through Americanization. At that point, publishers were required to file English translations of articles about governmental politics or international events as a result of the Espionage, Sedition, and Trading with the Enemy Acts. These laws fueled anxieties about the use of languages other than English and intensified an English-only campaign for public-school instruction, which continued until a 1923 Supreme Court decision that terminated these and other linguistic limitations (Miller 2009, 309–10).

Because of its importance to immigrant populations, study of the ethnic press provides one way of understanding the effects of language on borders and boundaries as well as the press's role as a means to a more inclusive multiculturalism. In the following pages, I will examine first the general environment of cultural contact and continuity in Chicago and then analyze one specific ethnic press that expresses cross-boundary ethnic identities within a larger cultural community. For this latter study, I selected a specific newspaper that appeals to a wider Spanish-speaking audience, and I focused on a particular feature that simultaneously acknowledges contact and continuity in its efforts to use language to transcend conventional borders and boundaries. In particular, this ethnic press mixes languages in ways that challenge conventional identity politics, and it creates alternative configurations, ones that cross conventional borders and establish new boundaries, thus reconfiguring relations of identity, community, and power.

CONTACT AND CONTINUITY IN CHICAGO

The metro Chicago area, in many ways, offers a useful site for studying cultural contact and continuity because it is a microcosm of cultural conditions across the United States. In particular, it both mirrors a national cultural diversity and suggests the nation's cultural future (see Table 3.1).

For example, the Hispanic population increased between 2000 and 2010 in every region of the United States, most significantly in the South and the Midwest, according to the US Census Bureau (2010). Among these increases, approximately three-fourths were Mexican (63 percent), Puerto Rican (9 percent), or Cuban (4 percent). By 2010, between one and two in ten people in the United States identified as Hispanic or Latino (16.3 percent), most of them Mexican (10.3 percent), Puerto Rican (1.5 percent), or Cuban (0.6 percent).

Throughout the metro Chicago area, communities that experienced this growth have been the focus of much research on cultural assimilation. Some researchers, for example, have documented how members of local Mexican American communities refashion disrespect into self-respect, rely upon extended social networks, and combine oral and literate practices to meet their needs both within and beyond schools in Chicago and in Mexico (Cintron 1997; Guerra 1998). Others have demonstrated how the experiences of those who have come from Mexico are different from those educated or born here, particularly in terms of their cultural traditions and identities as well as their relations to Spanish as a native or heritage language, with some studies including discussion of the impact of Spanish proficiencies upon thinking (e.g., contributors to Farr 2005).

Still other researchers have highlighted ways the experiences of local Mexican Americans differ from those of Puerto Ricans, whose presence in the metro Chicago area was established later and reflected the historical and economic relations between the territory of Puerto Rico and the United States mainland (Del Valle 2002). Some have documented how these different groups have different perspectives on the role of linguistic proficiencies in assimilation and authenticity (De Genova and Ramos-Zayas 2003). Others have identified differences among Chicago Mexican, Puerto Rican, and MexiRican Spanish, although some have suggested that even these distinctions represent generalizations about local experiences that are more complicated than the simple distinction would suggest (Del Valle 2005; Torres and Potowski 2008).

The researchers cited above along with other researchers have noted that there is an extensive context for understanding the ethnic press in

Table 3.1 Selected demographic and social characteristics of Chicago[1]

SELECTED DEMOGRAPHIC AND SOCIAL CHARACTERISTICS OF CHICAGO		
	METRO CHICAGO	UNITED STATES
HISPANIC OR LATINO (%)	16.9	12.8
MEXICAN	16.3	10.3
PUERTO RICAN	2.0	1.5
CUBAN	0.2	0.6
OTHER HISPANIC OR LATINO	2.1	4.0
LANGUAGE OTHER THAN ENGLISH (%)	28.4	20.6
SPANISH	16.9	12.8
OTHER INDO-EUROPEAN	7.2	3.7
ASIAN/PACIFIC ISLANDER	3.2	3.2
OTHER LANGUAGES	1.1	0.9
USE ENGLISH LESS THAN "VERY WELL" (%)	12.5	8.7

Source: 2010 American Community Survey (US Census Bureau).

Chicago. Throughout the metro Chicago area, numerous media outlets—television, radio, and newspapers—target Spanish speakers, as well as speakers of other languages. Some, such as WGBO (Univision) and La Raza, are relatively independent while others, such as Catolico, are more specific and specialized. For this project, I elected to study language practices in *EXTRA*, which is self-described as "a bilingual family-owned independent newspaper serving the Chicago Latino community" that has been publishing for thirty-one years with a 2011 circulation of 71,541, reportedly a 9 percent increase over the previous year. This independent newspaper is published on Fridays and distributed through street boxes and retailers as well as delivered to homes. In 2010, it won the José Martí Gold Award for being "the outstanding bilingual newspaper in the United States" as well as the Chicago Press Club's Peter Lisagor Award for General Excellence for a foreign-language newspaper, along with other design, editorial, and marketing awards (*EXTRA* 2011, 7). More than "an award winning weekly community newspaper," it intends to link "Chicago Latinos to their community," and it includes a "dynamic growing web presence," a "mobile platform including mobile web site, text messaging and mobile coupon delivery," and a "range of community event sponsorships, concerts, festivals, and activities" (*EXTRA* 2011, 2).

Given its conceptualization of its targeted audience, *EXTRA* is particularly appropriate for this study of cultural contact and continuity. By its own account, around two million Latinos live within the Chicago market, which represents about 20 percent of the total population, and more than nine in ten of these are Hispanics from either Mexico (82 percent) or Puerto Rico (almost 10 percent). These and other conditions reportedly make the Chicago market the fifth largest Hispanic market in the United States: 80 percent of Hispanics live in 20 percent of the zip codes, with 40 percent in only 14 zip codes. More than seven in ten (71 percent) are between the ages of eighteen and forty-four (48 percent between eighteen and thirty-four). The entire Hispanic market in Chicago has an overall estimated median household income (2007) of $45,597 (*EXTRA* 2011, 2). This newspaper, in other words, is particularly well suited to meet the needs of a large and concentrated market that represents a relatively young community with some disposable income.

"Today's Hispanic market," this newspaper suggests, "is multi-generational and multi-lingual," and the newspaper's "award-winning bilingual format," which "reaches 54% of the market neglected by Spanish-only media," is designed to enable readers "to choose their language of comfort" (*EXTRA* 2011, 4). In particular, this format allows "first-generation Hispanics and older Hispanics" to read in Spanish while "younger, higher educated Hispanics" can read in English: "One decision, one newspaper, one advertisement reaches the entire market" (4).

In keeping with its official mission and its marketing strategy, *EXTRA* offers print articles in both languages—a Spanish version and an English version—with a choice of languages on the website, though some posts can only be accessed in one language. However, *EXTRA* mixes these languages in the English versions of an advice column, which ostensibly features three *abuelitas* (literally translated as "little grandmothers"); the column is advertised to its readers thus:

> Mijitos,
>
> Te hace falta tu Abuelita? You have question about life, love, money, lo que sea, no te apures, your favorite Abuelita is here.
> There's three of us: Marta la Cubana, Lalita la Venezolana, y Dulce la Dominicana. Entre todas, te damos mas de 100 años de experiencia in Abuelitahood.
>
> Yo se que tienes una preguntita para las abuelitas y te prometemos que we'll give you the most thoughtful answer we can. Pero mira, si se ponen frescos, we gonna have to just tell you like it is. Atrevete- we can see you with the eyes we have in the back of our heads.

Submit your questions to DearAbuelitas@extranews.net.

Y remember: the question that makes us go "hmmmm" or "ehhhhh" the most, gets their pregunta answered with a very special video featuring all of the Abuelitas on the EXTRA Newspaper blog. Ahora . . . donde esta mi cafesito?

Sinceramente,
Tus Queridas Abuelitas (EXTRA n.d.)

Though once four, currently three *abuelitas* will individually respond to, for example, "a strong, independent woman" whose parents are concerned that she is still unmarried, or a sixth-grade girl who has known for some time that she likes "other girls" but can't talk with her parents about her sexual orientation.

The following sample submission and response illustrate the topics and tone of these exchanges.

Casada en Facebook/Married on Facebook

Dear Abuelitas:

I am going through a divorce right now and have been separated from my husband for two months now. However, on our Facebook profiles, it says we're still married. I want to prevent the awkward conversations that have started to pop up from people who don't know, but I also realize that not everyone on Facebook is a true "friend." When is the right time to update my profile?

Sincerely,

The Social Media Spouse

Querida "Social Media Spouse"

It's my advice to you that you do it in the middle of the day when people are posting the most and do it right away. Asi things keep moving along and too much attention isn't paid to your status change. I also think you need to delete the change to your profile or "remove" it, I don't know what they call it these days pero get rid of whatever FB wants to say about it.

When you change it go ahead and change it so that it doesn't show who you are with at all because it's nobody's business that you are single or not. In my opinion, no one on FB needs to know who you are with or not. A bunch of metiches anyway. If you want to get real sneaky, also make a little change in your "about" section so that the change becomes more important than the relationship status change. A friend of mine, Gloria, just went through the same thing, but she doesn't know how to use Facebook so she was getting calls all the way from Santo Domingo asking her why her and her enamorado broke up. You think family telephone game is bad . . . it gets worse when you have the Facebook. For the rest of you reading this, I say grow up and stop behaving like 13 year olds with who you're with and who you're not with, coño. Like my Mami used to say, a woman's secrets are a woman's secrets and not everyone needs to know your business. Talk about brushing your teeth if you must, but leave your relación out of it.

Your Abuelita Favorita,
Lalita (EXTRA 2012b)

Although other submissions remain as mixtures of Spanish and English, this particular submission also appears entirely in Spanish if the Spanish option of the web version has been selected.

One submission is particularly noteworthy because it was subsequently translated into an online video. Here is the initial print version, which remains the same in both the Spanish and English versions online:

Dear Abuelitas,

My aunt is visiting us and has been here for about a month. I notice that she has been gaining a lot of weight since she got here. She waits until everyone is in bed at night and then watches TV and eats her junk food—chocolates and Coke. She is beginning to waddle when she walks and if we go to the corner store.

I want to tell her that she needs to cut back on her junk food because it's making her unhealthy without hurting her feelings. How do I do that?

Signed,
The concerned niece who loves her Tia!

Querida "Concerned Niece who loves her Tia":

Pues sí. I like to eat también, y como me encanta la Coca-Cola, muchacha! It's criminal.

What worries me is that Latinos have the highest rate of Diabetes, mija, and the way your Tia is eating might lead her down that road if she's not careful. Pero your talking about how she walks funny y como she's gained weight and that's the fastest way to a cocotaso with a Latina. I say, talk to her about the amount of sugar and corn syrup y esa basura in the food she's eating. Tell her that it causes diabetes in Latinos and how difficult it is to live with diabetes and remember that knowledge is power, mamita. Pero please, no le digas que se está poniendo gorda. Because that would make you a mala and I write people out of my Will for things like that. So, piensa eso.

I think it's beautiful that you're worried though, cosita linda. Eso es family first mentality and I have a special place in my corazonsito for that kind of thinking.

-Tu Abuelita favorita, Lalita la Venezolana (EXTRA 2012a)

Although Lalita ostensibly provides the written response, *todas las abuelitas* respond in the video adaptation (*EXTRA* 2012a), which was posted later, and their video performances differ from the printed version. After opening with an introductory montage of *las tres abuelitas*, it features the three of them loosely following the print version (which is entirely attributed to Lalita), though the advice is distributed among them in the online video version; all three ad-lib their lines, sometimes in Spanish, sometimes in English.

CONTACT, CONTINUITY, AND CODE-SWITCHING IN CHICAGO

This paper and these columns are continuing an effort that began at least as early as the nineteenth century when the Cherokee were the first indigenous community in North America to own their own press and produce their own bilingual newspaper (O'Connell 2010, 497). At the same time, this paper's particular existence within Chicago and Illinois is also significant. Although Chicago declared in 1867 that official notices had to be published in other languages, this requirement was overturned by the Illinois Supreme Court in 1891, and as early as 1889, Illinois required English as the language of instruction in schools, which resulted in a "nativist reaction" that fragmented the state (Baron 1990, 119). Continuing in this direction, Illinois passed one of the first language laws in the nation that established its official language as *American*, and although state legislators changed it from the nationally and even internationally popular *American* to *English* in 1969, the message was nonetheless clear.

In this context of legal preference for English, this newspaper and these columns challenge tacit English-only language policies that reflect misunderstandings about the relative role of English within larger debates, according to political scientist Ronald Schmidt (2000), over the designation of an official language, linguistic civil and political rights, and educational policies for minority students. Some believe that the dominance of English is threatened by those who use a language other than English in public places and that English-only policies are necessary to ensure social unity and increase individual opportunity. Others maintain that the dominant status of English is the result of unequal competition among linguistic groups within a multilingual country and that multilingual policies and philosophies are the only means to ameliorate existing inequalities. Both perspectives cite data: the use of English is highly correlated with income, wealth, and occupational standing, and yet a second language is not correlated with low income as long as it exists alongside English proficiency (Schmidt 2000, 83–95).

These conventional perspectives about English use index language to cultural identity, or create symbolic links between the two, in ways that reflect larger historical and social disagreements over linguistic and cultural conditions. The assimilationist perspective of English only misunderstands the status of English in the United States, where immigrants since the 1960s have exhibited the same trend toward English monolingualism by the third generation as other US immigrants since World War II. At the same time, the assimilationist perspective reflects an incomplete and romanticized history of the United States as a land of opportunity, ignoring its history of imperialism and conquest. In contrast, the pluralist perspective that endorses multilingualism, although preferable, often overlooks the linguistic and cultural dilemmas created when the acquisition of English, which perhaps permits individuals to overcome a subordinate social status, subsequently overrides other proficiencies. This latter view is typically based in liberal individualism that ignores the instability of multicultural communities and their challenge of negotiating these linguistic and cultural differences, differences that rarely, if ever, offer choices among equally acceptable alternatives for them (Schmidt 2000, 198–203; Schroeder 2011, 196–206).

In a metro area where between one and two in ten identify as Hispanic and about the same percentage of residents use Spanish at home, the advice dispensed by *EXTRA*'s *las tres abuelitas* clearly represents the perspective of *EXTRA* as "Two Languages Una Voz." At the same time, these columns create *una voz* that not only transcends specific immigrant communities but also connects these with a larger community.

EXTRA and its columns, by extension, challenge official and unofficial language policies and cultural identities within Illinois and across the nation. While the bilingual content of the paper is significant, perhaps a more significant feature is the existence of code-switching exclusively within the English versions, a practice that seems to expand the function of the ethnic press to highlight cultural differences. These expansions and challenges are reinforced by the recognition of cultural differences in the online video, where the print response is merely a script and is delivered by the performers in ways that highlight these differences in phonetic, morphological, syntactic, semantic, and even pragmatic dimensions.

In general, these columns exhibit the full range of features researchers associate with code-mixing (code-switching): intersentential, or switching between languages at sentence or clause boundaries; intrasentential, or switching between languages with phrases, words, or morphemes; and even tag switches, or switching with tag forms that some linguists do not acknowledge as a separate category. (Although some distinguish between *code-mixing* and *code-switching*, many researchers use these terms interchangeably.) At the same time, these columns exhibit the deliberate use of first language (L1), second or subsequent language (L2), and mixed L1-L2 to express the idiomatic, attention-getting, and/ or emotional-cultural-evocative bonding that can be found in other national publications. In short, communicative characteristics in these columns suggest language change (e.g., Mahootian 2005; 2012).

The columns of *las tres abuelitas*, especially within larger linguistic, social, and cultural contexts, address the challenges of maintaining cultural continuity and acknowledging cultural contact by illustrating ways code-switching can shift power relations and privilege multilingual and multicultural identities. Such code-switching efforts can function, as the linguist Shahrzad Mahootian (2012) has suggested, as statements of political defiance, as evidence of globalization and deterritorializing of identity. Code-switching also reflects shifts in social status and, thus, social power; it is also a symbol of emerging ethnic identities and hyphenated communities. Not only do *EXTRA*'s mixed languages define and promote bi(multi)cultural identities, but they also suggest and represent new linguistic and cultural norms that can restructure existing power relations throughout society (195–98).

In particular, *las tres abuelitas* and *EXTRA* suggest ways code-switching can appeal to Spanish-English speakers in Chicago despite different cultural histories of these multilinguals. At the same time, it can function as a symbolic metaphor that cultural critic Ed Morales (2002) has argued is characteristic of Chicago's combined East- and West-Coast Spanglish culture. In so doing, code-switching can reconcile differences among distinctly different cultural identities across the United States. Spanglish, as both a linguistic phenomenon and symbolic metaphor, can invoke what Kwame Appiah (1997; 2006) has identified as a cosmopolitan culture that both celebrates differences and retains loyalties, respecting individuals while celebrating institutions where they live. Although such invocations sometimes neglect material realities, they nonetheless can challenge exclusionary calls for a national language and culture and suggest possibilities for new perspectives.

IMPLICATIONS

In a small yet public way, the code-switching by *las tres abuelitas*, including their synthesis of linguistic and cultural differences into *una voz*, contributes to larger debates about how our notions of language and literacy create borders and boundaries within and even beyond the United States.

More research is needed to document different ways code-switching crosses various borders and draws (new) boundaries in Chicago and elsewhere. Some, for example, have suggested that the code-switching among varieties of Chicago Spanish, which are generally expected to converge over time, still exhibits internalized differences that have tentatively been attributed to linguistic and ethnic differences among Spanish speakers (e.g., Torres and Potowski 2008). One potentially productive approach to researching characteristics and implications of code-switching has been employed by Barbara Johnstone (2010), who has explored how individuals index the local, which she has interpreted as reflecting the impact of globalization upon cultural production. In particular, she has documented how indexicals, or specific signs created through the lived experience of individuals, such as certain local phonemes or phrases, have been *enregistered*, or integrated within social norms. For instance, she describes *Pittsburghese* as a local language variety that requires a familiarity with the cultural and linguistic conventions of Pittsburgh to interpret (e.g., Johnstone 2011; Johnstone and Kiesling 2008).

Other researchers have acknowledged a lack of research on written code-switching as well as the need to analyze it from the perspective of literacy studies, link it to the formation of cultural identities, and consider layout, typography, and other often ignored aspects affiliated with code-switching (e.g., Sebba 2012). Another potentially productive approach has been outlined by Brandt and Clinton (2002), who have criticized situated models of literacy for overemphasizing the local. They have highlighted the *transcontextualized* and *transcontextualizing* aspects of literacy, or the features that allow literacy, which is locally realized, to "delocalize or even disrupt local life" (338). More specifically, they have argued for a more comprehensive account of literacy that recognizes its technological potential, including its ability to participate in, and thus shape, local experiences through what they have called *localizing moves, globalizing connects,* and *folding in,* accommodations that frame interactions by recognizing the immediate and the distant and that embed cultural relations in tools and products. Such accommodations are illustrated, they suggest, in the way that applying for a loan, for example, is shaped by "forms, files, documents, contract, calculator, computer, data bases" and other aspects and objects, even the furniture and building where the transaction occurs (344–45).

The link between the local and global is crucial to understanding the role of language and literacy in creating borders and drawing boundaries today among diverse communities. The result of these "local-global encounters" reflected in language practices, according to literacy theorist Brian Street (2003), is not "a single essentialized version of each language represented in these practices" but rather "a new hybrid" of literacy practices (80–82; see also Bartlett and Holland 2002; Collins and Blot 2003; and Hornberger 2003). These situations, in other words, are better understood as amalgamations of practices and norms with potentially local and global origins. Though some (e.g., Bizzell 2002) have criticized *hybridity* as a conceptual metaphor, it nonetheless offers one way to begin theorizing about the role of written and spoken language in the creation of borders and boundaries within a globalized world. For example, in his widely admired book *The World Is Flat,* Thomas L. Friedman (2007) has argued that "flattening forces" of new technologies in globalized societies are in fact "equalizing" because they empower increasing numbers of individuals "to reach farther, faster, deeper, and cheaper than ever before" (x). Such forces provide "an equalizing opportunity" that gives "so many more people the tools and ability to connect, compete, and collaborate" (x). More and more people in this increasingly flat world can "collaborate and compete in real time with more other people on more different kinds of work from more different corners of the planet and on a more equal footing than at any previous time in the history of the world—using computers, email, fiber optic networks, teleconferencing, and dynamic new software" (8). This "flat-world platform," as Friedman has described it, creates a more enabling and empowering world driven not only by individuals but also by more diverse—nonwhite and non-Western—individuals (11).

Friedman's book has been praised for its clear explanations and clever metaphor (e.g., Zakaria 2005). However, he largely ignores the effects of literal and figurative borders, including their relations to linguistic identities, even as he occasionally acknowledges linguistic identities as borders, in effect. For instance, he describes an "accent neutralization class" in which he, even with his "Minnesotan" accent, is asked to supply an "authentic" account of "a single phonetic paragraph" that has been prepared for students "to teach them how to soften their *t*'s and roll their *r*'s" (26–28). Later he reproduces alarmist statistics about the purported decline of college graduates' reading and writing proficiencies as a result, he suggests, of the Internet (353–54). In other words, Friedman acknowledges efforts to eliminate these borders, in the form of phonetic differences, in the first example even as in the second he clearly establishes others by distinguishing between those who read and write in college-educated ways and those who presumably do so in other ways.

Although his perspective seems to overlook the effects of linguistic borders and boundaries at a systemic level, Friedman nonetheless recognizes language and literacy as means to increase communication and collaboration, long central to social organization and cultural evolution (e.g., Wright 2000). Conventional accounts construct the notion of the nation, which is presumed to be congruent with the state, from linguistic boundaries and cultural traditions that, in their origins, had to be established and delimited (e.g., Wright 2004). These boundaries and traditions, which are harder to sustain in speaking than in writing, have been challenged by contemporary technologies, such as social media, that allow individuals to index cultural identities to competing centers, even ones increasingly distant from their geographical locations (de la Piedra 2010; Lam 2009; McLean 2010).

The outcomes of increased cultural contact and efforts to maintain cultural continuity are, at the moment, unclear at best. For example, some have suggested, despite widespread predictions about the Englishization of the world, that global-based markets are reducing the abilities of nation-states to control language use and change through standardization initiatives and other means, as illustrated by the ways individuals can watch television programming or surf the Internet in different languages (e.g., Dor 2004). Participants within this global market, these researchers have suggested, will adapt to local cultures and languages and produce culturally specific commodities. The outcome for language dominance in this global political economy could be neither global English nor multilingual freedom but market-imposed multilingualism within different language zones (111–12).

In these or other ways, linguistic borders and boundaries, established as a result of cultural contact and efforts to maintain cultural continuity, could be configured and reconfigured to provide increased access to social resources and sociocultural capital, as *las tres abuelitas* seem to do. While cultural diversity can challenge social solidarity and restrict social capital, these challenges and restrictions can be overcome, the sociologist Robert Putnam (2007) has argued, by establishing more expansive social identities and, through them, more extensive social and cultural capital that produces opportunities for people to build better democracies and economies as well as opportunities for the citizens within them to lead longer and happier lives (137–39).

Note

1. Perhaps in part as a result, Chicago neighborhoods generally and Chicago Latinos specifically have been the focus of much cultural and linguistic research (e.g., Cintron 1997; De Genova and Ramos-Zayas 2003; Del Valle 2002; Farr 2005; Guerra 1998).

References

Anderson, Benedict. 2006. *Imagined Communities: Reflections on the Origin and Spread of Nationalism.* Rev. ed. London: Verso.

Appiah, Kwame Anthony. 1997. "Cosmopolitan Patriots." *Critical Inquiry* 23 (3): 617–39. http://dx.doi.org/10.1086/448846.

Appiah, Kwame Anthony. 2006. *Cosmopolitanism: Ethics in a World of Strangers.* New York: Norton.

Baron, Dennis. 1990. *The English-Only Question: An Official Language for Americans?* New Haven, CT: Yale University Press.

Bartlett, Lesley, and Dorothy Holland. 2002. "Theorizing the Space of Literacy Practices." *Ways of Knowing* 2 (1): 10–22.

Bizzell, Patricia. 2002. "The Intellectual Work of 'Mixed' Forms of Academic Discourses." In *ALT DIS: Alternative Discourses and the Academy*, edited by Christopher Schroeder, Helen Fox, and Patricia Bizzell, 1–10. Portsmouth, NH: Heinemann.

Brandt, Deborah, and Katie Clinton. 2002. "Limits of the Local: Expanding Perspectives on Literacy as a Social Practice." *Journal of Literacy Research* 34 (3): 337–56. http://dx.doi.org/10.1207/s15548430jlr3403_4.

Cintron, Ralph. 1997. *Angels' Town: Chero Ways, Gang Life, and Rhetorics of the Everyday.* Boston, MA: Beacon.

Collins, James, and Richard K. Blot. 2003. *Literacy and Literacies: Texts, Power, and Identity.* Cambridge: Cambridge University Press. http://dx.doi.org/10.1017/CBO9780511486661.

De Genova, Nicholas, and Ana Y. Ramos-Zayas. 2003. *Latino Crossings: Mexicans, Puerto Ricans and the Politics of Race and Citizenship.* New York: Routledge.

de la Piedra, Maria Teresa. 2010. "Adolescent Worlds and Literacy Practices on the United States Mexico Border." *Journal of Adolescent & Adult Literacy* 53 (7): 575–84. http://dx.doi.org/10.1598/JAAL.53.7.5.

Del Valle, Tony. 2002. *Written Literacy Features of Three Puerto Rican Family Networks in Chicago.* New York: Mellen.

Del Valle, Tony. 2005. "'Successful' and 'Unsuccessful' Literacies of Two Puerto Rican Families in Chicago." In *Latino Language and Literacy in Ethnolinguistic Chicago*, edited by Marcia Farr, 97–131. Mahwah, NJ: Lawrence Erlbaum.

Dor, Daniel. 2004. "From Englishization to Imposed Multilingualism: Globalization, the Internet, and the Political Economy of the Linguistic Code." *Public Culture* 16 (1): 97–118. http://dx.doi.org/10.1215/08992363-16-1-97.

EXTRA. Two Languages Una Voz. n.d. "Las Abuelitas." http://extranews.net/abuelitas.

EXTRA. Two Languages Una Voz. 2011. "Media Kit." Extra News. http://extranews.net/media-kit.

EXTRA. Two Languages Una Voz. 2012a. "The Concerned Niece Who Loves Her Tia." Extra News. http://extranews.net/dear-abuelitas-the-concerned-niece-who-loves-her-tia-video.html.

EXTRA. Two Languages Una Voz. 2012b. "Married on Facebook." Extra News. http://extranews.net/married-on-facebook.html.

Farr, Marcia, ed. 2005. *Latino Language and Literacy in Ethnolinguistic Chicago.* Mahwah, NJ: Lawrence Erlbaum Associates.

Friedman, Thomas L. 2007. *The World Is Flat: A Brief History of the Twenty-first Century.* New York: Picador.

Guerra, Juan C. 1998. *Close to Home: Oral and Literate Practices in a Transnational Mexicano Community.* New York: Teachers College Press.

Hornberger, Nancy. 2003. *Continua of Biliteracy: An Ecological Framework for Educational Policy, Research, and Practice in Multilingual Settings.* Bristol, UK: Multilingual Matters.

Johnstone, Barbara. 2010. "Indexing the Local." In *The Handbook of Language and Globalization,* edited by Nikolas Coupland, 386–405. Oxford, UK: Wiley-Blackwell. http://dx.doi.org/10.1002/9781444324068.ch17.

Johnstone, Barbara. 2011. "Dialect Enregisterment in Performance." *Journal of Sociolinguistics* 15 (5): 657–79. http://dx.doi.org/10.1111/j.1467-9841.2011.00512.x.

Johnstone, Barbara, and Scott F. Kiesling. 2008. "Indexicality and Experience: Exploring the Meanings of /aw/-monophthongization in Pittsburgh." *Journal of Sociolinguistics* 12 (1): 5–33. http://dx.doi.org/10.1111/j.1467-9841.2008.00351.x.

Lam, Wan Shun Eva. 2009. "Multiliteracies on Instant Messaging in Negotiating Local, Translocal, and Transnational Affiliations: A Case of an Adolescent Immigrant." *Reading Research Quarterly* 44 (4): 377–97. http://dx.doi.org/10.1598/RRQ.44.4.5.

Mahootian, Shahrzad. 2005. "Linguistic Change and Social Meaning: Codeswitching in the Media." *International Journal of Bilingualism* 9 (3–4): 361–75. http://dx.doi.org/10.1177/13670069050090030401.

Mahootian, Shahrzad. 2012. "Repertoires and Resources: Accounting for Code-Mixing in the Media." In *Language Mixing and Code-Switching in Writing: Approaches to Mixed-language Written Discourse,* edited by Mark Sebba, Sharzad Mahootian, and Carla Jonsson, 192–212. New York: Routledge.

McLean, Cheryl A. 2010. "A Space Called Home: An Immigrant Adolescent's Digital Literacy Practices." *Journal of Adolescent & Adult Literacy* 54 (1): 13–22. http://dx.doi.org/10.1598/JAAL.54.1.2.

Miller, Sally M. 2009. "Distinctive Media: The European Ethnic Press in the United States." In *Print in Motion: The Expansion of Publishing and Reading in the United States, 1880–1940,* edited by Carl F. Kaestle and Janice A. Redway, 299–311. Chapel Hill: University of North Carolina Press.

Morales, Ed. 2002. *Living in Spanglish: The Search for Latino Identity in America.* New York: St. Martin's.

O'Connell, Barry. 2010. "Literacy and Colonization: The Case of the Cherokees." In *An Extensive Republic: Print, Culture, and Society in the New Nation, 1790–1840,* edited by Robert A. Gross and Mary Kelley, 495–515. Chapel Hill: University of North Carolina Press.

Putnam, Robert D. 2007. "E pluribus unum: Diversity and Community in the Twenty-First Century. The 2006 Johan Skytte Prize Lecture." *Scandinavian Political Studies* 30 (2): 137–74. http://dx.doi.org/10.1111/j.1467-9477.2007.00176.x.

Roeber, A. Gregg. 2010. "Readers and Writers of German." In *An Extensive Republic: Print, Culture, and Society in the New Nation, 1790–1840*, edited by Robert A. Gross and Mary Kelley, 471–82. Chapel Hill: University of North Carolina Press.

Schmidt, Peter. 2014. "Supreme Court Upholds Bans on Racial Preferences in College Admissions." *Chronicle of Higher Education*, April 22. http://chronicle.com/article/Supreme-Court-Upholds-Bans-on/146145/.

Schmidt, Ronald. 2000. *Language Policy and Identity Politics in the United States*. Philadelphia, PA: Temple University Press.

Schroeder, Christopher. 2011. *Diverse by Design: Literacy Education within Multicultural Institutions*. Logan: Utah State University Press.

Sebba, Mark. 2012. "Researching and Theorising Multilingual Texts." In *Language Mixing and Code-switching in Writing: Approaches to Mixed-Language Written Discourse*, edited by Mark Sebba, Sharzad Mahootian, and Carla Jonsson, 1–21. New York: Routledge.

Street, Brian. 2003. "What's New in New Literacy Studies? Critical Approaches to Literacy in Theory and Practice." *Current Issues in Comparative Education* 5 (2): 77–91.

Torres, Lourdes, and Kim Potowski. 2008. "A Comparative Study of Bilingual Discourse Markers in Chicago Mexican, Puerto Rican, and MexiRican Spanish." *International Journal of Bilingualism* 12 (4): 263–79. http://dx.doi.org/10.1177/1367006908098571.

Tucker, Andie. 2010. "Newspapers and Periodicals." In *An Extensive Republic: Print, Culture, and Society in the New Nation, 1790–1840*, edited by Robert A. Gross and Mary Kelley, 389–408. Chapel Hill: University of North Carolina Press.

US Census Bureau. 2010. "American Community Survey." http://www.census.gov/acs/www/

Wright, Robert. 2000. *Nonzero: The Logic of Human Destiny*. New York: Vintage.

Wright, Sue. 2004. *Language Policy and Language Planning: From Nationalism to Globalisation*. New York: Palgrave Macmillan.

Zakaria, Fareed. 2005. "'The World Is Flat': The Wealth of Yet More Nations." Review of *The World Is Flat: A Brief History of the Twenty-first Century*, by Thomas L. Friedman. *New York Times*, May 1, Sunday Book Review. http://www.nytimes.com/2005/05/01/books/review/01ZAKARIA.html.

4
HUMOR'S ROLE IN POLITICAL DISCOURSE
Examining Border Patrol in Colbert Nation

Jonathan P. Rossing

As many scholars have shown, disputes over immigration policy have generated public and vernacular discourses that shape and reconstruct rhetorical borders (Flores 2003; López 2006; Ono and Sloop 2002). One form of discourse not commonly examined is humor. Among the public policies, town-hall meetings, pundit debates, political speeches, and more, humor about immigration contributes vital critical perspectives with the potential to reshape attitudes toward immigration and change the meaning and understanding of borders. Examples of humor about immigration are abundant. Consider the following responses to the passage of Arizona Senate Bill 1070 in April 2010. The law rendered the failure to carry immigration documents a crime and granted police broad power to interrogate and detain any people they suspected to be "illegal." As debates about Arizona's legislation escalated, a photo of Dora the Explorer garnered national attention. The Latina children's cartoon character appeared in a mug shot with a black eye and bloodied lip (Friedman 2010). This dark humor relied on the comic incongruity of a beloved children's character fallen victim to racial profiling and brutality in order to raise questions about the overreaching law. In a similar vein, various comedians have filmed videos in which they stop Caucasians and demand their immigration papers on the grounds that they were not native to the land. These groups satirically cast white people in the role of illegal immigrant in order to contextualize current opposition to immigration within a history of violent displacement of native populations at the hands of immigrants.

Immigration debates and policy disputes provide fertile territory for examining humor's potential to blur borders and invite audiences to inhabit the often uncomfortable borderlands. Scholars of communication, psychology, sociology, anthropology, and more have long studied the role of humor as a critical, instructional, and political discourse (Hall, Keeter, and Williamson 1993). In this chapter, I argue that public discourse, particularly surrounding the most serious sociopolitical issues such as immigration, would benefit from a hybridity that includes sensibilities and strategies of humor. This argument does not seek to diminish the seriousness of immigration debates but rather to highlight ways humor productively intervenes in such serious sociopolitical discourses. To be certain, some uses of humor rightfully give pause to wholehearted celebration of its potential to problematize the status quo and contribute to progressive change. Humor has marked specific ethnic and racial communities as Other. Likewise, demeaning and degrading caricatures frequently reinforce social and psychological borders between "us" and "them." Such functions of humor too often create narrow, impermeable borders that trap and tame humor in public discourse and deny humor the opportunity to mingle productively with serious discourse on topics such as moral action or policy decisions. Moreover, when humor is relegated to "mere" entertainment, its potential to traverse and contest rigid social orders and borders is diminished. This chapter seeks to challenge the discursive boundaries that contain and limit humor, particularly as these boundaries constrain critical discourse that might cross and disrupt the borders that currently divide peoples residing in America. Thus, my dual purpose in this chapter is (1) to illustrate the potential of critical humor to problematize rigid and unreflexive borders, particularly in relation to race, nationality, and immigration, and (2) to expose and trouble the firmly guarded border erected between humor and serious political discourse.

To warrant my argument, I focus on the work of political satirist Stephen Colbert. Between 2005 and 2014, Colbert played a faux-conservative news anchor on the Comedy Central series *The Colbert Report*. His work includes two satirical books—*I Am America (And So Can You!)* and *America Again! Rebecoming the Greatness We Never Weren't*—and a children's book, *I Am a Pole (And So Can You!)*. He has garnered national awards and accolades including an Emmy, a Peabody, and recognition by the American Dialect Society and Merriam-Webster dictionary for coining the Word of the Year in 2005: *truthiness*. Stephen Colbert's humor is uniquely suited for a discussion of rhetorical borders because through his speech and performance he occupies multiple rhetorical spaces and enacts ambiguous performances that traverse sociopolitical borders. As a satirist, Colbert's performance is two faced. On one hand, his comic persona unabashedly espouses right-wing doctrine as he caricatures conservative pundits from cable news and talk radio such as Bill O'Reilly or Rush Limbaugh. On the other hand, Colbert the actor is decidedly liberal and left leaning as evidenced by his celebrated coverage on Huffington Post, Rachel Maddow, and other progressive news sources. He skewers political polarization and hypocrisy and undermines the logic of conservative ideologies through hyperbole and contradictory juxtapositions. Colbert also occupies and contests multiple positions of privilege. I am cautious not to exalt a white voice over others, particularly in relation to issues of race, at the risk of silencing voices who experience life from more marginal positions. However, I also recognize Colbert's role and performance as an ally: as I argue elsewhere, he makes visible and disrupts white privilege and postracial ideologies even through his guise of conservative, colorblind commentary (Rossing 2012).

Colbert regularly leverages his celebrity status to direct attention to and participate in serious political causes. For example, he participated in the national discussion about campaign financing when he formed a super PAC during the 2012 presidential elections and used the money he raised to air satirical ads during the primaries. His cultural capital provides a platform to bring attention to issues and stories that might not otherwise find their way into dominant media. In this chapter, I focus on Colbert's commentary on immigration debates on his Comedy Central news satire, *The Colbert Report*. In particular, I consider his participation in the United Farm Workers' (UFW) Take Our Jobs campaign in 2010. The UFW invited US citizens to work as migrant farm workers in order to contest the narrative that migrant workers "steal" jobs. Colbert accepted the challenge, and he featured his day of farm labor in a recurring segment on *The Colbert Report*. In October 2010, he testified in character about his experience for a Congressional committee hearing on the AgJOBS bill (H.R. 2414, 11th Cong. 2009), which would have granted a path to legal status for undocumented farm workers. Colbert's satire on *The Colbert Report*, his public advocacy for the UFW, and his in-character testimony before a Congressional subcommittee provide representative examples of the possibilities for political humor. These case studies illustrate humor's potential to problematize, redraw, and reshape not only rigid racial and national border constructions that exclude and divide but also the conventions of political discourse governed by an increasingly permeable border between serious public discourse and humor.

The chapter proceeds in two parts. First, I highlight three ways Stephen Colbert uses humor to bring attention to, unsettle, and advocate for new border constructions, particularly in relation to geographic and racial boundaries. Second, I describe the ways public discourse disciplined and minimalized Colbert's comic advocacy for the UFW's Take our Jobs campaign and the AgJOBS bill. The chapter concludes with a call for greater appreciation of and attention to hybrid discourses—at once serious and comic—and offers suggestions on how scholars and educators might productively engage such humor.

TROUBLING BORDERS IN COLBERT NATION

The Colbert Report, which aired on Comedy Central, regularly featured segments on immigration issues. For example, for this show, Colbert offered satiric commentary on topics such as the Minuteman Project, a 2011 Alabama law that required employers and schools to verify immigration statuses, and President Obama's Executive Order in 2012 to provide pathways to citizenship for students who immigrated to the United States as children. The following section recognizes three ways in which his satire participates in serious discourse regarding race, immigration, and border constructions. First, Colbert appropriates and then defamiliarizes common arguments about immigration so as to call into question their logic. Second, Colbert exposes the tenuous nature of border constructions, particularly racial and ethnic boundaries. Moreover, by highlighting the shaky ground of racial borders, this humor also calls into question the meaning-making processes that imbue the resulting groups and identities with meaning. Finally, he composes an argument in support of progressive immigration policy through satirical exaggeration.

APPROPRIATION AND DEFAMILIARIZATION

Scholars have documented the dehumanizing discourses that vilify immigrants as contaminants to the nation's purity, criminal threats, job takers, and more (Cisneros 2008; DeChaine 2009; Flores 2003). Colbert appropriates such discourses through his conservative persona, then defamiliarizes them with comic incongruities and exaggerations that render them untenable. In one segment, for example, he celebrated 101-year-old Eulalia Garcia Maturey, who became an official US citizen in 2010 after arriving in the States as an infant in 1909 (Colbert 2010b). Colbert invoked stereotypes of Mexican labor, noting, "Now she's eligible to work here legally: picking crops, paving roads, doing construction. No more racing away with her oxygen tank when immigration pulls up in front of the Home Depot." He appropriates identity constructs such as the peon and criminal (Flores 2003) to suggest that Eulalia worked illegally throughout her life and that only certain classes of jobs will be available to her. Colbert's persona uncritically applies racial stereotypes that continue to mark Ms. Maturey as Other. Similarly, in a segment titled "Labor Chains," Colbert (2011) satirized anxieties over pregnant women who are undocumented residents and who give birth in the United States. These women, Colbert claimed, "are the most devious [immigrants] because they sneak across our border with another immigrant hiding inside them. For all we know there's another one hiding inside the baby." His hyperbolic frame positioned expectant mothers, who in most cultural contexts would enjoy respect and reverence, as a hybrid of Russian nesting dolls and Trojan horses. Colbert recommended that these pregnant women be "shackled to a hospital bed" and taken to the US-Mexico border where they can "pop that baby out into Mexico." He concluded, "That way it's not an American citizen and I don't have to treat it with human decency."

In each of these commentaries, Colbert appropriates commonplace arguments that demean, dehumanize, and criminalize immigrants, thereby appearing to reinscribe divisive national and racial borders. Colbert uses humor to problematize these discursive borders and to rupture unquestioned "terministic screens"—to use Burke's (1966) famous category. Terministic screens shape our perception of reality and set parameters on what we say, what we question, and how we act. Colbert calls upon terministic screens that classify undocumented people from Mexico as contemptible and criminal. However, he disrupts these alienating and criminalizing discourses, which render immigrants unassimilable, and makes these discourses unpalatable by deploying them in unfamiliar contexts with unexpected agents in the narrative. He uses a 101-year-old woman who endured a 100-year path to citizenship as a symbol for day laborers who ostensibly divert labor from American workers. He casts an expectant mother as deviant and criminal. He positions an infant, a symbol of innocence and a source of compassion and joy, as abject and undesirable. Such discursive stretching of terministic screens has the potential to destabilize supposedly steadfast borders and to induce different action and attitudes (Critchley 2002). Said otherwise, appropriating these discourses and placing them in unfamiliar contexts creates conditions for reimagining identities, revising narratives, and shifting borders (Cisneros 2011).

This analysis suggests that neither humorous disruptions nor Colbert's satire, in particular, definitively redraw social boundaries and reshape attitudes. Humor is plagued by the problem of polysemy: one cannot be certain whether a critical message will resonate with the audience or whether the audience will identify with an opposing meaning. To be sure, Colbert's joke about Eulalia's employment opportunities or the newborn's exile into Mexico may confirm some audience members' biases and reinforce rhetorical borders. However, I offer two responses to this possibility. First, the humor is not constructing such biases and borders; they already exist in some audience members' minds. Humor is social and draws on familiar cultural scripts and beliefs (Charney 2005; Douglas 1999). While it may confirm, rather than refute, the very attitudes it seeks to subvert, it seems ill advised to hold humor responsible for the construction of these attitudes. Second, the significance and success of such humor is not in a definitive outcome or transformation but in the possibilities it creates for further disruption and destabilization. By constructing incongruous contexts such as a newborn unworthy of human respect and dignity, Colbert troubles the border constructions that create divisions between "us" and "them," desirable and undesirable. His absurd scenarios have the potential to challenge the audience to question the uncritical maintenance of these divisions and to imagine new possibilities.

TENUOUS CONSTRUCTIONS

Racial borders are often naturalized in public discourse through citizenship and immigration laws like Arizona's Senate Bill 1070 and then treated as given, recognizable, and stable. Critical race theorists in particular have illustrated how legal discourses construct the fiction of racial categories but then enable these constructions to concretize into material and social realities (López 2006). However, humor exploits this certainty in order to expose the inescapable permeability and contingency of constructed borders (Critchley 2002). Colbert exposes the tenuous nature of the constructed borders that public culture rigidly enforces. In the "Labor Chains" segment (Colbert 2011), he unsettled the divisions between exceptional Americans and dehumanized others. He explained that the moment a woman gives birth on US soil to "the illegal, resource-sucking immigrant inside them that's been stealing jobs from American embryos," the baby "instantly transform[s] into the greatest, best-est, freest baby in the world!" Colbert enthusiastically fawned over a photograph of a baby holding an American flag: "You are so cute! Yes you are! Who deserves a free education? You do!" Colbert continued, "I love this baby because he is an American citizen. But if that baby were born in Mexico . . ." He hinted at a more sinister alternative as a sombrero, a dark moustache, and a Mexican flag were superimposed on the same photograph. The greatest baby in the world who deserved boundless opportunity and freedom immediately became unworthy and unfit for participation in the nation. The juxtaposition revealed the high stakes of such a tenuous boundary: the meanings associated with physical, geographic, and racial borders determine human worth and dignity. These border constructions not only influence access to education, healthcare, and other social services but also shape attitudes about who is worthy of and entitled to such support.

In a segment titled "No Problemo," Colbert (2010a) championed Arizona's controversial Support Our Law Enforcement and Safe Neighborhoods Act (Senate Bill 1070). He reasoned that the law would drive not only immigrants but also many other citizens away from Arizona, and this mass exodus would cause the state economy to falter. Consequently, without an economic incentive to move to the state, the immigration problem would be solved. As he warranted his argument, he muddied the borders of the immigrant profile: "No illegal immigrant is going to want to be pulled over all the time; or for that matter, legal immigrants because they look the same and so you have to pull them over, too; or American citizens of Hispanic descent; or Italians because, you know, the olive skin . . . ; and come to think of it folks, Eskimos are basically ice Mexicans." Colbert's list of potential targets for this new law revealed that supposedly stable boundaries are anything but. He troubled the racial dynamics of the Arizona bill by exposing the far-reaching consequences of a bill that amounts to racial profiling. The list of targets who might be detained on suspicion of immigration and the absurdity of Eskimos as "ice Mexicans" revealed the implicit racial bias against brown-skinned bodies as foreign others and broke down the presumed stability of the immigrant profile. Colbert's performance highlighted not only how quickly and easily people make judgments about race based on supposedly rigid categories but also the foolishness of such reliance on stable border constructions.

Against the supposed certainty of racial and ethnic borders, Colbert's comic juxtapositions offer the countervailing claim that racial borders are ambiguous constructs saturated by racial ideologies. In short, Colbert problematizes overreliance on essentialized, racialized borders. In the "Labor Chains" segment, a child gains or loses her humanity and worth by virtue of tenuous borders. Colbert dramatizes how easily attitudes shift based merely on national origin—from resource sucking to deserving a free education, from criminal to exceptional. These segments invite the audience to question and resist the enforcement of rigid borders. Humor provides a safe way to demonstrate how easily borders and boundaries can be crossed as demonstrated through the ambiguous newborn whose worth and opportunity fluctuate with nationality. Humor also invites the audience to begin to understand how easily such supposedly rigid borders can be confused and muddied. As sociopolitical constructions of our making, borders can readily be undone. We can appropriate them for different purposes. This border-troubling characteristic of humor invites the audience to recognize the constant transitions and indeterminacy inherent in the lines we often perceive as stable. Colbert reminds his audience that borders overlap, dissolve, and shift: to assign meanings such as criminality and human dignity to such tenuous constructions is foolhardy.

ARGUMENT AND ADVOCACY

Colbert's most significant intervention in immigration debates included his advocacy for the United Farm Workers (UFW) Take Our Jobs campaign in 2010 and his subsequent testimony before a Congressional subcommittee. His advocacy epitomized the role of humor as a form of argument. Stephen Smith (1993) argues that humor is often purposeful and persuasive; it provides a sanctioned strategy for challenging dominant knowledge structures and opposing power relationships. Indeed, Colbert used the tactics of humorous appropriation and defamiliarization throughout his testimony to argue against majority viewpoints that opposed progressive immigration reforms. True to his character, Colbert positioned himself as a conservative and advocated the need to "secure our borders," maintaining that "we do not want immigrants doing this labor [farm work]" (*Protecting America's Harvest* 2010). However, his testimony called into question this rigid opposition to immigrants and migrant labor and used humor to argue for humanizing public policy as the best action. First, he emphasized once again the precariousness of rigid racial and national borders, arguing, "This is America. I don't want a tomato picked by a Mexican. I want it picked by an American, then sliced by a Guatemalan and served by a Venezuelan in a spa where a Chilean gives me a Brazilian." Colbert's play on nationalities exposed the tenuous nature of constructed borders and how easily different social identities can be excised from or included within the boundaries. Specifically, he laid bare before the Congressional subcommittee the underlying anti-Mexican bias that often informs debates over immigration policy. He problematized selective exclusion of immigrants from the nation with the simultaneous containment and confinement of laborers for the nation's benefit and its citizens' personal edification.

More significantly, Colbert's use of humor throughout the testimony created an argument in support of the AgJOBS bill. He presented illogical and absurd solutions to the problem so as to point toward the provisions in the AgJOBS bill as the most sensible solution. For example, he offered the "obvious answer" to eliminate the need for migrant workers: "Stop eating fruits and vegetables" (*Protecting America's Harvest* 2010). This solution cavalierly rejected dealing with the serious concerns surrounding migrant laborers and their work conditions. Instead, Colbert advanced a dietary boycott as the solution to complex policy debates over immigration. Colbert, however, gestured toward the lunacy of this option when he admitted his colonoscopy to the Congressional record as evidence of the need for "roughage." Next, he embraced a free-market argument: "Normally, I would leave this [the debate over migrant labor] to the invisible hand of the market, but the invisible hand of the market has already moved over 84,000 acres of production and over 22,000 farm jobs to Mexico and shut down over a million acres of US farmland due to lack of available labor because, apparently, even the invisible hand doesn't want to pick beans." Appropriating and extending the metaphor of the invisible hand, Colbert suggested that free-market ideologies are not suited to address problems such as working conditions and fair wages. Moreover, he implied that it is not migrant workers but free-market thinking that threatens the number of available farm jobs in this country. This incongruity complicates and undermines the argument that undocumented workers are stealing jobs and instead implicates current business practices and capitalism as responsible for harm to the workforce. Finally, Colbert suggested, "The easier answer is just to have scientists develop vegetables that pick themselves. The genetic engineers over at Fruit of the Loom have made great strides in human-fruit hybrids." Again, hyperbole highlights the implausibility of his supposedly sensible answer.

Colbert's nonsensical suggestions and his satirical appropriation of the commonplace argument for a free-market ideology worked to augment his ultimate support of the AgJOBS Bill. Near the end of his testimony, Colbert conceded that the government may need to offer more work visas for migrant farm workers. He reasoned that the legal status would afford recourse against exploitation, which itself would lead to better pay, working conditions, and benefits. In contrast to his previous suggestions, Colbert not only stressed the need for a bill designed to help migrant workers but underscored the seriousness of the issues facing these workers. Lest his comic persona give way, however, he quickly back-pedaled: "Or maybe that's crazy." The proposed actions of the AgJOBS bill were the only solutions dubbed "crazy," while his implausible and laughable solutions were offered as serious suggestions. However, these comic juxtapositions constructed an argument that positioned the proposed legislation as the sensible and necessary action.

In highlighting this use of humor as a strategy for advancing a particular argument, I mean to suggest neither that this strategy is universally successful nor that arguments must be humorous in nature. In this case, the AgJOBS bill was not even passed to the full Congress and was not enacted. To attempt to measure the success of Colbert's argument merely by the passage of the bill, however, is to conceive too narrowly of the purposes of such an argument. Once again, humor creates possibilities for new perspectives and new understandings, which may not immediately lead toward a direct action such as the passage of a Congressional bill. To look for a particular effect as a result of Colbert's argument through humor is also to ignore the powerful barriers and borders that public culture maintains between "serious" discourse and humor or entertainment.

CONTAINING HUMOR

Humor's contributions to serious sociopolitical concerns are curtailed by resistance to humor in public discourse. Reactions to Colbert's in-character testimony in support of the AgJOBS bill draw attention to a different kind of border anxiety. In response to Colbert's injection of humor into the political scene, as I will show, public discourse guarded and firmly reasserted boundaries between entertainment and politics. Such reactions illustrate how public culture disciplines humor as a viable participant in serious sociopolitical concerns. This section identifies two tactics used to discipline Colbert's political humor when he testified before the Congressional subcommittee: (1) maintaining a division between "seriousness" and "humor" and (2) perpetuating anxieties about reality versus performance.

Responses to Colbert's testimony enforced a bold line that marked humor as distinct from serious discourse. Public discourse in the form of media response marked the testimony as evidence of the uncertain borderlands between humor and politics and lamented this dangerous dissolution of borders. ABC News reported, "On Capitol Hill today, the line between politics and entertainment was completely wiped away after blurring for years" (Stephanopoulous and Karl 2010). Likewise, NBC News explained, "On Capitol Hill today a very serious political issue, immigration, was turned over, intentionally, to a scripted farce to make a point, as the comedian Stephen Colbert brought his fictionalized late night cable TV character to an actual congressional hearing" (Williams and Guthrie 2010). Similarly, columnist Ruben Navarette (*Contra Costa Times*, September 30, 2010) argued, "[Immigration] is a serious issue that impacts people's lives, and it shouldn't be treated as a punch line." Even the moment that marked Colbert's performance as a worthy, serious intervention became evidence of his impropriety. Asked why he wished to bring attention to the issue of immigration, Colbert responded, "It just seems like one of the least powerful people in the United States are migrant workers who come and do our work but don't have any rights as a result. . . . Migrant workers suffer and have no rights." Commentators identified this final statement as the only "serious" moment, primarily because this moment was perceived as a break in his character. For example, CBS News claimed, "At the end of the hearing, even Colbert acknowledged this issue is no laughing matter" (Couric et al. 2010). Setting aside this final moment as a uniquely earnest moment within an otherwise inappropriate farce only bolsters the boundary between humor and seriousness.

Public culture also disciplines humor because humor amplifies anxieties over the often uncertain distinction between performance and reality. Upon invitation to the hearing, Colbert (out of character) told Representative Zoe Lofgren, "I'm going to have to do it in character. There's no reason for me to go [out of character]. But my character really feels like he has something to say, and I'll do my best to say something through the character" (Gross 2011). Indeed, Colbert accepted UFW's Take Our Jobs challenge in character and he worked on a farm in upstate New York as his television personality; therefore, to share his knowledge and insight from these experiences in character arguably constituted the most authentic presentation he could offer. Nevertheless, much of the criticism surrounding his Congressional appearance took issue with Colbert playing a role rather than appearing as himself. Colbert was attacked and dismissed for delivering a routine instead of a testimony. For example, CNN reported, "He pretended that he was there to give serious testimony about migrant workers. Instead, he did a routine" (Sanchez et al. 2010). CBS evening news reported, "With Stephen Colbert at the witness table, this congressional hearing felt more like open mic night" (Couric et al. 2010). These frames emphasize the performative dimension of Colbert's testimony: when the humorist arrived and took the microphone, an otherwise serious hearing transformed into a performance. MSNBC's *Hardball* was concerned that political debate finally reached "a level I don't think any of us ever thought, where an actor or comedian decides to go in character on Capitol Hill" (Todd et al. 2010). Appearing as his onscreen persona rendered his words inappropriate and meaningless. As one reporter framed it, "The substance of the hearing was quickly overshadowed by Colbert's performance art" (Chen, *Houston Chronicle*, September 25, 2010). In other words, people perceived Colbert as pretending to be something he was not and consequently the comic performance lacked substance and seriousness.

These disciplinary responses assert expectations and conventions for serious subjects while clearly marking humor outside those boundaries. Humor allegedly violated the sobriety of the issue of immigration and disrupted the serious work of politics. Colbert's "excruciatingly inappropriate spectacle" was out of place and out of bounds (Goldberg, *Tulsa World*, October 3, 2010). Humor is relegated to something unreal, untruthful, and insincere while, by comparison, the serious work of Congress is maintained as pure and honest discourse. These condemnations of Colbert's testimony work to (re)construct and reify borders between serious and humorous discourse. Disciplining this unwelcomed breach of discursive borders served to reinforce a belief that humorous and serious discourses cannot intermingle. However, patrolling this rigid boundary ignores the dialectical tension that augments humor's potential for public argument and advocacy. Colbert's humorous testimony does not stand in opposition to his sudden turn to seriousness. Rather, it is the ongoing tension between seriousness and farce that drives the humor and strengthens the argument. Colbert's humor invites the audience to tack back and forth between his ludicrous, hyperbolic suggestions and his earnest call for justice, a movement that ultimately advocates for a humanizing immigration-policy solution. Moreover, such rigid divisions ignore the permeability and instability of the border between humor and politics. Pop culture unquestionably participates in struggles over social and political meaning (Brummett 2008; Street 1997). Humor, in particular, serves a vital, valuable purpose in public discourse about serious social and political issues despite its frequent trivialization and exclusion. Disciplining humor in these ways limits the benefits and possibilities of political humor and ignores the serious work of humor.

HYBRID DISCOURSES

A year after his testimony for the AgJOBS bill, Colbert shared an anecdote that exemplified borderland clashes between the serious and the comic. Representative John Conyers, the head of the subcommittee before which Colbert spoke, sent Colbert a letter thanking him for his "valuable" testimony and asking him to review the transcript of the hearing for accuracy. The transcript included Rep. Conyers's request for Colbert to leave the hearing before giving his statement. Colbert highlighted both the passage that thanked him and the portion of the transcript in which Conyers asked Colbert to leave. He framed these highlighted pages side by side and hung them in his office (Gross 2011). Colbert's whimsical juxtaposition of these conflicting reactions to his comedic testimony provides a symbol for the hybridity that public culture would do well to embrace.[1] In the context of a Congressional hearing, Colbert's performance represented a hybrid discourse: neither a purely playful triviality nor a perfectly serious intervention into immigration public policy. His humorous testimony was simultaneously an act of political engagement and an act of protest and contestation, both civic action and entertainment. By testifying on the AgJOBS Bill and affirming the rights of migrant workers, Colbert enacted a traditional mode of citizenship and political identity. Yet, by disrupting the decorum of Congress, mocking the contemporary dysfunctions of Congress, and appearing in character, Colbert disrupted the conventions of the political process. With humor that bespoke a serious purpose, Colbert created a mélange of informational testimony, cultural criticism, comedy performance, and spectacle. In conclusion, I claim that such blurring of borders between humor and politics creates opportunities for education and transformation.

Contemporary public, political discourse has become increasingly tragic: creating evil enemies, castigating scapegoats, and securing victories through the political "death" of the opposition. Such rigid borders are untenable, including those that protect serious forms of political discourse. Stephen Colbert's hybrid performances, both on *Comedy Central* and before Congress, offer an alternative mode of political and public discourse suited for challenging the rigidity of discursive conventions. Arguing for the intermingling of humor with serious, sociopolitical purpose, my point is not that political discourse must necessarily operate on a humorous register. Nor do I wish to elevate humor as an antidote to political ineffectiveness or conflict. Rather, humor serves as a vital style of political discourse. It should be valued as an equal participant in public deliberation and allowed to intersect and overlap productively with other styles of political discourse. Robert Hariman argues, "The key to achieving high-quality democratic discourse is not to institutionalize a single form of that discourse, but to support those practices that contribute directly to the sustainability of the public culture" (Hariman 2004, 226). In other words, it is vital for communication scholars and critics to uphold humor as a meaningful player in important sociopolitical debates and to continue exploring its unique contributions to public deliberation. I argue elsewhere, for instance, that humor is a necessary, though not sufficient, style of truth telling and social justice advocacy because it humanizes all stakeholders in a particular struggle and because it creates unique pathways for identification with marginalized perspectives (Rossing 2013, 2014). The goal is to identify how humor functions as a valuable and essential partner with other sociopolitical discourses and to embrace the flexibility to allow humor to interact with competing and opposing discourses.

Humor such as Colbert's also offers a way to challenge the rigidity of socially constructed borders that delineate race and ethnicity. These social and psychological borders continue to figure prominently in disputes about immigration and citizenship. On one hand, the playfulness inherent in such hybrid discourse invites audiences to see familiar categories, boundaries, and divisions from new perspectives and to recognize the contingency of those borders. Humor breaks boundaries and disrupts conventions (Berger 1993). Such provocative (ex)changes of perspective might work to reconstruct borders suitable for new, inclusive forms of political and social identity. On the other hand, the seriousness of such humor reveals both the stakes and the consequences of continuing to police or beginning to blur these vexing racial and ethnic borders. Too often the default position on humor regarding race and ethnicity is to denounce its reinforcement of dominant and oppressive ideologies. I urge a more charitable view of humor that not only maintains vigilant attention to its capacity for conserving the status quo but also equally recognizes its potential to resist, subvert, and reimagine the fictions and realities of race.

To be sure, humor alone will not redraw or reconfigure our geographic, political, social, and psychological borders. However, it possesses great potential to serve as a pedagogical resource for scholars, educators, and activists. Humor "shows us ourselves . . . as we are, with all the warts, scars, and other imperfections intact; and careful analysis can offer insights that are otherwise unattainable" (McIntire-Strasburg 2006, 5) In other words, one of humor's greatest contributions is educative error correction. When the borders people construct become too rigid, too constraining, or too oppressive to prove valuable, humor points out the flaws and models creative new modes of thought and action that might inspire ways to transform those borders. This invention holds promise for both the social and political boundaries that govern understandings of race or conversations about immigration and the discursive borders that frequently bar humor from mingling and mixing with serious public discourse. Communication scholars and educators might more readily turn to humor as a pedagogical resource to provoke new perspectives in the classroom and to guide discussions about the paradoxical rigidity and fluidity of identity borders. Communication critics might find models and inspiration in the work of humorists who engage in similar projects of cultural criticism. And while humor alone will not transform our political landscape, activists dedicated to progressive change might be well served by tactics that capitalize on humor's dialectical tensions between seriousness and folly. In short, if scholars, teachers, activists, and critics take seriously the work humor performs, I believe we will find it complements, sustains, and invigorates our projects.

Note

1. My use of *hybridity* is informed by Darrel Enck-Wanzer's (2006) discussion of intersectional rhetoric and Josue D. Cisneros's (2011) analysis of hybrid performances.

References

Berger, Arthur A. 1993. *An Anatomy of Humor.* New Brunswick, NJ: Transaction.
Brummett, Barry. 2008. *A Rhetoric of Style.* Carbondale: Southern Illinois University Press.
Burke, Kenneth. 1966. *Language as Symbolic Action: Essays on Life Literature and Method.* Berkeley: University of California Press.
Charney, Maurice. 2005. "Introduction." In *Comedy: A Geographic and Historical Guide.* Vol. 1, edited by Maurice Charney, 1–5. Westport, CT: Praeger.
Cisneros, J. David. 2008. "Contaminated Communities: The Metaphor of 'Immigrant as Pollutant' in Media Representations of Immigration." *Rhetoric & Public Affairs* 11 (4): 569–601. http://dx.doi.org/10.1353/rap.0.0068.
Cisneros, Josue D. 2011. "(Re)bordering the Civic Imaginary: Rhetoric, Hybridity, and Citizenship in *La Gran Marcha.*" *Quarterly Journal of Speech* 97 (1): 26–49. http://dx.doi.org/10.1080/00335630.2010.536564.
Colbert, Stephen. 2010a. "No Problemo." *The Colbert Report,* April 21. New York: Comedy Central. Television.
Colbert, Stephen. 2010b. "101-Year Old Woman Becomes US Citizen." *The Colbert Report,* October 22. New York: Comedy Central. Television.
Colbert, Stephen. 2011. "Labor Chains." *The Colbert Report,* September 28. New York: Comedy Central. Television.
Couric, Katie, Chip Reid, Kelly Cobiella, Heather Brown, Nancy Cordes, Dean Reynolds, Seth Doane, and Richard Schlesinger. 2010. *CBS Evening News,* September 24. New York: CBS. Television.
Critchley, Simon. 2002. *On Humor.* New York: Routledge.
DeChaine, D. Robert. 2009. "Bordering the Civic Imaginary: Alienization, Fence Logic, and the Minuteman Civil Defense Corps." *Quarterly Journal of Speech* 95 (1): 43–65. http://dx.doi.org/10.1080/00335630802621078.

Douglas, Mary. 1999. *Implicit Meanings: Selected Essays in Anthropology.* 2nd ed. New York: Routledge.
Enck-Wanzer, Darrell. 2006. "Trashing the System: Social Movement, Intersectional Rhetoric, and Collective Agency in the Young Lords Organization's Garbage Offensive." *Quarterly Journal of Speech* 92 (2): 174–201. http://dx.doi.org/10.1080 /00335630600816920.
Flores, Lisa A. 2003. "Constructing Rhetorical Borders: Peons, Illegal Aliens, and Competing Narratives of Immigration." *Critical Studies in Media Communication* 20 (4): 362–87. http://dx.doi.org/10.1080/0739318032000142025.
Friedman, Emily. 2010. "Is Dora the Explorer an Illegal Immigrant?" *ABC News*, May 21. New York: ABC. Television. abcnews.go.com.
Gross, Terry. 2011. "Stephen Colbert: In Good 'Company' on Broadway." *Fresh Air*, June 14. Washington, DC: NPR.
Hall, Stephen, Larry Keeter, and Jennifer Williamson. 1993. "Toward an Understanding of Humor as Popular Culture in American Society." *Journal of American Culture* 16 (2): 1–6. http://dx.doi.org/10.1111/j.1542-734X.1993.00001.x.
Hariman, Robert. 2004. "Civic Education, Classical Imitation, and Democratic Polity." In *Isocrates and Civic Education*, edited by Takis Poulakos and David Depew, 217–34. Austin: University of Texas Press.
López, Ian H. 2006. *White by Law: The Legal Construction of Race.* New York: New York University Press.
McIntire-Strasburg, Janice. 2006. "Introduction: Humor Is Serious Business." *Studies in American Humor* 3 (13): 3–10.
Ono, Kent A., and John Sloop. 2002. *Shifting Borders: Rhetoric, Immigration, and California's Proposition 187.* Philadelphia, PA: Temple University Press.
Protecting America's Harvest: Hearing before the Subcommittee on Immigration, Citizenship, Refugees, Border Security, and International Law of the House Judiciary Committee. 2010. 111th Congress.
Rossing, Jonathan P. 2012. "Deconstructing Postracialism: Humor as a Critical, Cultural Project." *Journal of Communication Inquiry* 36 (1): 44–61. http://dx.doi.org/10.1177 /0196859911430753.
Rossing, Jonathan P. 2013. "Dick Gregory and Activist Style: Identifying Attributes of Humor Necessary for Activist Advocacy." *Argumentation and Advocacy* 50 (2): 59–71.
Rossing, Jonathan P. 2014. "Critical Race Humor in a Postracial Moment: Richard Pryor's Contemporary Parrhesia." *Howard Journal of Communications* 25 (1): 16–33. http:// dx.doi.org/10.1080/10646175.2013.857369.
Sanchez, Rick, Wolf Blitzer, Casey Wian, Brianna Keilar, Brooke Baldwin, and Martin Savidge. 2010. "Stephen Colbert Brings Comedy and Controversy to Washington." *Rick's List*, September 24. New York: CNN. Television.
Smith, Stephen A. 1993. "Humor as Rhetoric and Cultural Argument." *Journal of American Culture* 16 (2): 51–64. http://dx.doi.org/10.1111/j.1542-734X.1993.00051.x.
Stephanopoulous, George, and Jonathan Karl. 2010. "Political Theater: Colbert to Congress." *World News with Diane Sawyer*, September 24. New York: ABC. Television.
Street, John. 1997. *Politics and Popular Culture.* Philadelphia, PA: Temple University Press.
Todd, Chuck, Vaughn Ververs, Richard Wolffe, Amanda Drury, Howard Fineman, and Lawrence O'Donnell. 2010. "Colbert on the Hill." *Hardball*, September 24. New York: MSNBC. Television.
Williams, Brian, and Savannah Guthrie. 2010. "Comedian Stephen Colbert Testifying on Capitol Hill." *NBC Nightly News*, September 24. New York: NBC. Television.

5
EMPLOYING ETHOS TO CROSS THE BORDERS OF DIFFERENCE
Teaching Civil Discourse

Karen P. Peirce

In February 2011, the National Institute for Civil Discourse (NICD) was founded at the University of Arizona. This founding occurred in the wake of a shooting at a Tucson shopping center that resulted in the deaths of six people and injury to fourteen others, including US Representative Gabrielle Giffords. After the shooting, both the media and political arenas were filled with strenuous debates and arguments about gun-control laws, background checks that would include mental-health screening, and the availability of mental-health treatment in the United States. Amid these strenuous debates and arguments arose a plea among many for more civility in public discourse, and the NICD was started in response to these pleas. As the NICD's mission statement explains, it is "a nonpartisan center for advocacy, research, and policy regarding civil discourse consistent with First Amendment principles" (University of Arizona 2012a). In the spirit of nonpartisanship, the Institute is chaired by Presidents George H. W. Bush and Bill Clinton (Cruz 2011). One of the main objectives of the institute is to "channel public demand for civil discourse in political campaigns and public policy deliberation" (University of Arizona 2012c).

A key term in this stated objective is *civil discourse*, which the NICD defines through the following description: "The Institute is predicated on a deep belief that vigorous but respectful debate, consistent with the First Amendment, is a necessary ingredient for successful problem solving in the civic arena. The Institute's role is to encourage civic leaders to embrace vigorous debate in a way that allows for diverse perspectives to be shared, for complex issues to be discussed thoughtfully, and for challenging topics to be explored without resorting to invective and personal attacks" (University of Arizona 2012b). Keywords for the

DOI: 10.7330/9781607324034.c005

NICD in defining *civil discourse* include: *respectful, problem solving, diverse perspectives, shared, complex issues, discussed thoughtfully, challenging topics, explored,* and *without resorting to invective and personal attacks.* These keywords might remind rhetorical scholars of work by such theorists as Deborah Tannen (1998), Jim Corder (1991), Richard E. Young (2003), and Thomas O. Sloane (1989), who advocate for exploration and openness in the process of reaching agreement instead of an emphasis on tactics for winning an argument between opposing sides. These theorists point out the need to cross the boundaries often established by sides. In this chapter, I explore these theoretical perspectives and also suggest ways to strengthen civil discourse through education. I ask two central questions: How can we shape the landscape of rhetorical education so winning and losing are not seen as the ultimate outcomes of discourse? How can we shape rhetorical education so reaching agreement across difference can be our objective? In response to these questions, the writing pedagogy I propose aims to teach people how to strive to understand others and at the same time be understood by them.

Differences of race, class, gender, opinion, and so on can create what seem to be insurmountable borders between people. These borders are erected when differences are emphasized above all else. To take an example from recent history, if one person thinks the healthcare system in the United States needs reform and another person disagrees, focusing only on that difference of opinion can make the chasm between the two people feel unbridgeable. Both sides can argue that their side is the correct side, and the opposing side could easily be seen as ignorant, corrupt, evil, or simply wrong. Avoiding this situation may seem impossible at times; however, the chasm might be crossed if participants could learn and apply ways to enter into civil discourse with others in order to reach mutual understanding. Such an education could lead to improved human relations and the possibility for more resolutions than impasses. This type of education would perhaps reduce the tensions and conflict that seem to pervade many disputes in contemporary American society.

Scholars and teachers of rhetoric are well positioned to construct such a reality by beginning in the classroom. We can draw on our rich theoretical traditions to help students move beyond the notion that those who disagree are simply wrong and move toward being more open to understanding many perspectives. I examine in this chapter some of the tools needed to participate in civil discourse with the aim of mutual understanding. I start with a review of composition textbooks to show that our common methods of teaching argumentation and ethos largely do not support the approach I advocate but rather support winning as opposed to losing an argument. I next build on the work of previous rhetorical scholars to extend classical and contemporary notions of ethos and explore what might build an ethos of openness. I suggest that to facilitate communication that allows for the opportunity to understand and to be understood—rather than just win or lose—we must theorize, teach, and practice an ethos that is both questioning and open to new possibilities rather than one that is always authoritative and limits mutual understanding. I conclude the chapter by considering how we might reshape rhetorical education so it centers on a rich conception of ethos that hopefully can extend beyond the contexts of the classroom and sustain rhetors as they engage in civil discourse beyond their educational experience.

To begin, let us turn to reviewing the state of contemporary rhetorical education. In "A Textbook Argument: Definitions of Argument in Leading Composition Textbooks," A. Abby Knoblauch provides a starting point. She "examines the definitions and practices of argument perpetuated by popular composition textbooks, illustrating how even those texts that appear to forward expansive notions of argument ultimately limit it to an intent to persuade" (Knoblauch 2011, 244). "In doing so," Knoblauch claims, such textbooks "help perpetuate constricted practices of argument within undergraduate composition classrooms" (244). In her introduction, Knoblauch illustrates the reliance on textbooks by inexperienced instructors in first-year composition courses, explaining that such reliance allows textbooks to become the dominant instructional voice, adding urgency to the need for well-constructed texts (245–46). Knoblauch then provides a review of several of the most popular composition texts and ultimately focuses on two of them for detailed analysis. She finds "the discussion questions, examples, and more detailed explications . . . privilege an intent to persuade, illustrating for students the primacy of persuasion and either marginalizing or functionally erasing alternative processes or outcomes" (262). The danger in such practices is that, in Knoblauch's words, "as we attempt to help students negotiate differences, both within the classroom and in the larger social realm, we do them a disservice if we limit definitions and practices of argument . . . solely to conversion and an intent to persuade" (263).

Knoblauch's findings add support to my claim that an emphasis on communicating with the goal of winning rather than with the goal of achieving mutual understanding stands in stark contrast to the aims of the NICD and others who hope to strengthen civil discourse. To achieve these aims, we must teach students how to communicate across borders established due to difference rather than solely how to win arguments. We must teach students communicative strategies that focus on an open, inquiring ethos receptive to alternate realities and perspectives.

In research I conducted on the treatment of argumentation in popular composition textbooks from the past few decades, I found that their authors tend to equate ethos with assertiveness rather than with the openness or inquiry needed to communicate across differences. In a survey of four popular textbooks, I found a bias toward an Aristotelian notion of rhetoric. This bias is not surprising given the intersections of the fields of composition and rhetoric in the United States. Nonetheless, the extent of this emphasis on classical rhetoric in composition courses, while seen by some as beneficial, has its costs. One of these costs is a single-minded focus on persuasion based on Aristotle's definition of rhetoric. In *On Rhetoric,* Aristotle defines rhetoric as "an ability, in each [particular] case, to see the available means of persuasion" (Aristotle 1991, 36). In the Aristotelian tradition, to be successful speakers, students of rhetoric must identify what makes some speeches in particular contexts persuasive and what makes others not so persuasive. The hope is that with this knowledge, students will be able to create persuasive speeches of their own. The primary aim of communication in this tradition is persuasion, which carries the cost of deemphasizing other aims, such as achieving mutual understanding.

A persuasion-heavy focus is just one cost of emphasizing Aristotelian rhetoric in contemporary textbooks. Another is that the definition of ethos is limited to credibility. According to Aristotle, portraying a credible ethos is an important strategy speechmakers can use to achieve persuasion. He explains that persuasion occurs "through character whenever the speech is spoken in such a way as to make the speaker worthy of credence" (38). Certainly if the aim of communication is to persuade an audience, seeming credible to that audience is essential. After all, if speakers do not appear to know what they are talking about, nobody is likely to believe their lines of argument. If speakers do not have knowledge, experience, or other authority upon which to base their assertions, their assertions are not likely to be very persuasive. However, my analysis will show that emphasizing persuasion and credibility at the expense of other communicative aims carries the cost of limiting our ability to teach other skills, such as civil discourse aimed at reaching mutual understanding across difference.

I have found that, with persuasion as their primary goal, many writing, rhetoric, and composition texts teach students to adopt an Aristotelian credible ethos in their writing. The first of the four textbooks I examined was Annette Rottenberg's *Elements of Argument*. As the title of the book and the headings of its four main parts—"The Structure of Argument," "Writing and Researching Arguments," "Opposing Viewpoints," and "Classical Arguments"—clearly announce, the entirety of Rottenberg's text focuses on "explaining and defending [one's] own beliefs and opposing those of others" (Rottenberg 1991, 4). Rather than teaching students to reach mutual understanding with those who hold different viewpoints, Rottenberg's text instructs, "Refuting an opposing view means to attack it in order to weaken, invalidate, or make it less credible to a reader" (Rottenberg 1991, 260). The violence of the language used here as students are taught to refute and attack opposing views is troubling, as it leaves no room for achieving mutual understanding. Instead, persuasive argument in which one side wins and another loses is the primary goal of communication. Furthermore, Rottenberg emphasizes the need for a credible ethos in order to achieve such persuasion. She writes, "All arguments are composed with an audience in mind" (Rottenberg 1991, 13), going on to explain that "success in convincing an audience is almost always inseparable from the writer's credibility, or the audience's belief in the writer's trustworthiness" (14). Rottenberg suggests that if a writer has researched carefully and can present evidence of that research through citations, the audience is more likely to be persuaded on the strength of the authoritative voices used to support the writer's argument. Throughout the text, Rottenberg instructs students in how to persuade readers to accept one point of view by refuting other points of view. As a result, Rottenberg's text, with its emphasis on an ethos of credibility with the aim of persuasion, limits the possibility for teaching students about the aims of civil discourse because it neglects to emphasize an ethos of openness and inquiry, the type of ethos necessary to communicate with the aim of crossing boundaries that might exist between those with opposing viewpoints.

An emphasis on credibility for achieving persuasion is also reflected in David Jolliffe's text *Inquiry and Genre*. As Jolliffe explains, his text "guides students through a series of five related, sequenced writing projects" (Jolliffe 1999, xiii), culminating in what he calls "the Working Documents Project" in which "writers try to get a certain group of readers to think and act in a specific way in regard to the subject at hand" (4). Although the text offers students the opportunity to "use writing to clarify... ideas and feelings about a subject" (4), as well as to "illustrat[e] the process involved in exploring [their] subject" (4), these types of writing are offered in service to the final stage, which is writing to persuade. Therefore, these other types of writing and the purposes behind them are presented as subordinate to persuasion. Jolliffe explains that after writers clarify their ideas and feelings and explore their subjects, "The first step in writing to change people's minds or actions is obvious. You need to decide . . . your *persuasive goal* and . . . your *audience*" (139). Jolliffe explains that shaping writing for an audience involves addressing "those ideas, attitudes, and beliefs that the audience holds that you, the writer or speaker, must bring up and capitalize on if you hope to influence the audience's thinking or behavior in the way you want" (140–41). Here we see a clear emphasis on helping a writer convert an audience to a desired position, as opposed to helping a writer and audience achieve mutual understanding.

One of the means for achieving persuasion as presented in this text is through a credible ethos. As Jolliffe explains, "In addition to appealing to the feelings and interests of your audience, you can also influence their minds and actions by appealing to yourself as a credible person. Teachers call this an appeal to the writer's *ethos*" (146). Jolliffe advises, "You should do everything you can to suggest to your readers that you have their best interests in mind when you propose your persuasive goal, when you try to get them to think and act in a different way about your topic" (147). What should be clear here is that ethos, as it is portrayed to the student in this text, becomes a tool for achieving persuasion to the potential detriment of other communicative aims, such as the aim of civil discourse. In Jolliffe's text, as in many others, ethos is presented as a strategy that can be employed to make the author appear knowledgeable so as to achieve a persuasive effect on the audience.

The role of a credible ethos in achieving persuasion is also explored in Patsy Callaghan and Ann Dobyns's *A Meeting of Minds*. Like Jolliffe's text, Callaghan and Dobyns's (2004) text moves through sequenced instruction. The first two chapters of Callaghan and Dobyns's text discuss dialogue, community, inquiry, and shared inquiry, which would seem to stand in sympathy with the approach I advocate. Yet overall, an emphasis on persuasiveness is clear in their text. In a chapter titled "Taking a Position: The Academic Argument," Callaghan and Dobyns explain that the purpose of "explor[ing], respond[ing], or account[ing] for the positions of other writers" is to "begin the process of taking a position of your own about a question at issue" (Callaghan and Dobyns 2004, 218). Therefore, the inquiry and dialogue emphasized at the beginning of the text is ultimately presented in service to an argumentative aim. In this text, as with the others already presented, again we see rhetoric's main purpose defined as "get[ting] your reader to see your subject the way you do" (6). Callaghan and Dobyns elaborate on this point, writing, "A person using this kind of rhetoric is . . . trying . . . to convince the other person to consider the strength of a position" (9–10). In an academic setting, they explain, such an outcome is achieved through assignments that require students to "study a problem, take a position, and give good reasons for [their] opinion" (12). The aim of this kind of writing is to "convince a reader to see the subject the way [the writers] do" (60). The focus here is on communication that lays claim to a stance and tries to convince others of that stance, while other types of writing are seen as being useful for leading to this aim. Students are shown that the ultimate outcome of communication is to convince an audience.

Like the other authors noted so far, Callaghan and Dobyns introduce students to a key strategy for convincing the reader: the use of ethos. Students are taught in the Aristotelian manner that ethos is a tool for achieving a persuasive aim. As Callaghan and Dobyns put it, "To appeal ethically: Identify for readers the beliefs and values they (should) share with you, the writer, and then show how your argument is connected to those values and beliefs. . . . Argue that your position is the 'right' one" (128). An effective use of ethos, then, contributes to giving "the reader reasons to accept the writer's argument" (128). As with the previous texts I analyzed, the focus of the instruction here is on using ethos as a means to achieve persuasion. Where inquiry and dialogue are addressed, these approaches are presented in service to the ultimate aim of making an argument, again downplaying the importance of communicating to achieve mutual understanding.

My claim that writing textbooks place undue emphasis on a credible ethos as a means to achieve persuasion is also illustrated by *Ancient Rhetorics for Contemporary Students* by Sharon Crowley and Debra Hawhee. In the preface to their text, Crowley and Hawhee (2004) explain that "the need to compose arises from the composers' desire to insert their voices into the differences of opinion that occur with the discourse of a community. When they are read or heard, compositions enter into that discourse, either to maintain and reinforce it or to disrupt it" (2004, xiv). As with the other texts analyzed, here we see an emphasis on argument, for writing is viewed as having the purpose of entering into existing debates by taking one side or another. Rather than rhetors being depicted as seeking to resolve differences of opinion or to reach mutual understanding, rhetors are portrayed as participating in ongoing disputes that can be won through persuasion. Instruction about the means rhetors can use to achieve this persuasion is what makes up the bulk of the text. One of the means addressed is ethos, and in Crowley and Hawhee's conception, "A rhetor who uses invented *ethos* . . . constructs a character for herself within her discourse" (Crowley and Hawhee 2004, 169). They go on to write, "People tend to believe rhetors who either have a reputation for fair-mindedness or who create an *ethos* that makes them seem fair minded" (170); in short, in a conception of rhetoric based on persuasion, learning how to construct a fair-minded ethos so as to appeal to the reader is an important task for students. Crowley and Hawhee instruct, "Rhetors who are preparing to argue a case should ask: What would or did it take to move someone who is/was indifferent toward acceptance or rejection of my position?" (198–99). In other words, students should reflect on their constructed ethos to be sure they can avoid rejection and gain acceptance. Crowley and Hawhee go on to instruct the student to ask, "Can I move someone from a position of acceptance toward rejection, or vice-versa?" (199). Again, students should be sure they have constructed their ethos so that it helps them ensure acceptance of their own positions and rejection of other possibilities. Here we clearly see a limitation of communicative possibilities to one option: convincing the audience to adopt the rhetor's stance and reject others. Such a goal weakens the potential for civil discourse by neglecting to teach students how to focus on reaching mutual understanding or agreement.

Imagine what could be achieved if teachers of writing emphasized reaching mutual understanding instead of achieving persuasion. What possibilities could we achieve as individuals dealing with other individuals, as communities dealing with other communities, as nations dealing with other nations? Could we minimize disagreements between coworkers, friends, or families? Could we avoid political filibusters, religious persecution, or even war? In order to imagine such possibilities, we must revamp our teaching of ethos. Because mutual understanding requires sensitivity, patience, and a desire to learn from one another, an ethos that presents the rhetor as certain, strong, and focused on persuasion can actually work to the detriment of coming to understanding. Such an ethos can erect barriers rather than build bridges across difference, and with so much emphasis in composition and rhetoric textbooks on this sort of ethos aimed at persuasion, we have not equipped students to consider other alternatives.

How can we change this situation? How can we foster the development of an inquiring, questioning, curious ethos? How can we use such an ethos to communicate successfully across difference? To answer these questions, I draw on several theorists, first turning to Deborah Tannen's analysis of argument in contemporary American culture and her call for changes to our educational practices. I next turn to Jim Corder, who establishes the importance of ethos for communication and who analyzes the ethos used in much academic writing. I then draw from Richard E. Young, who provides a case study illustrating the prevalence in academic writing of prematurely adopting an ethos that is certain and who calls for changes in writing pedagogy. I conclude this review with a look at Thomas O. Sloane's work with Ciceronian invention as a means to making changes in our writing pedagogy that can alter our conception of ethos and in turn ensure more successful communication across differences. After reviewing the work of these theorists, I describe a writing pedagogy designed to implement the changes they call for.

Deborah Tannen highlights the danger to society caused by an overreliance on argumentation and calls for changes to educational practices in human communication. In *The Argument Culture: Moving from Debate to Dialogue*, Tannen claims that in the United States we are living in "a pervasive warlike atmosphere that makes us approach public dialogue, and just about anything we need to accomplish, as if it were a fight" (Tannen 1998, 3). She continues by explaining that this tendency "has served us well in many ways but in recent years has become so exaggerated that it is getting in the way of solving our problems" (3). She goes on: "Our spirits are corroded by living in an atmosphere of unrelenting contention—an argument culture" (3). Not much has changed in the years since Tannen made these observations, as witnessed by the founding of the NICD and its goal of encouraging civil discourse. To move away from an overtendency toward argument, Tannen would like to see a change to our educational system. As Tannen points out and as my review of textbooks illustrates, in contemporary classrooms we teach students that the most important skill they can gain is to express their opinions in a convincing manner. As my analysis shows, we neglect to teach students how to listen to divergent opinions and wrangle meaningfully with those opinions. Instead, we teach them to be assertive in their single-minded opinions on matters. We teach students to write in order to convince an audience rather than teaching them to write in order to better understand others and be better understood by them. Shifting the aims of our teaching could shift the results we see in our students, making us more likely to reach the goal of achieving mutual understanding and appreciating difference.

Along with shifting the overall goal of our teaching away from persuasion and toward achieving civil discourse aimed at reaching mutual understanding across difference, we must also shift our teaching of ethos away from advocating one that is assertive, argumentative, and closed and toward advocating one that is open, inviting, and sincere.

We can see the importance of this kind of ethos when we look at the work of Jim Corder. In "Academic Jargon and Soul-Searching Drivel," Corder (1991, 317) writes, "To demand that others accept our particular experience is arrogance and dogma. To offer our experience to another may be the only plenitude we have." Corder goes on to suggest, "Perhaps instead of confronting each other with truths already found, we can learn to accompany each other toward what we'll find" (1991, 319). Here Corder shows the contrast between an ethos useful for achieving persuasion—one that portrays "arrogance and dogma" and is the type of ethos that appears to be rewarded in textbooks—and an ethos that "offer[s] our experience to another" and helps us "accompany each other" in working out differences between rhetor and audience. My foregoing survey of textbooks shows that we emphasize to students primarily how to assume an ethos of authority, just the sort of emphasis Corder laments. We teach students how to be steadfast, sure, and clear. We teach students to write with assertion, make claims with confidence, and construct a persuasive argument. Corder worries about how such teaching encourages disconnections between people, writing, "A perpetual sorrow in human communication, I think, is that often we only announce ourselves to each other, declare ourselves to each other, write as authorities before and at each other, but don't give each other much time" (317). Such a tendency in communication worries me as well because it closes off the possibility of civility in discourse before it has the chance to begin. Because civil discourse aimed at mutual understanding requires communicators who can listen to each other, work together to solve problems, and be open to multiple perspectives, I think we must shift our teaching about ethos to better match these aims.

I wonder what could happen if, instead of proving points and making cases, we shared our thoughts with one another. What could happen if, instead of winning arguments, we focused on asking questions? We will never know what other types of possibilities could occur through academic writing if we continue to place primary focus on teaching persuasive writing to our students in the composition classroom. By teaching students how to construct arguments that project a closed, confident ethos, we in turn close them to possibilities that could result from maintaining openness in their writing. As a result, we close them to possibilities that could lead to understanding across differences.

My thinking about this situation has been enriched by the work of Richard E. Young. In a chapter titled "Toward an Adequate Pedagogy for Rhetorical Argumentation: A Case Study in Invention," Young makes points similar to Corder's. Using his own experience of teaching an "upper-level course in argumentation," Young examines the difficulties he had in teaching students to "develop a considered judgment on an issue" (Young 2003, 159). As he explains, he began the course by introducing his students to formal logic and argumentation, asking them to write persuasive essays articulating their positions on euthanasia (160–61). Later in the course, Young introduced his students to a real-life scenario about a man badly burned in an accident who wished to die but was instead kept alive. Young shared with his students graphic descriptions by the burn victim of the painful treatments he endured and his wishes for death. He also exposed them to successes (such as earning a law degree) that the burn victim achieved after many surgeries and a long recovery, though people eventually seeking legal assistance from the burn victim were often put off by the extensive scarring that remained evident. Young hoped such exposure to first-person testimony would open up his students to reconsider or problematize the formal arguments they had learned to construct earlier in the course.

To Young's dismay, he found by the end of the course that he had not managed to teach his students the kind of openness he had wanted to teach. As Young puts it,

> The students had simply become more expert at arguing their initial positions. Apparently, I had taught them to be more articulate about their positions, to explain them better, to perhaps be more persuasive about them, and to be more effective in their criticisms of other positions. I see now that they had learned quite well what I had actually taught, which was not without value; however, it wasn't what I was trying to teach, what I thought I was teaching. That is, I had not taught them to be more critical of their own positions and more sensitive to the complexities of the controversy. (Young 2003, 161)

What Young notices is the same thing Corder notices and that my analysis of textbooks helps substantiate: the emphasis in our classrooms on persuasive writing at the expense of writing aimed at mutual understanding. When we focus solely on teaching persuasion, the end result appears to be that students do not open themselves to other opinions and do not cross beyond differences of opinion to reach mutual understanding. Young's students became quite skilled at the argumentative writing so valorized in the academy. But, like Corder, Young had hoped for more. Young wanted his students to rethink their conceptions and be open to change. Young and Corder both want students to be more open to inquiry, more open to questioning, more open to curiosity. Taking up their calls for change, I later propose a different way to teach writing so perhaps students will be better able to communicate with the aim of reaching mutual understanding, a hallmark of civil discourse.

Young does not investigate what implications his disappointment in the course might have beyond the sphere of the writing classroom, but he does make points that seem applicable to my claims about civil discourse. For instance, he posits, "Certitude tends to induce a predisposition to look no further, confirming the mind in its habitual grooves and encouraging it to ignore whatever might threaten to dislodge it. Certitude, then, subverts dialogue as discussion and encourages debate" (Young 2003, 165). How do we avoid this type of outcome? In addressing this question, Young states,

> We need an art of rhetoric that encourages inquiry and discussion; the present art, the one I relied on in the course, while valuable for many purposes, does not do this well. It emphasizes abstract principle, the self-evident, and the axiomatic in contrast to the particular, the practical, and the probabilistic . . . . It tends to devalue shared experience, communal belief, the situational and contingent, and the prudential. The dominant rhetorical tradition and our textbooks on argumentation, which are informed by this tradition, have been and still are essentially eristic. (166)

Young's claim here is that we need to value just what our present art of rhetoric tends to devalue. We need to value "shared experience, communal belief, the situational and contingent, and the prudential" in order to encourage "inquiry and discussion" (166). In order to make changes that would help us understand people from across the borders of difference and make ourselves understood to them as well, I think we must teach students how to adopt a more open ethos. Such openness can lead to less disagreement and less hostility. We must shape our educational practices to better achieve a rhetoric that emphasizes an open ethos for use in civil discourse.

Young agrees that the time has come for a new way of teaching rhetorical ethos. He states, "Because certitude tends to transform discussion into debate, I think we need to build into rhetorical invention what for want of a better term might be called a problemology. We need to find ways of moving students beyond easy notions and into . . . a state of mind where questioning rather than asserting and bolstering assertion characterizes thinking" (Young 2003, 166). Again, while Young's analysis focuses only on the writing classroom, it seems to me that if we move into the realm of questioning and away from the realm of assertion as we teach students to communicate across borders, we can help them have more positive interactions beyond the classroom as well. If we can move students into a way of thinking in which assertion is not their primary aim, in which their goal is not to prove themselves right and the other wrong, the inquiring, questioning, curious ethos they will create as a result should help them reduce hostility and enable them to carry out dialogues rather than arguments that have winners and losers.

For insights into how to make developing an open ethos a reality, I next turn to Thomas O. Sloane's discussion of Ciceronian invention. According to Sloane, Cicero's later-life conception of invention "is dialogic and it must be pursued pro and con, prosecution and defense, affirmation and negation" (Sloane 1989, 462). He continues, "One must, that is, debate both sides—or, for that matter, all sides—of any case or one's own invention will remain not fully invented" (462). Sloane here moves beyond two-sided debate to suggest that we must open-mindedly investigate as many aspects of each situation as possible in order to come close to fully understanding them. As Sloane remarks, not choosing sides too early is key to developing a rich understanding of complex situations. Instead of choosing sides immediately, students should learn to see all sides involved. Sloane writes, "This continual practice of debating one side and then the other . . . is a key to Ciceronian invention . . . for it helps students form new resolutions and reexamine the ones they already hold" (466, 467). Unlike Young's students, who refuted opposing arguments in order to bolster their own, as Sloane envisions Ciceronian invention, each student must stand in the place of others. In this way they come to know the multiple sides of any issue and can use this knowledge to reach new conclusions. Unlike Young, who started his course by using the common pedagogy of the composition classroom that calls for students to make judgments, choose sides, and construct arguments, Ciceronian invention in Sloane's conception calls for students to hold off on making judgments, hold off on choosing sides, hold off on constructing arguments so they can investigate the complexities involved in any situation.

When using Ciceronian invention to investigate not only one's own viewpoints but also the viewpoints of others, according to Sloane, "the student's rhetorical task is always to put the matter into debate, voicing the multiplicity of issues until the stasis, the point of crucial difference, is reached, the point beyond which discussion cannot proceed until agreement between people is attempted" (Sloane 1989, 467). I think it is this reaching for agreement between people that is key. When we are already closed to what others might offer before they utter their opinions, our chances of reaching agreement are diminished. Remaining open to the variety of opinions voiced by multiple people, listening for the places where they clash, then moving beyond that clash are all moves that encourage civil discourse and understanding. Reaching for agreement allows us to see the opposing side not just as something against which to argue but as a positioned statement from a human being or beings with reasons, emotions, and values. By conceptualizing a position as coming from human beings, as coming from people who think, feel, and are authentic, we can show the audience, through an open ethos, that we want to communicate across difference. The pedagogy I propose next capitalizes on these Ciceronian strategies for developing an open ethos in order to equip students to seek mutual understandings through civil discourse.

The pedagogy I describe here is grounded in the principles of inquiry and mutual understanding. As detailed elsewhere (Peirce 2007), my teaching in several composition courses shifted attention away from the principles of winning an argument and toward the principles of considering multiple viewpoints. Based on the framework proposed by Linda Flower in "Talking across Difference: Rhetoric and the Search for Situated Knowledge," in which she describes the "story behind the story," "rivaling," and "options and outcomes" strategies for considering multiple viewpoints (Flower 2003, 51), I expected students in these courses to question more than assert, consider as many possible solutions as feasible, and investigate potential outcomes to various scenarios. The multimodal inquiry projects students developed showed creativity, curiosity, and openness to varied perspectives. For example, one student who was homeschooled as a child designed a project to investigate multiple perspectives on schooling. He created a choose-your-own-adventure type of video game in which the player encountered various scenarios while moving through a school setting. In one scenario, upon encountering a disaffected teacher in a public school setting, the player could choose to go to private school, be homeschooled, or persist in public school. The player's choice determined what would be presented next, and in this way, the student created an inquiry into education that explored multiple perspectives and offered multiple choices for proceeding. Rather than reaching the conclusion that one approach to education is superior to others for all people at all times, by creating this game the student learned that multiple perspectives on education have merit. Rather than using a forceful, self-assured ethos to argue one perspective over all others, this student's video game employed and conveyed an open, questioning ethos to demonstrate that people with differing perspectives on education have valid reasons for those differences and that those perspectives are worthy of respect.

Another student also wanted to investigate public education, but her main question centered on her future role as a teacher. To investigate educational theories and practices, this student created an essay in a fairly traditional format, but rather than writing a solo-voiced argument that aimed to convince the reader that one approach is correct while all others are wrong, this student designed her text in such a way that it allowed room for varied perspectives. In the margins of her text, she inserted images and words to represent alternate possibilities, personal insights, questions, and resources the reader could use to do more research into the topic. Rather than reaching an absolute conclusion that favored one approach to education, this student enriched her understanding of educational practices by allowing room for multiple perspectives, acknowledging the contingent nature of what she discovered. She conveyed an ethos in her project that was open to differing opinions, thereby drawing her readers with her on an investigation into a significant issue while allowing those readers to reach different conclusions.

Not all students in these courses investigated questions surrounding education. For example, one student wanted to explore the role ethnicity plays in the creation of personality, and to investigate this topic, he wrote a multivoiced dialogue that represented different aspects of his personality as well as his varied ethnic background. Rather than claiming definitively that certain of his personality traits could be traced to specific elements of his heritage, the dialogue he created was filled with questions that examined multiple possibilities. He investigated various hypotheses, keeping open to the potentials that were inherent in each. As did the other students, this student maintained an inviting ethos through his use of questions more than assertions, possibilities rather than answers, and multiple perspectives rather than one certain viewpoint. Because of this approach, his readers could join him on a journey of discovery, thereby promoting mutual understanding.

A final example involves a student who was interested in the connection between colors and mood. This student created a series of colorful posters filled with terms used to describe the colors, and quotations that depicted the moods different people associate with those colors. The posters were accompanied by a sound track that included songs with lyrics and titles that had the names of colors in them. His project depicted not one correct term for each color, not one correct mood to feel in association with each color, not one correct song to perfectly represent each color and associated mood, but rather it displayed the multiplicity of terms, moods, and music associated with different colors. This student, like the others, approached his subject with openness and curiosity, creating a multimodal project that conveyed an open, curious ethos that invited the audience to accompany him on a quest for mutual understanding rather than a closed, certain, assertive ethos that shut down dialogue before it could begin.

As these examples show, students in these courses strove to reach mutual understanding by exploring multiple perspectives with an open ethos rather than striving solely to use an assertive ethos to win arguments. In their course evaluations, students reported experiencing "freedom, openness, and exploration" as main themes of the course, stating, "I learned how to . . . write an inquiry without always asserting," "It really helped me become more inquisitive," and "It opens up one's mind to new ideas and perspectives" (Peirce 2007, under "Student Reactions"). As such, these students came to embody the goals of the NICD in that they shared diverse perspectives, considered complex issues thoughtfully, and explored challenging topics while maintaining civility in discourse. Further research in the form of follow-up surveys or analysis of the students' writing after completing the course would be needed to show whether or not students were able to sustain beyond the classroom the lessons they learned about an open, inquiring ethos. However, the fact that one student stated "I will use the inquiry-based writing in my own teaching and future writing" (Peirce 2007) leaves me hopeful that my approach could have lasting effects.

With so many calling for the types of changes I implemented in my own courses, why do we not see movement away from the predominant teaching of argument toward the teaching of civil discourse, as I have envisioned it here? Further research is needed to discover why we hear theorists from Sloane in 1989 to Knoblauch in 2011 and all those in between making the same plea for altering our teaching of rhetoric and ethos without seeing significant change across all those years. Is the answer simply because change is difficult? Is it because maintaining the status quo is simpler? Is it because teachers aren't sharing their pedagogical innovations in public ways? Finding answers to these questions could perhaps bring widespread change to our educational practices that could result in increasing civil discourse across the borders of difference.

References

Aristotle. 1991. *On Rhetoric: A Theory of Civic Discourse.* Translated by George A. Kennedy. New York: Oxford University Press.
Callaghan, Patsy, and Ann Dobyns. 2004. *A Meeting of Minds: A Brief Rhetoric for Writers and Readers.* New York: Pearson.
Corder, Jim W. 1991. "Academic Jargon and Soul-Searching Drivel." *Rhetoric Review* 9 (2): 314–26. http://dx.doi.org/10.1080/07350199109388936.

Crowley, Sharon, and Debra Hawhee. 2004. *Ancient Rhetorics for Contemporary Students.* 3rd ed. New York: Pearson.

Cruz, Johnny. 2011. "Bush, Clinton to Chair New National Institute for Civil Discourse at the University of Arizona." University of Arizona. http://uanews.org/story/bush-clinton-chair-new-national-institute-civil-discourse-university-arizona.

Flower, Linda. 2003. "Talking across Difference: Intercultural Rhetoric and the Search for Situated Knowledge." *College Composition and Communication* 55 (1): 38–68. http://dx.doi.org/10.2307/3594199.

Jolliffe, David A. 1999. *Inquiry and Genre: Writing to Learn in College.* Needham Heights, MA: Allyn & Bacon.

Knoblauch, Alison Abby. 2011. "A Textbook Argument: Definitions of Argument in Leading Composition Textbooks." *College Composition and Communication* 63 (2): 244–68.

Peirce, Karen P. 2007. "Building Intercultural Empathy through Writing: Reflections on Teaching Alternatives to Argumentation." *CEA Forum* 36 (2). https://web.archive.org/web/20100610035944/http://www2.widener.edu/~cea/362peirce.htm.

Rottenberg, Annette T. 1991. *Elements of Argument: A Text and Reader.* 3rd ed. Boston, MA: Bedford.

Sloane, Thomas O. 1989. "Reinventing Invention." *College English* 51 (5): 461–73. http://dx.doi.org/10.2307/378000.

Tannen, Deborah. 1998. *The Argument Culture: Moving from Debate to Dialogue.* New York: Random.

University of Arizona. 2012a. National Institute for Civil Discourse. http://nicd.arizona.edu.

University of Arizona. 2012b. "Frequently Asked Questions." National Institute for Civil Discourse. http://nicd.arizona.edu/faq-page#n52.

University of Arizona. 2012c. "Objectives." National Institute for Civil Discourse. http://nicd.arizona.edu/objectives.

Young, Richard E. 2003. "Toward an Adequate Pedagogy for Rhetorical Argumentation: A Case Study in Invention." In *Beyond Postprocess and Postmodernism: Essays on the Spaciousness of Rhetoric,* edited by Theresa Enos and Keith D. Miller, 159–69. Mahwah, NJ: Erlbaum.

6
CROSSING LINGUISTIC BORDERS IN THE CLASSROOM
Moving beyond English Only to Tap Rich Linguistic Resources

Anita C. Hernández, José A. Montelongo, and Roberta J. Herter

For more than a century, people have been crossing the US–Mexican border from south to north to find work in the United States. Many of those who have found work have brought their families to reside and be educated here. While immigrants in general have been subjected to many forms of prejudice, the concern of this chapter is with discriminatory policies and practices that Latino English learners encounter in US public schools; 80 percent of emergent bilinguals in the United States are Spanish speakers (NCELA 2011). We argue that Latino English learners have been seen as inferior and deficient with respect to language development and that English-only approaches lead to maltreatment rather than support of these English learners. Such approaches tend to be pervasive—a huge and needless issue for all learners within the schools.

Another victim of the pervasive English-only climate is the Latin-based Spanish language itself because of its association with the social status of its speakers. Even though it is the third-ranked language in terms of number of speakers, teaching students to learn and develop their knowledge of Spanish is not often encouraged in the schools. This is particularly troubling because a major thrust in education concerns the learning of "academic vocabulary," most of which is also Latin based.

In the following pages, we first examine the politics of language that have shaped the current language policies. Next, we examine models of biliteracy in terms of the speaker's needs. Finally, we introduce a vocabulary research program we designed to develop English-Spanish biliteracy for all students using cognates, words orthographically and semantically identical or nearly identical in both English and Spanish, as conduits to biliteracy. In presenting this review of language policy and our classroom research, we hope to show how barriers created by law—if not prejudice—thwart the efforts of second language learners. Such issues can be overcome in the classroom through crossing language borders in the specific ways we recommend.

THE POLITICS OF BILINGUAL EDUCATION

On the fiftieth anniversary of the Civil Rights Act, April 2014, President Obama paid tribute to President Lyndon Johnson, who signed the Civil Rights Act of 1964. In 1968, President Johnson moved bilingual education into prominence by signing the Bilingual Education Act. This legislation recognized the needs of limited-English-speaking students and provided grant money for schools to develop bilingual education programs, teaching students both in their native language and in English, to accommodate their needs.

In 1974, the US Supreme Court ruled in *Lau v. Nichols* that there is no equality of treatment achieved by merely providing students with the same facilities, textbooks, teachers, and curriculum. Limited-English-speaking students were therefore entitled to supplemental assistance in order for them to participate equitably in schools, guaranteeing their rights under the Civil Rights Act of 1964 (Crawford 1995; *Lau v. Nichols* 1974). In other words, when it came to addressing English-language learners, public schools were to eliminate sink-or-swim educational practices.

The Ford (1974–76) and Carter (1976–80) administrations endorsed the Lau Remedies (*Lau vs. Nichols* 1974; US Office for Civil Rights 1975) by reauthorizing the Bilingual Education Act. In 1994, the Clinton administration also reauthorized the Bilingual Education Act and actively promoted approaches that cultivated bilingualism through enrichment programs known as *dual immersion* or *two-way bilingual education* with the intent of providing all students full access to the curriculum. For example, as Spanish-speaking students learned English in bilingual classrooms, their English-speaking classmates learned Spanish in the same classrooms. The advantage of these programs was that they were designed for *all* students instead of focusing only on disadvantaged children who were English-language learners and were thus defined as deficient (Howard and Sugarman 2010; Lindholm-Leary 2000). The administration recognized that the two-language approach provided advantages for English-speaking populations (e.g., helping them to meet language requirements for college attendance) and that there were equal advantages for the less privileged. This approach acknowledged the permeability of language borders.

ENGLISH-ONLY POSITION

Opposed to these bilingual programs are the advocates of the English-only position, which seeks declaration of English as the country's official—and only—language to be used in business, government, education, and similar contexts. This argument is actually nothing new in American politics but in fact has a long political and academic history. Theorists and researchers such as Geoffrey Nunberg (2007) suggest that the growth of the English-only movement has more to do with cultural anxieties than it has to do with English losing its primacy. This anxiety has been reflected at the highest level of American government; as early as 1907, President Theodore Roosevelt announced, "We have room for but one language here, and that is the English language, for we intend to see that the crucible turns our people out as Americans, and not as dwellers in a polyglot boarding house" (Roosevelt 1926, 554).

The one-language position reemerged in the 1980s as the contemporary English-only movement, whose intellectual founder was Senator S. I. Hayakawa, a professional linguist and semanticist by training. In 1981, Hayakawa introduced an English Language Amendment to a Senate bill in response to a national study by Danoff, Coles, McLaughlin, and Reynolds (1978), which suggested that English learners were not achieving well academically in federally funded, language-maintenance bilingual programs. Hayakawa and several of his fellow senators voiced their displeasure over the fact that 86 percent of bilingual programs in the nation at the time had the achievement of fluency in Spanish as one of their academic goals. These English-only advocates supported using transitional bilingual education programs to teach English to minority-language students, but they argued against the language-maintenance bilingual education programs, which continued through high school. The latter programs were believed to only encourage Spanish-language enclaves, similar to the French Canadian Quebec-style separatism, instead of promote assimilation into "mainstream America" (Crawford 2008). Later executive involvement was reported by the *New York Times* with President Reagan's pronouncement: "It is absolutely wrong and against the American concept to have a bilingual education program that is now openly, admittedly, dedicated to preserving [students'] native language and never getting them adequate in English so they can go out into the job market" (Clines, *New York Times*, March 3, 1981).

The Reagan administration never fully examined the research evidence, yet it charged that bilingual education fostered ethnic identity at the expense of teaching students English. The Reagan administration relaxed the enforcement of the Lau Remedies and greatly expanded funds for English as a second language (ESL) programs while reducing funds for bilingual education programs.

In the next iteration of the English-only movement, new opponents to bilingual education presented themselves as mainstream conservatives advocating for immigrant children instead of nativist fanatics attacking bilingualism as un-American. For example, Ron Unz, California entrepreneur and aspiring conservative politician, recognized that garnering public opposition to bilingual education would be an easier endeavor than convincing state legislators who for years had been deadlocked over bilingual education. In 1998, Unz positioned himself as an advocate and financed the English for the Immigrant Children campaign to limit bilingual education by replacing it with English-only policies. The California vote opened the way for similar English-only legislation in other states, such as Arizona, Massachusetts, and Colorado, though Colorado's antibilingual education initiative of 2002 was defeated. Ironically, many Anglo voters feared that immigrant children would take the teachers' time away from their own children because extra time was needed for immigrant children to learn English (Escamilla et al. 2003), ignoring the advantages that a bilingual program could provide for all children.

The bilingual approach to education in this country was essentially brought to an end in 2002, and as James Crawford (2008) so aptly stated, "it died a quiet death" when the George W. Bush administration pushed Congress to pass the No Child Left Behind (NCLB) Act. Further, the NCLB Act required that all testing be conducted in English—one of its accountability provisions that also pushed bilingual education and dual-language programs against the wall. In addition, control of education in effect was seized from the hands of teachers and placed instead in the hands of corporations that sold millions of dollars worth of scripted curricula to schools across the nation for basal readers, standardized tests, and test-prep materials.

The English-only ideology fosters the assimilation of an Anglo-American majoritarian perspective, which makes people who are bilingual or who speak a language other than English feel belittled and subordinated (Macedo 2000). While English-only legislation that comes before Congress often touts English as the "common language" of the nation, the legislation typically not only promotes English but also prohibits the use of other languages in government documents, thereby limiting the rights of minority groups and condemning immigrants for many of today's problems (Crawford 2008, 111).

Not all states have accepted the English-only movement. For instance, while the English-only and antibilingual education law was passed in

Massachusetts, some parents in Cambridge whose own children were learning a second language (Spanish) in dual-language programs lobbied against the law. In California, Anglo parents also sought to have dual-language programs exempt from the antibilingual ballot initiative. These parents recognized the value and sought the advantages of bilingualism for their children (Gándara and Contreras 2010). New Mexico requires teachers to become proficient in Spanish and English to help Spanish-speaking children in schools through historical state legislation dating back to 1911. Four states—New Mexico, Oregon, Rhode Island, and Washington—adopted an English-plus resolution in which use of diverse languages in business, government, and private affairs, along with the presence of diverse cultures, is welcomed, encouraged, and protected. In addition, Hawai'i is officially a bilingual state recognizing native Hawaiian and English as the official languages.

BILINGUALISM: CROSSING LINGUISTIC BORDERS

Bilingualism is a common phenomenon in borderlands where the peoples of two regions, such as Mexico and the United States, come into contact. Individuals may become bilingual through *circumstances* or because they *elect* to do so (Valdés and Figueroa 1994). Bilingualism developed as a result of circumstances is a common phenomenon in immigrant communities in which individuals or families of minority groups learn the language of the host country in order to function, succeed in school, and achieve financial stability. Contradistinctively, native speakers of a host country usually do not have a need to learn the minority language because of the power differential they have over immigrant minority groups (Hamers and Blanc 2000). Historically, the children of immigrant families are the ones who learn the language of the host country to which they immigrated, and hence these children not only become bilingual and transnational but also become language brokers for their parents (Faulstich Orellana et al. 2001), thereby weaving in and out of linguistic borders. For example, these bilingual children translate and broker meaning for their parents in doctors' offices, with representatives of service agencies, and with teachers during parent-teacher conferences.

Others learn a second language not because they have to but because they elect to do so. In the United States, these are generally children whose middle-class parents wish for them to become bilingual and place them in dual-language programs to learn Spanish with native Spanish-speaking classmates. In addition, some adolescents and young adults elect to learn a language such as French, German, or Spanish in high school, college, or language institutes. Still others are individuals who elect to learn and improve their heritage languages, such as Navajo and Cherokee, in order to preserve their cultures and to interact with their elders. Still other adults teach themselves an additional language through online language programs, community education programs, or contact with speakers of other languages.

Society treats its elective bilinguals differently from its circumstantial ones. Elective bilinguals are generally privileged and praised for their bilingual skills, however incipient, whereas circumstantial bilinguals are often criticized for not being able to speak one of their languages well or are perceived as not being able to speak either language well. Further, circumstantial bilinguals are expected to learn the host language in order to earn a living, be successful in school, and conduct everyday transactions. In contrast to circumstantial bilinguals, the well-being of elective bilinguals is not tied to becoming bilingual.

The many types of bilinguals and their use of languages can be described on a continuum in terms of an individual's listening, speaking, reading, and writing skills in the two languages (Valdés and Figueroa 1994). At one end of the continuum are those who are predominantly fluent in Language A; at the other end of the continuum are those who are primarily proficient in Language B. In between these two poles are the bilinguals who vary in their listening, speaking, reading, and writing competencies. Those rare individuals who have command of both languages equally across an array of topics, social situations, academic knowledge, and cultural experiences represent the center of the continuum. A different perspective, one common in foreign-language departments, considers bilingualism to be two monolinguals in one person, an ideal almost impossible to reach in the United States (Grosjean 2010).

SECOND LANGUAGE STUDENTS

In the US educational context, the number of schoolchildren who speak a language other than English has mushroomed. Of the 5.3 million children who speak a language other than English, 80 percent are Spanish speakers (NCELA 2011). Schools across the nation are seeing an increase in second language learners, even in states—for example, California, Texas, Florida, Illinois, and New York—other than those generally known for having large numbers of second language learners.

Regardless of where they are located, children who speak a language other than English have been referred to as either English-language learners or English learners. Escamilla and Hopewell (2010) suggest such labels define these children in terms of a deficiency. Instead, they propose these schoolchildren be described in a more positive light as "emergent bilinguals." Following Escamilla and Hopewell, we refer to English learners as emergent bilinguals, with a shift toward acknowledging the benefit of bilingualism. This advocacy stance on the part of teachers repositions learners in the process of acquiring a second language.

In many countries, the ability of children to speak more than one language is seen as important. Such is not generally the case in the United States. As sociolinguist Joshua Fishman and his coauthors have claimed, "Many Americans have long been of the opinion that bilingualism is 'a good thing' if it was acquired via travel (preferably to Paris) or via formal education (preferably at Harvard) but that it is a 'bad thing' if it was acquired from one's immigrant parents or grandparents" (Fishman et al. 1966, 122–23). In cities such as El Paso, Texas, a city on the US-Mexico border, the ability of thousands of Latino children to speak Spanish is often not seen as a resource but rather as a deficit to be remedied in the service of English by means of a transitional model. Despite the existence of such deficit thinking, more and more dual-language programs that promote biliteracy are being started every year through grassroots efforts.

BILINGUAL EDUCATION MODELS

Dual-language abilities can be fostered in several ways. Some educators believe the two languages should be separated entirely as in the increasingly popular dual-language models (Howard and Sugarman 2010)—navigating language borders separately and in parallel fashion. Others advocate transitional models in which students learn to read and write in their first language in order to develop a stronger second language (Crawford 2004; Cummins 1981). Finally, others suggest both languages should be learned strategically and simultaneously in bilingual programs (Escamilla and Hopewell 2010; García 2008).

Dual-language programs that focus on developing children's bilingualism and biliteracy are organized so children receive their Spanish instruction from a designated Spanish-language teacher and their English instruction from an English-model teacher. Dual-language programs use an additive model of language in that students develop two languages. The two languages are not mixed so students will develop independent bilingual and biliteracy skills. Undergirding this language model is the belief that bilinguals are two monolinguals in one person and that a separation of languages is necessary for developing balanced bilingual individuals and for maintaining language purity (Howard and Sugarman 2010). Critics of this model suggest that this language practice goes too far and does not take advantage of cross-linguistic transfer; it ignores the interrelationship of the two languages. For example, Bertha Pérez (2003) recommends that students in the later years of dual-language programs engage in hybrid language practices to show how bilingual individuals in communities use their two languages in translanguaging practices. Teachers can also encourage talk in two languages and position such bilingual language practices as resources (Martin-Beltrán 2009).

Bilingual education models vary. For instance, two primary models emphasize learning languages sequentially. The main goal of these models is to develop children's first-language literacy in the service of acquiring higher levels of the second language. One transitions the children from Spanish to English literacy as quickly and as early as possible, in the first and second grades, while a second model waits until the students are more academically advanced in the third or fourth grades. Both models lead ultimately to a subtractive bilingualism: underlying this language model is the ideology that bilingualism is a temporary state and that the first language is not to be developed any more than necessary.

In contrast, a third model focuses on developing bilingual minds simultaneously (Escamilla and Hopewell 2010). This model shifts the two language paradigms from strict separation of languages or from the lines implicitly drawn in dual-language and transitional models. This third model makes strategic use of two languages by concurrently providing students with rich opportunities to develop their two linguistic and literacy repertoires, in effect allowing learners to cross borders that tend to be established between their languages. Escamilla and Hopewell (2010) believe that emergent bilingual children can grow both languages simultaneously and make crossover language connections throughout their elementary schooling. Because the literature shows a strong and positive correlation between Spanish and English literacy, bilingualism and biliteracy in schools can therefore be realized to its full potential.

In any case, around the country, children in dual-language and bilingual education models have shown greater gains in reading and academic achievement in comparison to children in English-only programs (see Greene 1998; Ramírez, Yuen and Ramey 1991; Willig 1985). Those who encourage these programs support an ideological perspective on dual-language learning that views language as a resource and as beneficial to the individual, to the community, and to the wider society (Ruiz 1988).

Grounded in the theoretical position taken by Kathy Escamilla and her associates, we espouse a framework for bilingual education that argues for the simultaneous development of bilingualism, biliteracy, and cross-linguistic connections, especially for those students whose first language is Spanish. In adopting this position, we place ourselves squarely against the predominant English-only movement that fails to respect the first languages schoolchildren bring to school.

In this next section of the chapter, we describe the professional work we do to encourage bilingualism in English and Spanish. While the major goal of our work is to develop the bilingual and biliterate capabilities of emergent bilinguals, the approach we advocate can also be used to great effect with native speakers of English.

USING COGNATES AS BRIDGES TO BILITERACY

English-Spanish cognates are an important subset of English and Spanish languages. They are words that possess identical or nearly identical spellings and meanings in both languages. Cognates are typically multisyllabic words derived from Latin and Greek (Corson 1997). Many of the more than twenty thousand English-Spanish cognates are academic words—that is, terms needed for success in school. Elfrieda Hiebert (2007) found that over 61 percent of the words in the General Service List (Bauman and Culligan 1995) are cognates. The General Service List includes over two thousand base words identified as most useful to English learners. Averil Coxhead (2000) further extended the General Service List to include 570 more base words in her Academic Word List. Similarly, in an analysis of the Academic Word List, Hiebert and Lubliner (2008) found that 70 percent of these 570 words are English-Spanish cognates. The importance of these words is further supported by the fact that most of the subject headings in the Dewey Decimal System are English-Spanish cognates (Montelongo 2012).

One limiting language-acquisition factor in schools is that many of the words taught in early grades and encountered in early basal readers are one-syllable words of Anglo-Saxon origin (Corson 1997). These words are especially difficult for Latino emergent bilinguals because the words are not a part of their listening or speaking vocabularies in their native language of Spanish. In contrast to the early-grade basal readers that emphasize Anglo-Saxon words, picture books found in the early grades as well as content-area texts encountered in the later grades include many English-Spanish cognates. Through these cognates, Latino emergent bilinguals can better grasp many unknown academic-English words.

Many of the academic words in English are also academic words in Spanish. Teaching Latino emergent bilinguals about cognates taps into their preexisting knowledge and enables them to engage with literacy more effectively than do strategies that ignore or denigrate their rich linguistic knowledge (Cummins 2005). Lubliner and Hiebert (2011) further suggest that the influence of Latin provides bilingual students with "funds of knowledge" (Moll et al. 1992) that put them at an advantage over English-only speakers for acquiring academic vocabulary. Cognates drawn from the Spanish speakers' linguistic funds of knowledge can provide a lifelong resource for learning English, particularly academic English (Lubliner and Hiebert 2011).

Learning to recognize Spanish cognates in English words in effect gives Latino emergent bilinguals an edge over students who do not recognize these cognates. One of the ways in which knowledge of Spanish gives Latino emergent bilinguals an edge over their English-speaking peers is revealed through the morphological analyses of words. In practical terms, when taught to recognize cognates drawn from Spanish, Latino emergent bilinguals are better able to dissect these cognates into roots and affixes in order to arrive at the meanings of previously unknown words. For example, the cognate *intolerable* may be divided into the prefix *in*, which means "not," the suffix *able*, which means "able to," and the base word *tolerate* in order to yield the meaning "not able to be tolerated." David Corson (1997) suggests that members of sociocultural and language groups who have more frequent practice with the morphological and semantic features of academic words taken from Latin and Greek will differ from others in their readiness or ability to see the semantic transparency often evident in multisyllabic words. Corson further proposes that "student language awareness, especially knowledge of word semantic transparency, seems an important area for teachers and learners to concentrate on," adding that "student opportunities to learn words in motivated contexts, talking about academic texts, provide another priority area for pedagogical change" (Corson 1997, 672).

In order to take advantage of the morphological structures of cognates, Montelongo and Hernández (2012) have recommended that cognates be taught early and often through picture-book read-alouds and accompanying vocabulary activities. Picture books may be defined as those books for young children that include text and illustrations, which are often more important to the understanding of the story than are the words. *Where the Wild Things Are* (Sendak 1963) and *The Polar Express* (Van Allsburg 1985) are examples of some of the picture books commonly read aloud to primary school children.

Picture books are an excellent source when selecting vocabulary words to enrich student vocabularies because they contain so many words primary schoolchildren do not encounter in their basal readers (Beck, McKeown, and Kucan 2002, 2008). In their original books, Beck, McKeown, and Kucan (2002) listed several enrichment vocabulary words taken from each of over eighty picture books. An analysis of their word lists revealed that more than half of the words (53 percent) were English-Spanish cognates, such as *commotion, enormous*, and *murmur* (Montelongo, Durán, and Hernández 2013). In a subsequent book, Beck, McKeown, and Kucan (2008) listed seven to nine words for each of twenty picture books. Just fewer than half of the words listed by the authors (49 percent) were cognates, such as *harmony, dignity*, and *peculiar* (Montelongo, Durán, and Hernández 2013). The significant number of cognates in the books by Isabel Beck, Margaret McKeown, and Linda Kucan provides further evidence of the pervasiveness and importance of English-Spanish cognates.

COGNATES: EVIDENCE FROM THE CLASSROOM

Equally important, using the English-Spanish cognates found in picture books to expand students' vocabularies can benefit all learners, not just Latino emergent bilinguals (Montelongo, Hernández, and Herter, unpublished manuscript). General knowledge of the meanings of words or their roots or affixes can improve all students' abilities to make meaning from texts.

Experimental studies have shown that recognizing English-Spanish cognates in this way in the classroom is not an automatic mental process for students (Nagy et al. 1993). Explicit instruction is required in order for students to develop cognate recognition (Jiménez and Gámez 1996). Teachers can instruct their students to use cognates as clues for decoding the meanings of an unfamiliar words in context (Montelongo et al. 2011). Effectively, this entails teaching students to try to deduce the meaning of a word by treating the word as a cognate and then deciding whether the guess makes sense in that context. Empirical studies have repeatedly demonstrated that, on tests of comprehension, bilingual students who adopt such a cognate-recognition strategy while reading texts outperform those who have not developed this skill (Jiménez 1997).

USING COGNATES: A CLASSROOM EXAMPLE

In this section, we provide an example of how teaching students about cognates can benefit all learners. In an observational study of a classroom near the Texas-Mexico border, Hernández et al. (2011) found that cognate morphology instruction additionally led to the improved spelling of English words. In the study, fourth-grade teacher Ms. Parra (a pseudonym) introduced her students to English-Spanish cognates. Because of the interest students displayed in learning about cognates, Ms. Parra created additional lessons on morphology. The lessons incorporated cognate words to scaffold the learning of Latin and Greek roots and affixes such as the root *audi*, which means "to hear," and may be found in the English-Spanish cognates *audible-audible*, *audio-audio*, and *auditorium-auditorio*. Through these lessons, Ms. Parra observed that several of her students improved their spelling of English and Spanish words. They became conscious of their spelling in each of their two languages. Ms. Parra attributed the improvement in spelling to the English-Spanish cognate instruction and the students' interest in these words. Specifically, Ms. Parra observed a marked improvement in the English words having the word endings *sion* and *tion* as in the words *confusion*, *vision*, *graduation*, and *civilization*.

As another example, in a fourth-grade bilingual classroom in California that was focusing on an investigation of context clues, several English-dominant students commented that they wished they knew Spanish because they saw how easily their bilingual counterparts answered many questions about word meanings of multisyllabic academic words so quickly.

In addition, Latino emergent bilinguals have been found to demonstrate enthusiasm for learning cognates. For instance, in the aforementioned study of Ms. Parra's class, Hernández et al. (2011) found that students exhibited high levels of engagement while learning cognates. Once, as Ms. Parra read aloud to her class, a student raised his hand to inform her that she had just read a cognate. Before she finished the chapter, five other students had informed Ms. Parra that they recognized a number of cognates, such as *community-comunidad*; *defense-defensa*; *excellent-excelente*; *impossible-imposible*, and *interest-interés* (all words affiliated with academic vocabulary).

A week later, Ms. Parra observed that a group of boys remained in the classroom to compare lists of cognate words instead of going to recess. These students had initiated a contest among themselves to see who would be the first to identify one hundred cognates. Soon after this, the girls wanted to be a part of the competition and began compiling their own lists of cognates. As the weeks passed, the entire fourth-grade class maintained their interest in cognates—consistently identifying them in the books they read and the lessons the teacher taught. To boost their word consciousness, Ms. Parra dedicated a bulletin board for students to post their completed cognate word lists. At each recess, the fourth graders continued comparing their lists of new cognates with each other. These cognate words represented their identity as bilingual learners who could go between two language worlds while creating their own bilingual third space (Gutiérrez 2008).

Beck, McKeown, and Kucan (2002) suggest that children who develop an interest in and an awareness beyond school vocabulary assignments help themselves to grow their own vocabulary repertoire, which is important for reading comprehension. Evidence of this advantage was also observed in Ms. Parra's fourth-grade class. Once the bulletin board became crowded with the lists of cognates the students had compiled, students transitioned to recording cognates in their own cognate notebooks. Furthermore, they shared this new word knowledge with other classmates, their teacher, and their parents. One of the girls, who served as a language broker for her mother, began teaching her mother the English-Spanish cognate equivalents she had learned in school as a way to support her mother's goal to learn English.

During the introduction of a lesson, conversations about whether certain words were cognates arose. For example, Ms. Parra observed two children debating whether the pair of words *red* and *rojo* were cognates. Ms. Parra taught the children how to use the Find-A-Cognate database (Montelongo 2010a) to verify cognate pairs. This online resource allows a user to find a cognate for an English or Spanish word if one exists (Montelongo 2010b; Montelongo, Hernández, and Herter 2011). The ease of access for children to the database makes it an effective instructional and assessment tool since teachers can use it to track a student's access based on types and numbers of words.

James Cummins (1981) and Anita Hernández (2002) indicate that although a first language supports the second, the second language can also support the first. In other words, languages can serve as bidirectional linguistic resources. Evidence of this may be seen in the discussions and debates of Ms. Parra's fourth-grade students. The students were using their knowledge of Spanish cognates to understand previously unknown English words and vice versa. For example, while studying language arts, the students who knew the word *tranquilo* equated it to *tranquil* as the English equivalent. In science, students learned that the English word *system* had as its Spanish equivalent *sistema*. As the results in Ms. Parra's class illustrate, the use of cognates is a means for Latino emergent bilinguals to improve their English and, more important, to develop a curiosity about their two languages and how they can use them for learning—in short, crossing borders—drawing from existing borders between languages and then eliminating borders simultaneously. This approach allows emergent bilinguals to view the linguistic border as permeable, in many cases finding passage between their two languages to be seamless.

For language learners and bilingual children, cognate word play and cognate word study create an interest in their native and nonnative languages and provide a cross-linguistic awareness of words that allow them to grow their own vocabulary so they can become more proficient readers, writers, and learners. The evidence from a fourth-grade classroom suggests that cognate word study leads to engagement and improved performance in language abilities necessary for literacy. The affirmation of a student's home language within the school can serve to encourage Spanish-language speakers to view their multilingual talents as a valued component of their identities (Cummins 2005). At a time when Latinos are losing their ability to communicate in their native Spanish, teachers like Ms. Parra do all they can to encourage making connections between English and Spanish explicit. As may be seen from the enthusiasm for word learning in Ms. Parra's class, all students can feel empowered by learning cognates.

ACCESS FOR ALL TO THE ACADEMIC CURRICULUM

In conclusion, there are a variety of ways for teachers to subtly cross linguistic borders in English-only settings when working with Latino emergent bilingual students. Teaching all students about cognates in the primary grades facilitates biliteracy. Moreover, cognates tap into Spanish-speaking students' preexisting knowledge and enable them to engage with literacy much more effectively. Since so many cognates are academic words, they are essential to academic success. Making students aware of cognates in the early grades during literacy and content-area instruction gives them a foundation for comprehending and using academic English words.

For native speakers of English, instruction about cognates also provides access to an academic vocabulary. Cognates provide access to the Latinate vocabulary that dominates disciplinary knowledge, benefiting all students. Many teachers do not use cognates as part of their practice because they are unaware of the utility of having over twenty thousand potential words at their disposal to scaffold the learning for all students—Latino emergent bilinguals and native speakers alike. Teachers do not see the potential of cognates to give native English speakers access to the Latinate vocabulary of various academic disciplines. Furthermore, many teachers do not feel competent enough in their knowledge of Spanish to use cognates for interdisciplinary teaching.

To overcome these barriers and to make biliteracy a real possibility, we have created online databases of cognates using award-winning books. For example, Montelongo and Hernández (2013) created a database for 180 of the International Reading Association's Teachers' Choices books. Similarly, José Montelongo created a database for all of the forty-five Geisel Award winners (Montelongo 2013) and for the forty-eight New Mexico Award winners and nominees (Montelongo, Hernández, and Ruiz 2013). All teachers, whether they are fluent in Spanish or not, can use these cognates within the databases to create vocabulary lessons that help Latino emergent bilingual students and native speakers access the interdisciplinary curriculum. Furthermore, teaching cognates to all students gives them access to academic Spanish. This highlights the advantage of biliteracy for all students. More important, it is a move toward language equity for all.

English-only schools have failed to close the gap between Latino emergent bilinguals and their English-speaking peers. Despite this failure, critics undermine bilingual education models by casting doubt on the benefits they provide (Macedo 2000). Clearly, the time has come to embrace bilingualism and biliteracy in order to create an educational system that encourages the crossing of linguistic borders. The English-only mindset obstructs linguistic border crossing; it also obstructs possibilities for building a nation on the strengths of all who live here, to the benefit of all who live here. Use of bilingual teaching techniques, such as instruction in cognates, facilitates the learning of a second language and allows both native and nonnative speakers of English to see the merits of crossing language barriers to improve their language learning. If our nation overcomes fear of language difference (if not the Other), we all stand to benefit.

References

Bauman, John, and Brent Culligan. 1995. "About the General Service List." http://jbauman.com/aboutgsl.html.

Beck, Isabel, Margaret McKeown, and Linda Kucan. 2002. *Bringing Words to Life: Robust Vocabulary Instruction.* New York: Guilford.

Beck, Isabel, Margaret McKeown, and Linda Kucan. 2008. *Creating Robust Vocabulary: Frequently Asked Questions and Extended Examples.* New York: Guilford.

Corson, David. 1997. "The Learning and Use of Academic English Words." *Language Learning* 47 (4): 671–718. http://dx.doi.org/10.1111/0023-8333.00025.
Coxhead, Averil. 2000. "A New Academic Word List." *TESOL Quarterly* 34 (2): 213–38. http://dx.doi.org/10.2307/3587951.
Crawford, James. 1995. *Bilingual Education: History, Politics, Theory, and Practice.* Trenton, NJ: Crane.
Crawford, James. 2004. *Educating English Learners: Language Diversity in the Classroom.* Los Angeles, CA: Bilingual Educational Services.
Crawford, James. 2008. *Advocating for English Learners: Selected Essays.* Clevedon, England: Multilingual Matters.
Cummins, James. 1981. "The Role of Primary Language Development in Promoting Educational Success for Language Minority Students." In *Schooling and Language Minority Students: A Theoretical Framework*, California State Office of Education, Office of Bilingual Bicultural Education, 16–60. Los Angeles: Evaluation and Dissemination and Assessment Center, California State University.
Cummins, James. 2005. "A Proposal for Action: Strategies for Recognizing Heritage Language Competence as a Learning Resource within the Mainstream Classroom." *Modern Language Journal* 89 (4): 585–92.
Danoff, Malcolm, Gary Coles, Donald McLaughlin, and Dorothy Reynolds. 1978. *Year Two Impact Data, Educational Process, and In-Depth Analysis.* Evaluation of the Impact of ESEA Title VII Spanish/English Bilingual Education Programs, vol. 3. Palo Alto, CA: American Institutes for Research.
Escamilla, Kathy, and Susan Hopewell. 2010. "Transitions to Biliteracy: Creating Positive Academic Trajectories for Emerging Bilinguals in the United States." In *International Perspectives on Bilingual Education: Policy, Practice, and Controversy*, edited by John Petrovic, 69–94. Charlotte, NC: Information Age.
Escamilla, Kathy, Sheila Shannon, Silvana Carlos, and Jorge García. 2003. "Breaking the Code: Colorado's Defeat of the Anti-Bilingual Education Initiative (Amendment 31)." *Bilingual Research Journal* 27 (3): 357–82. http://dx.doi.org/10.1080/15235882.2003.10162599.
Faulstich Orellana, Marjorie, Barrie Thorne, Anna Chee, and Wan Shun Eva Lam. 2001. "Transnational Childhoods: The Participation of Children in Processes of Family Migration." *Social Problems* 48 (4): 572–91. http://dx.doi.org/10.1525/sp.2001.48.4.572.
Fishman, Joshua, Valdimir Nahirny, John Hofman, and Robert Hayden. 1966. *Language Loyalty in the United States: The Maintenance and Perpetuation of Non-English Mother Tongues by American Ethnic and Religious Groups.* The Hague, Netherlands: Mouton.
Gándara, Patricia, and Frances Contreras. 2010. *The Latino Education Crisis: The Consequences of Failed Social Policies.* Cambridge, MA: Harvard University Press.
García, Ofelia. 2008. *Bilingual Education in the 21st Century: A Global Perspective.* Oxford, England: Wiley-Blackwell.
Greene, Jay. 1998. *A Meta-Analysis of the Effectiveness of Bilingual Education.* Claremont, CA: Tomás Rivera Policy Center.
Grosjean, François. 2010. *Bilingual: Life and Reality.* Cambridge, MA: Harvard University Press. http://dx.doi.org/10.4159/9780674056459.
Gutiérrez, Kris D. 2008. "Developing a Sociocritical Literacy in the Third Space." *Reading Research Quarterly* 43 (2): 148–64. http://dx.doi.org/10.1598/RRQ.43.2.3.
Hamers, Josiane, and Michel Blanc. 2000. *Biliguality and Bilingualism.* Cambridge, England: Cambridge University Press. http://dx.doi.org/10.1017/CBO9780511605796.
Hernández, Anita. 2002. "The Expected and Unexpected Literacy Outcomes of Bilingual Students." *Bilingual Research Journal* 25 (3): 251–76.
Hernández, Anita C., José A. Montelongo, Patricia Minjarez, and Aurora Oblack. 2011. "English-Spanish Cognate Phenomena in a Fourth-Grade Classroom." *New Mexico Journal of Reading* 32 (2): 7–11.

Hiebert, Elfrieda H. 2007. "A Core Academic Word List for the Middle Grades." Presentation at the International Reading Association, Toronto, ON, May 17.
Hiebert, Elfrieda H., and Shira Lubliner. 2008. "The Nature, Learning, and Instruction of General Academic Vocabulary." In *What Research Has to Say About Vocabulary*, edited by Alan Farstrup and S. Jay Samuels, 106–29. Newark, DE: International Reading Association.
Howard, Elizabeth, and Julie Sugarman. 2010. *Realizing the Vision of Two-Way Immersion: Fostering Effective Programs and Classrooms*. Washington, DC: Center for Applied Linguistics.
Jiménez, Robert T. 1997. "The Strategic Reading Abilities and Potential of Five Low-Literacy Latina/o Readers in Middle School." *Reading Research Quarterly* 32 (3): 224–43. http://dx.doi.org/10.1598/RRQ.32.3.1.
Jiménez, Robert T., and Arturo Gámez. 1996. "Literature-Based Cognitive Strategy Instruction for Middle School Latino Students." *Journal of Adolescent & Adult Literacy* 40 (2): 84–91.
Lindholm-Leary, Kathryn. 2000. *Dual Language Education*. Clevedon, England: Multilingual Matters.
Lubliner, Shira, and Elfrieda H. Hiebert. 2011. "An Analysis of English-Spanish Cognates as a Source of General Academic Language." *Bilingual Research Journal* 34 (1): 76–93. http://dx.doi.org/10.1080/15235882.2011.568589.
Macedo, Donaldo. 2000. "The Illiteracy of English Only." *Educational Leadership* 57 (4): 62–67.
Martin-Beltrán, Melinda. 2009. "Cultivating Space for the Language Boomerang: The Interplay of Two Languages as Academic Resources." *English Teaching* 8 (2): 25–53.
Moll, Luis C., Cathy Amanti, Deborah Neff, and Norma Gonzalez. 1992. "Funds of Knowledge for Teaching: Using a Qualitative Approach to Connect Homes and Classrooms." *Theory into Practice* 31 (2): 132–41. http://dx.doi.org/10.1080/00405 849209543534.
Montelongo, José A. 2010a. *Find-a-Cognate Database*. http://www.angelfire.com/ill/monte/findacognate.html.
Montelongo, José A. 2010b. "Library Instruction and Spanish-English Cognate Recognition." *Teacher Librarian* 38 (2): 32–6.
Montelongo, José A. 2012. "Spanish-English Cognates and the Dewey Decimal System." *California Reader* 45 (2): 11–6.
Montelongo, José A. 2013. "Online Cognate Databases for Picture Book Read-Alouds to Latino ELLs." *School Library Monthly* 30 (3): 35–37.
Montelongo, José A., Richard Durán, and Anita Hernández. 2013. "English-Spanish Cognates in Picture Books: Toward a Vocabulary Curriculum for Latino ELLs." *Bilingual Research Journal* 36 (2): 244–59. http://dx.doi.org/10.1080/15235882.2013.818074.
Montelongo, José A., and Anita Hernández. 2012. "Using Picture Books to Develop English-Spanish Cognate Recognition in Primary School English Learners." *New Mexico Journal of Reading* 33 (1): 14–19.
Montelongo, José A., and Anita Hernández. 2013. "The Teachers' Choices Cognate Database for K–3 Teachers of Latino English Learners." *Reading Teacher* 67 (3): 187–92. http://dx.doi.org/10.1002/TRTR.1194.
Montelongo, José, Anita Hernández, and Roberta J. Herter. 2011. "Identifying Spanish-English Cognates to Scaffold Instruction for Latino ELs." *Reading Teacher* 65 (2): 161–4. http://dx.doi.org/10.1002/TRTR.01019.
Montelongo, José A., Anita C. Hernández, Roberta J. Herter, and Jaime Cuello. 2011. "Using Cognates to Scaffold Context Clue Strategies for Latino ELs." *Reading Teacher* 64 (6): 429–34. http://dx.doi.org/10.1598/RT.64.6.4.
Montelongo, José A., Anita C. Hernández, and Roberta J. Herter. "Using Cognates in K–4 Classrooms: A Guide for Teachers and Resource for K–4 Students Learning English and Spanish." Unpublished manuscript, Philadelphia, PA.

Montelongo, José A., Anita C. Hernández, and Marisol Ruiz. 2013. "The New Mexico Book Awards and a Cognate Database." *New Mexico Journal of Reading* 33 (3): 39–44.

Nagy, William E., Georgia E. García, Aydin Y. Durgunoglu, and Barbara Hancin-Bhatt. 1993. "Spanish-English Bilingual Students' Use of Cognates in English Reading." *Journal of Reading Behavior* 25 (3): 241–58.

National Clearinghouse for English Language Acquisition (NCELA). 2011. *What Languages Do English Learners Speak? NCELA Fact Sheet.* Washington, DC: NCELA.

Nunberg, Geoffrey. 2007. *Talking Right: How Conservatives Turned Liberalism into a Tax-Raising, Latte-Drinking, Sushi-Eating, Volvo-Driving, New York Times-Reading, Body-Piercing, Hollywood-Loving, Left-Wing Freak Show.* New York: Public Affairs.

Pérez, Bertha. 2003. *Becoming Biliterate: A Study of Two-Way Bilingual Immersion Education.* Mahwah, NJ: Lawrence Erlbaum.

Ramírez, David, Sandra Yuen, and Dena Ramey. 1991. *Final Report: Longitudinal Study of Structured English Immersion Strategy, Early-Exit and Late-Exit Transitional Bilingual Education Programs for Language Minority Children.* San Mateo, CA: Aguirre International.

Roosevelt, Theodore. 1926. *Works. Memorial edition.* Vol. 24. New York: Charles Scribner's Sons.

Ruiz, Richard. 1988. "Orientations in Language Planning." In *Language Diversity: Problem or Resource?* edited by Sandra Lee McKay and Cynthia Wong Sau-ling, 3–25. New York: Newbury House.

Sendak, Maurice. 1963. *Where the Wild Things Are.* New York: Harper and Row.

US Office for Civil Rights. 1975. *Task-Force Findings Specifying Remedies Available for Eliminating Past Educational Practices Ruled Unlawful Under Lau v. Nichols.* http://www.stanford.edu/~hakuta/www/LAU/IAPolicy/IA3ExecLauRemedies.htm/.

Valdés, Guadalupe, and Richard Figueroa. 1994. *Bilingualism and Testing: A Special Case of Bias.* Westport, CT: Ablex.

Van Allsburg, Chris. 1985. *The Polar Express.* Boston: Houghton Mifflin.

Willig, Ann C. 1985. "A Meta-Analysis of Selected Studies on the Effectiveness of Bilingual Education." *Review of Educational Research* 55 (3): 269–317. http://dx.doi.org/10.3102/00346543055003269.

7
TRAVERSING RHETORICAL BORDERS OF SPIRITUALITY IN ACADEMIC SETTINGS

Susan A. Schiller

On the first day of college courses, most students are eager to see the projected plan outlined in the syllabus. They never expect that a daily practice of fifteen minutes of silence will be assigned. It is fun for me to watch their responses when we get to that part of the syllabus, for their eyes open a little wider, grow somewhat confused, or roll in disbelief. The less fearful ask such questions as "What is a practice of silence?" "What does it mean?" "What counts to fulfill this assignment?" "Isn't this just meditation?" "You mean I have to do this every day?" I answer by asking them to think about other words that might describe practicing silence—words such as *relaxation, contemplation, meditation, spirituality*. I also answer by promising that fifteen minutes of silence each day will help them in ways they never imagined, and as a countercultural activity, it will guide them to new points of view.

The students I see in a public state institution have been deeply conditioned by a culture that values coercion rather than choice and promises success for those who conform. They have learned that to venture beyond those cultural borders involves serious risk. The practice of silence I assign is a safe first step beyond the border and comes with no risk, but students must feel that for themselves before we—student and teacher—may openly and safely discuss what I refer to as a *spiritual approach to learning*. In this way, we challenge borders, and we ease into this spiritual approach. We also begin to counter mainstream approaches to learning that I argue inhibit creativity and promote conformity. In this chapter, I show the value of highlighting democratic choice through what can be considered a spiritual approach to teaching and learning. First, I share a sampling of efforts that educational theorists have made toward fostering what I term *spiritual intelligence*

DOI: 10.7330/9781607324034.c007

as a means to facilitate student learning and creativity. Next, I take up the restrictive borders common in educational settings, including those affiliated with rhetoric and composition. Finally, I draw on my own experiences of teaching composition and literature from a holistic and spiritual approach.

SCHOLARS DEFINING BORDERS FOR A SPIRITUAL PEDAGOGY

The word *spiritual* is a loaded word in nearly the same way as the word *God*. When *spirituality* is used, most listeners immediately link the term to God and expect some connection to fundamentalism, proselytizing, religious dogma, or worse. People automatically think and feel *religion*, and these thoughts are either positive or negative depending on their personal background. It is just the way it is, a point of rhetorical reality.

But as a scholar and educator trying to cross that rigid border, I know one's way of receiving the word *spiritual* is constructed and shaped by cultural boundaries. Over the years, I have learned that using the word *spiritual* as a secular construct nearly always requires a parenthetical aside that defines new boundaries, new tenets of meaning that will replace the automatic response with a new response—a response that embraces awe, inspiration, creativity, and joy in learning as the new rhetorical markers for the word. Once this border is crossed by the respondent, new ways of speaking about what is spiritual enter the vista. Today, I am more choosy as to when and with whom I use the word *spiritual*, but as a teacher and a scholar, I continue to embrace spiritual approaches that lift and lighten the soul, that invite creativity and inspiration, that embrace the inner life of learners, and that delicately lead students and readers beyond the borders of their own cultural limitations as well as those imposed by the academy. Traversing such borders through a spiritual approach to learning is easily accomplished without fear or coercion when teachers purposely create opportunities for transcendence and awe. A spiritual approach requires more than tolerating alternative perspectives in learning styles and activities; it requires making room for, and trusting in, breakthrough vision that can occur when democratic choice and creativity are prioritized more highly.

Joining me in such practice are many educators around the United States, Canada, Great Britain, Mexico, and other Latin American countries who now use the word *spiritual* to describe teaching and learning that comes from the heart and soul. The works of Parker Palmer (1998), James Moffett (1994), Linda Lantieri (2001a), Regina Foehr (and Schiller 1997), Rachael Kessler (2000), Nell Noddings (1992),

Mary Rose O'Reilley (1998), Ron Miller (2000), Richard Graves (1997), and John P. Miller (1996, 2000, 2006, 2012) have particularly informed my research, my teaching, and my personal investment in promoting a spiritual approach to writing and learning. Their wisdom and courage to cross borders surpasses mine; they have helped me develop not only courage but intention to encourage my students to live with spirit at the center of their lives. Their reported individual experiences with a spiritual approach to learning reveal that such an approach is essentially fluid, intuitive, liberating, and democratic because it can be shaped to suit the individual, not only by the teacher but by the student as well.

To reduce the connotative weight attached to *spiritual*, these educators are seeking broader definitions—definitions that promote breakthrough visions and that lead us away from borders that oppress growth. For example, Linda Lantieri says, "Spiritual experience can be described as the conscious recognition of a connection that goes beyond our own minds or emotions," and spiritual approaches are "the kinds of approaches that encourage a commitment to matters of the heart and spirit that are among the positive building blocks of healthy development" (Lantieri 2001b, 16). Parker Palmer tells us the spiritual voice is "the voice of soul, that sacred place in every human being where suffering is transformed into creativity and from which generosity can flow" (Palmer et al. 2001, 132). John P. Miller writes in *The Holistic Curriculum* that spirituality is the "sense of awe and reverence for life that arises from our relatedness to something both wonderful and mysterious" (Miller 1996, 2). This is similar to Ron Miller's statement that spirituality is "some even larger dimension of cosmic purpose, which many people term as the 'spiritual' dimension" (R. Miller 2000, 11). I believe a spiritual pedagogy is founded upon and develops our wonder and awe of the infinite energy of the cosmos—an energy tapped by us when we blend our inner and outer ways of knowing in creative acts that result in wonder-filled manifestations. When such manifestations inspire awe in ourselves and in others, borders to the spiritual side of learning have been crossed. Public dialogue becomes wide open, more inclusive, more welcoming of difference. Crossing this border serves to strengthen and protect democratic choice in our schools because we ask learners, as creative decision makers, to internalize a value for hope and possibility in the future.

National and international professional groups have also entered the scene, offering alternatives to mainstream education. For example, the Royal Society of the Arts (RSA) is a British organization that offers a broad approach to cultural change, and the Alternative Education

Resource Organization (AERO) supports educators seeking to develop learner-centered and democratic schools and approaches to learning. In addition, creativity dominates the curriculum in Waldorf schools, Montessori schools, Sudbury schools, and Albany Free schools, and students are encouraged to take responsibility for their own learning through decision making reserved for adult administrators in mainstream public schools. Sudbury students choose content they want to learn and are expected to form contracts with those capable of helping them learn it. In matters of school governance, their vote is equal to an adult vote. They are trusted to make informed decisions and live with the consequences of those decisions.

Other organizations also emphasize democratic approaches to learning. In 1993, the first International Democratic Education Conference (IDEC) was held in Israel. This annual conference is organized by members of the International Democratic Education Network (IDEN) and is dedicated to promoting the Democratic Education Movement around the world. Each conference is hosted by a different country and organized by various schools or other organizations such as AERO; in some cases the conference has been completely organized by students. Obviously, democratic education has enough power to equalize people and evaporate borders.

Within the National Council of Teachers of English (NCTE), which generally supports mainstream approaches to education, educators wishing to move beyond the mainstream founded the Assembly on the Expanded Perspectives of Learning (AEPL) in 1992 to promote pedagogies and theories that would add to cognitive domains of learning. Their annual conference and journal include secular understandings of spiritual approaches to learning among their topics of interest. Through personal development with AEPL charter members, Regina Paxton Foehr and I contributed to the beginnings of spiritual approaches in composition and rhetoric, releasing an edited collection titled *The Spiritual Side of Writing: Releasing the Learner's Whole Potential* (Foehr and Schiller 1997). We aimed to fill a gap in mainstream education and propel a serious affirmation of the topic. Richard Fulkerson, who reviewed it for *College Composition and Communication*, said it was part of a "mini-groundswell" (Fulkerson 1998, 101) even as he staunchly held to a traditional viewpoint.

In Mexico, the World Holistic Education Forum is sponsored by the International Foundation for Holistic Education founded in 1992 by Dr. Ramon Gallegos. The Foundation is a private organization, partially funded by the Mexican government, and offers doctorate and master's level degrees in holistic education and in meditation practices. The curriculum is offered in a hybrid format that requires face-to-face and online courses. While Dr. Gallegos has written many books, a principle book translated into English is *Holistic Education, Pedagogy of Universal Love*. Dr. Gallegos (2001) sees Holistic Education as a "social movement" rather than as an educational one and seeks to spread the holistic vision across the world. People from twenty-five countries, especially from Latin America, have attended the foundation's annual forum, as have people from America, Asia, Oceania, Europe, and Canada. In past years, invited keynote speakers included Jack Miller, Ron Miller, Jeffrey Kane, Sam Crowell, and Dale T. Snauwaert. For the December 2013 forum, Dr. Gallegos invited Mary Beattie from the University of Toronto, Bob London from CSU-San Bernardino, and myself. We each gave a ninety-minute keynote and served on a panel titled "Happiness and Holistic Education," and Bob and I facilitated interactive workshops with students. When Ramon Gallegos invited me with a request to feature spirituality in education, my thoughts turned immediately to a new chapter on the subject I had just finished for the second edition of my book *Sustaining the Writing Spirit: Holistic Tools for School and Home* (Schiller 2014). Thanks to Dr. Gallegos's generosity and recognition of my work, I crossed new borders (for me) to contribute to the advancement of spirituality in education.

Since 1997, in Canada, Dr. John (Jack) P. Miller, faculty of the Ontario Institute for Studies in Education (OISE) at the University of Toronto, and colleagues have facilitated an international conference titled Holistic Learning: Breaking New Ground. Dr. Miller also linked this group to ASCD (formerly the Association for Supervision and Curricular Development), an organization that serves 150,000 educators in more than 145 countries and aims at democratic education around the globe. By creating an ASCD Professional Interest Community (PIC) for Holistic Learning and Spirituality in Education, Dr. Miller found an international site where holistic education could receive wider recognition. For the same reason, he also initiated the PIC's newsletter titled the *Holistic Educator* (Babiuk and Schiller 2012). In 2011, when Dr. Miller asked me to take his place as team member with Dr. Gary Babiuk (from the University of Manitoba) to coedit the newsletter, I agreed, seeing this as a way to give back to a group that continues to influence and support my work. Crossing the US-Canadian border for professional development at the Breaking New Ground conference over the past twelve years has been important to my career and eventually led me to writing a second book.

For the PIC's newsletter, Dr. Babiuk and I do not focus on the whole-child revolution; we take a broader view as we encourage others to cross borders, to embrace a pedagogical practice that values the inner life of learners, and to share success stories that further motivate our readership. For example, in the spring 2012 issue, we included information from Dr. Miller about his experiences with helping the government of Bhutan develop holistic education as part of its educational policy. In April 2012, Dr. Miller was invited to attend a one-day meeting of the United Nations to support a statement written and presented by Bhutan titled "Realizing a World of Sustainable Wellbeing and Happiness." It includes the statement that education should promote "holistic life-long learning, including vital literacies required for wellbeing, such as ecological, civic, cultural, health, nutrition, science, financial, and other literacies" (J. Miller 2012, 7). Six hundred people from around the globe in attendance heard Bhutan ask the United Naions to consider adopting it in whole or in part.[1] Of course, the United Nations was founded for the purpose of crossing borders and uniting people, but a proposal about policies grounded in holistic education must be considered as supportive evidence for spiritual approaches to learning because the student's spirit is at the core of holistic education. Clearly, as we can see by this example, innovative educators all around the world are turning to holism as a means to evoke and recover the spiritual center in learners. Lantieri reports in her essay "A Vision of Schools with Spirit" that when 272 global thinkers from around the world were surveyed, "five shared values emerged: compassion, honesty, fairness, responsibility, and respect" (Lantieri 2001b, 11). These values are at the heart of a spiritual approach to learning, and teachers who advocate for it understand that a true democracy provides room for a range of approaches. For our part, we specifically want to create a forum for approaches that value and support spirituality in education. Within this forum, spirituality is grounded in awe, wonder, transcendence, joy in learning, and breakthrough vision from educators and students. In addition, the work Dr. Babiuk and I engage in to produce the biannual newsletter dovetails nicely with ASCD's whole-child revolution.

What ASCD refers to as a *revolution* (their term) is built upon five interconnected tenets for educational settings: healthy, (and) safe, (and) engaged, (and) supported, (and) challenged. ASCD rhetoric does not specifically draw out spirituality in learning, but the inner life of the learner is embedded in each tenet. Health includes mental and emotional health in which the inner life is active. A child's sense of safety is again connected to emotional reactions to the environment in which learning occurs. Children cannot be engaged if they are upset or afraid. When they are supported by the learning environment and by the adults responsible for that environment, their willingness to be challenged by new experiences may be fearlessly encountered. When unencumbered, wonder, awe, and creativity can emerge. When this happens, learning transcends the status quo and becomes a spiritual experience. Learning, not schooling, is the ASCD focus, and although ASCD does not directly state that it is enlivening the spiritual center of the learner, it is doing just that.

ASCD is effectively, albeit slowly, changing ways we educate young people. Whole-child schools now integrate the ASCD tenets across all grade levels. At the same time, when I think of my own growth in finding a breakthrough vision, I have found dialogues from Canada and Mexico to be spiritual and profound, while I have found those at ASCD professional-development workshops to be politically cautious, not fully breaking free from the testing craze that threatens democratic and spiritual approaches to learning. Progress toward breakthroughs does occur slowly.

Yet because many educators are accepting that holistic education integrates all ways of learning available to us, international interest in holistic methods continues to grow. We know inherent social and spiritual characteristics create contexts in which the mind, emotion, and body are integrated. Within the rich context created by wholeness, one's spirit assumes a central and vital role because it is the source of our motivation for growth and learning. It is no surprise then that the holistic educator does not see the learner as an independent agent but rather as a part of the greater whole that includes the family, the community, the natural environment, and the universe (Rocha 2003, xi). Holistic educators use wholeness as a means through which to teach, and they create methods through which wholeness fosters our full awareness.

Our inner and outer lives are no longer considered, or treated, as isolated but are integrated so we come to a meaningful understanding of our spirits, our souls. In this context, spirit or soul can be understood as that energy that expresses our center, or as the core of our being. Some educators also consider spirit or soul to mean the inner life of the learner. While many (not all) mainstream educators relegate spiritual experiences to sites outside the classroom (due largely to a nonsecular connotation attached to the word *spiritual*), holistic educators agree that learners also need opportunities for spiritual experience inside the classroom. Creating learning experiences that evoke the *sacred*, defined by Parker Palmer as "that which is worthy of respect" (quoted in Lantieri 2001a, xiv), is a primary goal among holistic educators. Palmer's (1998) seminal book, *The Courage to Teach*, is probably the most widely read book that advocates a spiritual approach to teaching and learning; however, there are many more, such as *The Soul of Education* by Rachael Kessler (2000); *Education and the Soul: Toward a Spiritual Curriculum* and *Educating for Wisdom and Compassion: Creating Conditions for Timeless Learning*, both by John P. Miller (2000, 2006); Dawn Emelie Griggs's (2003) *Spirit of Learning*; Nel Noddings's (1992) *The Challenge to Care in Schools: An Alternative Approach to Education*; *Schools Where Children Matter: Exploring Educational Alternatives* by Doralice Lange DeSouza Rocha (2003); *Teacher*, by Sylvia Ashton-Warner (1963); and *The Spiritual Side of Writing: Releasing the Learner's Whole Potential*, which I edited with Regina Paxton Foehr (Foehr and Schiller 1997). Holistic educators believe that the spiritual, the sacred, is not isolated to religion but indeed infuses all daily life, particularly the soul of the learner. It only needs awakening. The educators above understand this need, and each suggests awakening the inner life of the student in a variety of ways. One path we all seem to embrace advocates creativity and transcendence of limitations.

As I present in the text *Sustaining the Writing Spirit* (Schiller 2014), within the teaching of composition, the first border to move beyond is a cultural value for logic and analysis as the *preferred* ways of knowing. This value is reinforced by the academy in a variety of ways, and it almost always subordinates creativity to a lesser position. This subordination is most visible in writing programs where composition and creative writing are separated; composition is situated as a service course, a requirement generally perceived as a skill one must learn to succeed in multiple professions promising financial bounty, while creative writing is situated as an "elective" that rarely prepares one for financial rewards that can sustain a lifetime career of creativity. As a result, most students of writing never study creative writing, and creativity as a mode of thinking and/or being does not make it into master course syllabi. Instead, students learn to rely on analysis and argumentation, and the rhetorical border between creativity and analysis remains heavily guarded.

Analysis and argumentation, from the commonly held perspective, are rhetorical acts wherein the parts are separated from the whole for closer scrutiny of their solitary function within the whole rather than for their interconnections with other parts. In analysis, the sum of the parts equals the total of the whole. This view (and practice) of analysis contains a reductionist quality that weakens the act of knowing. This quality is too restrictive and causes writing to become an arduous time-intensive task that allows little room for original thought or creativity, especially when such analysis becomes the primary element or preferred model for knowing. It is not holistic because it features disconnections rather than interconnections. However, analysis and argumentation from within a holistic perspective see the sum of the parts as greater than the total of the whole. In fact, the whole cannot be completely understood solely by investigating the parts; we must also review and understand the connections within the parts, the connections within the whole, and the connections to the exterior elements surrounding the whole. The connections and inclusion of the exterior elements enrich the phenomenon and enliven knowledge making. Therefore, the potential for a spiritual experience when approaching writing in this way is more likely.

Even within mainstream education, creative-writing programs, differing from composition programs, move beyond the logical and linguistic ways of knowing to include and connect with creative processes of the writers. As students discover their own creative processes, they learn that the act of creativity *refreshes their souls and then ignites cognition*; objective data simply functions to support and supplement the creative impulse. They learn to value creativity as highly as, or even more highly than, logical and linguistic ways of knowing. As a result, this approach inculcates in students a reliance and a dependence *on their ability to be creative*, and their creative process becomes *a routine natural way of learning*. This is a holistic way of learning that balances multiple intelligences; it includes a broader field of rhetorical and social choices; it connects writers to their own creative processes; and, it leads students to surpass—to transcend—borders of restriction.

CROSSING COMMON BORDERS IN EDUCATIONAL SETTINGS

Unfortunately, within mainstream education today, information, analysis, and persuasion, the essential modes in research, are still valued more than creativity despite the work in multiple ways of knowing documented by Howard Gardner. Although Gardner's seven types of intelligence—"linguistic, logical mathematical, spatial, musical, kinesthetic, interpersonal, and intrapersonal" (quoted in J. Miller 1996, 20)—have received general acceptance, they have not gone uncontested. However, Gardner's work has opened doors for later scholars who have theorized about emotional intelligence and spiritual intelligence. Even so, mainstream education still relies primarily on linguistic and logical mathematical ways of knowing (Noddings 1992, 31). This reliance seems to be most unwise considering what we know about creativity. We must move closer to a holistic form of education—one that equally values analysis and creativity and one that uses creativity as a primary learning strategy made available to large numbers of students, particularly students of writing.

Modifications to existing writing programs that would transform the logic and linguistic foundation into one that is more holistic are not necessarily difficult to make if we focus on the use of creativity as the primary learning strategy. We do not need to cut or replace composition courses with creative writing courses; we must *redesign* composition courses so that creativity can *dominate* the curriculum in a way that also invites objective data to function in a *supportive* role. First, a working definition of creativity should inform and frame the new design, and second, the creative process(s) should be identified so writers have a clear behavioral model to inform their decisions.

Activity in the field of creativity studies (what it is and how it works) has increased over the last seventy years and is usually dominated by psychological approaches. Social, psychological, emotional, cultural, and biological factors are most often featured. Studies tend to fall into two categories: idiographic research that relies on individual case studies and nomothetic research that seeks discovery of general or universal laws that can be applied to all (Gardner 1994, 143).[2] Howard Gardner attempts to construct a bridge that spans idiographic and nomothetic research and presents a more holistic perspective, although he fails to account for the spiritual side of knowing. In our view, he should have taken one step further, risking even more than he has. Instead, he stresses cognitive and developmental psychological frames that take into account social and motivational aspects of creativity. These frames bind him in a culture that tends to connect religion to the word *spiritual*, so it is not at all surprising that he omits ideas about spiritual intelligence. However, his approach is "inherently interdisciplinary" (Gardner 1994, 145), and this is a feature that leans into holism. About his definition and approach, Gardner says,

1. I focus equally on problem solving, problem finding, and the creation of products, such as scientific theories, works of art, or the building of institutions.

2. I emphasize that all creative work occurs in one or more domains.[3] Individuals are not creative (or noncreative) in general; they are creative in particular domains of accomplishment and require the achievement of expertise in these domains before they can execute significant creative work.

3. No person, act, or product is creative or noncreative in itself. Judgments of creativity are inherently communal, relying heavily on individuals expert within a domain. (Gardner 1994, 145)

To accept Gardner's view requires a broadening of perspective that lets us see that "creativity emerges by virtue of a dialectical process among *individuals* of talent, *domains* of knowledge and practices, and *fields* of knowledgeable judges" (Gardner 1994, 145–46). His work further relies on two general positions: one, that people can develop all seven intelligences he has already identified, and two, that creative people "are characterized particularly by a tension, or lack of fit, between the elements involved in a productive work" (146). He labels this tension "fruitful asynchrony" and says that it is "the conquering of these asynchronies that leads to the establishment of work that comes to be cherished" (146).[4] In other words, fruitful asynchrony provides the initiating impulse for creativity.

What does this mean for people who seek to produce a piece of writing? According to Gardner, we move through three phases of creativity. First, writing can be identified as problem solving and/or the creation of a product (the written document). The beginning step is to decide which task descriptor applies or whether both apply. For example, when I ask my students to create a screenplay from a scene in a novel, they see this assignment as a problem to be solved. They must understand the literary content first and then decide which scene would transfer well to film. Second, the domain, or set of practices one needs, should be identified. Since this is the first experience my students have had with writing a film adaptation, I set the domain in the assignment guidelines, and we explore practices published experts have demonstrated. At this point, the students determine whether or not their expertise is sufficient or whether it needs development before the screenplay can be manifested. Their actions may be self-motivated or externally motivated by me, whom they consider as an expert in the domain. Self-development may involve additional reading, collaborative exploration, or consultation with me. In most cases, actions that manifest the creative work increase their level of expertise.

Third, since judgments of creativity are inherently communal, writers need connections with experts within the domain who can articulate previously set standards for determining the emergence of creativity. Teachers recognized as experts in the domain articulate the academic standards; clarify the assignment requirements such as genre, length, style; and reinforce students' actions as the creative process progresses. While standards may serve to direct the creative action, they may inhibit creativity if a student cannot imagine meeting or surpassing them. For other students, the standards may appear too limited and too easy to meet or surpass. In this case, the standards might initiate a new level of achievement, but if the achievement is too extreme for the community of judges, a different type of tension can arise (Gardner 1994, 147). Students who fear this risk ask the teacher, "What do you want in this assignment?" But the student who is excited by this risk often crosses borders set by assignment guidelines and creates amazing responses. These students have an internal set of standards that are fluid and malleable when finding and creating solutions to problems. The cliché often applied to such people is that they are ahead of their time. Yet, many of our greatest thinkers and creators have been labeled as such and have depended on their own standards; they became their own judges and worked to please their own innate need to create something new.

It is easy to see that fruitful asynchrony can begin in all three categories and that no people, acts, or products are creative or noncreative in themselves. Since external and internal elements in the creative act are interconnected, holism is strong. Moreover, the creative act in all of the three categories requires writers to *imagine* they can accomplish something new. At the root of *imagine* is *image*. According to the research completed on imagery and creativity by George Ainsworth-Land (J. Miller 1996), the relationship between creativity and imagery is developmental. People can identify and use a creative process, this researcher claims, outlining the process in four steps.

The first step is sense related and arises out of physical need. This trait can be seen in the students above who find it difficult to believe they can write original screenplays, but the physical need to produce one is compelling. The second involves improvement of an idea or artistic product through analysis and evaluation. When my students reread a text for the purpose of creative adaptation, they read with a different purpose and begin to evaluate the text from within borders set by the genre they are to produce. The third requires synthesis, not just revision or modification. Something new or novel must be discovered through the synthesis before there is a breakthrough to new knowledge or understanding. Synthesis of text occurs when students resee it for their own creative goals, which leads to a new way of seeing and understanding. As they write the screenplay, new knowledge presents itself within their creative product. The final step, Ainsworth-Land states, occurs when "one's whole being comes into play with the conscious and unconscious minds, reason and intuition, inner and outer, subsumed into a kind of meta-consciousness." At this point, "The self is part of a larger reality. [Here, one is] building new perceptual order" (quoted in J. Miller 1996, 94).

When the students complete their screenplays, they have built a new perceptual order about literature, about writing, and about their own ability to be creative. Ainsworth-Land's process casts creativity as a self-motivated action that connects the individual inner life of the creator with the exterior social and environmental exigencies described so thoroughly by Gardner. Both Gardner and Ainsworth-Land provide models that can help us understand and implement creativity as the primary and dominant strategy for writing, regardless of any specific rhetorical genre we seek to produce.

The process described by Ainsworth-Land *naturally* activates learning, and with creativity as the dominant strategy, students awaken to the innate and universal human desire for learning. When students complete creative projects, they naturally combine analytic thinking, critical thinking, research, creativity, and reflection. They must imagine their projects completed and then attempt to reach the images they have mentally created. As they reach toward completion, they participate physically and socially when choosing collaboration with peers and then again during the presentations of their completed projects. Their intellect and spirit are awakened by work they choose, create, and design, and their intellectual abilities are stretched with the challenge of synthesizing material into a creative artifact they judge to be aesthetically pleasing. A transcendent unity occurs when, through the creative impulse, these parts of the learner are integrated and harmonized within their expressive projects. The students writing screenplays experience this harmony when their processes of creativity produce the solution (the screenplay) to the problem (the assignment to adapt a literary scene) and when they, and I, judge their projects as complete and beautiful. Every time we create something new, this process emerges and enlivens our spirits; we are engaged in spiritual learning, for our inner selves and the outer community in which we exist are united by awe and wonder at creativity.

Through creativity, students further develop a holistic worldview—one that provides "an ability to see connections between diverse things and see the bigger picture" (Zohar and Marshall quoted in Lantieri 2001b, 17). Sir Ken Robinson calls this ability "divergent thinking" (Robinson 2010, n.p.). He defines creativity as "the process of having original ideas that have value." Divergent thinking is the capacity to see lots of possible answers to a question rather than just one right answer, and Robinson says it is an "essential capacity" for creativity.[5] I believe creativity is also a pathway that provides opportunities for students to develop spiritual intelligence,[6] which Danah Zohar and Ian Marshall define as "intelligence with which we address and solve problems of meaning and value, the intelligence with which we can place our actions and our lives in a wider, richer meaning-giving context. It is the intelligence with which we can assess that one course of action or one life path is more meaningful than another" (quoted in Lantieri 2001b, 18). Zohar and Marshall "call spiritual intelligence the ultimate intelligence because it is the necessary foundation for the effective functioning of the other intelligences and because it has a transformative power" (quoted in Lantieri 2001b, 18).

Creativity, as a dominant learning strategy, fosters an environment in which the "basic [human] need to create" (Gifford 1956, 32) *can thrive*. It also facilitates a spiritual approach to learning because it entices holism and *invites transcendence*. Students rise into the realm of imagination and possibility. They imagine originality. This transcendence happens every time I assign creativity as part of the assignment as demonstrated above with students writing screenplays. While facilitating processes of creativity, learners naturally connect their inner beings, their souls, to their exterior world. Their processes take them across borders by uniting their whole beings into the learning experience. Creativity asks that they find meaning and purpose in what they do and imagine powerful results that will transform their current condition. Through creativity, they can transcend the contextual limitations of specific rhetorical activities and experience the spiritual in secular ways that promote learning and self-development. Sir Ken Robinson recognizes they will wake "up to what they have inside themselves" (Robinson 2010, n.p.). These are the reasons creativity should be a valued partner with logic and analysis and the reasons it works so well to traverse the borders that work to keep spiritual ways of knowing out of the classroom.[7] It seems imperative to me, then, that we incorporate creativity more frequently in the teaching of composition. We need holistic assignments to awaken students *or* we need to redirect students' perceptions of writing so they see it as a creative act regardless of the genre they produce. The massive cultural shift a change in perception requires seems daunting to me as a first step. I think it more feasible to start with holistic assignments that eventually *will lead to perceptual shifts*. Holistic assignments can activate the process of creativity, and the students who internalize creativity benefit for life.

SPIRITUAL PEDAGOGY ACTIVATED

Classroom practice based on these ideas asks for careful planning. In most of the classes I teach, the first activity is always a self-reflective ice breaker. It relies first on words, then metaphor, then abstract images to represent students' immediate conditions (physical, emotional, intellectual, spiritual). Students are asked to write tenets from holistic education—spiritual, emotional, physical, aesthetic, intellectual—on one side of a notecard. Then, in order to tap intuition, they quickly write next to each word the first adjective that occurs in their minds. On the card's reverse side, they draw abstract designs that represent every word they wrote. Discussion that follows features the inner self and ways it is linked to our exterior experiences. This little ice breaker leads to more challenging interconnected activities as the semester moves forward.

While I rely more heavily on visual arts, sometimes we use sound and movement to express energy used in what we just wrote. It is essential to combine student experience, course content, and any cultural roles the content may contain in the activities. By the end of a sixteen-week semester, students manifest a creative synthesis of the content through projects and demonstrations of their work. From literature classes, I have seen beautiful quilts, intricate scrapbooks, cooking demonstrations, model houses, tool demonstrations, tree grafting, original songs sung and recorded on CDs, graphic novels, newspaper and magazine design, period clothing design, oil and water paintings, sculpture, plans for starting a holistic school, and many more creative projects.[8] From writing courses, essays and portfolios have provided a range of nonfiction examples that were joyful to produce and had personal significance for the writer. Essays of place, personal memoir, literary reportage, and social justice exposés are popular choices. When students orally present their work to the class, transcendence and awe, the spiritual side of their learning, are easy to observe, *and* it is just as easy to observe which students did not experience transcendence or awe. These projects are further supported by a written analysis that explains the connections students have made between their creative processes and the course content. The written analysis values logical thinking, and as such it provides a comfort zone for the student who struggles with new ways of learning.

In every class, there are resistant students who seem to be unable or unwilling to imagine anything original. These students prefer the standard approach. I believe they have been conditioned to perform by giving the teachers what they want in order to get good grades. This approach teaches them to assume little or no responsibility for their own learning and to distrust their inner selves. A teacher's assessment gains more control while their inner selves lose power. Without any doubt, a holistic approach attempts to reverse this learned value, and students must self-motivate, self-discover, and cross new borders. When standard borders (logical and linguistic learning) are replaced with finding and creating transcendence and awe, some students fear the outcomes, for in their earlier experience, creativity and risk taking too often led to bad grades or negative criticism. However, their gate of resistance can be opened when positive rewards for risk taking are integrated with course activities. After a time, most students begin to feel safe. At that safety point, they often experience an epiphany that further propels them into creativity. It is as if they are suddenly set free to learn in ways that speak to their spirits. They begin to value what they have inside them as something precious and beautiful. I love watching fearful, resistant students cross this border when they get to it. These are true moments of transcendence and awe, true moments of spirituality in action—in the classroom—for the students—for me.

My interest in spiritual approaches to learning began in the early 1990s and continues today in various scholarly goals that include crossing borders and filling gaps within the academy. In the early years, I adamantly proclaimed that the word *spiritual* had to be used because I believed its repeated use would weaken the rhetorical and cultural borders contained in connotative values attached to the word. I wanted to weaken this border to a point that allowed educators to engage in a spiritual pedagogy without fear of reprisals from other teachers, administrators, students, parents. Now, some twenty-plus years later, my position has both softened and solidified. On one hand, I am more comfortable with not using the word *spiritual*; on the other hand, I am even more ardent about crossing the border. Indeed, I work to destroy the border. Eradicate it. Make it history. Is this goal reasonable? Yes. Is it possible? I still hope so. However, I admit I occasionally lapse into teaching practices that primarily value logical thinking. Mainstream habits I began my career with kick in as do the institutional pressures to follow the master course syllabus (MCS). When I do lapse, I choose to transcend the limits of the MCS even as I seek to preserve its objectives. I choose a spiritual approach to teaching with creativity and transcendence at its heart. These choices bring me back to crossing borders, and it is an ongoing source of growth for me.

I have been crossing borders of one kind or another all my life, and I expect to cross a few more in the future. The rhetorical borders attached to a spiritual approach to learning have presented varying challenges that I tenaciously tended, always aiming at the students' growth. The personal and professional growth I have enjoyed continue to inspire my efforts as well. This I will not deny, for it is gratifying to know I have contributed to the emergence of a growing acceptance of these ideas. Yet, broader acceptance is still needed, for the current dichotomy between mainstream and holistic methods pits one against the other by establishing separation, disconnection, and unnecessary rhetorical borders.

Fortunately, these borders can be traversed—the dichotomous conditions dissolved—when we embrace spirit as a natural human condition, and when we initiate spiritual approaches to learning that are *infused* with, and *evoke*, creativity, transcendence, and awe.

Notes

1. More details about the meeting and the complete statement can be accessed at https://Sustainabledevelopment.un.org.
2. For a fuller view of creativity studies than this space allows, see Margaret Boden 1994.
3. "A domain is a set of practices associated with an area of knowledge; the field consists of the individuals and institutions that render judgments about work in a domain" (Gardner 1994, 152).
4. In this study, Gardner goes on to use even well-known creators: Sigmund Freud, Albert Einstein, Pablo Picasso, Igor Stravinsky, T. S. Eliot, Martha Graham, and Mahatma Gandhi—each exemplifying at least one of the seven intelligences Gardner identifies.
5. See the Youtube video "RCA Animate" for Robinson's (2012) fuller discussion of divergent thinking and why creativity is part of a paradigm shift in education reform.
6. Gardner's intelligences, developed within cognitive psychology, do not include spiritual intelligence. Within the field of holistic education, however, spiritual intelligence is essential. Without the spiritual core, there is no holism.
7. The argument I make here on creativity is from *Sustaining the Writing Spirit: Holistic Tools for School and Home* by Susan A. Schiller (2007, 13–20).
8. See the *Willa Cather Newsletter & Review* (2005) for an example of what is possible. I presented student projects at the Willa Cather Summer Symposium in Red Cloud in 2005 to demonstrate ways creativity promotes a holistic approach to learning. A quilt made by student Carrie Jones is featured in the newsletter, and particular panels from the quilt are distributed throughout to illustrate contributors' works. Carrie's quilt now hangs in my campus office. Other students have gifted me with scrapbooks, smaller quilts, oil or water paintings, CDs, and photographs.

References

Ashton-Warner, Sylvia. 1963. *Teacher*. New York: Simon and Schuster.
Babiuk, Gary, and Susan A. Schiller, eds. 2012. *The Holistic Educator* 22 (1).
Boden, Margaret A., ed. 1994. *Dimensions of Creativity*. Cambridge, MA: MIT Press.
Foehr, Regina P., and Susan A. Schiller, eds. 1997. *The Spiritual Side of Writing: Releasing the Learner's Whole Potential.* Portsmouth, NH: Boynton/Cook.
Fulkerson, Richard. 1998. "Call Me Horatio: Negotiating Between Cognition and Affect in Composition." *College Composition and Communication* 50 (1): 101–15. http://dx.doi.org/10.2307/358358.
Gallegos, Ramon. 2001. *Holistic Education: Pedagogy of Universal Love*. Brandon, VT: Psychology Press/Holistic Education Press.
Gardner, Howard. 1994. "The Creators' Patterns." In *Dimensions of Creativity*, edited by Margaret A. Boden, 143–58. Cambridge, MA: MIT Press.
Gifford, Donald C. 1956. "The Creative Process in the Classroom." In *Conference on Creativity as a Process*, 32–38. New York: Arden House.

Graves, Richard. 1997. "Grace in Pedagogy." In *The Spiritual Side of Writing: Releasing the Learner's Whole Potential*, edited by Regina P. Foehr and Susan A. Schiller, 15–24. Portsmouth, NH: Boynton/Cook.

Griggs, Dawn Emelie. 2003. *Spirit of Learning*. Blairgowrie, Australia: Jubilation.

Kessler, Rachael. 2000. *The Soul of Education: Helping Students Find Connection, Compassion, and Character at School*. Alexandria, VA: Association for Supervision and Curriculum Development.

Lantieri, Linda, ed. 2001a. *Schools with Spirit: Nurturing the Inner Lives of Children and Teachers*. Boston, MA: Beacon.

Lantieri, Linda. 2001b. "A Vision of Schools with Spirit." In *Schools with Spirit: Nurturing the Inner Lives of Children and Teachers*, edited by Linda Lantieri, 7–20. Boston, MA: Beacon.

Miller, John P. 1996. *The Holistic Curriculum*. Toronto: Ontario Institute for Studies in Education.

Miller, John P. 2000. *Education and the Soul*. Albany: SUNY Press.

Miller, John P. 2006. *Educating for Wisdom and Compassion*. Thousand Oaks, CA: Corwin.

Miller, John P. 2012. "Happiness and Well-Being: A New Economic Paradigm—Up-Date." *The Holistic Educator* 22 (1): 7.

Miller, Ron. 2000. *Creating Learning Communities: Models, Resources, and New Ways of Thinking about Teaching and Learning*. Brandon, VT: Foundation for Educational Renewal.

Moffett, James. 1994. *The Universal Schoolhouse*. San Francisco: Jossey-Bass.

Noddings, Nel. 1992. *The Challenge to Care in Schools: An Alternative Approach to Education*. New York: Teachers College.

O'Reilley, Mary R. 1998. *Radical Presence: Teaching as Contemplative Practice*. Portsmouth, NH: Boynton/Cook.

Palmer, Parker. 1998. *The Courage to Teach*. San Francisco: Jossey-Bass.

Palmer, Parker, March Jackson, Rick Jackson, and David Slyter. 2001. "The Courage to Teach: A Program for Teacher Renewal." In *Schools with Spirit: Nurturing the Inner Lives of Children and Teachers*, edited by Linda Lantieri, 132–47. Boston, MA: Beacon.

Robinson, Sir Ken. 2010. "Changing Paradigms." *YouTube*. Accessed July 31, 2013. www.youtube.com/watch?v=zMCbdS4hSaOs.

Robinson, Sir Ken. February 15, 2012. "RCA Animate," *YouTube*. Accessed July 31, 2013. http://www.youtube.com/watch?v=zMCbdS4hSaOs.

Rocha, Doralice Lange DeSouza. 2003. *Schools Where Children Matter: Exploring Educational Alternatives*. Brandon, VT: Foundation for Educational Renewal.

Schiller, Susan A. 2007. *Sustaining the Writing Spirit: Holistic Tools for School and Home*. 1st ed. Lanham, MD: Rowman and Littlefield Education.

Schiller, Susan A. 2014. *Sustaining the Writing Spirit: Holistic Tools for School and Home*. 2nd ed. Lanham, MD: Rowman and Littlefield Education.

Willa Cather Newsletter & Review. 2005. 49 (2).

8
DIFFERENCE AS RHETORICAL STANCE
Developing Meaningful Interactions and Identification across Racial and Ethnic Lines

Mónica Torres and Kathryn Valentine

A growing number of scholars in the last two decades have argued that verbal interactions across racial and ethnic lines are valuable for college students. Essentially, their research, as discussed below, demonstrates that cross-racial interactions productively position students to develop both intellectually and socially. It is important to note, however, that cross-racial interactions on college and university campuses—whether they occur as a natural consequence of students occupying the same spaces or as a result of faculty/staff interventions—are not isolated events. They occur within a broader context: the United States, with an increasingly diverse demographic profile, with a complicated and painful racial history, and with complex—and often divisive—discursive practices on issues of race. It is both the tremendous potential and the complex context of cross-racial interactions that make our attention to this issue such an important one.

Recent conversations with two colleagues illustrate, for us, the range, the texture, and the complexity of diversity issues as they occur on our campuses and in our classrooms. In these conversations, two powerful, if exceptionally dissimilar, responses to cultural differences reveal the discomfort that may emerge or develop when we ask or expect students to engage diversity in our learning environments. One instance exposes the threat of violence that may undergird a particular kind of engagement with differences; the second instance makes clear a reluctance to acknowledge differences even when they are more than evident. Our discussion of these incidents follows.

At the end of the spring semester in 2013, a young college student who works with a colleague of ours reported an incident to his professor. For his final project in an art class, he had painted a large image—a stylized image of a man carrying what appears to be an automatic rifle—on the external wall of a campus building. Below the image was an inscription, "Corrupción." Situated on a campus along the US-Mexico border, this image offers rich possibilities for discussion: about violence that disrupts community life, about corruption within law enforcement, and about militarization on the US-Mexico border. The complexity of the image, however, is reduced by what happened next. Within twenty-four hours of the image's completion, another person, very likely a student, scrawled an inscription at the bottom of the painting: "English motherfucker Do you speak it?!" From our perspective, this represents a particular kind of response to cultural difference: direct acknowledgment of and aggressive confrontation with.

While this first instance suggests the potential for violent confrontation, a second reflects a different problem: that of nonconfrontation. Graduate students enrolled in a composition studies course taught by another colleague in the summer of 2012 were asked to produce and then introduce their literacy narratives. The first student to talk provided a compelling story, much of which was related to her distinctly bilingual and bicultural circumstances, including a story of how she missed a great deal of elementary school as a result of her family's migratory movement. Interestingly, when prompted to highlight differences and similarities with previous narratives, the students whose narratives followed in the discussion, despite radically different cultural experiences, confirmed only that their own narratives were similar to those described by the first student. When prompted, the students simply seemed unable or unwilling to highlight or focus on differences, and, when asked, one student reported he did not feel comfortable pointing out the differences between his literacy narrative and that of the bilingual student. Here, he equated different as a negative, and he chose not to explicitly acknowledge such difference.

We find these two examples striking. While the first instance reveals an impulse to focus only on difference, the second exposes a desire to attend only to similarity. Both, we believe, risk a sort of violence—physical and/or epistemological. In an increasingly diverse world, neither seems to be a productive approach. Furthermore, these examples push our agenda further. There is no doubt we are concerned with the intellectual and social development of our students. These examples make clear we cannot attend to that development outside the complex circumstances of contemporary society. And interactions about race/ethnicity and across racial/ethnic boundaries will certainly be among the most complex students will deal with.

If our goal as faculty members is to support student development, and clearly it is, cross-racial interactions may prove to be an intellectual and pedagogical landscape worthy of thoughtful exploration and teacher intervention. Almost as soon as we make that decision to intervene, questions form on the horizon: What sort of interactions prompt the sort of intellectual and social development scholars suggest can occur? What personal and social circumstances might lead to more (and less) successful interactions? How might we productively encourage and employ cross-racial interactions to help students most fully benefit from diversity on college campuses?

In this chapter, we seek to better understand what occurs when students attempt to interact across racial and ethnic differences, and we draw on rhetorical theory to do that. Specifically, we use key theoretical and methodological concepts developed by Kenneth Burke—dramatism generally, and identification more specifically—as well as more contemporary critique and development of these concepts by rhetorical scholars Krista Ratcliffe and Bryan Crable to construct a framework through which to consider the complications, the difficulties, and the potentials of cross-racial interactions. In addition, we use the work of Gloria Anzaldúa to productively extend the framework. And finally, we employ that expanded framework to "read" an exchange between three undergraduate students. We have two goals in mind in doing so: to encourage rhetoricians to further explore the ways in which rhetorical theory can be used to theorize race and to offer educators a framework that might assist them to productively intervene in pedagogical environments where cross-racial interactions occur.

A PROPOSED THEORETICAL FRAMEWORK FOR ANALYZING INTERACTION

To achieve the goals mentioned above, we demonstrate how perspectives from four theorists provide a useful framework for analyzing conversations about the borders of race and racism, especially when those conversations involve moments of agreement and moments of dissent. It is well known that Kenneth Burke, one of the foremost thinkers of the twentieth century, considered literature as "equipment for living." Following Burke's sociological approach, forms of literature "would be treated as *equipments for living*, that size up situations in various ways and in keeping with correspondingly various attitudes" (Burke 1967, 304). Others, including Barry Brummett (1993), argue that a cursory glance at Burke's theoretical and critical writings reveals that rhetoric can be seen in the same light. What tools, then, might rhetoric provide not only for living but also for negotiating the borders of different experiences of race and ethnicity?

Kenneth Burke's foundational concept of dramatism, simultaneously a philosophy of language and a technique of analysis, can be one such tool. Generally speaking, several fundamental principles undergird this notion: (1) language shapes how we perceive the world around us; (2) communication can be systematically studied as a form of action; and (3) specific elements of drama—act, scene, agent, agency, purpose (and, later, attitude)—can serve as tools of analysis. Essentially, Burke asserts that language can help us see, understand, and navigate the social and political world that surrounds us. And his works, both theoretical and critical, many argue, are the very analytic tools that help us do that.

More specifically, one of Burke's most critical concepts is identification. For Burke, identification cannot be understood apart from the idea of division: "Identification is affirmed with earnestness precisely because there is division. Identification is compensatory to division" (Burke 1969, 22). Essentially, Burke asserts that humans, given our embodiment and material conditions, are divided from each other. Identification is a rhetorical attempt to overcome that division. Burke writes, "You persuade a man only insofar as you can talk his language by speech, gesture, tonality, order, image, attitude, idea, *identifying* your ways with his" (Burke 1969, 55). Several things strike us about this claim. First, Burke makes identification a strategy of persuasion, fully situating it within rhetorical function. And second, identification is an inclusive activity: "[A speaker's] act of persuasion may be for the purpose of causing the audience to identify itself with the speaker's interests; and the speaker draws on identification of interests to establish rapport between himself and his audience" (Burke 1969, 46). What seems important to note here is the mutuality of the effort—interests of both rhetor and audience are considered. This sense of identification asserts, at the very least implies, that persuasion is about both understanding perspectives and building relationships based on these perspectives.

In more recent years, contemporary scholars dealing with cross-cultural issues have embraced, resisted, and extended Burke's foundational concepts. Bryan Crable asserts the value of Burke's "study of symbolicity" for a "strong, rhetorically-based theory of race and identity" but also argues that other views such as Ralph Ellison's "critical reading of race within the institutions, norms, literature, and hierarchies of American culture" (Crable 2003, 22) are essential for a theoretical project on race and racism. Krista Ratcliffe values Burke's concept of identification, but she also understands it can be a challenging prospect in cross-cultural environments. Ratcliffe writes, "But identifications, especially cross-cultural identifications, are sometimes difficult to achieve. Such identifications may be troubled by history, uneven power dynamics, and ignorance" (Ratcliffe 2005, 2). Both scholars assume Burke's value but also suggest his work must be combined with the work of others to effectively engage cross-racial, cross-cultural issues.

In using Burke's work as a tool to understand cross-racial conversations, it is useful to balance his view of difference as fundamental, and in that sense universal, with attention to how difference manifests itself culturally and historically. In this light, Crable suggests Burke's *Rhetoric of Motives* is significant even beyond its historical value for the field of rhetoric. He writes that Burke's "recasting of rhetoric in terms of identification continues to influence contemporary scholarship on the relationship between discourse, social formations, and individual identity" (Crable 2003, 5). Essentially, Burke's rhetoric can be useful when navigating identity and the cultural context in which identities are embedded. Crable more specifically explains that *A Rhetoric of Motives*, "as a work on inter-group conflict and symbolic identification, is well-suited to consideration of discourse surrounding racial difference and racist violence" (5).

Crable also argues, however, that such a view of Burke's rhetoric is not possible without refracting Burke's ideas through thinkers like Ralph Ellison. In fact, it is Burke's relationship with Ellison, Crable suggests, that helps us to understand how his work might be applied to race. Crable posits a fundamental agreement between Burke and Ellison: symbolicity, the potential of the symbol using/symbol misusing animal. Ellison writes, "It is through the symbolic capacities of language that we seek simultaneously to maintain and evade our commitments as social beings" (quoted in Crable 2003, 21). At the same time, Burke and Ellison had significant differences that shaped their approaches to race and racism. Crable goes on to elaborate a fundamental one between the two men: Burke's belief that a universal terminology, one that "moves beyond the binary conflict between the white and black races" (18), will move the "black race" toward freedom and Ellison's view that a terminology based on race, an approach aware of and sensitive to "the racist legal and social system which decisively shapes the attitude of those in an oppressed social group," would be needed to address the significant racial issues of the time (20). Essentially, Crable, working to develop a new direction for current scholarship that addresses questions of race and identity, draws on both Burke and Ellison for a new approach, "an approach to race grounded in Burke's study of symbolicity, but with a vocabulary . . . ever-alert to the manifestations and functions of race in American culture" (23).

Along with focusing on race historically and culturally in using Burke's approach as a tool for analysis, it is also important to focus on how differences might not always be productively bridged and, in contrast, might more usefully be listened to and sustained. In this light, Krista Ratcliffe also notes Burke's work as foundational in rhetoric and composition studies. Specifically, in *Rhetorical Listening: Identification, Gender, Whiteness*, she takes up his concept of identification. She writes that when rhetoric and composition scholarship invokes identification, it most commonly cites Kenneth Burke. She notes two characteristics of his take on this concept that she finds particularly important. First, she notes his emphasis on consubstantiality, essentially common ground that can be established between rhetor and audience. Second, she suggests that Burke's interpretation of this concept allows space for agency, even in a postmodern age. She quotes Frank Lentrichia to make the point: "The rhetorician is the not-always-knowing carrier of historical and ideological forces, while at the same time he acts within and upon the present and thereby becomes an agent of change" (quoted in Ratcliffe 2005, 58).

Having said that, however, Ratcliffe finds that a strict Burkean version of identification, given certain cultural contexts, is not enough to do the work she wants to do, which is to facilitate thoughtful, conscious, productive cross-cultural communication. In her second chapter, she describes Burke's notion of identification and then generally situates it vis-à-vis modernist and postmodernist frameworks. Then, employing the work of Diana Fuss, Ratcliffe describes two concepts—disidentification and nonidentification—that interrogate and further develop the concept of identification.

At the core of Ratcliffe's disagreement with Burke is the tension between commonalities and differences. She writes that although Burke's view emphasizes common identifications to bridge human differences, these commonalities often come at the expense of differences. She writes, "Burke's identification demands that differences be bridged. The danger of such a move is that differences and their possibilities, when bridged, may be displaced and mystified" (Ratcliffe 2005, 53). Ratcliffe goes on to explain that common ground may have a coercive function. She asks, for example, "Who defines and who decides what is *necessary* and *unnecessary*—or in other words, who defines the terms of commonality, and who decides which differences must be bridged and which differences must be deemed excess and relegated outside the consubstantial place of identification?" (59). Ratcliffe is interested in identification that acknowledges the coercive potential of commonalities and allows for the inventive potential of difference in ways Burke's work does not. For that, she turns to the work of Diana Fuss and her concepts of disidentification and nonidentification.

Ratcliffe writes, "Invoking Butler's theory . . . Fuss claims that *disidentification* signifies an identification that is not so much 'refused' as 'disavowed'; in other words, a disidentification is 'an identification that has already been made and denied in the unconscious'" (Ratcliffe 2005, 62). Disidentification, from Ratcliffe's perspective, may not be a positive direction to travel if our goals are productive cross-cultural interactions. She highlights the difficulty of disidentification in several important questions: "How accurate are mental images that drive our identifications and disidentifications? Who decides and defines what is accurate?" (62). From her perspective, disidentification may be problematically enabled by power differentials and the representations that emerge from those differentials. However, it is important to note that Ratcliffe also sees potential in disidentification—if used reflexively: "If such disidentifications can be brought to consciousness (and obviously not all of them can), then places for negotiating coexisting commonalities and differences may emerge" (63). Used reflexively, disidentification can serve a purpose: to create spaces that allow us to acknowledge both commonalities and differences.

Ratcliffe finds even more potential in Fuss's notion of nonidentification, which relies on the metonym. Ratcliffe argues that in contrast to the metaphor, which "foregrounds resemblances based on commonalities," the metonym "foregrounds resemblances based on juxtaposed associations, thus foregrounding both commonalities *and* differences" (Ratcliffe 2005, 68). This metonymic juxtaposition creates space between them. From Ratcliffe's perspective, this space, which Fuss calls nonidentification, is an inventive space, "a place wherein people may *consciously choose* to position themselves to listen rhetorically" (72). Ratcliffe further describes this space as "a place of pause, a place of reflection, a place that invites people to admit that gaps exist" (72–73). She goes on to specify what we might find in that place: an opportunity to recognize our cultural positions, a partiality of our visions, and our interdependencies. In this place, identification becomes a more conscious, more thoughtful process that will more fully serve us in cross-cultural, cross-racial interactions.

In conceptualizing border spaces, Gloria Anzaldúa also offers a way to rethink places of interaction as bordering both identification and nonidentification. This way of thinking is more than evident in her now iconic book *Borderlands/La Frontera: The New Mestiza*. It is clear in her work that she thinks cross-cultural/cross-racial relationships are important: "Many women and men of color do not want to have any dealings with white people. It takes too much time and energy to explain. . . . Many feel that whites should help their own people rid themselves of race hatred and fear first. I, for one, choose to use some of my energy to serve as mediator. I think we need to allow whites to be our allies" (Anzaldúa 1999, 107). Here, Anzaldúa not only articulates value for relationships between whites and people of color, she also exhorts both groups to engage in those relationships, to pursue those alliances. In this regard, she pushes individuals and groups to create and inhabit places of identification and nonidentification.

Moreover, we argue that Anzaldúa develops strategies for engaging this work. We can read her work as productively exploring the question at the center of our inquiry: how do we create identifications attuned to the "functions and manifestations of race" in the United States (as Crable calls for) that don't sacrifice racial differences (as Ratcliffe suggests)?

In her well-known chapter on "mestiza consciousness," Anzaldúa addresses and challenges both people of color and white people to see identification as a crossing of borders, a process that is likely never complete. This suggests that for Anzaldúa, identification never fully resolves differences or creates connections in the way it does for Burke. In the chapter, she outlines several rhetorical strategies that will be necessary in order to encourage successful, transformative interactions: engaging others, acknowledging our complicity in our complicated racial histories, and working (and working hard) to build relationships. From Anzaldúa's perspective, we must choose to engage. She acknowledges that cross-racial interactions are often embedded in confrontation and, more specifically, in confrontation that often goes on across a substantial divide. She suggests we not let the divide, whatever form it takes, stop us from engaging. She says, "It is not enough to stand on the opposite river bank" (Anzaldúa 1999, 100). And later, she declares, as noted above, "I, for one, choose to use my energy to serve as a mediator" (107). In this regard, Anzaldúa helps us to see the importance of Burke's concept of identification. She points to the need for those willing to acknowledge and mediate differences.

At the same time, the second rhetorical strategy she suggests more fully addresses Crable's call for attention to how experiences of difference are situated in particular cultural contexts. It is important from Anzaldúa's perspective that people take inventory of context, honestly acknowledge the role that they (and their ancestors) have played in racial conflict and hegemony. For example, at one point she asks white people for this acknowledgment: "We need you to own the fact that you looked upon us as less than human, that you stole our lands, our personhood, our self respect" (Anzaldúa 1999, 107–8). At the same time she asks people of color to consider how they may have colluded in systems of domination by using questions such as: How have white people colonized people of color? How have people of color colluded in these systems of domination? By extending racist, sexist, classist, homophobic insults to feel better about ourselves? By not acknowledging some of us have benefitted from historical acts of oppression? By not voicing our needs vis-à-vis white people? Anzaldúa asks all people to take stock of our historical and social circumstances, however painful, because she posits this as an important aspect of identification and nonidentification.

Finally, Anzaldúa suggests that to effectively build relationships, we must speak and listen. In one of the most interesting rhetorical moves of the chapter, she demonstrates this work by writing, "We need to voice our needs" (85), and then she voices her own. She writes eight sentences essentially calling out white people for injustices to Chicanos. And she asks white people to listen by addressing them directly: "We need you" (107–108). It's important to note, however, that she doesn't stop there. She closes the paragraph and the section with, "And finally, tell us what you need from us" (108). Here, Anzaldúa enacts the kind of inventive space Ratcliffe hopes for: she voices her needs, acknowledges differences without sacrificing them, and recognizes that those different from her also have needs they can voice.

It seems clear Anzaldúa is interested in one of the key divisions between humans: race. Our sense of her work is that she is very much traveling the landscape that Burke, as well as Crable and Ratcliffe in their extensions of Burke, works in. She asserts that we can use language to narrow the divisions between humans. She is interested in "racial manifestations and functions" in our lives. And while she assumes basic human commonalities, she asserts that we must acknowledge and share historical and cultural differences in our communications with each other. Most important, she offers and demonstrates specific rhetorical strategies to engage this work.

APPLYING THE FRAMEWORK TO STUDENT CONVERSATIONS ABOUT RACE

In what follows, we discuss a moment from a conversation with students that struck us as a place where rhetorical theory might offer useful perspectives on cross-racial interactions. We use this moment to explore how rhetorical theory helps us to make sense of border crossing in conversations. In particular, in order to begin to understand how rhetorical strategies can be used either to open up spaces for listening and self-reflection or to close down such spaces, we look at the rhetorical strategies students employ to communicate about negative experiences with people from different races or ethnicities.

This conversational moment is drawn from our research on students' experiences with cross-racial interactions in college (Arellano, Torres, and Valentine 2009; Torres et al. 2013; Valentine et al. 2012; Valentine and Torres 2011). Our study was a multiphase mixed-methods project[1] that included perceptions of students and faculty at two universities and two community colleges on the US side of the US-Mexico border. We surveyed over nine hundred students and facilitated focus groups with thirty-five undergraduate students and twenty-seven faculty. Each phase, though slightly different in orientation, was focused on the value of cross-racial interactions for college and university students attending institutions situated in the US borderlands. Based on substantial research being produced largely in colleges of education, we took as our founding assumption that cross-racial interactions productively position college students for social and intellectual development. Based, in most cases, on analyzing multi-institutional data sets resulting from longitudinal surveys related to student learning on college campuses, researchers (Antonio 2001; Chang 1999; Chang et al. 2006; Gurin et al. 2002; Milem 2003; Reason, Terenzini, and Domingo 2006; Terenzini et al. 2001) suggest students benefit from cross-racial interactions both socially and intellectually in areas such as critical thinking, engaging multiple perspectives, and developing democratic leadership abilities and problem-solving abilities. In our research project, we specifically wanted to know whether students at campuses situated on the border were engaging in the sorts of interactions researchers posited as socially and intellectually productive, particularly those informal, interpersonal interactions that allowed students to get to know each other well enough to discern both commonalities and differences.

We have included below a short excerpt from one student focus group we conducted as part of this research project. Just prior to the conversation represented in the passage, students had been asked how they describe their race or ethnicity. Interestingly, all three students in this excerpt seemed to wrestle with identifying themselves with a single race or ethnicity, perhaps because they identified with multiple races or identities. The first student to respond, Amber,[2] had previously described herself as "mixed" in the focus-group interview. In this excerpt she seems to identify herself as black. The second student, Sarah, also described herself as "mixed" in the focus-group interview. She noted she grew up in a white community, and had white, Native American, and Hispanic ancestors. The third student, Anna, also noted difficulties in characterizing her race or ethnicity. She stated, "Mine's hard. I guess whenever I have to say, I declare myself as Hispanic." What seemed important to us about this ambivalence is that students may have been presenting an awareness that communicating who one is vis-à-vis race or ethnicity can be a complex rhetorical task—with one student even explaining that she understands that how she describes herself might depend, in part, on geographical location. At the same time, it may suggest these students are not used to thinking or talking about how they name and describe their race and ethnicity and that they are less practiced, so to speak, in reflecting on these aspects of their identity.

As noted above, the excerpt we analyze next comes from a focus-group interview conducted with undergraduate students to explore their experiences with cross-racial interactions as part of their college education. The specific interview question that prompted this particular conversation was the following: "When you think about your experiences on campus with people of other races and ethnicities, what has bothered you or troubled you about those experiences?"

> AMBER: The thing that troubles me the most is it seems like every time I walk in a room, people stop and stare. I don't know what it is, but I've noticed it with other black people, too. Every time somebody walks in the room that's black, everybody just stops and stares. They wait, I guess, until they see what they're going to do. It kind of bugs me . . . I'll say it: I'll be like, "I hate it when people stare." My friends will just start laughing, because they know it bugs me. It just . . . I don't know why they do it. It's just like, "I'm not going to flip out! I just came to get a seat—came here for the lecture." I don't know . . . it really gets annoying after awhile.
>
> SARAH: I've kind of noticed that, too, that people do just stop and stare. I've also kind of noticed that it doesn't really matter what nationality you are: if you just walk in the room, people are going to shut up what they're doing and look to see who it is. Most of the time because they're wondering, "Is the teacher going to come in the door yet, or do we still have time to talk?"
>
> AMBER: But I'm talking about anywhere on campus: when I go into Taos [the primary campus cafeteria], or if I go into that little one [cafeteria] in the Health and Social Services building, people just stop. I'm like, "What are you looking at? Seriously! Is there something on my face? Do I need a napkin?" It's just so annoying.

SARAH: I've never seen anybody do that . . .

AMBER: I notice it all the time.

ANNA: [to Sarah] You're not in that position . . . I've never noticed it either . . .

SARAH: Even when I'm walking with my friend . . . I never notice that. It's just kind of strange. Maybe it's just the group of people you hang out with? That they think it's kind of odd or something . . .

AMBER: I don't know.

We found this passage striking for a variety of reasons during our initial stages of data analysis for the larger project. We found it even more striking after discussions about how rhetorical theory and criticism might be useful in helping us think about cross-racial, cross-cultural interactions. It seemed clear to us that each student recorded in the passage was making compelling statements about racial identities and cross-racial identifications based on assumptions they held about each. It seemed interesting to put these students/statements in conversation with Burke's, Crable's, Ratcliffe's, and Anzaldúa's ideas. We believe these theorists/critics help us understand the conversation quoted in the passage above—help us understand both how students represented their experiences with cross-racial identities and interactions and what rhetorical strategies they employed in those representations.

We thought Burke's (1969) dramatistic approach could be useful in helping us to understand the "dramas" through which students present their views on race and racism. Three specific elements of dramatism seem most applicable in this context: that the language we use shapes (both enables and constrains) how we see the world, that communication is a form of action in the world, and that using specific dramatic elements (act, scene, agency, etc.) can tell us something about the rhetorical moves/motivations in an interaction.

By using a dramatistic approach to analyze this passage, we can highlight how what might seem to be subtle disagreements (such as whether or not students' actions might be motivated by racial concerns) draw on larger cultural narratives about race and racism (such as the idea that we have moved beyond race). It can help us to more carefully map where individuals hold different perspectives (such as individuals in conflict over the idea that race affects how we perceive and act in the world). It can also help us to understand how those perspectives may seem more certain the closer they are to "mainstream" cultural narratives, as with Sarah, or how those perspectives may seem more tentative—and yet dramatic—the farther they are from those same narratives, as with Amber.

In drawing on Burke's rhetorical concepts, we can see a number of ways in which the disagreement between Amber and Sarah can be understood as competing or conflicting dramas. Race is a clear presence in Amber's drama at the same time as it is a clear absence in Sarah's. Amber names blackness almost immediately after the question is asked. Sarah never acknowledges the difference Amber names as "race" or the circumstances Amber describes as racially motivated. In fact, Sarah doesn't use the term *race*. In responding to Amber, she uses "nationality." For Amber, race marks clear hierarchies. For example, Amber's drama suggests that black students occupy a lower place in the student hierarchy so much so that they are watched carefully or cautiously: "Every time somebody walks in the room that's black, everybody just stops and stares." For Amber, this seems to indicate a motive for the people who stare: "They wait, I guess, until they see what they're going to do." At the same time, this motive is somewhat mysterious to her: "I don't know why they do it." Whatever the motive, Amber makes clear that a border, situated in hierarchy, separates black students from other students.

For Sarah there seems to be no hierarchy among students. She notices that people stare, as Amber suggests, but not for the reason Amber suggests. Rather, Sarah explains that it is the teacher, the authority figure, who is object of students' stares. For Sarah, students are not motivated to stare based on race, or as she calls it, "nationality": "I've also kind of noticed it doesn't matter what nationality you are." She posits an entirely different motive: "Most of the time because they're wondering, is the teacher going to come in the door yet?" It is possible to employ two other Burkean concepts to explain this passage: scapegoating and transcendence. Sarah suggests a scapegoat for Amber's drama: "Maybe it's just the group of people you hang out with?" This statement also offers the possibility of transcendence. Amber can avoid experiencing this treatment if she hangs out with a group of people like Sarah's friends.

Turning more specifically to identification as Burke conceptualizes it, we can see that this conversation starts with identification—with the assertion of a commonality in order to move the listener toward agreement. This happens when Sarah identifies with Amber's experience, at least initially, by sharing that she too has seen what Amber sees, as she states: "People just stop and stare." Sarah, too, has noticed that people stop what they're doing and stare when other students walk in the room. However, at this point, Ratcliffe's work may suggest that Burkean identification doesn't go far enough. While Sarah asserts a commonality, that commonality risks coercion. This identification becomes coercive when Sarah offers a different drama, a different explanation for what they both have experienced, one that denies Amber's perspective. As Ratcliffe notes, disidentification is a disavowal that, invoking Butler, is often unconscious. Sarah disidentifies with Amber in several ways in this short passage. First, she makes several claims that directly deny Amber's experience. As noted above, she agrees she has seen people stare but posits an entirely different reason for the behavior. Later in the passage, after Amber has reiterated her experience, Sarah claims, "I've never seen anybody do that." Second, Sarah also uses others to create disidentification. She not only creates a divide between her and Amber but also creates a divide between Amber and other black people. Sarah does this by claiming an identification with her friend, also a black person, as justification for her position: "Even when I'm walking with my friend I never notice that. It's just kind of strange." Sarah employs identifications only in support of her view or perspective. She does not see the possibility of, in Crable's terms, "manifestations and functions of race in American culture" (Crable 2003, 23).

Finally, we also see a third strategy of identification, from Ratcliffe's (and Fuss's) perspective: nonidentification in the contribution of Anna to the conversation. As Sarah and Amber seem to move further apart in their perspectives on troubling experiences with students of other races, Anna's brief comment toward the end of the excerpt suggests a third rhetorical strategy for bridging differences—one that relies on engaging both commonality and difference. The movement here is twofold. Anna's remarks to Sarah, "You're not in that position . . . I've never noticed it either," imply the possibility of both identification and nonidentification. In the first half of the statement, she recognizes, and asks Sarah to recognize, that they are not in the same position as Amber. She does not claim to know Amber's experience, but she creates space for it nonetheless. In the second half of the statement, Anna then suggests a common ground with Sarah in stating she hasn't noticed this either. Anna creates identification with Amber in that she acknowledges she does not have the same experiences as Amber and yet makes room for listening to those experiences. She also creates identification with Sarah in affirming she has also not seen what Sarah insists she has never seen. In doing this, she creates space for Sarah's perspective. Interestingly, "I've never noticed it either" is an almost word-for-word reiteration of Sarah's earlier statement, one we identified as disidentification. This time, however, in combination with the second half of the statement, it allows for identifications based on both commonalities and differences.

While Ratcliffe advocates for the inventive potential for space that includes both commonalities and differences, Gloria Anzaldúa serves as an additional resource for thinking about what it means to focus on differences. Specifically, Anzaldúa offers three concepts—engagement, recognition of complicity, and relationship building—through which we can explore the exchanges among Amber, Sarah, and Anna.

At the most basic level, the three participants in this excerpt are engaged. They volunteered to come to a focus group and discuss their experiences with students from other races and ethnicities. Apparently, they did not believe it was enough to "stand on the opposite river bank" (Anzaldúa 1999, 100). In short, they showed up. In a more challenging form of engagement, Amber participated in much the same way Anzaldúa recommends in chapter seven of *Borderlands/La Frontera.* She articulates what she sees as a racialized experience. She makes two attempts to represent this experience. Anna also engages at a deeper level in two distinct directions—as noted in the earlier discussion. She creates space for both Amber's experience and Sarah's perspective and seems to demonstrate the tolerance for ambiguity Anzaldúa champions in her chapter.

It is important to note there are serious disengagements in this interaction as well. While Sarah engages by entering the conversation, she seems unable to listen to and make sense of Amber's experience *from* Amber's perspective. In this sense, we see her as disengaged from Amber's experience, and we see Amber disengaging herself from Sarah at the end of the conversation.

It is possible to understand, at least in part, these disengagements through one of Anzaldúa's fundamental concepts: complicity. For Anzaldúa, it is essential to reflect on one's positionality. For Anzaldúa, acknowledging our complicity goes beyond merely recognizing our position; it also means coming to terms with our role in the circumstances of oppression, whether that move is based on our individual choices and actions or on the broader experiences of the groups with which we are affiliated. It appears from relatively early in the focus group that these students may have been struggling with how they define themselves by race and ethnicity and in turn with what positions they occupied in relation to cross-racial and ethnic interactions. These struggles are at least partially evident when the students are asked to describe their racial and ethnic background. Each has some difficulty doing this. Then, while Amber clearly articulates what she thinks is racialized experience, Sarah seems to have difficulty hearing this or identifying this experience as a racialized one. And while Anna creates space for the experience, she, too, says she has never observed what Amber describes. These responses suggest that these students struggle with the "manifestations and functions of race in American culture" (Anzaldúa 1999, 23), particularly with employing (or not employing as the case may be) rhetorical strategies that might help them navigate discussions and reflection on race. These responses also suggest that these students are not yet positioned to more directly ask for what they need in cross-racial interactions, as Anzaldúa calls for.

CLASSROOM IMPLICATIONS AND DIRECTION FOR FUTURE STUDY

Given the short-term nature of a focus group, it may not be possible for the development of deeper understanding of identity or of productive cross-racial identifications in encounters such as the ones we observed. Having said that, it is still possible to use this kind of exchange as a learning opportunity, particularly for those of us who teach and for those of us who conduct research in a diverse democracy.

While we cannot guarantee as teachers that students will continue relationships outside of our classrooms, we do know they are often engaged in sustained and focused relationships with each other for the length of a semester. And we can use this time and focus to help students develop rhetorical approaches and strategies that support crossing the divides or borders that exist around race in this country. We believe this excerpt, read through the lenses or frameworks offered by Burke, Crable, Ratcliffe, and Anzaldúa, reveals several opportunities for a teacher in the classroom. It illuminates spaces where intervention to help students more fully learn from and benefit from such interactions is possible. We take as our starting place that, like Burke, identification is an important approach for human communication. Like Crable and Ratcliffe, we believe teaching strategies that encourage identification cannot do so without taking into consideration how power relations potentially shape the ways in which identifications are made (or not made) and the historical events from which those power relations emerge. And finally, we value Anzaldúa's strategies that encourage us to cross borders even if doing that requires some level of discomfort.

If this exchange were to happen in our classrooms, we would see several moments in which intervention could be productive. First, we might encourage all students to explore their identities more fully. What does it mean to be "mixed"? Why is describing one's identity "hard"? Second, we might encourage Amber to explore her experience more fully. Why does she think people are staring at her because she is black? What has led her to this conclusion? Third, we might ask Sarah to listen more fully to Amber's experience, and we might ask her to talk about why she is so sure Amber's experience is not about race. Fourth, it might be important to invite Anna to talk more. What does she mean when she says to Sarah "You're not in that position . . . I've never noticed it either"?

In analyzing an exchange like the first one between Amber and Sarah, for example, teachers might learn to employ additional strategies of engagement to move the conversation away from calling into question one student's experience. We see another opportunity when Anna speaks. She gestures toward complicity in that she suggests she and Sarah are differently positioned because of their race and/or ethnicity, which implies an acknowledgment that race and racism might be operating in Amber's life in a way she does not experience. At the same time, Anna also makes an attempt to bridge the disagreement by, as mentioned above, briefly pointing to positionality and to both similarities and differences among the three students. We conjecture that if this attempt had been taken up in a classroom setting, it could have led to Sarah's being able to recognize Amber's experience while still maintaining her position that she had not had such an experience.

As teachers analyzing this conversation, we recognize Anna's attempt at engagement does not seem to be effective, yet we want to acknowledge that it does offer a place where a teacher might also engage by taking up Anna's comment and asking her and others in the classroom to extend it. We believe opening up conversations like these would prompt students to notice the borders, boundaries, and divides that exist all around us and by which racial identities in the United States have been defined. We also believe situating these conversations within a broader rhetorical context—one that minimally includes the work of Burke, Crable, Ratcliffe, and Anzaldúa—could serve as a foundation for students developing the sort of border-crossing skills we're interested in.

At the same time that we view this interaction from our perspective as teachers, we also continue to trouble it from our perspective as researchers. While applying rhetorical theory to the focus-group excerpt, we could have simply labeled students as rhetorically unsophisticated when it came to cross-racial conversations. We could have labeled them as unreflective about their identities (we, in fact, revised our analysis to move away from this idea) and unreflective about each other's experiences with race and racism. We might have wanted to label behavior as racist. But recalling Anzaldúa, we realized we, too, needed a tolerance for ambiguity: we needed to "shift out of habitual formations; from convergent thinking, analytical reasoning that tends to use rationality to move toward a single goal (a Western mode), to divergent thinking, characterized by movement away from set patterns and goals and toward a more whole perspective, one that includes rather than excludes" (Anzaldúa 1999, 101). As both teachers and researchers who occupy positions of oppression and dominance, we needed to see these students as negotiating the same complicated borders of race and other aspects of identity, of self and other, that we too negotiate. And a tolerance for ambiguity helped us to see that we didn't fully know their experiences even in the short time of this focus group. It helped us, too, to see that we had responsibilities to all the students to think about how to support and challenge each of them if we imagined this as a teaching and learning moment.

This realization then leads to potential new directions for research: What is the role of ambiguity in conversations about race and racism? When does ambiguity lead to productive conversations in which we learn from each other while also recognizing our differences? When does ambiguity fail? In short, what are rhetorical strategies of ambiguity that might promote the kind of hospitality and democratic discourse this collection discusses in its opening chapter?

It seems to us, then, that applying rhetorical theory to a cross-racial interaction illuminates the potential that key concepts around identification—Burke's and others—offer for helping us to make sense of those interactions. Notably, the strategies we found most important seek to build identification but do not ultimately focus on eliminating or even fully bridging differences. This then suggests that strategies of ambiguity are all the more important to employ and to understand in becoming a diverse democracy.

Notes

1. Each phase of the study was conducted with approval from the NMSU Institutional Review Board.
2. All student names are pseudonyms.

References

Antonio, Anthony L. 2001. "The Role of Interracial Interaction in the Development of Leadership Skills and Cultural Knowledge and Understanding." *Research in Higher Education* 42 (5): 593–617. http://dx.doi.org/10.1023/A:1011054427581.

Anzaldúa, Gloria. 1999. *Borderlands/La Frontera: The New Mestiza*. San Francisco: Aunt Lute Books.

Arellano, Eduardo Casillas, Mónica F. Torres, and Kathryn Valentine. 2009. "Interactional Diversity in Border Colleges: Perceptions of Undergraduate Students." *Journal of Hispanic Higher Education* 8 (3): 282–97. http://dx.doi.org/10.1177/1538192708326396.

Brummett, Barry. 1993. Introduction to *Landmark Essays on Kenneth Burke*, edited by Barry Brummett, xi–xix. Davis: Hermagoras.
Burke, Kenneth. 1967. *The Philosophy of Literary Form*. Baton Rouge: Louisiana State Press.
Burke, Kenneth. 1969. *A Rhetoric of Motives*. Berkeley: University of California Press.
Chang, Mitchell J. 1999. "Does Racial Diversity Matter? The Educational Impact of a Racially Diverse Undergraduate Population." *Journal of College Student Development* 40 (4): 377–95.
Chang, Mitchell J., Nida Denson, Victor Sáenz, and Kimberly Misa. 2006. "The Educational Benefits of Sustaining Cross-Racial Interaction among Undergraduates." *Journal of Higher Education* 77 (3): 430–55. http://dx.doi.org/10.1353/jhe.2006.0018.
Crable, Bryan. 2003. "Race and *A Rhetoric of Motives*: Kenneth Burke's Dialogue with Ralph Ellison." *Rhetoric Society Quarterly* 33 (3): 5–25. http://dx.doi.org/10.1080/02773940309391257.
Gurin, Patricia, Eric L. Dey, Sylvia Hurtado, and Gerald Gurin. 2002. "Diversity and Higher Education: Theory and Impact on Educational Outcomes." *Harvard Educational Review* 72 (3): 330–66. http://dx.doi.org/10.17763/haer.72.3.01151786u134n051.
Milem, Jeffrey F. 2003. "The Educational Benefits of Diversity: Evidence from Multiple Sectors." In *Compelling Interest: Examining the Evidence on Racial Dynamics in Higher Education*, edited by Mitchell Chang, Daria Witt, James Jones, and Kenji Hakuta, 126–69. Stanford, CA: Stanford University Press.
Ratcliffe, Krista. 2005. *Rhetorical Listening: Identification, Gender, Whiteness*. Carbondale: Southern Illinois University Press.
Reason, Robert D., Patrick T. Terenzini, and Robert J. Domingo. 2006. "First Things First: Developing Academic Competencies in the First Year of College." *Research in Higher Education* 47 (2): 149–75. http://dx.doi.org/10.1007/s11162-005-8884-4.
Terenzini, Patrick T., Alberto F. Cabrera, Carol L. Colbeck, Stefani A. Bjorklund, and John M. Parente. 2001. "Racial and Ethnic Diversity in the Classroom: Does It Promote Student Learning?" *Journal of Higher Education* 72 (5): 509–31. http://dx.doi.org/10.2307/2672879.
Torres, Mónica F., Mary Prentice, Kathryn Valentine, Eduardo C. Arellano, and Robin L. Dankovich. 2013. "So Close, and Yet So Far: Cross-Racial Interactions among Undergraduate Students in Two Neighboring Borderland Communities." *International Journal of Qualitative Studies in Education: QSE* 26 (3): 369–89. http://dx.doi.org/10.1080/09518398.2012.762478.
Valentine, Kathryn, Mary Prentice, Mónica F. Torres, and Eduardo C. Arellano. 2012. "The Importance of Student Cross-Racial Interactions as Part of College Education: Perceptions of Faculty." *Journal of Diversity in Higher Education* 5 (4): 191–206. http://dx.doi.org/10.1037/a0030109.
Valentine, Kathryn, and Mónica F. Torres. 2011. "Diversity as Topography: The Benefits and Challenges of Cross-Racial Interaction in the Writing Center." In *Racism and Writing Centers: A Call for Sustainable Dialogue and Change*, edited by Laura Greenfield and Karen Rowan, 192–210. Logan: Utah State University Press.

PART II

Living Borders

Rhetoric Confronting/Erasing Physical Boundaries

9
"I AM THE 99 PERCENT"
Identification and Division in the Rhetorics of the Occupy Wall Street Protests

Randolph Cauthen

Admirers of Kenneth Burke cannot help but wish he had lived long enough to observe the Occupy Wall Street movement in the fall of 2011. Occupy Wall Street, a leaderless, nonsectarian protest against the massive influence of the United States' wealthiest citizens on its government's policy, began as an encampment of perhaps one thousand people in Zuccotti Park in lower Manhattan on September 17, 2001 (Writers for the 99% 2011, 16) and rapidly grew to a nationwide and even worldwide movement. In doing so, it—and the varied reactions to it by the press, by professional politicians, and by private individuals—tested a number of Burke's ideas about how human beings define themselves in groups, how they establish borders between their own groups and those of others, and how the symbolic acts that erect borders between groups might be channeled to build a society more congruent with American political ideals of equal opportunity and justice.

Burke's reactions to the Occupy movement would have been complex in keeping with his strong philosophical commitment to the idea that no single perspective can render a correct view of reality. Since Burke's concerns with social hierarchy, rhetoric, and the interfaces between them was lifelong and would be nearly encyclopedic in reference, my brief exposition of those concerns here will necessarily be more than a little reductive. From the many possibilities for Burkean analysis of the Occupy movement, I have chosen his theories regarding identification, division, and consubstantiality, as well as those regarding ontological guilt and the means by which we expiate it, as being most in keeping with the themes of this volume since these theories examine how we establish borders between ourselves and other social entities and how we dissolve them. To contextualize both those theories and the Occupy

DOI: 10.7330/9781607324034.c009

movement, however, I will begin with a short analysis of the movement using Burke's familiar dramatistic pentad.

SCENE, AGENCY, AND PURPOSE IN THE OCCUPY WALL STREET PROTESTS

Dramatism is simply the idea that any purposeful human action, including any use of language, can most fruitfully be analyzed in terms of the drama and specifically in terms of the interactions, or as Burke (1969a) calls them, "ratios," among the aspects of the dramatistic pentad: act, agent, agency, scene, and purpose. Here, I will concentrate in particular on the last three of these as being most relevant to analyzing the circumstances of Occupy Wall Street. One useful feature of the pentad is that we can specify these aspects in many ways and thus propagate a large number of interpretations. For instance, we can define the scene of Occupy Wall Street very broadly as taking place in the context of the American Dream mythos, somewhat broadly as taking place in a political context in which the right has succeeded, since the 1960s, in exploiting racial anxieties (Edsall and Edsall 1992), or very narrowly in terms of its immediate geographic and temporal context—with any number of possibilities in between.

By locating in Zucotti Park—or, as they renamed it, Liberty Square—the Occupiers were able to confront multinational capital at its very center. The fact that the park was a "privately owned public space"—its owner, Brookfield Properties, having received a zoning variance from the City of New York to build higher and more densely in the area on the provision that it would provide an open space close by for public use (Gitlin 2012, 19)—gave the Occupiers a tactical advantage because it was legally open to the public twenty-four hours a day. The space also made a political point in that the Occupiers were therefore able to take as a commons—as being free to all—a space created by the convergent interests between Big Capital and government that they were protesting. The ratio between the scene (the paradoxically private/public space they took as their own, with "Whose park? Our park!" being one of the protestors' favorite chants) and the agency ("occupying," living there as a group) was also powerfully symbolic. Participant Yotam Marom characterized Occupy Wall Street as

> a dual-power movement . . . on the one hand—trying to form the values and institutions that we want to see in a free society, while at the same time creating the space for that world by resisting and dismantling the institutions that keep us from having it. Occupation in general, as a tactic, is a

really brilliant form of a dual-power struggle because the occupation is both a home where we get to practice the alternative—by practicing a participatory democracy, by having our radical libraries, by having a medical tent where anybody can get treatment, that kind of thing on a small level—and it's also a staging ground for struggle outwards. It's where we generate our fight against the institutions that keep us from the things that we need, against the banks as a representative of finance capitalism, against the state that protects and propels those interests. (Klein and Marom 2012)

The Occupy movement asserted itself as a utopian community at the very center of the society it was critiquing rather than withdrawing to some periphery and thus being easily ignored. In one of his earliest books, *Counter-Statement*, Burke describes the artist's task as acting as a counterweight, advocating values antithetical to the current values of the particular time in society. Given an American emphasis on efficiency, money, and progress (seemingly unchanged from the 1930s to the 2010s), the artist, he said, must speak for *inefficiency* and against the motives of property and social organization (Overington 1977, 98). Giving away free social services in an egalitarian community that lived "homelessly" in a celebratory fashion was a means of throwing into new perspective the idea that American life consists of atomized individuals or single-family units socially independent of one another. It spoke to inefficiency, as an act of what Burke calls "perspective by incongruity" (Burke 1984, 308), a means of gaining perspective through defamiliarization, by metaphorically fusing together previously unrelated concepts.[1]

As they evoked social and economic inefficiency by living in Zucotti Park, Occupy Wall Street participants evoked *political* inefficiency by not asserting specific policy proposals. That the protestors did not know their own purpose was the theme of the first major media notice of the encampment; in the September 23 *New York Times* article "Gunning for Wall Street with Faulty Aim," Ginia Bellafante described the movement as "noble but fractured and airy," an "intellectual vacuum" and as having a cause that was "in specific terms, virtually impossible to decipher." This topos quickly became a media cliché, forefronted particularly by the commentators of *Fox News*; for instance, Kimberly Gullifoyle characterized the protestors as "people with absolutely no purpose or focus in life." Gullifloyle went on: "No wonder, they have nothing but free time to be down there. They make up a slogan or a cause as they go along. . . . And they really don't have any, like, idea about what they are doing there" (Berrier and Rudman 2011, under ". . . Who Don't Know What They Want . . ."). In some ways, this critique was specious, as the overall point of the group's demands was clear: the financial and especially political power of the wealthiest Americans must be curbed in the name of democracy and the financial malefactors responsible for the great recession be brought to justice.[2]

But the critique was also relevant because members of the Occupy movement itself resisted the formation of specific demands, and for good reason. Mark Bray, a member of the Occupy Press Relations Working Group, stated in a CNN interview that what the movement actually sought was a wide-ranging conversation about the country's social goals and present conditions, and "making a list of three or four demands would have ended the conversation before it started" (Writers for the 99% 2011, 81). A Demands Working Group within the movement proposed, in early October, that the group formalize a demand for a federal public-works program, but the proposal was rejected by the group at large on the grounds that the group should not be making any specific demands (Gitlin 2012, 106).[3] The movement was asking for deep changes to current ways of thinking—not reducible to a simple set of policy options—and to put forward a legislative program would in any case have endorsed the legitimacy of the current ruling structures. Building their own structure, in the midst of the world's financial capital but in absolute inversion of that capital's ethos, was more important; exactly how they tried to build that structure runs directly counter to some of Burke's root beliefs, as I will now attempt to show.

HIERARCHY, IDENTIFICATION, PURE PERSUASION, AND THE PEOPLE'S MIC

Burke's famous "Definition of Man" reads as follows:

> Man is
> the symbol using (symbol making, symbol misusing) animal
> inventor of the negative (or moralized by the negative)
> separated from his natural condition by instruments of his own making
> goaded by the spirit of hierarchy (or moved by the sense of order)
> and rotten with perfection. (Burke 1966, 16)

Human beings under conditions in which a need for order inevitably leads to hierarchy must work continuously to relieve the goad—to justify their current position in the hierarchy, to move within it, or to replace whatever current hierarchy exists with a new one—using their symbolic (i.e., rhetorical) tools. Rhetoric is necessary because human beings are necessarily divided from one another, and not only by the "spirit of hierarchy"; Burke notes that division is a physiological fact prior to being a political and psychological fact (Burke 1969b, 130, 146). Therefore, rhetoric operates through identification, a key Burkean concept he defines as being "compensatory to division" (22) and exemplifies as ranging "from the politician who, addressing an audience of farmers, says, 'I was a farm boy myself,' through the mysteries of social status, to the mystic's devout identification with the source of all being" (xiv). "You persuade a man," Burke says, "only insofar as you talk his language by speech, gesture, tonality, order, image, attitude, idea, *identifying* your ways with his" (55). A successful rhetorical act leads the audience into a state of consubstantiality, "the identifying of one's own substance with something larger and more comprehensive" (Henderson 1988, 29), but identification and consubstantiality are never final because division always reasserts itself.

Or so Burke believes. The Occupy movement, on the other hand, attempted to organize itself nonhierarchically as a matter of fundamental principle. The protestors' means of ordering themselves was one of consensus in decision making that insisted against any leadership structure, continuous with the long history of anarchist-influenced protest in the United States and taking many of its specific techniques from Quaker precedents (Writers for the 99% 2011, 29). The group's general assembly met nightly, usually at 7 p.m.; these meetings were run by "facilitators" who effaced their quasileadership roles by never taking them two days in a row and by referring to themselves only by their first names.[4] Meetings began with a set agenda of announcements, proposals for consensus approval, and reports from various working groups within the camp; afterwards came the "soapbox" period during which anyone who wished to speak was allowed to do so (25–32). Significantly, many Occupiers who were asked the inevitable question about the group's overall purpose evoked the participatory process itself: Gitlin quotes three of them as saying "I think the conversation is one of our goals," "Just being able to say what you feel is one of the most empowering things," and "The process is the message" (Gitlin 2012, 68).

Due to a police ban on the use of electronic amplification in the park, the meetings were forced to use a technique that became known as *the people's mic*, which required the speaker to use a brief phrase then pause to wait for it to be repeated outward by all those around them, and, in a large crowd, it was echoed yet again by all those who could hear the first group (Asher 2011). Thus, not only was anyone allowed to speak during the general assembly, but also all those present were continually speaking each other's words. As such, the people's mic became an important means of building empathy and solidarity within the movement as a whole, as Gitlin points out: "By repeating other people's words we are forced to actively engage with them—to actually hear them" (Gitlin 2012, 78). It was often used, seemingly almost liturgically, when it was not strictly needed (e.g., indoors) and was generally used in concert with a range of hand signals (called *twinkling* and derived from American Sign Language) to designate approval, disapproval, and ambivalence without interrupting the echoing discourse (Writers for the 99% 2011, 28). All told, the people's mic worked as a powerful invitation to consubstantiality; as Burke says in his discussion of the enthymeme and its use in identification, "Could we not say the audience is exalted by the assertion because it has the feel of collaborating in the assertion?" (Burke 1969b, 58).

If the act of collaboration and the consubstantial dissolution of borders in itself was actually the point, if the process of the Occupy movement was indeed the message, the group seems to have come close to what Burke calls "pure persuasion"—"the saying of something, not for an extraverbal advantage to be got by the saying, but because of a satisfaction intrinsic to the saying" (Burke 1969b, 269).[5] Richard Dienst believed the tendency toward pure persuasion in the Occupy movement to be a function of agency, specifically of the movement's debt to online social networking: "Here the medium really matters: the sheer profusion of messages circulating on social media has turned the whole movement into an open-ended experiment in political expression. On the ground and on the Internet, the protestors address their most radical questions to each other: who are we, really? what do we have in common? what do we want?" (Dienst 2011). A sympathetic reading of Occupy's pure persuasion might see it as a necessary means of self-assertion in an economic and political climate that was severely alienating, especially to the young, or as a necessary antihierarchical statement toward a society in the condition that Burke calls "hierarchical psychosis" (Burke 1984, 374), that is, a condition in which alternatives to a particular ruling hierarchy are so taboo as to be inconceivable. Less generously, we might see it as simple naïveté, particularly because the group seemed to be courting its own destruction by encamping itself on Wall Street in the path of the most powerful members of our society's current hierarchy.

Nevertheless, it asserted itself in a remarkably optimistic way, most notably through a symbolic identification that worked both internally and as external outreach—the movement's self-definition as being the 99 percent. Always a strongly dialectical thinker, Burke emphasizes that our status as "inventor of [and] moralized by the negative" forces us to define through opposition (Burke 1966, 16). In the case of the Occupy movement, the 99 percent definition seems to have been drawn from economist Joseph Stiglitz's article, "Of the 1%, by the 1%, for the 1%," in the May 2011 issue of *Vanity Fair*. Here, Stiglitz noted that the wealthiest 1 percent of Americans earned nearly one-quarter of the country's income and owned 40 percent of its wealth, "an inequality even the wealthy will come to regret" (Stiglitz 2011, n.p.). The chant "We are the 99 percent" was adopted early in the Occupy protests (Gitlin 2012, 108) and gained enormous cultural currency in the early fall of 2011, with Google searches for the phrase *the 99%* multiplying sevenfold between September and October, and with that number being invoked by advertisers and by Democrats in Congress (Stelter, *New York Times*, Nov. 30, 2011). The 99 percent trope had many powerful advantages for the movement: it was radically condensed (and thus was congenial to posting on social networking sites such as Twitter) but gave a very clear summation of the movement's goals by invoking a United States not democratically divided almost equally between far-right and center-right political parties but divided between a tiny political and economic elite and the remainder of the population and thus fundamentally undemocratic. The phrase acted as an identification trope, inviting and assuming the support of the overwhelming majority of the population, as John Nichols described: "The brilliance of Occupy Wall Street's message, 'We are the 99 percent,' is that it invites just about everyone who isn't a billionaire to recognize themselves as members" (Nichols 2011). The implication of near but not total unity, in turn, reinforced the fundamental optimism of the Occupiers themselves; one sign in Zucotti Park read: "99 to One: Those Are Great Odds" (Gitlin 2012, 26–27).

By all accounts, these various means of identification promoted an extraordinary degree of consubstantiality within the movement. A very large number of the participants in the Occupy movement spoke of it as being personally redemptive in terms of helping them find some sort of meaning to their existence when, as participants in the American Dream ideology, they had been discounted by their own lack of economic success. Many other members of the movement besides Marom believed they were indeed in the process of building the better world they wanted to inhabit through their consensus decision-making process, celebratory ethos, and provision of food, medicine, and social services monetized ruthlessly elsewhere in the American economy (Gitlin 2012, 73, 111–12; Writers for the 99% 2011, 30). Cynics, of course, might take exception to that belief, seeing Occupiers' statements to be saccharine, like those of Naomi Klein, who told the general assembly on October 6 that the occupation was "the most important thing in the world" and also said,

"My favorite sign here says, 'I care about you.' In a culture that trains people to avoid each other's gaze . . . that is a deeply radical statement" (Klein 2011).

In fact, as Burke would predict, the movement was not immune to borders within itself. There was a certain class structure reflected in the physical layout of the Zuccotti Park encampment, with the east side of the park primarily populated by white, middle-class protesters of a reformist bent and the west side primarily populated by less affluent people of color, who tended toward a more radical point of view. One Latino Occupier noted that the geographical split along ethnic and class lines was "just like New York City" (Writers for the 99% 2011, 90). There was also continuing, fundamental disagreement in terms of tactics, with some members of the movement convinced that its stubborn adherence to its model of direct democracy at best rendered decision making "frustratingly clumsy and time consuming" (Writers for the 99% 2011, 27) and, at worst, ran the risk of turning the entire movement into an exercise in "collective narcissism" (Gitlin 2012, 94). More than one analyst believes the Occupy movement essentially failed largely because its ethos of full participation and pure persuasion left it unable to find a path forward after the Zuccotti Park encampment was evicted by the New York Police Department on November 15, 2011—specifically, the group was unable to reorganize itself due to a very small minority of disruptive voices in meetings, whether they were intentional provocateurs or those whose personal need to be heard overrode more important business (Gitlin 2012, 135–36; Gupta, *Guardian*, July 5, 2012). Perhaps these observers were too focused on the improbable possibility of a short-term victory for the movement; perhaps they did not sufficiently note the possibility that, in dramatistic terms, the agency/purpose of direct democracy was predicated upon the scene, upon the fact that the encampment was a functioning physical community, living together twenty-four hours a day.

THE 99 PERCENT, THE 53 PERCENT, CONSUBSTANTIALITY, AND SCAPEGOATING

I have to this point concentrated solely on that particular community in lower Manhattan because that encampment was generally seen as first among equals in the Occupy Wall Street movement by the media, the public at large, and members of the movement itself, and as such it is most thoroughly documented and discussed. However, the Zucotti/Freedom Park community represented just one aspect of a worldwide and continuing protest and was in temporal terms not even first among equals. The blog *We Are the 99 Percent* (n.d.) on Tumblr.com took on an iconic status concurrently with the physical protests, but it was actually first posted in late August 2011; in fact, several early postings encouraged viewers to join the forthcoming protest on September 17. As of July 2012, the site consisted of 228 pages with fifteen postings on each page; it is thus useful as a large, stable corpus of discourse contributed by those sympathetic with the Occupy movement and taking up its various themes. Examination of the postings reveals a large number of ways in which these writers persuade by identifying their ways (in order, attitude, image, and idea) with their audience.

Contributions to the *We Are the 99 Percent* blog are highly stylized: with very few exceptions, they consist of a photograph of a single individual holding up a handwritten (or, rarely, word processed) statement that partially or completely obscures their face.[6] The actual written discourse very often contains direct statements of consubstantiality in which the speaker subsumes their own identity into the 99 percent; typical examples are the posts on November 15 and December 17, 2011: "I am the 99%. You are the 99%. And together we can create change!" and

> I'm so happy to know we're in this together. It's been so difficult struggling alone, trying to find a way to get ahead and only falling behind.
> The 1% took away our
> -Democracy
> -Pride
> -Hope.
> Let's take it back.
> With interest.
> We deserve it. We are the 99%.

But even more striking evidence of consubstantiality is what Burke would call the "repetitive form" of the postings—"the consistent maintaining of a principle under new guises" or the "restatement of the theme by new details" (Burke 1968, 125). Almost every posting describes the writer's economic circumstances and a few other biographical details in generic terms and ends with the statement "I am the 99%" or a close variation of that phrase.[7] The contributors to *We Are the 99 Percent* attenuate their individual identities verbally as well as by hiding their faces behind their words; in terms of the Burkean pentad, each subsumes their individual status as agent to become a collective agent. They elide the specific details typical to conversational introductions; identification by first name is quite infrequent, and I have noted only three instances of a writer including their surname (posts on October 2 and 6 and on November 21). Most often, the writers identify themselves by job title and/or by age. Location is seldom given in terms more specific than "I live in Central Wisconsin" (December 17).

Furthermore, the stories the writers tell fall, most frequently, into two relatively specific categories correlating with age group. Older writers depict middle-class lives sabotaged by the economic malfeasance of the 1 percent. An October 3, 2001, post on *We Are the 99 Percent* reads,

> I am 62 years old. I have worked honestly and hard my whole life (since I was 14) because that is how you "realize The American Dream."
>
> I was a home builder and designer.
>
> In 1980, the "Savings & Loan Crisis" forced me out of work and out of business. (the government helped the banks survive . . .) I slowly rebuilt my life and business.
>
> In 2007, the "Sub-Prime Mortgage Crisis" crushed me again. I lost my business, my home, my wife and my belief in that American Dream. (The government saved the banks again . . .)
>
> WE ARE THE 99%

Considerably less frequently, older contributors describe themselves as still being relatively comfortable but precariously so, knowing that an unexpected illness or job loss would cause them to lose everything they have.

Younger contributors to *We Are the 99 Percent* convey a sense that they will never be able to achieve the American dream of financial independence in the first place. This message was posted on November 25, 2011:

> I am 26 years old. I have worked at the same job since I was 17. The money I earn is not enough to cover my monthly expenses and I don't even have a car. Dreams of getting a college education have passed as 50+ hours a week working are still not enough to pay for groceries.
>
> I am not a celebrity or star athlete who gets paid millions a year. I am a normal person literally working myself to the bone and still unable to provide adequate food and shelter. There are many much worse than myself, but I am tired of struggling. I am tired of having no voice and watching people suffer, while knowing there are people with much more than what would ever be needed. I work to live and it is still not enough.
>
> I am the 99%!

In keeping with Burke's definition of repetitive form, the postings on *We Are the 99 Percent* vary in detail but essentially tell the same story again and again: of slow suffocation under debt, of families dislocated by foreclosure or the need to search for work, of the sense that "I've done everything right, and no one will hire me" (post on January 10), of a promise made to the writers—that if they attained educations and worked hard at their jobs, they would reach the American Dream—that has been revoked. Plaintive and moving, the postings clearly perform psychological work for their authors as well as rhetorical work in promoting the interests of the 99 percent, but they do so anonymously by subsuming individual identity into narrative consubstantiality.

The *We Are the 99 Percent* Tumblr quickly became such a prominent outreach mechanism of the Occupy movement that the Right felt an imperative to respond. One such response was a blog replicating the 99 percent Tumblr's design and conceived by right-wing blogger and CNN correspondent Erik Erickson. This site, also on Tumblr, called *We Are the 53%* (n.d.) debuted on October 5, 2011. The percentage of 53 evoked in the blog's name is derived from the fact that, as of 2010, 47 percent of American households ended up owing no federal income tax—a fact oversimplified by right-wing commentators to imply that a relatively huge number of Americans were on the dole (Leonhardt, *New York Times*, April 13, 2010) and one that gained infamy through Mitt Romney's use of it to an audience he believed to be private during the 2012 presidential campaign (Rucker, *Washington Post*, Sept. 17, 2012).[8] In contrast to the Occupy movement's assertion of itself as an overwhelming majority, *the 53 percent* seems an odd, rhetorically unpowerful choice, but it does evoke the implication of a *precarious* majority that must constantly guard its borders against the other, the 47 percent. In the wake of fifty years of racialized demagoguery against social-assistance programs, it is easy for the blog's intended audience to associate this dangerous, expensive Other with the "welfare queen" mythos (Boris 2007). Edsall and Edsall (1992) demonstrate how the American Right has exploited racial anxieties to persuade lower- and middle-class white Americans to dismiss their economic circumstances as a basis for voting; Thomas Frank (2004) similarly shows how the Right uses anxieties surrounding sexuality, religion, gun control, and similar social issues to gain votes for its economic program. Any attempt to have the white lower classes identify with their actual economic interests constitutes an extreme threat to the political survival of the American Right. Although the Right did initially attempt to write the Occupy movement off as a manufactured, top-down phenomenon, with Rush Limbaugh calling it "a construct of the media-Democrat complex, industrial complex" (Taibbi 2011), it soon became a clear threat representing a genuine, growing sentiment—and so it became necessary to scapegoat the movement.

The scapegoating process is a central theme in Burke's later work; he describes it as a means by which people expel unwanted individuals or groups by first acknowledging an identification with them and by then purging them to atone for the perceived sins of their own community.

Scapegoating occurs, Burke says, because human beings are "moralized by the negative" (Burke 1966, 16) and because the standards set up by the moral system derived from the negative, from the central imprecation of "thou shalt not" (Burke 1970, 279), are essentially unattainable, leading to universal guilt. The guilt must be expiated, Burke says, either in terms of scapegoating or "purification by disassociation" (Burke 1973, 202) or through mortification, scapegoating turned inwardly toward the self (Burke 1970, 248). The scapegoating process, Burke says, occurs through three stages: "(1) an original state of merger, in that the iniquities are shared by both the iniquitous and their chosen vessel; (2) a principle of division, in that the elements shared in common are ritualistically alienated; (3) a new principle of merger; this time in the unification of those whose purified identity is defined in dialectical opposition to the sacrificial offering" (Burke 1969a, 406).

The *We Are the 53%* blog enacts the first stage of Burkean scapegoating through publishing stories that are, in their description of economic hardship, extraordinarily consubstantial with the stories that appear on the *We Are the 99 Percent* blog. This post appeared on October 5, 2011:

> I am a former Marine.
> I work two jobs.
> I don't have health insurance.
> I worked 60–70 hours a week for eight years to pay my way through college.
> I haven't had four consecutive days off in over four years.
> But I don't blame Wall Street.
> Suck it up you whiners.
> I am the 53%
> God bless the USA!

And this one on October 17, 2011:

> I was laid off from a great paying job 12 years ago, after 16 years. I went back to work and have been working for another 12 years. Then my dad died, then my mom died, then I got breast cancer and I am still here and still working. For all you whiners,—get off the dole, quit asking for everything to be given to you, get a job. The jobs are out there. Life is not easy or fair!

Less frequently, postings convey success stories in terms of the American Dream ideology,[9] and a very few turn the guilt inward toward mortification.[10] The repeatedly shared topos of hard work without economic security makes it clear exactly what guilt the 53 percent is trying to expiate: it is contained in the syllogism implicit in the American Dream ideology that *if anyone who works hard enough in America will succeed, then if you have not succeeded, you have not worked hard enough.*

The exact rhetorical means by which the 99 percent are cast out often reflect characterizations of the Occupy movement familiar from right-wing media and congruent with the long history of racial scapegoating—the protestors are seen as dirty, overly sexualized, and overly fond of marijuana. Elsewhere on *We Are the 53%*, an antifeminist topos is most prominent: "That womyn's studies major not paying off for ya?" (post on October 22, with similar imprecations on October 14, 18, 20, and 27). But by far the most common means of scapegoating the Occupy protestors is through the "whiners" topos shown above; a brief sampling includes examples such as "America is a place for winners, not whiners" (October 17), "bums sitting on the street whining" (October 11), "I am the 53% and pissed off at the whining 99%ers. Suck. It. Up. Wimps!" (October 20), "a few thousand whiny babies mewling in the streets" (October 13), "whiny babies masquerading as adults" (October 14), and "whiny babies crying for socialism" (October 17).

A very clear parallel to this whiny-baby topos is shown in the ethnographic data Jennifer Seibel Trainor gathered in a suburban, 97-percent-white public high school in the mideastern United States. Trainor interviewed a large number of students about the considerable resistance they demonstrated against claims about racism made by African American writers and found that a majority of the students simply dismissed the claims as being "whiny" (Trainor 2008, 91) or "complaining" (94) and as such were negated by the enforced optimism of the American Dream ideology their school inculcated: "Students were repeatedly told that their destiny was in their hands if only they maintained the right attitude" (97). The ubiquity of this critique, both in the high school Trainor studied and in the *We Are the 53%* text, implies that it is a central topos in American ideology. And in fact the whiny-baby topos as applied to the Occupy movement enjoyed considerable success in two different ways. First, it became important to the Obama administration's (and to political and media elites as a whole) response to the Occupy protests. On November 22, 2011, during a speech in New Hampshire, President Obama was interrupted by chanters who, using the people's-mic echoing technique, said, "Mr. President, over 4000 peaceful protesters have been arrested. While bankers continue to destroy the American economy. You must stop the assault on our First Amendment rights. Your silence sends a message that police brutality is acceptable. Banks got bailed out. We got sold out." Obama responded by saying, "A lot of folks who've been down in New York and all across the country in the Occupy movement, there is a profound sense of frustration, a profound sense of frustration about the fact that the essence of the American dream . . . feels like it's slipping away. . . . Families like yours, young people like the ones here today—including the ones who were just chanting at me—you're the reason that I ran for office in the first place" (Gitlin 2012, 191–92).

Rather than addressing either the First Amendment issue or the issue of bank malfeasance, Obama simply attempted to soothe feelings, as one would try to calm an upset child. Similarly, he had told *ABC News* on October 18, "I understand the frustrations being expressed in those protests" (Dwyer 2011), a response perhaps strongly influenced by Bill Clinton's success in telling a member of the audience at the 1992 presidential debate in Richmond, "I feel your pain" (Levine 1993, 23). We might also speculate that the Occupy protestors—by implying, if not stating outright, that their communicative process actually constituted their protest—left themselves open to this kind of rhetorical ploy.

In addition, the whiny-baby topos does double service in terms of Burke's theory of guilt and expiation. It allows the *We Are the 53%* writers to scapegoat the Occupy movement and mortify themselves *at the same time*, identifying themselves as consubstantial with the American Dream not because they have gained any sort of financial independence but simply because they can disassociate themselves from the whiners. Many of the posters seem to be welcoming severe financial hardship as a badge of righteousness, mortifying themselves and accepting their suffering as a sacrifice for the greater good.

THE ENDS OF THE OCCUPATION

Despite efforts to discredit them, the writers of the *We Are the 99 Percent* blog explicitly reject the role of scapegoat, refusing the guilt that would be foisted upon them. This rejection of guilt occurs specifically in response to the accusation of whining—as if they recognize its centrality in the critique against them—with a large number of them expressing the sentiment of the twenty-six-year-old quoted above, by saying, "There are many much worse [off] than myself"; in fact, in his post to the blog *Rortybomb* on October 9, 2011, Mike Konczal's quantitative analysis of the *We Are the 99 Percent* Tumblr, done relatively early in the history of the blog, found *lucky* to be the most frequently used adjective and fourteenth most frequently used content word.[11] More generally, those who write in to the Tumblr turn attributions of guilt made against them toward the 1 percent, with discourse like this post on October 20, 2011:

I AM the 99%. I have worked too hard for this to be the end. I am pissed. I'm tired of being screwed over and of attempts to make ME feel bad about it to alleviate YOUR guilt or greed, or to prop up your overinflated sense of self importance. I do not care about being in the 1%."

This, of course, raises the question of whether these writers are scapegoating their own adversaries. The answer to this seems to be no because their rejection of these adversaries does not begin in a sense of consubstantiality; the 1 percent is seen as completely Other, both in their circumstances and in their morality, a view expressed as the October 20 post continues:

> The 1% sold my future, polluted my planet, bought my "elected" leaders, looted our treasury, holds our health hostage, wiped out my Grandparents' life savings, made over 1 Million US citizens homeless through foreclosure. No arrests, no prosecutions. 700 peaceful protesters spoke out and were locked up.
> I demand JUSTICE. I am the 99%.

In his book-length Burkean analysis of Martin Luther King's "I Have a Dream" speech, David Bobbitt argues that King expiates African American guilt "by transforming the very conditions of that guilt, oppression and socioeconomic inferiority, into a virtue," taking on martyrdom in fulfillment of Burke's principle of mortification (Bobbitt 2004, 43). The Occupy movement's use of this principle shows a difficult, but possible, means of identification with the mortification of the suffering, but uncomplaining, 53 percent, and, in fact, no less of an authority on contemporary American politics than Barack Obama was one of many observers who noted that the Occupy movement shared a large number of economic concerns with the rightist Tea Party movement (Dwyer 2011).

In this, and in many of its other rhetorical tactics, the movement may yet achieve a strategic victory despite its tactical defeat in the late fall of 2011. On the night of November 14–15, police forcibly evicted Occupiers from encampments in Manhattan, Denver, Oakland, and Portland; other encampments nationwide were shortly afterwards removed. Documents later emerged showing these police actions to be coordinated by an entity called the Domestic Security Alliance Council, a partnership between elements from the FBI, the Department of Homeland Security, and the private sector—including the selfsame financial corporations whose influence the movement was protesting (Wolf, *Guardian*, Dec. 29, 2012). In the wake of this crackdown, the *New York Times* stated, "Whatever the long-term effects of the Occupy Movement, protesters succeeded in implanting 'we are the 99 percent' into the cultural and political lexicon" (Stelter, *New York Times*, Nov. 23, 2011). This is no small achievement because in Burkean terms our "terministic screens" (Burke 1966, 44ff) determine exactly what it is we see. It's notable that even the writers of the *We Are the 53%* blog occasionally accept it as a frame for contemporary economic reality, saying things such as "I am part of the 99% but you do not speak for me" (post on October 18) and "I am part of the 99%, but I am NOT 'the 99'" (October 20). The larger, and more important, issue of whether the partisans of the Occupy movement can bring their class equivalents among those who call themselves the 53 percent into a truly consubstantial relationship—whether the guilt attendant to failure to reach the American Dream can be consistently redirected away from social, sexual, racial and religious anxieties and toward needed economic and political reforms—remains open. Burke wrote early in his career that "criminality . . . is actually *transformed, transcended, transubstantiated*, by incorporation into a wider context of symbolic action" (Burke 1973, 51–52). That the 99 percent trope has become a terministic screen for many Americans suggests a wider context and a more profoundly inclusive community are possible.

But it is also clear that a great deal of work remains to be done, by the American citizenry as a whole and by rhetoricians of good conscience in particular, for us to achieve this community. One important first step would be to examine the successes and failures of the Occupy movement much more thoroughly than I have been able to do here. One particular topic I have only briefly touched upon is the shifting relationships among the Occupy movement, the general public, and the American mass media; it remains very much an open question whether any mass movement truly critical of the economic status quo can receive ongoing attention in this corporatized media environment. In large part, the movement tried to elude this difficulty through the use of "people-powered" new media—but this raises another vital question, that of the nature of an effective polis in the Internet age and what constitutes a "public space" in the twenty-first century. As I have noted above, many observers attributed the decline of the movement to its forcible eviction from the physical spaces it occupied. Furthermore, there has been an ongoing controversy as to how and even whether Internet activism can convert into effective political action in "real life," but the discussion regarding this question has been largely theoretical or advocatory (see Gladwell 2010; McCafferty 2011) or else derived from experimental, nonnaturalistic studies (such as Lee and Hsieh 2013). Some qualitative rhetorical analysis of the interface between Internet activism and "real life" has been published—most notably in McCaughey and Ayers (2003)—but this important work has really just begun, and we should note that, since it is centered in the relationships among scene, act, agent, agency, and purpose, it is work highly amenable to Burkean dramatistic analysis.

We also need much more thorough scholarly examination and public discussion of how, exactly, the mechanisms of Burkean scapegoating establish boundaries within our democracy. One fundamental question regarding this theme I hint at above by noting that the scapegoating of Occupy used similar strategies to those used against African Americans. Scapegoating of African Americans may very well be fundamental to the contemporary success of the American Right. Contemporary discourse on both the Right and the Left, as is shown by Tim Wise (2010), proclaims a "postracial" society that brings African Americans (as well as other ethnic minorities such as Latinos) into a state of Burkean identification. It does so through "dog-whistle politics" (i.e., politics based on coded racist assertions; see López 2014) by which the sins of the American polity as a whole—laziness and criminality foremost among them—are shunted onto the racialized Other and purged from the American Dream. As the percentage of people of color in America rises, and as the opportunities for middle-class employment decline, resistance against these scapegoating strategies will be more and more urgently needed.

Burke's theories remind us that, because division continually reasserts itself in human affairs and borders are continually configured and reconfigured through symbolic actions, to create a more inclusive community, we must continually reassess the discourses around us. We must realize these borders exist within a continuing human drama driven by human purpose, and we must take rhetorically cogent actions against division. Burke's methods also provide us with the means to do this by fully and flexibly contextualizing these discourses through the dramatistic pentad, by understanding the process that establishes cultural boundaries through the attribution of guilt to scapegoated groups, and by realizing that the opportunities for consubstantial identification "by speech, gesture, tonality, order, image, attitude, idea" (Burke 1969b, 55) proliferate throughout the entire range of our human identities.

Notes

1. Grieg Henderson's gloss is useful here: "Perspective by incongruity is a de-familiarization strategy akin to Brecht's alienation effect. Its political genius resides in its ability to co-opt the hegemonic vocabulary of the dominant class—the ideology of

the status quo that converts the historical into the natural—and to form it into a counterstatement, a rhetoric of social change. By allowing us to translate back and forth between conceptual schemes that are traditionally kept apart, perspective by incongruity is both a methodological device for giving us a handle on the bewildering dense diversity of interpretations with which we are bombarded and a rhetorical technique for subverting a given hegemonic discourse from within by transvaluing its symbols of authority" (Henderson 1988, 21).

2. The nadir of the they-don't-know-what-they-want topos was, perhaps, reached when a correspondent on *Forbes*'s web page sniffed that the protestors did not know whether they were angry with Wall Street's retail traders, flow traders, or execution traders (Hirschhorn 2011).

3. In any case, the editorial board of the *New York Times*—certainly no great enemy of current government structures—pointed out that it was not really the protesters' job to make specific policy proposals; that was the job of the nation's political leaders, and they had not been doing it. Under those circumstances, "the public airing of grievances is a legitimate and important end in itself." They continued, "It is also the first line of defense against a return to the Wall Street ways that plunged the nation into an economic crisis from which it has yet to emerge" ("Protestors against Wall Street," *New York Times*, October 8, 2011). Eventually, on January 3, 2012, the Occupy Wall Street General Assembly did officially adopt the measure that "corporations are not people and money is not speech" and called for public funding of elections (Gitlin 2012, 109).

4. The Occupy Denver encampment performed a trenchant act of perspective by incongruity in regard to the perceived need for leaders when it, upon being told by the mayor of Denver that he would negotiate with the group if provided with a single leader with which to speak, elected as its leader a Border Collie named Shelby (Mitchell 2011, 82).

5. Although Burke says that the idea of pure persuasion is a utopian one, that it is an ultimate rather than normative term, he does allow that it can be an ingredient in persuasion of all types no matter how "advantage seeking such a rhetoric may be" (Burke 1969b, 269).

6. The visual rhetoric of the blog was evocative enough to be quickly taken up for other purposes—for example, it was repeated almost exactly in the *Who Needs Feminism* (n.d.)Tumblr started by women's studies students at Duke University as well as on the *We Are the 53%* (n.d.) blog I will discuss momentarily.

7. The blog's first posting (August 23, 2011) specified guidelines for contributions, but those guidelines were very quickly overridden. One in particular that was done away with almost immediately was the request that posters restrict their description of their particular circumstances to a single line.

8. According to the Tax Policy Center, only 23 percent of Americans incurred no income tax because of low income; another 23 percent had their federal income tax liability cleared by a variety of exemptions and credits (Johnson et al. 2011).

9. An October 14, 2011, post on *We Are the 53%* read, "I worked for two years after college at a below poverty wage. I worked hard to grow in my expertise. I took a job making more than double my poverty wage. 4 years later I was upper middle class. I have helped make other people rich. I am grateful for the opportunity."

10. An October 20, 2011, post on *We Are the 53%* read, "I was careless. I worked but didn't save. I ate out almost every weekend, I had a bar tab in the triple digits. I don't blame Wall Street for my lack of judgment. . . . Good judgment comes from experience. Experience comes from bad judgment. I regret nothing!"

11. Those more frequently used were *job(s), debt(s), work, college, pay, student, loan(s), afford, school, insurance, body, money,* and *home.*

References

Asher, Levi. 2011. "Occupy Wall Street: How the People's Mic Works." *Literary Kicks.* http://www.litkicks.com/PeoplesMic.
Berrier, Justin, and Chelsea Rudman. 2011. "A Guide to the Smear Campaign against Occupy Wall Street." *Media Matters for America.* http://mediamatters.org/research/2011/10/18/a-guide-to-the-smear-campaign-against-occupy-wa/181591.
Bobbitt, David A. 2004. *The Rhetoric of Redemption: Kenneth Burke's Redemption Drama and Martin Luther King, Jr.'s "I Have a Dream" Speech.* Lanham, MD: Rowman and Littlefield.
Boris, Eileen. 2007. "On Cowboys and Welfare Queens: Independence, Dependence, and Interdependence at Home and Abroad." *Journal of American Studies* 41 (3): 599–621. http://dx.doi.org/10.1017/S002187580700401X.
Burke, Kenneth. 1966. *Language as Symbolic Action.* Berkeley: University of California Press.
Burke, Kenneth. 1968. *Counter-Statement.* Berkeley: University of California Press.
Burke, Kenneth. 1969a. *A Grammar of Motives.* Berkeley: University of California Press.
Burke, Kenneth. 1969b. *A Rhetoric of Motives.* Berkeley: University of California Press.
Burke, Kenneth. 1970. *The Rhetoric of Religion.* Berkeley: University of California Press.
Burke, Kenneth. 1973. *The Philosophy of Literary Form: Studies in Symbolic Action.* 3rd ed. Berkeley: University of California Press.
Burke, Kenneth. 1984. *Attitudes Toward History.* 3rd ed. Berkeley: University of California Press.
Dienst, Richard. 2011. "Listening to Zuccotti Park." *Verso.* http://www.versobooks.com/blogs/748-listening-to-zuccotti-park.
Dwyer, Devin. 2011. "Obama: Occupy Wall Street 'Not that Different' from Tea Party Protests." *ABC News.* http://abcnews.go.com/blogs/politics/2011/10/obama-occupy-wall-street-not-that-different-from-tea-party-protests/.
Edsall, Thomas Byrne, and Mary Edsall. 1992. *Chain Reaction: The Impact of Race, Rights, and Taxes on American Politics.* New York: Norton.
Frank, Thomas. 2004. *What's the Matter with Kansas? How Conservatives Won the Heart of America.* New York: Metropolitan Books.
Gitlin, Todd. 2012. *Occupy Nation: The Roots, the Spirit, and the Promise of Occupy Wall Street.* New York: It Books.
Gladwell, Malcolm. 2010. "Small Change: Why the Revolution Will Not Be Tweeted." *New Yorker.* http://www.newyorker.com/magazine/2010/10/04/small-change-malcolm-gladwell.
Henderson, Greig E. 1988. *Kenneth Burke: Literature and Language as Symbolic Action.* Athens: University of Georgia Press.
Hirschhorn, Doug. 2011. "Occupy Wall Street? Do You Even Understand Wall Street?" *Forbes.* http://www.forbes.com/sites/doughirschhorn/2011/10/03/occupy-wall-street-do-you-even-understand-wall-street/.
Johnson, Rachel, James Nunns, Jeffrey Rohaly, Eric Toder, and Roberton Williams. 2011. "Why Some Tax Units Pay no Income Tax." *Tax Policy Center.* http://www.taxpolicycenter.org/UploadedPDF/1001547-Why-No-Income-Tax.pdf.
Klein, Naomi. 2011. "Occupy Wall Street: The Most Important Thing in the World Now." *Nation.* http://www.thenation.com/article/occupy-wall-street-most-important-thing-world-now/.
Klein, Naomi, and Yotam Marom. 2012. "Why Now? What's Next? Naomi Klein and Yotam Marom in Conversation About Occupy Wall Street." *Nation.* http://www.thenation.com/article/why-now-whats-next-naomi-klein-and-yotam-marom-conversation-about-occupy-wall-street/.
Lee, Yu-Hao, and Gary Hsieh. 2013. "Does Slacktivism Hurt Activism?: The Effects of Moral Balancing and Consistency in Online Activism." In *CHI '13: Proceedings of the*

SIGCHI Conference on Human Factors in Computing Systems, 811–20. http://dx.doi.org/10.1145/2470654.2470770.

Levine, Richard M. 1993. "I Feel Your Pain." *Mother Jones* 18 (4): 22–26.

López, Ian Haney. 2014. *Dog Whistle Politics: How Coded Racial Appeals Have Reinvented Racism and Wrecked the Middle Class*. New York: Oxford University Press.

McCafferty, Dennis. 2011. "Activism vs. Slacktivism." *Communications of the ACM* 54 (12): 17–19. http://dx.doi.org/10.1145/2043174.2043182.

McCaughey, Martha, and Michael D. Ayers, eds. 2003. *Cyberactivism: Online Activism in Theory and Practice*. London: Routledge.

Mitchell, Greg. 2011. *40 Days That Shook the World: From Occupy Wall Street to Occupy Everywhere*. New York: Sinclair Books.

Nichols, John. 2011. "The 99 Percent Rise Up." *Nation*. 2012. http://www.thenation.com/article/99-percent-rise/.

Overington, Michael A. 1977. "Kenneth Burke and the Method of Dramatism." *Theory and Society* 4 (1): 131–56. http://dx.doi.org/10.1007/BF00209747.

Stiglitz, Joseph E. 2011. "Of the 1%, by the 1%, for the 1%." *Vanity Fair*.http://www.vanityfair.com/society/features/2011/05/top-one-percent-201105.

Taibbi, Matt. 2011. "Why Rush Limbaugh Is Freaking Out about Occupy Wall Street." *Rolling Stone*. www.rollingstone.com/politics/blogs/taibblog/why-rush-limbaugh-is-freaking-out-about-occupy-wall-street-20111018.

Trainor, Jennifer Seibel. 2008. "The Emotioned Power of Racism: An Ethnographic Portrait of an All-White High School." *College Composition and Communication* 60 (1): 82–112.

Wise, Tim. 2010. *Colorblind: The Rise of Post-Racial Politics and the Retreat from Racial Equity*. San Francisco: City Lights.

Writers for the 99%. 2011. *Occupying Wall Street: The Inside Story of an Action that Changed America*. New York: OR Books.

10
AMERICAN RHETORICS OF DISAPPEARANCE
Translocal Feminist Problem-Solving Rhetorics

Tricia Serviss

Ciudad Juarez, in the Mexican state of Chihuahua and across from the city of El Paso in the US state of Texas, is an American[1] city that became famous for disappearances—sometimes called forced disappearance— when reports of missing women circulated widely in 1993. The women were often last seen in transit to school, work, or home as they moved through public spaces (buses, sidewalks, and desert streets). Some murdered women were discovered, often alongside evidence of their rape, torture, mutilation, and death, in mass graves in desert areas between the factory regions (the *maquiladoras* and surrounding temporary housing) of Ciudad Juarez and El Paso (Luevano 2012; Pineda-Madrid 2011; Salzinger 2003; Staudt 2008; Staudt, Payan, and Kruszewski 2009; Valdez 2006; Wright 2001, 2006). In response to these devastating circumstances, the women of Juarez invented a number of rhetorical practices that were uniquely tied to their situation and brought attention to the tragedies that affected their lives. Those of us invested in understanding how language wields power, especially as we determine and cross borders, need to delineate rhetorical systems of disappearance, like those of these women and others in the Americas; teach our students to see them at work; and respond to these systems not only as legal or feminist problems but also as rhetorical problems with, perhaps, rhetorical solutions.

To defend my claim above, in this chapter I begin by defining the phenomenon of disappearance and how it has played out in Juarez, resulting in a popularized, dramatized rhetoric of disappearance that obscures the specific nature of the rhetoric of the activists themselves. I next go on to introduce rhetorical problems that arise from such disappearances in Juarez and Argentina. I explain how women rhetors in the Americas have invented rhetorical solutions to these material

DOI: 10.7330/9781607324034.c010

problems and how we need to consider them as translocal practices, studying them through a transcontextual approach. As a demonstration of why this approach is important, I next examine the advocacy efforts of Amnesty International, showing how their tactics—while helpful in protesting disappearance—obscure and often erase the distinct rhetorical approaches of women in Argentina and Juarez and important dimensions of their unique circumstances, and I explore further how approaches of the women in Juarez, often thought to have origins in Argentinian rhetorics, are in fact uniquely their own. Ultimately, I argue that we can learn from the rhetorical problem-solving strategies of these women as citizens, scholars, and students, claiming that we not only need to better understand and value the critical stakes for women in the Americas who are rhetorically and physically facing disappearance but also that we need to recognize the rhetorical solutions activists generate that expand current rhetorical traditions.

THE PHENOMENON OF DISAPPEARANCE AND ITS EMERGENCE IN JUAREZ

Disappearance Defined

While *disappeared* or *disappearance* are terms used differently across many organizations, institutions, and academic disciplines involved with Latin American issues, the term *disappearance* gained some stability when, in 2006, the International Convention for the Protection of All Persons from Forced Disappearance was formed as an instrument of the United Nations during the 2006 United Nations Convention against Torture. The ratified United Nations resolution not only makes "disappearance" an international crime, but also defines "enforced disappearance" as "the arrest, detention, abduction or any other form of deprivation of liberty by agents of the State or by persons or groups of persons acting with the authorization, support or acquiescence of the State, followed by a refusal to acknowledge the deprivation of liberty or by concealment of the fate or whereabouts of the disappeared person, which place such a person outside the protection of the law" (United Nations 2006, 2).

Disappearance is internationally defined, then, as the result of organized actions of the state or groups allowed impunity from the general laws of that state. Disappearance, as a cultural activity, is often tied to colonialism and the rhetorical traditions of state-sponsored boundaries and borders. It is helpful to consider notable American historical moments—from the removal of indigenous groups in both North and Latin America from ancestral homes to the state-authorized annexation of territories in documents such as the Treaty of Guadalupe Hidalgo—in the context of American *disappearance* or *enforced disappearance*. While removal, displacement, and disappearance happen in various settings in the world, incidents of disappearance in the Americas have coherence across political borders in unique ways, even as we live in an era marked by transnational living.

While phrases like *forced disappearance* can evoke a far-off landscape—the so-called western frontier in the United States or civil wars in Argentina or El Salvador—for many people living in contemporary Northern America, *forced disappearance* has greater resonance here when contextualized with ongoing life in the Americas. We can look back to our recent—and ongoing—histories to see how American disappearance continues as a rhetorical phenomenon with material consequences. Rhetorical ecosystems that bind the stories of American disappearance abound: events in New York City on 9/11, the continual deployment of US soldiers to wars in the Middle East, narco wars blanketing northern Mexico, and more engage rhetorics of disappearance. When we look back still further, we can relate these incidents and show how the disappearances of women in Ciudad Juarez that began to receive attention in 1993—what we now understand as a large-scale phenomenon known as *femicide*[2]—might best be understood in the context of a rhetorical tradition of *disappearance* in the Americas. Understanding Juarez femicide as a site of American disappearance rhetorics helps us both to understand—and contemplate appropriate responses to—the American rhetorical tradition of *disappearance*, which we interpret as an often horrific attempt to manage, manipulate, and tame particularly unruly physical boundaries in the Western Hemisphere.

Disappearance in Juarez

Ciudad Juarez was imagined from the early 1960s as the "laboratory" of a newly globalizing economic system of the Western Hemisphere (Bowden 1998). It was imagined as a primary site for understanding the boom of a twentieth-century industrializing Mexico and greater Latin America, where foreign-owned factories, known as *maquiladoras*, were constructed in the 1960s and 1970s. By the 1980s, Juarez was the fastest-growing city in Mexico, with the population increasing annually by 166 percent (Nevins 2001). The more than four hundred *maquilas* of Juarez transformed the landscape, the demographics, and the culture of Juarez itself as new ecosystems—cultural, economical, environmental, rhetorical—formed. Economic boom, transnational cultural leadership, regional drug-cartel violence, and border-security policies contributed to a dramatic shift in the city. When 383 women were internationally reported as victims of Juarez femicide in 1993, Ciudad Juarez also emerged as the seat of globalized, gender-based, transnational violence, attracting attention from a wide audience (de Alba 2005).

The entertainment industry fixated on the "story"; Juarez femicide narratives began to *write over* the lives of the murdered women, their families, and the writings of the families about femicide (Duarte 2008; Rodriguez 2007). Films (see *The Virgin of Juarez, Bordertown, Juarez Mexico*, and *Backyard*), novels (such as *Desert Blood: The Juarez Murders, Juarez: A Novel, 2666*), and popular publications (see articles in the *New Yorker, Harper's*, and more) reported and dramatized the femicides. In addition, artists invited consciousness raising and engaged in epideictic odes as they explained their work (see Lisa Bjorne Linnert [2006] on the international collaborative art project called *Desconocida Unknown Ukjent* and the work of Arianna Garcia-Fialdini [2011] for helpful examples). Unfortunately, Juarez femicide resistance rhetorics and writings were absorbed into this wider sensationalized tradition of Latin American disappearance as fiction and creative nonfiction confused facts and cast doubt on the events (Partnoy 2008). Disappearance, as or infused with a set of American tropes, is an often-simplified discourse with conquest as a foundational premise and accessible analytic stance (Arditti 1999; Mignolo 2003). Missing-person fliers, monuments, legal appeals, narratives of secret mass atrocities, proceedings of inter-American councils, and more embody those tropes. The roots of these genres of disappearance are deeper and more diverse than is often obvious; scholarship about them has previously been limited to those in the anthropological, sociological, and political science disciplines (e.g., Crenzel 2011; Grandin, Levenson, and Oglesby 2011; Guest 2000).

JUAREZ FEMICIDE AND ARGENTINE DISAPPEARANCE RHETORICS: A SITE FOR TRANSCONTEXTUAL APPROACHES TO TRANSLOCAL RHETORICS

Two dominant origin stories are often used to understand Juarez activist rhetorics. One origin story casts the rhetorics of Juarez mothers as descended from Amnesty International. The Urgent Action appeals of Amnesty International (AI)—letters that petition governments to intervene into a human rights concern within their jurisdiction—is central to this discussion. In this narrative, activists who emerge, organize, and respond to Juarez femicide merely inherit the rhetorical traditions of AI, born in Europe decades before. A second origin story of Juarez activism, less obvious and less popular but crucially important, explains Juarez activist rhetorics as connected to the rhetorical traditions of other American activist women, most directly the Argentine Mothers of the Plaza.³

This chapter deciphers these narratives and connections, taking care to avoid conflating these traditions. Upon first glance it may seem that Juarez activist rhetorics are simple imitations of existing activist responses to disappearance and femicide in the Americas. Yet it is important to complicate such simplification and explore the notion that rhetorics and literacies are always local as well as translocal—always premised upon rhetorical traditions and literacy practices already at play in other places and simultaneously developing locally. Thus, the emergence of these activist writings is truly constituted by their duality, both tied to local context and influenced by transcontextual American rhetorical traditions. To associate the writings of Juarez women with the rhetorical strategies of both AI and Mothers of the Plaza is a logical assumption, but assuming such a genealogy is also troubling in that Juarez women activists are then removed from their work within the rhetorical materiality of Ciudad Juarez. As an alternative to this view, I argue that Juarez activism isn't simply inherited from AI; Juarez rhetorics are translocal and transamerican rhetorical adaptations and inventions. This kind of translocal orientation disrupts views of the world as demarcated by clear political and cultural borders. The translocal perspective, for those of us interested in rhetorical practices, requires us to view the world as inherently both local and networked; we must focus first on situated practices of activists to understand local ecosystems, yet we must also simultaneously approach those local ecosystems as connected to networks often disjointed by traditional notions of borders in all forms (time, language, geography). With this view in mind, I argue that the Juarez activist is defined in Juarez by circumstance and practice but best understood and valued by contextualizing Juarez rhetorical problem solving with similar rhetorical problems of disappearance in other localities.

In some discourses about activist rhetoric, the rhetoric of Juarez women is celebrated as the result of Western advocacy groups like AI. Such scholarship pursues accurate description of such high-stake situations, shedding light on happenings in areas difficult to access and work in to advocate for women's rights (Fragoso 2002; Wright 2006;). The result, however, is that wider audiences often fail to recognize the unique literacies and rhetorics developed by Juarez women to make influential public arguments about the femicides (see Serviss 2013;

Wright 2001). It is crucially important that we investigate these kinds of rhetorical spaces and movements, discovering even more "little narratives of literacy" (Daniell 1999) that help us better understand new rhetorical situations such as transnational activism. We need to see and understand how rhetorical problem solving in these contexts is working to develop useful and ethical rhetorical solutions to serious problems. We need to explore both the local, little narratives of writing and rhetoric in the Americas as well as their interactions and transcontextual lives beyond those sites. In an effort to begin this work, in this chapter I describe related rhetorical strategies developed both locally and transcontextually as American mothers in Juarez and Argentina respond to the horrors of American forced disappearance.

A place to begin is to understand forced disappearance as a global historical reality and a continuing problem with local dimensions. Forced disappearance is an old human warfare tactic; it is also one that has come to be directly associated with the "idea of Latin America" (Dussel 2008; Mignolo 2003, 2005). Yet, disappearance is often dangerously cast as a *new* and emerging genre of violence, the result of globalization and transnational living. This casting can simplify discussions, as transnational feminist rhetorical studies scholars (Dingo 2012; Hesford 2005, 2011; Rice 2012; Schell 2006; Wingard 2012) rightly point out. Misattribution, co-opting, and heroic rescue narratives abound as local and translocal agents interact, transfer, and exchange rhetorical strategies, genres, and practices. In these exchanges, much can be gained to advance the activists' cause, but the lineages, genealogies, and therefore agencies of the actors involved are at risk in engaging in such exchanges. In some cases the risks are tied to materiality and even symbolic capital, but in other cases the risks of engaging in such exchanges can have troubling consequences. Wendy Hesford's (2005) discussion of the "pornographic" photographs that circulated and drew commentary by journalists and academics alike is a helpful example. Hesford (2011), in her text *Spectacular Rhetorics: Human Rights Visions, Recognitions, Feminisms*, recognizes the fixation on Abu Graib abuse images as a repurposing of representations of suffering; she calls this rhetorical move "an act of spectacular rhetoric." The photos, depicting human-rights abuse at the hands of United States soldiers, become an additional layer of exploitation their circulation was theoretically meant to interrupt. The photos capture and expose abuses but also revise them as Western audiences hyperfocused on these images, rewriting the Western viewer as both a victim and aggressor in the era of terrorism. The images, arguably in circulation to stop such abuses, problematically encourage viewers to trade in their role as potentially allied witness for the role of complacent participant. Rather than witnessing and halting abuses, the images become an additional form of abuse themselves in this way. Thus, much is at stake when working with representations of others and their suffering, even for well-intended, alert audiences.

Even as we acknowledge such dangers of simplifying, conflating, or appropriating the practices of others in these kinds of (mis)exchanges, we as scholars can all too easily collapse various American women's rhetorics together, and, unfortunately, therefore essentialize the work of those women that our scholarship works to disentangle from such global conflations. Thus, it is crucial that we distinguish between transnationalism and a different orientation I call *translocalizm* (see Brandt and Clinton's 2009 treatment of transcontextual literacy research). Key differences between transnational and translocal orientations are important to the inquiry described in this chapter. If we adopt a transnational orientation similar to AI's stance—advocating use of similar strategies to analyze discourse in very different sites of disappearance—we might sacrifice important local differences in hopes of creating a systematized tradition. AI's primary goals are aligning issues and strategies as more shared than divergent, arguing that the femicides happening now in Guatemala, for example, are *very nearly the same* as femicides happening in northern Mexico (Amnesty International 2009a, 2009b).

While a useful promotional technique, this essentializing also obscures some of the local specifics (strategies of Juarez activists addressing the unique context created by the proximity of *maquiladoras*, for example) that exist. While Juarez strategies can become useful to other activists in other contexts, it is important that those strategies be appreciated as both a local solution to a local problem and a potentially transportable solution for others to adopt and adapt. To achieve such aims, I specifically take up the work of Brandt and Clinton (2009) as they call for more intentionally "transcontextualized" and "transcontextualizing" literacy research that alleviates the polemics that comparative rhetorics and essentializing narratives of Western activist rhetorics can often generate. This kind of translocal orientation to understanding these incidents and their contexts, I argue, changes the conversation dramatically; translocal orientations are driven by strategic synthesis, an ecological approach to understanding rhetorical practices as embedded in networks rather than stretched across borders. Thus, strategically considering the activist writings of Juarez and Argentine mothers as both groups respond to local mass disappearances—alongside but separate from AI activist instruction—is an attempt to both synthesize and parse out local and translocal rhetorics from one another. This kind of translocal research illuminates a key tension in the study of writing and rhetorical practices across contexts, highlighting the required conceptual and methodological border crossing for continued study of American rhetorics. This latter position is developed from inquiries about literate and rhetorical practices that are interpreted as inherently social and local, tied to situated practices (Barton and Hamilton 1998; Besnier 1995; Cintron 1997; Gee 1990; Heath 1983; Scribner and Cole 1981; Street 1984).

AMNESTY INTERNATIONAL, THE TRANSNATIONAL EPISTOLARY APPEAL, AND THE ERASURE OF TRANSLOCAL RHETORICS

Founded in 1961 by London lawyer Peter Benenson, AI has historically relied upon legal genres to pressure nation-states into international human-rights laws adherence (Ron, Ramos, and Rodgers 2005). Direct Action campaigns were developed early in the organization's history (first used in 1965, which culminated in the successful release of a prisoner in 1973) as letter-writing campaigns focused upon freeing citizens imprisoned for dissidence. These were legal requests written as civic epistles and modeled after Western *habeas corpus*. The letters, written by attorneys, were signed and submitted to local governments by citizens around the world. Direct Action epistles were designed to bring about the release of imprisoned individuals. AI imagined its campaigns as "undertaking research and action focused on preventing and ending grave abuses of the rights to physical and mental integrity, freedom of conscience and expression, and freedom from discrimination, within the context of its work to promote all human rights" (Amnesty International 2013). Such AI efforts relied upon a genre I call the *epistolary appeal* and AI now calls "Urgent Action" campaigns. I forward the term *epistolary appeal* to describe how AI's Urgent Action campaigns depended upon large numbers of citizens submitting the *same* letter (or epistle) with the *same* message to government officials in solidarity and mass congruence. The genre comes from the "letters" of the *writ of habeas corpus* that evolved by the end of the thirteenth century with the passage of the Magna Carta. Epistolary appeals are, by historic use and design, both deeply locally focused, addressing a local problem, and translocally constituted. The epistolary appeal is valued because of its ability to travel while retaining its integrity, because of its ability to unite people separated by physical distance, and because of its ability to affect the contexts it traverses all at once.

According to AI, the Urgent Action campaign began as a transcontextual epistolary appeal (Amnesty International 2007). Citizens first in

London and then around the world wrote letters similarly composed of two sections per letter: each letter housed both an individual (local) statement expressing concern to the government and a section that appeared in every letter in the same way (creating translocal cohesion), expressing the citizens' shared concerns to the government. The letters, housing both the local and translocal manifestation of an epistolary appeal, expressed grievances about the country's detention of the political prisoner and requested release. The first campaign began in 1965 when letters were sent to the Brazilian government requesting the release of academic Luiz Basilio Rossi,[4] who was eventually released in 1973. The circulation and submission of the letters, written on precomposed, preaddressed postcards, was credited for Rossi's release. AI began to offer "appeal kits" to chapters around the West and Westernized world, providing necessities for epistolary campaigns advocating the release of political prisoners. From conception, the goal was transnational civic involvement in campaigns, enlisting an international citizenry in the regulation of human rights. AI was credited with the genre's formation and success once kits popularized the tradition of epistolary appeals. While the work of AI is admirable and crucially important to the development of human rights advocacy in the twentieth century, the monolithic representation of the epistolary appeal—a fluid, adaptive genre and rhetorical strategy that emerged well before the twentieth century—obscures how American activists can use it translocally.

*Amnesty International and the Translocal Rhetoric
of the Argentina Mothers of the Plaza*

By the late 1970s, AI targeted American disappearances—in Chile, Argentina, Peru, and Guatemala—using the same epistolary-appeals approach. AI arrived in Argentina in 1977 following several national events there: La Noche de los Lápices,[5] the Night of the Pencils, and the start of the Argentinian Dirty War[6] (Bouvard 1994; Fisher 1989). What does not appear in AI's own history is *how* AI's involvement there began. One history suggests that AI imported epistolary-appeal kits that enabled the Mothers of the Plaza to protest, arming them with rhetorical strategies they would not have otherwise had. Other accounts complicate this model of simple exportation and depict the Argentine mothers' rhetorical strategies as more translocal, transcontextual attempts to solve problems.

On April 30, 1977, Argentine mothers walked together in Plaza de Mayo near the presidential palace, protesting the disappearance of their children (Fisher 1989). By November, over one hundred mothers gathered every Thursday afternoon, even as nineteen mothers were themselves forcibly disappeared. Initially, according to mother Aida de Suarez, the Mothers of the Plaza first gathered to perform what they considered subtle public appeals (Fisher 1989). They met and walked together in small circles for hours. They created a physical appeal, rooted in implicit solidarity rather than explicit confrontation. Over time, the Mothers performed more explicit gestures of protestation, using symbols—roses, Catholic prayer books, and knitting projects—to unify themselves, highlighting their shared Catholic faith and woman/motherhood to attract empathetic attention. Eventually the emboldened Mothers wore white head scarves in symbolic solidarity with their innocent children (alluding to their infancy and diapers, reportedly) (Fisher 1989).

White head scarves were also worn as symbols of their shared resistance to the continued disappearances of their children and an appeal for their children's release. So many Argentinians began gathering that it became difficult to identify the Mothers among the crowds, so Aida de Saurez reports, "We circulated a message: Bring something of your child to the Plaza to identify yourself as a mother" (Fisher 1989, 88). Many brought childhood mementos. The white head scarves—and these mementos—evoked their rights as mother-citizens. The display of the scarves became a different kind of epistolary appeal that implicated all mothers in the struggle. The epistolary appeals of 1977 Argentina complicated the rhetorical traditions of disappearance. Rather than the simple implementation of AI appeal kits, the white-scarf appeals are the result of converging strategies and rhetorical traditions. The Mothers of the Plaza invented and deployed their own appeals to their peril. Alongside appeal genres already in circulation, their strategies for protestation in the Plaza emerged from their contexts, agency, and positionality as Argentine women.

Dora de Bazze, an Argentine Mother of the Plaza, describes the emergence of their strategy and the "problems" of "organizing" the Mothers. She writes, "We tried to produce leaflets . . . and little stickers saying the mothers will be in such and such a place on such a day and 'Where are our disappeared children?' or 'The military have taken our children.' We went out at night to stick them on the buses and underground trains. And we wrote messages on peso notes so that as many people as possible would see them" (Fisher 1989, 53). While these campaigns helped, de Bazze describes their ambulatory appeals—walking together, physically representing their children—to be their most successful appeals. At the end of each walk they presented officials with an official epistolary appeal, a form letter listing grievances and redresses along with a list of their children's names.

Two years after the Mothers of the Plaza campaigns began, AI sent delegates to Argentina a second time to design a supporting campaign. AI's campaign was an Urgent Action campaign. With AI's presence, methods shifted in Argentina, overwriting one another, becoming transformed and even reformed. The Mothers' arguments were suddenly recognized and valued more readily, highlighted by AI and international press. The use of epistolary appeals—or any form of that appeal's genre—was considered the result of AI's activist curriculum that AI argued was a tool for export and use in creating democracy anywhere. Even as Argentine mothers continued their own campaign practices, their rhetorical strategies began to be attributed to AI. The "export" of AI methods was celebrated; rhetorics and campaigns emerging from the Argentine Mothers were subsumed by such praise.

The rhetorics of the Mothers of the Plaza, rooted in the everyday practices of their culture, language, histories, religion, gender, and class, were condensed and simplified as the result of AI's campaigns. The consequence of such conflation and reduction is the decontextualization and therefore dismissal of the actual rhetorics invented and deployed by the Mothers of the Plaza. Here we see the erasure of the local in favor of the transnational.

To suggest AI or any other organization constitutes the universal rhetoric of American disappearance activism is to disenfranchise and conceal the discrete though interconnected—the transcontextual—rhetorical strategies developed by groups such as the Mothers of the Plaza. Yet, the trend continues. AI itself does not claim to be a centralizing, parental rhetorical force. Yet the discourses surrounding AI as a transnational, Westernized, nongovernment organization (an NGO) often explain these seemingly shared genres and practices as authoritatively derived from AI, reading activist rhetorical acts and artifacts in the Americas as unified and even imitative of activist practices of Western-style democratic countries embodied by the United Kingdom and the United States.

This altered vision of transnational rhetorics of disappearance deflates the rhetorical practices of individual groups, making the Mothers of the Plaza seem standard alongside American disappearances in entirely different contexts. The recognizable conventions used by AI in the epistolary appeals—the portraiture, the descriptions of the disappearance, the pleas for the return of the disappeared—obscure the specific work of local rhetors. This work is most often obscured by NGOs like AI operating in borderlands where rhetorical inventions are often overlooked in favor of established traditions. AI deeply influences how borderlands are understood and imagined by scholars and citizens alike who don't access borderlands physically or conceptually. AI attributes the rhetorical inventions of the Mothers of the Plaza to existing traditions (like the Direct Action appeals developed by AI collaborators in the early 1970s) in favor of the more difficult task of learning about the Mothers' practices and contributing strategies. In this context, borderland NGO observers, AI specifically in this case, attach emerging practices to ongoing traditions to sort out, stabilize, and quickly explain what is happening in the between spaces of the borders. These representations that favor tradition, stripping local rhetors of their agency, are flawed and thwart the development of productive relationships between and across activist groups working in localities themselves.

Another Translocal Rhetoric: The Emergence of the Juarez Appeal

In 1993 a coalition of Juarez activist organizations joined to form *Coordinadora de organismos no gubernamentales contra la violencia hacia las mujeres* (Coordination of Non-Governmental Organizations against Violence toward Women), a local and transnational NGO. Their declared goal was more rigorous policing and investigation of the Juarez femicides (Wright 2004). At the same time, Esther Chavez Cano, founder of the Juarez rape-crisis center *Casa Amiga*, archived reporting of the femicides[7] to document fallacious representations (Wright 2004). The coalition's work and Chavez's archive still vastly inform local understandings of the femicides. The coalition was made of several conjoining organizations such as *Justicia para nuestra hijas*[8] (Justice for Our Daughters), *Nuestras hijas de regreso a casa*[9] (May Our Daughters Return Home), and *Casa Amiga* Rape and Crisis Center. Juarez mothers developed campaigns that brought international attention focused upon the femicides as reports circulated in local newspapers such as the *El Paso Times* and *Diaro* as well as broader venues such as the *New Yorker*, the *New York Times*, the *Los Angeles Times*, and the *Guardian*—all depicting activist work in Juarez. Most of these reports described the work as AI designed and directed. Three main campaigns were eventually given the most international attention (indicated here as the Cross Campaign, March of the Weeping Women, and the Postcard Campaign); yet these three campaigns were all products of local rhetors and rhetorical traditions of the Americas even as AI was often assigned authorship.

A notable example of the erasure of translocal activist rhetorics in favor of transnational NGO activist campaigns is the Cross Campaign of voces sin eco (Voices without Echo), a group formed in 1998 by Juarez mothers Irma Perez and Guillermina Gonzalez. The campaign is recorded as the first to use the now iconic symbol of the pink cross to represent women killed by femicide. Perez describes the development of the cross campaign of Voces:

> We had to find a way to take control of the voices of our daughters. We who had no hope of finding our children alive, we at least had hope of recovering their lives in this way . . . [yet] sometimes our members couldn't make the meetings because they didn't have the money for bus fare . . . [and then] one of the larger organizations would step in. Amnesty International would offer us materials to use and plans to follow, but mostly we needed them for the money. To make our own statements in ways that would be heard in Juarez. (Valdez 2006, 37)

Voces sin eco's own website, now defunct, describes activist projects—such as the campaign to create and erect pink crosses to interrupt Juarez public discourses that depicted those killed in the femicides as "loose women" or "prostitutes"—as working toward several goals (Voces 1998b, 2001). They describe their mission as an "attempt to rectify the violence of the women's voicelessness, by speaking for and on behalf of the dis(re)membered remains." They write, "Perhaps unsurprisingly (given the need for Voces sin eco's existence and also given predominant narratives of rape in Western legal culture) investigations into the murders often become investigations into the women's own lifestyles instead of searches for killers" (Voces 1998b). The crosses, Voces reason in their 1998 "Cross Campaign" entry, simultaneously represent individual women and bring greater consideration to their collective deaths. Hundreds of crosses, distinguished only with names, eventually lined open fields, de facto garbage heaps, city sidewalks, and church plazas in Juarez; they remain in hypervisible places today (such as the base of the Santa Fe Bridge that connects Juarez and El Paso). Activists erected crosses where bodies of femicide victims were once found, creating monuments within landfills and alleyways. The crosses, Perez remarks on the Voces website, were meant to "startle" and "surprise" Juarez citizens into reconsidering the "merely sexual nature of the crimes so that our daughters might become more similar to their own daughters than prostitutes and Americanized working women" (Voces 1998a). The crosses were also drawing on the flexibility of symbolic systems, signaling participation across linguistic and cultural borders. The crosses were beyond English/Spanish or Christian/*curanderos* (indigenous) binaries.

Put another way, these crosses were designed to be translocal; the crosses were both drawing on and forwarding a rhetorical situation that was deeply transcontextual (Brandt and Clinton 2009). The crosses were deeply local as they emerged from the materiality of Juarez femicide. Yet the crosses were also designed to be persuasive beyond the locale of Juarez femicide. They are meant to be translocally useful in other contexts (used by activists in response to Guatemalan femicide and recently in Honduras as a sign of unjust violence and mass disappearance) as well, contributing to the accumulation of both local and translocal contexts and arguments.

Artifacts from the Voces cross campaigns now populate both Juarez and El Paso landscapes; they even reach beyond that to places like Los Angeles and Buenos Aires. Gonzalez comments on the strategies behind such a translocal campaign, writing, "We must not accept the shame that they attempt to paint on our daughters. We repaint them today as a cross . . . so that every Christian who encounters the crosses will recognize [our daughters] as suffering as Christ suffered. We draw on traditions that are bigger than Juarez, bigger than Mexico, bigger than maquiladoras" (Valdez 2006, 38). Perez and Gonzalez explain their cross campaigns as a rearticulation and reinvention of the belief systems that contribute to the murders of their daughters.

A prime example of this expansive strategy is the establishment of what Gonzalez calls an "altar" at the base of the Santa Fe Bridge in Juarez. The display is a physical and conceptual intersection between Catholic and *curandera* or indigenous healing rhetorics, an accumulation of argumentative layers. Gonzalez talks about the "use of the crucifix" along with "curandero traditional altars" as a representation of their daughters as both traditional and revolutionary Mexican women (Valdez 2006, 77). While Gonzalez and Perez both acknowledge their strategic use of traditional Catholic discourse, iconography, and practices, they simultaneously talk about their disappointment at the lack of church critique of femicide. Yet they express gratitude to some church leaders who encouraged them to "use Catholic discourse" to make powerful arguments of resistance in public discourse, even as the church does nothing to officially support their cause. Perez explains, "The Church is a site of resistance in Mexico, but not in obvious ways. They are more like [hidden] sponsors of our campaigns. They encourage us to use Catholic teachings and symbols, especially ones that show the Church's sympathies. To emphasize our points. But they don't tell us how" (Valdez 2006, 42).

Thus, Voces created a crucifix-like image at the Santa Fe Bridge. A metal cross with nails represents the simultaneous passion of Christ and the passion of the murdered women. Likewise, Gonzalez cites intentional connections between the passion of their daughters and the lives of the Virgin of Guadalupe, Latina/o American martyrs (such as Bishop Oscar Romero[10]), and saints. Voces reports maintenance of a familiar "mestiza presentation" in the cross campaign as a way to utilize the general *lack* of church involvement. "The presence of the crosses around the city creates more possibility than any letters to the government would. The crosses require other Mexicans to take ownership of their shame. It requires the Church to notice our daughters as martyrs," Perez says (Valdez 2006, 44). Voces mothers craft rhetorical performances and lasting artifacts that recast the vilified murdered women of Juarez, using symbols of pain in Catholic Mexico (the crucifixion), corrupt relationships between Catholicism and governments in Latin America (embodied by references to Oscar Romero, who spoke out against governmental abuses even as the church officially avoided the conflict), and redemption (all that follows the crucifixion). The crosses comment directly on Juarez femicide but also convey meaning about women's lives in translocal, related settings as they accumulate layers of meaning born from Latin American Catholicism and its tensions. They both specifically signify Juarez femicide and femicide more broadly, as well as Juarez disappearances and American disappearances more broadly. Thus, the cross campaigns are intentionally both local and translocal, evoking locally specific events and tensions while also drawing on broader American rhetorical traditions[11] in hopes of reaching local and broad audiences in meaningful ways.

CONCLUSION AND IMPLICATIONS

In 2007, Juarez mothers were invited to speak with actress and international performer Jennifer Lopez to support the launch of her AI-sponsored film *Bordertown*. Juarez mothers reportedly explained to journalists during their accompanying speaking tour, "We were invited here to support the work of Amnesty International. We would rather tell you about our daughters. They are still missing . . . and more every day. We appreciate interest from far away places, but our goal is for the end of impunity here. We work for changes here. We speak for ourselves. We work on our own behalf" (Amnesty International 2009b). What we learn from this moment—and our study of the rhetorical problems of American disappearance—is the importance of seeing local activities in translocal contexts, adopting methodological stances that allow us to see rhetorical happenings this way as researchers, and using transnational perspectives that make witnessing and intervening in such horrific situations as citizens probable, a key feature of rhetoric itself.

The Juarez mothers, while clearly bringing to attention the material reality of their losses, also bring to our attention, as rhetoricians, the consequences of dismissing a local perspective on the rhetorical work of activists in dire situations. To acknowledge such work, we must adopt a different orientation toward our work, one more sensitive to both translocal and transnational discourses and the physical situations that inspire them. Virgilio Elizondo's (1997) *Guadalupe: Mother of the New Creation* concretizes just such an orientation in his translation, from Nahuatl to English, of Juan Diego's 1531 narrative near Tepeyac Hill, just outside of modern-day Mexico City. Elizondo includes extensive footnotes explaining the importance of particular translation decisions and interpretations. What is crucial, he implies, is the simultaneity of contexts pressing upon Juan Diego and others working to stabilize the stories of the Virgin of Guadalupe. Elizondo explains the lamentation of Juan Diego's layers of world views—those before and after contact with Catholic Spaniards— that become fused together. Diego's world became, Elizondo writes, *mestizo*—a word used to describe a mixture of cultures and, in the context of Mexico specifically, the mixture of Catholic Spanish and indigenous Mesoamerican cultures after the Spanish invasion—in that moment, unknowable without an appreciation for the compressed layers of meaning systems. Diego was using a screen. Recognizing those layers, those analytic moves and rhetorical instincts, is foundational to *mestizo* epistemologies, Elizondo suggests, and, I would add, *mestizo* rhetorics. In that *mestizo* context, rhetorical strategies became not only local but also translocal by necessity as colonization created an inherently networked world. When Elizondo (2000) declares the *Future is Mestizo* in a later work, he is forwarding this exact sentiment, drawing attention to the Western Hemisphere as a land of translocality. Elizondo is also challenging scholars interested in such tensions to reorient our intellectual and research strategies to account for that *mestizo* world. In that world there is room, value, and perhaps even an imperative to seek out these translocal accumulations that repurpose borders and boundaries themselves.

And if we indeed adopt the orientation I have proposed, what then can be done in the face of such terrible situations to appropriately describe and interpret the rhetorical problems they pose for those who suffer them? The partnerships between local activists and transnational NGOs like AI are imperfect but important for addressing rhetorical and material realities in the Americas. As citizens, we can listen, triangulate, and ultimately insist upon the establishment of inter-American infrastructures such as the Inter-American Human Rights Council (created by the Organization of American States in 1959 to mediate between nations in Latin America) to help sufferers address material realities; as rhetoricians and researchers, we can ask our colleagues to adopt an inter-American perspective that views American countries as connected and perpetually in exchange so we can more effectively interpret the work of local activists; we can ask our students to get involved from a point of inter-American citizenship (positioning themselves as interested in not just their own country but the ecosystem that surrounds it as well) themselves. As researchers, this might mean adopting a trans-contextual view methodologically, not only in the representation of our research materials as derived from multiple sources but also in the documentation of our analysis as derived from multiple analytic and research traditions. For me, as a researcher, this means deliberately pursuing synthesis across research sites and looking for opportunities to create productive, conceptual foils across sites of activist rhetorical activity. This kind of research is very different from what some call *comparative* or *contrastive* studies of rhetoric that look at two separate rhetorical spheres. The research I hope we'll begin to pursue, most simply, will work to value relationships and networks between research sites and materials where traditional boundaries (cultural, geopolitical, genre based) once isolated our focus, making rhetorical activities seem singular, constricted by the borders we assign to them to make our research orderly and easily defined. We might consider that our fields of study—those of us interested in rhetoric as well as those of us studying the Americas—ought to be permeable, inter- and trans-, as we attempt to solve complicated, transnational problems. We begin this work when we consider these American sites of activism that bring to light rhetorical problems—in Juarez and Argentina—and, most important, bring rhetorical problem-solving strategies together across localities, genres, and the complicated problems associated with rhetorics of American disappearance.

Notes

1. I use the term *American* throughout the piece to mean a transnational space spanning the American continents, areas usually seen as distinct due to nation-state borders. Since "American" human rights laws will be discussed throughout this chapter, it is appropriate to emphasize the ways that *American* works as an adjective.
2. The term *femicide* is typically defined as the "assassination of women" via disappearance, murder, and sexual violence. The term *femicide* was also used by scholars in the fields of geography, economics, political science, anthropology, and women's studies as early as the 1970s to convey the idea that the systematic murder of women is a form of "female genocide" or "gender murder" (Fragoso 2002; Russell

1992; Wright 2001). The term *femicide* argues that women are being killed based upon their femininity, their lack of cultural value as female bodies, their cultural positionality as worker bodies that reproduce more workers, the instability of the region revealed by the perilous position of a female body in a patriarchal system, and so on. Activist groups such as *Nuestras hijas* and *Justicia* use the term to mean "assassination of women" with "impunity" for male perpetrators.

3. The Argentine Mothers of the Plaza are internationally recognized for their organized response to the abduction—the forced disappearance—of their children during the so-called Dirty War of Argentina that took place between 1976 and 1983.
4. Amnesty International's history explains that Professor Luiz Basilio Rossi was arrested for political reasons. Luiz Rossi wrote, "[I] knew that my case had become public, I knew they could no longer kill me. Then the pressure on me decreased and conditions improved." It was the first Urgent Action campaign. Rossi was eventually freed in October 1973, according to Bryan Subherwal in a post to the blog *Human Rights Now* on May 25, 2011.
5. The Night of the Pencils refers to September 1976 when, after months of protests, ten student leaders were disappeared by state order, accused of insurrection. It is primarily the mothers of these disappeared student leaders who became known as the Mothers of the Plaza de Mayo (Hodges 1991).
6. The Dirty War was a campaign launched by the leaders of Argentina who overthrew the democratically elected president in a coup and established a military dictatorship in March 1976.
7. The archive is now housed in the library of the University of New Mexico.
8. *Justicia* was founded by several mothers, notably Irma Perez, Soledad Aguilar, and Ramona Morales, in conjunction with a network of eight female attorneys. Throughout this chapter I will reference activists related to Juarez femicide based upon their affiliation to an organization. The preference of many Juarez rhetors is attribution and allusion to their organization rather than to individuals, as requested by the organizations themselves.
9. *Nuestra hijas* is one of the first organizations formed by the mothers of Juarez. They operate through the funding of organizations in both Mexico and the United States (Mexico Solidarity Network, *Casa Amigas*, and others) and devoted much of their energy, initially, to public demonstrations meant to draw regional attention to the government's inaction in response to the murders.
10. Oscar Romero was an El Salvadorian priest who criticized the corruption of the El Salvadorian government and called for an end to state-sponsored human-rights violations throughout the 1970s. A liberation theologian, Romero condemned the Roman Catholic Church in El Salvador, accusing them of aiding the government. He was assassinated, dying on the altar during mass. Romero is often idealized as a modern-day martyr and was officially beatified by the Catholic Church in 1997. The nature of Romero's assassination—in the midst of a Catholic mass and at the hands of state-sponsored violence—is often offered as a metaphor for the role of Catholicism in Latin America, where Catholic leaders either affirm state-sponsored violence or become victims of it. Significantly, Romero's image is often accompanied by what has come to be called the Virgin of the Disappeared, a depiction of the Catholic Mary created by Robert Lentz.
11. The organization known as Voces sin eco disbanded in 2001, publishing a statement on their own website and in *Diaro* explaining their decision to disband.

References

Amnesty International. 2007. "Amnesty's History." http://www.amnestyusa.org/About_Amnesty/Amnestys_History/page.do?id=1101298&n1=4&n2=63&n3=124.

Amnesty International. 2009a. "Guatemala Annual Report." http://report2009.amnesty.org/en/regions/americas/guatemala.

Amnesty International. 2009b. "Mexico Annual Report." http://report2009.amnesty.org/en/regions/americas/mexico.

Amnesty International. 2013. "Our Mission." http://www.amnestyusa.org/about-us/our-mission.

Arditti, Rita. 1999. *Searching for Life: The Grandmothers of the Plaza de Mayo and the Disappeared Children of Argentina*. Berkeley: University of California Press.

Barton, David, and Mary Hamilton. 1998. *Local Literacies: Reading and Writing in One Community*. New York: Routledge. http://dx.doi.org/10.4324/9780203448885.

Besnier, Niko. 1995. *Literacy, Emotion, and Authority: Reading and Writing on a Polynesian Atoll*. New York: Cambridge University Press. http://dx.doi.org/10.1017/CBO9780511519864.

Bouvard, Marguerita G. 1994. *Revolutionizing Motherhood: The Mothers of the Plaza de Mayo*. New York: Rowman and Littlefield.

Bowden, Charles. 1998. *Juárez: The Laboratory of Our Future*. New York: Aperture.

Brandt, Deborah, and Katie Clinton. 2009. "Limits of the Local: Expanding Perspectives on Literacy as a Social Practice." *Journal of Literacy Research* 34 (4): 337–56.

Cintron, Ralph. 1997. *Angel's Town: Chero Ways, Gang Life, and the Rhetorics of Everyday Life*. Boston, MA: Beacon.

Crenzel, Emilio. 2011. *The Memory of the Argentine Disappearances: The Political History of Nunca Mas*. New York: Routledge.

Daniell, Beth. 1999. "Narratives of Literacy: Connecting Composition to Culture." *College Composition and Communication* 50 (3): 393–410. http://dx.doi.org/10.2307/358858.

de Alba, Gaspar. 2005. *Desert Blood: The Juarez Murders*. Houston: Arte Publico.

Dingo, Rebecca. 2012. *Networking Arguments: Rhetoric, Transnational Feminism, and Public Writing*. Pittsburgh, PA: University of Pittsburgh Press.

Duarte, Stella P. 2008. *If I Die in Juarez*. Tucson: University of Arizona Press.

Dussel, Enrique. 2008. *Twenty Theses on Politics*. Durham, NC: Duke University Press. http://dx.doi.org/10.1215/9780822389446.

Elizondo, Virgil P. 1997. *Guadalupe: Mother of the New Creation*. Maryknoll, NY: Orbis Books.

Elizondo, Virgil P. 2000. *The Future is Mestizo*. Boulder: University Press of Colorado.

Fisher, Jo. 1989. *Mothers of the Disappeared*. Boston, MA: South End.

Fragoso, Julia M. 2002. "Serial Sexual Femicide in Ciudad Juárez: 1993–2001." *Aztlán* 28 (2): 153–78.

Garcia-Fialdini, Arianna. 2011. *Korporeal*. Installation. Ireland, September–December. http://www.garfiart.com/murals.html.

Gee, James P. 1990. *Social Linguistics and Literacies: Ideology in Discourse*. 2nd ed. Philadelphia, PA: Falmer.

Grandin, Greg, Deborah Levenson, and Elizabeth Oglesby, eds. 2011. *The Guatemala Reader: History, Culture, Politics*. Durham, NC: Duke University Press. http://dx.doi.org/10.1215/9780822394679.

Guest, Iain. 2000. *Behind the Disappearances: Argentina's Dirty War against Human Rights and the United Nations*. Philadelphia: University of Pennsylvania Press.

Heath, Shirley B. 1983. *Ways with Words: Language, Life, and Work in Communities and Classrooms*. New York: Cambridge University Press.

Hesford, Wendy. 2005. *Just Advocacy?: Women's Human Rights, Transnational Feminisms, and the Politics of Representation*. Piscataway, NJ: Rutgers University Press.

Hesford, Wendy. 2011. *Spectacular Rhetorics: Human Rights, Visions, Recognitions, Feminisms.* Durham, NC: Duke University Press. http://dx.doi.org/10.1215/9780822393818.

Hodges, David. 1991. *Argentina's "Dirty War": An Intellectual Biography.* Austin: University of Texas Press.

Linnert, Lisa Bjorne. 2006. *Desconocida unknown ukjent.* Traveling exhibit. http://www.lisebjorne.com/art_projects/desconocida-unknown-ukjent/.

Luevano, Rafael. 2012. *Woman-Killing in Juarez: Theodicy at the Border.* Maryknoll, NY: Orbis Books.

Mignolo, Walter. 2003. *The Darker Side of the Renaissance: Literacy, Territoriality, and Colonization.* Ann Arbor: University of Michigan Press.

Mignolo, Walter. 2005. *The Idea of Latin America.* London: Blackwell.

Nevins, Joseph. 2001. *Operation Gatekeeper: The Rise of the "Illegal Alien" and the Making of the U.S.–Mexico Boundary.* New York: Routledge.

Partnoy, Alicia. 2008. *The Little School: Tales of Disappearance and Survival.* Berkeley, CA: Cleis.

Pineda-Madrid, Nancy. 2011. *Suffering and Salvation in Ciudad Juarez.* Minneapolis, MN: Fortress.

Rice, Jenny. 2012. *Distant Publics: Development Rhetoric and the Subject of Crisis.* Pittsburgh, PA: University of Pittsburgh Press.

Rodriguez, Teresa. 2007. *The Daughters of Juarez: A True Story of Serial Murder South of the Border.* New York: Atria Books.

Ron, James, Howard Ramos, and Kathleen Rodgers. 2005. "Transnational Information Politics: NGO Human Rights Reporting, 1986–2000." *International Studies Quarterly* 49 (3): 557–88. http://dx.doi.org/10.1111/j.1468-2478.2005.00377.x.

Russell, Diana. 1992. *Femicide: The Politics of Woman Killing.* Farmington Hills, MI: Twayne.

Salzinger, Leslie. 2003. *Genders in Production: Making Workers in Mexico's Global Factories.* Berkeley: University of California Press.

Schell, Eileen. 2006. "Gender, Rhetorics, and Globalization: Rethinking the Spaces and Locations of Women's Rhetorics." In *Teaching Rhetorica*, edited by Kate Ronald and Joy Ritchie, 160–73. Portsmouth, NH: Heinemann-Boynton/Cook.

Scribner, Sylvia, and Michael Cole. 1981. *The Psychology of Literacy.* Cambridge, MA: Harvard University Press. http://dx.doi.org/10.4159/harvard.9780674433014.

Serviss, Tricia C. 2013. "Expanding Rhetorical Traditions in the Americas: *Coadjuvantes* and Femicide in Ciudad Juarez." *College English* 75 (6): 608–28.

Staudt, Kathleen. 2008. *Violence and Activism at the Border: Gender, Fear, and Everyday Life in Ciudad Juarez.* Austin: University of Texas Press.

Staudt, Kathleen, Tony Payan, and Anthony Kruszewski. 2009. *Human Rights along the U.S.–Mexican Border: Gendered Violence and Insecurity.* Tucson: University of Arizona Press.

Street, Brian V. 1984. *Literacy in Theory and Practice.* New York: Cambridge University Press.

United Nations Treaty Collection. 2006. *International Convention for the Protection of All Persons from Enforced Disappearance.* United Nations. https://treaties.un.org/doc/source/RecentTexts/IV_16_english.pdf.

Valdez, Diana Washington. 2006. *The Killing Fields: Harvest of Women, the Truth about Mexico's Blood Border Legacy.* Los Angeles, CA: Peace at the Border.

Voces sin eco. 1998a. "Cross Campaign." http://www.angelfire.com/in2/qualm/voces.html (site discontinued).

Voces sin eco. 1998b. "Who We Are." http://www.angelfire.com/in2/qualm/voces.html (site discontinued).

Voces sin eco. 2001. "Group Disbands." *Diaro* http://www.womenontheborder.org/Articles/no%20echo.htm (site discontinued).

Wingard, Jen. 2012. *Branded Bodies, Rhetoric, and the Neoliberal Nation-State.* New York: Lexington Books.

Wright, Melissa W. 2001. "A Manifesto against Femicide." *Antipode* 33 (3): 550–66. http://dx.doi.org/10.1111/1467-8330.00198.

Wright, Melissa W. 2004. "From Protests to Politics: Sex Work, Women's Worth, and Ciudad Juarez Modernity." *Annals of the Association of American Geographers* 94 (2): 369–86. http://dx.doi.org/10.1111/j.1467-8306.2004.09402013.x.

Wright, Melissa W. 2006. *Disposable Women and Other Myths of Global Capitalism.* New York: Routledge.

11
"A MELTING POT THAT'S CONSTANTLY BEING STIRRED"
Rhetorics of Race and Tolerance at a Regional Museum

Cori Brewster

With its acknowledgment of racial diversity and discrimination, the Four Rivers Cultural Center (Ontario, Oregon) is a rarity in the rural West—not the sort of small-town museum and interpretive center one finds in many predominantly white, agricultural communities between the Rocky Mountains and the Cascades. Conceived originally as a memorial to Japanese Americans forcibly relocated during World War II, the cultural center museum introduces visitors today to "the constant flow of people of varied ancestries—American Indian, Basque, European, Hispanic and Japanese—people," the center's website explains, "who have made this a diverse and vital region that has opened its arms to many cultures and accepted their differences" (Four Rivers Cultural Center 2015, n.p.).

There are reasons the cultural center is in Ontario, of course, claims to unity and acceptance notwithstanding. As town boosters miss few opportunities to point out, Ontario and surrounding Malheur County (pop. 31,313) do have a unique racial and cultural history, especially when compared to the rest of the state. With just 62.9 percent of the population identifying today as "White persons not Hispanic" on the 2010 Census (United States Census Bureau 2013, n.p.), Malheur County is the second-least white county in a very white state. At 53.5 percent "White persons not Hispanic," Ontario, likewise, is home today to a far larger number of people of color than all neighboring Oregon communities of comparable size. By contrast, 88.7 percent of La Grande residents identified themselves as white on the 2010 census, despite the four-year public college and two nearby reservations, Baker City is 92.4 percent white, and John Day is 94.4 percent white, to give just three examples. With 41.3 percent of the community identifying as "Hispanic or Latino

DOI: 10.7330/9781607324034.c011

origin," 2.2 percent as Japanese and other Asian American, 1.3 percent American Indian and Alaska Native, and fractions of a percent as black, Native Hawaiian, and Pacific Islander, rural, far eastern Malheur County has long been one of the most racially diverse counties in the state—a difference overtly marked and remarked upon in Ontario in a number of ways. From the trilingual storefront of the Red Apple Market to the city's annual Global Village festival, signs and stories of Ontario's racial and cultural distinctiveness are a central if not uniformly embraced element of community branding and self-representation.[1]

Opened in 1997, the cultural center museum formally assembles and authenticates the area's "unique" history, offering visitors a clearly articulated path from community past to present demonstrated by a wide range of artifacts, photographs, and personal accounts. Drawing on the mainstream, nonconfrontational multiculturalism of the mid-1990s, museum exhibits follow local characters through a familiar script featuring heroic white pioneers, regrettably mistreated Indians, and nonwhite immigrants whose perseverance and hard work in the face of prejudice past has ostensibly taught us all a thing or two about what it means to be American. As the brochure puts it, the museum introduces visitors to a "melting pot that is constantly being stirred," a "potpourri of people from all walks of life" who "continue to a build a strong community by focusing on their similarities, while respecting and celebrating their unique origins and traditions."[2] Racism of the present is typically cast in terms of individual pathology, and the workings of capital in terms of mutually beneficial, opportunity-based relations among individual workers, land owners, government agencies, and benevolent, community-minded businesses, both big and small. Indeed, *progress, technology,* and *industry* work here as god terms so seamlessly and so familiarly at times that they seem hardly worth mention at all.

But it is all worth mention, surprises or not. As Amy Levin argues and fellow contributors corroborate in *Defining Memory: Local Museums and the Construction of History in America's Changing Communities*, "Far from playing a minor role in the creation of contemporary America, . . . local museums are central to understanding the forces that create communities in the United States" (Levin 2007, 25). Indeed, Levin stresses, "local museums *are* museums of influence, deserving critical and public attention, because they may ultimately tell scholars more about contemporary life than all the branches of the Smithsonian put together. All museums tell narratives about culture—no matter how quirky, or dusty, or unprofessional they might seem" (25; italics mine). Whether the cultural center's writing of racial and economic history is wholly accepted by community members or not, whether or not it is commonplace or unconvincing from various academic perspectives, it is an official and widely circulated local telling—the museum records more than 2,800 visitors a year, at least half of them schoolchildren—and as such it wields significant rhetorical and imaginative weight.[3]

The stories of race and tolerance told in the Four Rivers Cultural Center museum serve as an important locus for examining how constructions of race and racism *become* commonplace in particular settings, how they articulate with other dominant community narratives, and how tightly local efforts to address race-based conflicts and inequities are rhetorically bound. My interest in studying the museum was motivated initially by my work with a local grassroots organization struggling to understand its repeated failure to organize residents across race and class lines and also by the patent refusal of otherwise progressive white organization members and community leaders—many of whom routinely invoked the story of Ontario's "unique racial tolerance"—to acknowledge race- and language-based inequities in the schools, the courts, and public services.[4] It has led, if not ended, here: to a closer examination of local rhetorical barriers to progressive community organizing, including how locally institutionalized histories help rationalize rhetorical and material "borders" in communities like Ontario and how they might better open such borders up, if not break them down.[5]

In (re)assembling the view of Ontario as a uniquely diverse and tolerant community, the cultural center museum brings together and reinforces several racialized storylines with significant implications for organizing around issues of social and economic justice. To illustrate, I begin here with a detailed overview of museum scripts and exhibits, tracing ways in which the museum "peoples" the area rhetorically and maps the borders between and ostensibly constitutive of racial and cultural groups. At the end of the chapter, I return to a more focused analysis of what this might mean for addressing race-based conflicts and inequities in Ontario and other communities like it, given a "tyrannizing image" of racial and economic harmony, to borrow Richard Weaver's (1964, 1970) term, that may serve more to disarm than to legitimize local residents who would challenge it on the ground.

WEAVING "A HUMAN TAPESTRY": *CULTURAL COLLISIONS*, PROGRESS, AND PROVING UP

Built in the spirit of reparations for the internment of Japanese Americans and the sincere desire to "encompass all the minorities"

(Cockle, *Oregonian*, Feb. 16, 1992) and "develo[p] cultural ties" (Cockle, *Oregonian*, Dec. 7, 1991), the Four Rivers Cultural Center aims today to weave "a human tapestry," as the brochure puts it, "of the diverse groups that have met and overcome discrimination [in the region]" (Four Rivers Cultural Center n.d.). A visit to the museum begins with a thirteen-minute video (not available for sale) shown in a small theater between the admissions desk and the entrance to the first exhibit. A combination of interviews with area residents, still shots of historic photographs, and footage of present-day landscapes and events, the video introduces viewers to the key themes and organizing principles that structure the exhibits ahead and help rationalize periodic migrations into the area: principally land, technology, war, and water. As in the exhibit space to follow, the five "cultures" represented in the museum are introduced in the video roughly in order of arrival—Native American, European American, Basque, Japanese American, and Hispanic—each group's relationship to and dependence upon the area's natural resources emphasized above all.[6] We learn, for example, that for "thousands of years, this region was home to a people who moved from place to place, living peacefully off the land." When "Euroamericans came and began to work the land," however, it "became clear that they had a different approach." In fact, the Native people and "white" cattlemen "didn't always get along": "Indians were forced to choose between losing their culture or starving or going to war." The arrival of Basque sheepherders "brought additional conflict over land and water," as did the steadily increasing numbers of white settlers from the East.

Following a brief discussion of ditch- and dam-building efforts, the video shifts to World War II and the forced relocation of Japanese Americans to the area. Framing anti-Japanese sentiment primarily in terms of the war with Japan, rather than within the broader context of anti-Asian sentiment across the western United States, the narrator explains that "there was a great deal of paranoia and prejudice against the Japanese during the war." Nonetheless, many Japanese Americans contributed to the war effort both as soldiers and in the fields: "During the war, the country desperately needed food," and Japanese Americans played a valuable role in helping to harvest it. This segment leads neatly into a discussion of the Bracero program in which the narrator explains briefly that imported Mexican laborers were also "segregated in camps and lived in poverty." Strikingly, the video directs no attention to Japanese American residents who lived in the area prior to World War II and mentions only briefly that "Vaqueros" had been coming to the area "for a long time." In place of a more nuanced history of cultural migrations, coexistence, and conflict, the need for agricultural labor in the service of national security becomes a rationale in the video for the "arrival" of Japanese Americans, which is extended, during wartime at least, to Mexicans and Mexican Americans, too.

At its close, the video provides visitors the moral to be learned in the museum, the conclusion toward which the exhibits that follow are inductively meant to led: "We have all come a long way since businesses posted signs [such as 'No Japs Allowed' and 'Mexicans Go Home']. . . . To live in healthy communities, we must respect each other's differences." While this is certainly a good sentiment and one worthy of repetition, it is also troublingly reassuring. As sociologist Eduardo Bonilla-Silva points out, the racial storyline "the past is the past" prepares viewers to enter the museum and understand that the few instances of racism past that they are about to see are neither indictments of present-day residents nor calls to pay contemporary racism more mind. Instead, they are just the opposite: markers of how we, like the land, have "improved" (Bonilla-Silva 2001, 157–59; 2003, 77–79).

Following the video, visitors enter the main museum space and move through the exhibits chronologically, economically, and, again, "culturally"—from the Northern Paiutes, to white cattlemen and Basque sheepherders, to white merchants and townspeople, to the forced relocation and internment of Japanese Americans, to successive "waves" of Mexican and Mexican American farmworkers. With the exception of the final section of the museum that focuses on the community present, the titles of each major exhibit space all center on land: *Living with the Land*, *Claiming the Land*, *Opening the Land*, and *Defending the Land*, followed by the culminating exhibit, *Faces of the Community*. As in the video, land, technology, war, and water are used to structure the human relationships addressed in the exhibits and to reinforce the borders constructed between each cultural group.

The first twenty feet of exhibit space in the museum, for example, are devoted to the Agaidka and other Northern Paiutes, who, "like the land they have lived on for countless generations . . . have witnessed centuries of dramatic change." "However," the opening placard explains, "both people and land have adapted and endured." Significantly, the first piece of technology in this exhibit to which visitors are explicitly directed is a water bottle, circa 1880, tying the museum's first cultural group into the larger narrative and introducing them according to its terms: the Paiute people depended on such technologies to survive in this "dry land," and they too stood to benefit from ongoing technological development.[7]

Various tools and technologies are highlighted in the next subsection of the museum as well, which is titled simply *Cultural Collisions*. In the first plexiglass case are miners' lanterns and picks, a miner's pan, a beaver pelt and trap, trade beads, an axe, and a kettle. The sole photograph in the case is captioned as follows: "Arrastra operated by Idaho Clearwater Co, Northern Idaho, late 1800s. . . . The technology was brought north from Mexico where it had been used for centuries by Native Americans, Spaniards, and Mexicans." In the next case, such "cultural collisions" are reframed to more strongly emphasize race-based hierarchies and "evolutionary" progression: "The handmade shovel contrasts with the traditional stone tools of the Northern Paiute," one caption reads. "The beginnings of an evolution from camp fires and bows and arrows to modern times," reads another.

Ironizing the pioneer historian's view of progress and entitlement to some extent, the next section goes on to assign some responsibility to white agents for the dispossession and extermination of Native people. One placard explains, "The Agaidka and other Paiute peoples were viewed by the new intruders as an obstacle to progress. In 1872, many Paiutes were confined on the Malheur Reservation. While keeping a large portion of their homeland, they lost the freedom of movement that was a key element of their traditional lifestyle." Later we learn that the Malheur Reservation was terminated in 1882 to open up a million more acres for white settlement and that the Paiutes were then pushed off what remained of their lands. As the panel *Stockman's Paradise* reports, "Enterprising cattlemen built their ranches courtesy of inexpensive land provided by the United States Government. The 'Indian Land Giveaway' began with the Homestead Act of 1862 and continued with the Oregon Swampland Act, the Timber Culture Act and the Desert Land Act of 1877." From photographs of corrals and white cattlemen, we move on to displays titled *Roads, Bridges, and Ferries* and *Sheepherders*, which include a reconstructed stagecoach and a diorama of a sheepherders' camp, ostensibly Basque. Once the next section of the museum begins, Native characters vanish from the museum's story of local history until the final exhibit.[8]

Next come three subsections dedicated to the rapid white settlement of the area: *The Rail Meets the Range*, *The Engine of Change*, and *Building Communities*. It is here that the museum's story of community building and belonging begins in earnest and that the symbolic ties among water systems, agricultural development, and community values are most explicitly laid out. In the *Building Communities* section, for example, visitors learn that the "scattered ranch families developed a new sense of community," sharing "common bonds of isolation, adversity, and the willingness to lend a neighbor a hand in time of need." *The Promise of Water* highlights the critical role access to water played in development of the region. A life-sized water wheel squeaks and splashes in one corner, followed by a large section of irrigation pipe in another. Visitors who walk through the pipe come out face to face with a floor-to-ceiling photograph of the nearby Owyhee Dam. The placard *Taking Root* represents this section's main themes most completely: "By the late 1880s, the railroad was helping to build farming communities in the area. Promoting both ticket and land sales, the rail company lured new settlers by painting a picture of the region as an agricultural paradise. Settlers came with high hopes and many left disappointed. But those who stayed put down deep roots working from sunup to sundown to make their dreams a reality. *Early irrigation projects symbolized the values of this new farming community that was built on cooperation and close ties to the land*" (italics mine). Given the dam and greatly expanded network of irrigation pipes and ditches, we are to understand, a whole new set of human relationships was made possible.

At this point, as in the video, the museum's narrative shifts dramatically to World War II and the forced relocation and internment of Japanese Americans. It is the largest rupture in the museum's scripts—where the story of melting-pot-minded pioneers meets the story of the internment, and the naturalization of "progress" and "civilization" must momentarily stop and back up. The first subsection, *The Home Front*, includes ads for war bonds from a 1942 Ontario newspaper in which racist caricatures of Japanese soldiers with guns pointed to their heads are captioned simply, "Make Him Remember." Multiple photos and panels documenting local residents' contributions to the war effort set the stage for the next exhibit, *Forced Removal.* Arguably the centerpiece of the whole museum, this reconstructed scene of an assembly center departure platform features life-size cutouts of area residents; most pictured are children and grandchildren of locals who were interned or who moved to Malheur County's "free zone" during the war. The following sections *My World Fell Apart, Disruption of Families, Leaving the Camps, Your Country Before Yourselves, Southeast Asia,* and *The Ultimate Sacrifice* tell the story of the internment through photographs, excerpts of internees' letters and diaries, and captions documenting the role Japanese Americans played in the war effort, both overseas in the military and at home in the fields.[9]

FACES OF A COMMUNITY: FROM "CRUEL CIRCUMSTANCES" TO A CULTURE OF ACCEPTANCE

The next major section of the museum begins in a short hallway that roughly marks the shift from community past to community present. "People of many different cultures have made their homes at the meeting of the Four Rivers," the main caption reads, and continues, "Come visit these places that tell stories of our journeys here, of the barriers we have overcome, and of our families, our traditions, and our communities. Many of our experiences are common to people all over this country and the world. We welcome you and hope that what you see here reminds you of your own stories." On one wall, five flags bearing the names of the five cultural groups the museum centers on hang from the ceiling. On the opposite wall is a collage of thirty-two photos titled *Lives Made and Stories Remembered*. From "Ore-Ida invites you to meet Miss Tater Tot," to Basque and Mexican dancers, to a mixed-race group of children in a playground, these photos provide visual evidence that many different cultures have indeed "made their homes at the meeting of the Four Rivers."

With the exception of the photo of children on the playground, however, the pictures don't provide much evidence of the racial and cultural integration the video suggested we would find here. Of the thirty-two pictures, all but three feature apparently monocultural, monoracial scenes. There is no Japanese American barrel racer here, no "diversity" among the fiddlers, only one group of adults of different races interacting in a nonworkplace environment in this collage. Though one of the final exhibits in the museum illustrates how one local woman "belongs to many communities," the five cultural groupings established in the museum are largely represented as distinct, fixed, and exclusive. While different cultures and traditions may be valuable, the museum seems to say, and while accepting those differences may be the mark of a "strong community," the overarching script very much reflects Bonilla-Silva's (2001, 2003) description of the "biologization of culture," a narrative frame through which traits labeled *cultural* rather than *biological* are naturalized nonetheless, presented just as innate, representative, and unlikely to change.

The remaining exhibit space includes a replica internment camp barracks, a "'European American' kitchen typical of the 1950s" (Highberger, *Observer*, Jan. 19, 2007), displays on contemporary Native and Basque events, photos of local families, and an exhibit titled *Barriers*, the museum's most direct attempt to address racism and other forms of discrimination experienced by people in the community today. "Drought, war and prejudice are among the barriers and hardships people in this region faced," the exhibit caption begins, and continues, "Men and women of diverse groups survived through struggle and sacrifice as they sought to make homes here. Members of this community continue to confront and adapt to new challenges while learning to live with the land and one another." In following panels, each group is shown to have experienced some such challenge, with separate displays illustrating how representative group members have faced "cruel circumstances" and worked to overcome them. Consequently, even as the exhibit attempts to call attention to discrimination in the community, it tends to minimize it at the same time, putting poor farming weather on the same level as racism and xenophobia in order to identify each of the museum's five groups separately as victims and sacrificers—a move, incidentally, that allows scriptwriters to avoid pointing fingers or making any explicit connections between the struggles of one group and the intentional or coordinated actions of another.

Accordingly, the most straightforward display in the *Barriers* exhibit is the one directed to children. As *Personal Prejudice: Hispanics Confront Ignorance and Fear* explains,

> When people of different races and cultures don't understand or respect one another, individuals may make judgments about whole groups of people based on fear or stereotypes. Prejudiced words and actions can hurt a person and make them feel worthless. People overcome prejudice by speaking up, finding common ground, looking for and listening to another point of view.
>
> Hispanic Americans in this region have faced many forms of prejudice from people who are insensitive, unkind or cruel. Prejudice might be hidden in a comment, look, gesture or joke in schools, stores and at work. As targets of discrimination, Hispanic Americans have made choices to ignore or confront prejudice.

Beneath the caption are four small wooden panels, each of which depicts an instance of discrimination and asks visitors how they would respond. "What would you do if store employees watched your every move when you were shopping?" one panel asks, for example. Behind the door visitors find sample answers given by area schoolchildren, ranging from "Say something" to "Ignore it." As in the museum's brochure and other adult-level communications, racism is presented as an individual pathology that manifests in personal interactions between more and less sensitive or respectful people. The need for coordinated, community-level response to a deeply institutionalized problem with significant social and material consequences for current residents is neither addressed here nor implied.

In this way and others, the museum effectively minimizes and contains racisms both present and past, limiting significantly how visitors might understand the way highly unequal relations of power and wealth have developed in the community or the pervasive, interlocking ways in which those inequities continue to be naturalized and sustained. Indeed, for a museum dedicated to addressing how the community has overcome "discrimination," there is surprisingly little acknowledgment of the explicitly racist policies and organizations that shaped who came to the state and who remains there. Oregon laws such as those denying blacks immigration into the state, for instance, are simply not mentioned in the museum. Because African Americans make up only a fraction of a percentage of the population of Malheur County today, their "group" is not included in the cultural center at all. Chinese Americans are similarly left out of the museum, despite the major role Chinese men in particular played in the early economic development of this part of the state (see Edson 1974, 71–73). The El Dorado Ditch, for example, which was dug almost exclusively by Chinese laborers between 1863 and the mid-1870s, stretches for 130 miles across present-day Malheur and Baker counties. Used initially for mining purposes, the El Dorado and a number of shorter ditches not only made mining more practical for both white and Chinese investors but spurred increased white settlement and agricultural development of the area as well. Nonetheless, there is no reference in the museum to the Chinese Exclusion Act of 1882, the Scott Act of 1888, or any local anti-Chinese sentiment or activity despite well-documented incidents of white violence against Chinese men in nearby communities, all of which contributed at least in part to the near total exodus of Chinese and Chinese Americans from the area.[10] Ultimately, the people we are presented within the museum appear less those who have chosen to struggle, sacrifice, and overcome difference and more a combination of the most privileged and most desperate few who, in the wake of ongoing racial, economic, and cultural conflict, are actually left.

Similarly, conspicuously absent from the museum's history of racial progress is any discussion of local nativist and white supremacist organizations, which clearly also affected who migrated to the area and who stayed. Admittedly, the history of such groups is often poorly documented and hard to trace. With a little digging, however, there are plenty of clues to be found. It took me less than an hour at the microfilm machine in the nearby Payette, Idaho, public library to find multiple references to local Ku Klux Klan activities in the *Payette Independent*, including an advertisement for the June 16, 1924, "Great Inter-Klan Meet" to be held less than ten miles from Ontario (June 5, 1924). According to the ad, the full-day "public program, open to all" would bring together "Big delegations from Boise, Baker City and other towns of Idaho and Eastern Oregon" for lectures, a parade through downtown Payette, and "the Greatest and Most Spectacular Display of Fireworks and Aerial Features Ever Given in the Intermountain Country." An article in the *Independent* titled "10,000 K.K.K. To Be Here" (April 24, 1924) published two months before the event reports that "Payette Klansmen, in conjunction with the Ontario, Oregon, Klan, have secured the great Inter-Klan meet of the Northwestern Klans which will be held in this city on Sunday and Monday, the 15th and 16th of June":

> The Payette Klan had to bid against many larger and more powerful organizations in the scramble for the convention, but won out and it is to their credit that they captured the big meeting, and that Payette will have the privilege of entertaining for two days so many visitors.
>
> A full detail of the program is not available as yet, but it is understood to include public lectures by men of national repute, a barbecue, parade, public nateuralization [sic] ceremony, and the holding of the entire Klan review, a symbolic feature of fireworks lasting two hours and depicting all phazes [sic] of the Klan ideals. Imperial officials have assured the Payette and Ontario Klans that this will be the most impressive Klan convention and ceremony ever held by the order west of the Mississippi river, and will mark a new epoch in Idaho and Oregon Klan history.

While the *Ontario Argus* had come out strongly against Ku Klux Klan candidates and anti-Catholic ballot measures in 1922, urging readers that "there is no place for intolerance and bigotry" in a nation "where every man has the right to worship his God after the dictates of his own conscience" (Aiken, Sept. 28, 1922), they did not, as far as I can tell, report on the "Great Inter-Klan Meet" of 1924 or other Ontario Klan activities. The *Independent*, however, provided consistent—and positive—coverage of local Klan activities in the 1920s, providing clear evidence of connections between area churches, the American Legion, and the Klan on both sides of the Oregon-Idaho border (see "K. K. K. Held Big Meeting," April 10, 1924, and "Klans Held Big Konklave," July 10, 1924).

Ignoring the coordinated and public, even if not representative, nature of such organizations in the museum hardly serves visitors well, allowing longtime white residents in particular to continue pointing blame for discriminatory practices past to aberrant or outside forces (as in the case of the internment) rather than coming to a better understanding of the local architecture of white supremacy and white privilege. Without further contextualization, that is, artifacts like the "No Japs Allowed" and "Mexicans Go Home" signs shown in the video at the beginning of the museum remain frozen in the past, isolated and apparently separable from current conflicts in the community over issues such as immigration and public language policy. To borrow David Roediger's (1999) term, the "wages of whiteness" remain unseen in the museum, as do the multiple imbrications of white supremacist, religious, nationalist, agrarian, and other narratives and worldviews.

Through this combination of overgeneralization, overdetermination, and exclusion, the museum effectively grafts contemporary colorblind storylines to longstanding rationalizations for community membership and entitlement. The basic plotline remains the pioneer-society history; the story of the Japanese American internment, though it aims to expand the definition of what it means to be a citizen, is simply laid over the top.[11] The pioneer narrative as it is invoked in the museum also provides all the rhetorical tools necessary for understanding such present-day "incivilities" as discrimination and racial intolerance: for communities moving ever forward, "progressing" through ongoing technological development and other "improvements," racism can simply be recoded as "backwards" and "uncivilized," too—the same tropes used against Native people and fellow Others in the first place. It's a marvelous if unintended feat of accommodation—a way to preserve the current racial and economic order in the community even in the face of marked disparities in income, political representation, and other resources.[12] Rather than moving visitors to radically rethink area history, in other words, or to better understand local relationships among race, racialization, and power, the museum simply refigures a staple white supremacist tale: those who "progress" are most entitled. The story of overcoming prejudice remains tightly grafted to the pioneer story of "proving up," implying again and again that participants need look only forward, never particularly critically back.

TO IGNORE OR CONFRONT: ENGAGING LOCAL RHETORICS OF OMISSION

Not understanding the way race and economics are storied in this community (or are not storied at all) has led to dead end after dead end for the community organization whose struggles to organize across race and class lines motivated this study. One might think residents who buy into the dominant imaging of Ontario as uniquely diverse and tolerant would be well positioned to hear fellow community members' concerns about discrimination in schools and social services, or about the need for bilingual documents in the justice system, or about the importance of providing pesticide applicators' training in both Spanish and English when a significant number of those handling such chemicals on area farms are Spanish-language dominant. But, in fact, quite the opposite has repeatedly shown to be the case. Why? What steps toward such conversations do institutionalized constructions of history and identity like those in the cultural center help to pave? What barriers do they help to prop up or create?

To be sure, as Richard Sandell and other museum scholars argue, "it is problematic to establish a direct, causal relationship between museum practices and contemporary manifestations of social inequality or their amelioration" (Sandell 2007a, 100). It is likewise problematic to assume that even if a significant majority of residents visit a local museum, they will read or respond to it in similar ways. "While [museums] might create contexts that encourage and lead toward particular understandings," as Corinne Kratz remarks, "ultimately exhibitions cannot control visitors' engagements and experience" (Kratz 2011, 29). Still, Sandell points out, "museums and other cultural organisations cannot be conceived as discretely cultural, or asocial—they are undeniably implicated in the dynamics of (in)equality and the power relations between different groups through their role in constructing and disseminating dominant social narratives" (Sandell 2007a, 100). The question we ought to be asking, he suggests, is what "political role . . . museums might play, alongside other organisations within civil society, in promoting equality of opportunity and pluralist values?" (100). Among these possible roles are sponsoring public forums about issues raised in museum exhibits; sharing space, resources, and expertise with community groups; and creating greater opportunities for visitors to actively engage with exhibits and contribute to their ongoing revision. Even if funds are not available for updating exhibits, as is the case in so many small local museums, calling more explicit attention to ways in which exhibits are constructed, perspectival, and open to contestation can help spur discussion and prevent dominant narratives from simply dominating in other spheres of public decision making and debate (see also Casey 2007; Crooke 2007; Sandell 2007b).

What is needed in Ontario and communities like it, no doubt, is more historicizing, more stories, more analysis, more participation—a messier, broader, more reflexive rendering of ways in which residents have raced and classed one another over time in this particular locale. If museums like the cultural center are to aid rather than inhibit efforts to shift, cross, or eliminate borders, both rhetorical and material, they must create spaces for dialogue and ongoing public interrogation of how those borders are made. Where they cannot, or will not, it remains up to residents, community organizers, scholars, and teachers to continue to unpack locally institutionalized tellings and leverage the sites in which those tellings are most visible to generate wider discussion ourselves.

Notes

1. When Ontario residents are asked about the racial and cultural makeup of their community, the area's agricultural economy and ongoing need for short-term labor are recurrent themes, as is whites' "relative tolerance" of Japanese Americans during World War II. This latter story, central to cultural center promoters' arguments to Congress and other funders for locating the museum in Ontario, ranges from the whole community "welcoming" displaced Japanese Americans to the magnanimity of individual patriotic, uniquely tolerant, and/or forward-thinking town leaders and employers. Of these, white former mayor and newspaper editor (and later governor) Elmo Smith, is typically given the most credit. For sample versions of this story in print, see Florangela Davis (Seattle Times, Feb. 17, 2002), Bob Rost (2006), and multiple chamber of commerce-generated fliers and brochures (Ontario, Oregon, Chamber of Commerce n.d.). Malheur County was one of few "free zones" on the West Coast to which Japanese Americans could opt to relocate for a period during World War II; the reasons it became a gathering place of sorts both during and after the internment are somewhat more complex than this local mythos would suggest.
2. To be sure, promotional materials for the museum call upon an array of conflicting metaphors to describe the region's racial and cultural makeup, from "melting pot" to "human tapestry" to "potpourri," all of which emphasize a kind of blending, or at least coexistence, but none of which direct attention to the tensions or imbalances of power that characterize such blending and that unfortunately very much remain.
3. In an area of this size, 2,800 visitors a year is a significant number. Though there are no available data identifying what percentage of the area's residents have been to the museum, most students enrolled in the region's public schools have visited (or will visit) the museum at least once as part of an official school trip, and many residents routinely bring out-of-town visitors to tour the museum, one of very few local attractions. The museum is also housed within the larger Four Rivers Cultural Center, which includes a high use conference facility and which abuts the area's community college and branch campuses of Eastern Oregon University and Oregon State.
4. This study of rural community organizing was conducted under the supervision of the Institutional Review Board at Washington State University from 2006 to 2007.
5. In *White Supremacy and Racism in the Post-Civil Rights Era*, sociologist Eduardo Bonilla-Silva identifies four dominant tropes or "frames" of colorblind racist ideology in circulation in the United States today: "abstract liberalism," "biologization of culture," "naturalization of racial matters," and "minimization of racism" (Bonilla-Silva 2001, 141–62). According to Bonilla-Silva, the most common of these is abstract liberalism, a frame through which white speakers rationalize racial inequality via "elements of political liberalism (equal opportunity, meritocracy, equal rights) and economic liberalism (free market, competition, individuals' preferences, little government intervention)" (141). Only slightly less common is the biologization of culture, ways of explaining racial inequality that replace the essentialization of color with the essentialization of "culture." "Although some analysts regard the demise of

biological or Jim Crow racism as a tremendous sign of racial progress," Bonilla-Silva explains, "whites' contemporary view of blacks as culturally deficient is as problematic because (1) it is as extensive as biological racism used to be among whites, (2) it is regarded by whites as fixed or as something very hard to change . . . and (3) . . . it allows whites to express resentment and hostility safely since, in their view, blacks are where they are as a group because they do not want to get ahead" (148).

Though the studies upon which Bonilla-Silva based these conclusions focus primarily on whites' attitudes toward blacks, white Americans use ostensibly culture-based explanations of inequality against all groups of color, particularly, as he notes, against "dark-skinned minority groups such as blacks, Puerto Ricans, Mexican Americans, and some Asian Americans" (138). Through the naturalization of racial matters and minimization of racist frames, likewise, whites consistently ascribe wage gaps, neighborhood segregation, disproportionate dropout and graduation rates, and other disparities along racial lines to individual preferences, motivations, and cultural norms—to anything, in effect, but racism or white privilege (149–53). While direct assertions of white supremacy may no longer be as socially acceptable in the United States, in other words, more than a few rhetorical detours for articulating and reinforcing it remain.

Bonilla-Silva's attempt to map how white supremacy is discursively sustained strongly informs my reading of the racial and economic history constructed in the cultural center and in the rearticulations of this history in the community of Ontario at large. Thus, when I refer here to white-supremacist discourse, it is not the rhetoric of the Ku Klux Klan or any other explicitly racist organization that I mean per se, but, more broadly, prevailing ways of making sense of the world and white racial identity that help legitimate the racial order in the contemporary United States. This more expansive definition includes all ways of storying place, history, economics, and other human relations in which white speakers either overlook or openly deny the joint experiences of people of color and the privileges earned by virtue of whiteness in ordering their own and others' identities and relationship with the world. "The mechanisms that continue to maintain racial and gender hegemonies are many and complicated," as Patricia Penn Hilden remarks. She continues, "But I'd like to suggest that perspective—the location of 'us' and 'them'—is inculcated early on until dozens of little-questioned assumptions veil both practice and theorizing about the quotidian acts of exclusion" (Hilden 2006, 160).

6. To be sure, the racial and cultural categories constructed in the video and following exhibits raise immediate questions of their own. How Basque people are not also European American is never made clear, for instance, while the rest of the undifferentiated European Americans are typically cast simply as white. Hispanic is likewise used fairly unproblematically and anachronistically throughout the museum, even as specific exhibits point to the many different parts of the world from which someone labeled Hispanic might have "arrived." With the exception of one photo display in the present-day section of the museum, moreover, no attention in the museum is given in the cultural center to multiracial families or to individuals who identify mixed or multiple cultural heritages. Nor is the ongoing role intermarriage has played in shifting constructions of race and culture in the western United States over the past several centuries anywhere to be found. For more on this, see Arnoldo De Leon (2002, 82–84), *Racial Frontiers*.

7. See Patricia Penn Hilden (2006, 41–99), *From a Red Zone* and C. Richard King (1998), *Colonial Discourses, Collective Memories, and the Exhibition of Native American Cultures and Histories in the Contemporary United States* for a more extensive discussion of ideology and the "Indian diorama" than I have space for here.

8. No doubt this reflects in part just how successful the US military and white settlers were in forcing the surviving Paiutes out of the Four Rivers region—to far southern Malheur County, to the Burns area, and to the Yakama and Warm Springs Reservations, primarily. But as suggested earlier, it speaks, too, to the way popular white pioneer histories have been recrafted in an attempt to mollify critics and fit a more inclusive multicultural moment: if the crimes against Native people are at least partially recognized, it is acceptable to go on with the rest of the story. In effect, "the past is the past," and it is too late to turn things around now.

9. Notably, the section is closed by a reminder that "many valiant and courageous men and women of all ethnic backgrounds fought bravely or worked hard on the homefront." *They Also Served*, a collection of photos, uniforms, and war memorabilia of local residents, points out that the "story of Japanese American contributions to the World War II effort, at home and in combat, is just one of many stories. . . . We pay tribute here to all the men and women of the Four Rivers Region for their service during WWII."

10. See for example Christopher Edson (1974), *The Chinese in Eastern Oregon, 1860–1890*; Arnoldo De Leon (2002), *Racial Frontiers*; David Horowitz (1999), *Inside the Klavern*; and Roger Daniels (2004), *Prisoners Without Trial*. The murder of a group of Chinese miners in Hells Canyon in 1887 and the expulsion of Chinese residents of Pendleton and La Grande by white mobs in the 1890s are two of the most well-known incidents of anti-Chinese violence in Oregon. The Idaho Historical Society Museum in Boise, Idaho, also has several newspaper articles on permanent display on the persecution of Chinese residents of Boise and nearby towns, at least one of which refers to white teenagers routinely pelting Chinese adults with rocks; similar incidents occurred in Baker City and John Day, Oregon (Edson 1974, 51).

11. That is to say, the internment story as it is constructed in the cultural center museum and in many other sites is explicitly about recognizing and expanding the definition of "Americanness" beyond white settlers' claims to the land: the Japanese Americans who were interned were US citizens, but the color coding of authentic citizen-ness led to their being rounded up and jailed indefinitely on the basis of race and national origin. Japanese Americans' contribution to the war effort via military service as well as through agricultural labor operates both within the museum and without to "prove" their people-ness, their citizenship and rightful place in the community. As an Ontario, Oregon, Chamber of Commerce (n.d.) flier tells the story, "A few Japanese Americans came before World War II with many coming to the 'free' area during and after the war. They provided much needed farm labor and went on to become businessmen and women and owners of some of the finest land in the area." This same theme is repeated by Hugh and Lorraine Lackey, "fourth-generation Ontarians" interviewed for the 2002 *Seattle Times* article reprinted on the Ontario Public Schools website: "Married since 1944, the couple says the Japanese were good farmers, helpful people who never got into any trouble. And they spoke English, Lorraine Lackey points out, which is a lot different, she adds, from the Mexican immigrants who have arrived here in the past decade" (Davis, *Seattle Times*, Feb. 17, 2002). Needless to say, this perspective forgets the very different conditions under which Japanese Americans, Mexican Americans, Mexicans, and other Latin American immigrants have come to this area over the past century. For Japanese Americans, however, the pioneer-society history's moralizing about hard work and just desserts absorbs the story of the internment quite handily after all.

12. Not only is Malheur County the lowest income county in the state of Oregon, it is also the most economically stratified by race. See US Census data for further details.

References

Bonilla-Silva, Eduardo. 2001. *White Supremacy and Racism in the Post-Civil Rights Era.* Boulder, CO: Lynne Rienner.

Bonilla-Silva, Eduardo. 2003. *Racism without Racists: Color-Blind Racism and the Persistence of Racial Inequality in the United States.* Lanham, MD: Rowman and Littlefield.

Casey, Dawn. 2007. "Museums as Agents for Social and Political Change." In *Museums and Their Communities*, edited by Sheila Watson, 292–99. New York: Routledge.

Crooke, Elizabeth. 2007. "Museums, Communities and the Politics of Heritage in Northern Ireland." In *Museums and Their Communities*, edited by Sheila Watson, 300–12. New York: Routledge.

Daniels, Roger. 2004. *Prisoners without Trial: Japanese Americans in World War II.* Rev. ed. New York: Hill and Wang.

De Leon, Arnoldo. 2002. *Racial Frontiers: Africans, Chinese, and Mexicans in Western America, 1848–1890.* Albuquerque: University of New Mexico Press.

Edson, Christopher H. 1974. *The Chinese in Eastern Oregon, 1860–1890.* San Francisco: R and E Research Associates.

Four Rivers Cultural Center. n.d. "Four Rivers Cultural Center and Museum." Ontario, OR: Four Rivers Cultural Center.

Four Rivers Cultural Center. 2015. "Four Rivers Cultural Center." http://www.4rcc.com.

Hilden, Patricia P. 2006. *From a Red Zone: Critical Perspectives on Race, Politics, and Culture.* Trenton, NJ: Red Sea.

Horowitz, David. 1999. *Inside the Klavern: The Secret History of a Ku Klux Klan of the 1920s.* Carbondale: Southern Illinois University Press.

King, C. Richard. 1998. *Colonial Discourses, Collective Memories, and the Exhibition of Native American Cultures and Histories in the Contemporary United States.* New York: Garland.

Kratz, Corrine A. 2011. "Rhetorics of Value: Constituting Worth and Meaning through Cultural Display." *Visual Anthropology Review* 27 (1): 21–48. http://dx.doi.org/10.1111/j.1548-7458.2011.01077.x.

Levin, Amy K. 2007. "Why Local Museums Matter." In *Defining Memory: Local Museums and the Construction of History in America's Changing Communities*, edited by Amy K. Levin, 9–26. Lanham, MD: Rowman and Littlefield.

Ontario, Oregon, Chamber of Commerce. n.d. *Brief History of Ontario* (brochure). Ontario, OR: Chamber of Commerce.

Roediger, David. 1999. *The Wages of Whiteness: Race and the Making of the American Working Class.* New York: Verso.

Rost, Bob. 2006. "The Ring of Success." *Oregon's Agricultural Progress.* http://oregonprogress.oregonstate.edu/spring-2006/ring-success.

Sandell, Richard. 2007a. "Museums and the Combating of Social Inequality: Roles, Responsibilities, and Resistance." In *Museums and Their Communities*, edited by Sheila Watson, 95–113. New York: Routledge.

Sandell, Richard. 2007b. *Museums, Prejudice, and the Reframing of Difference.* New York: Routledge.

United States Census Bureau. 2013. "Community Facts." American Fact Finder. http://factfinder2.census.gov/.

Weaver, Richard. 1964. *Visions of Order: The Cultural Crisis of Our Time.* Bryn Mawr, PA: Intercollegiate Studies Institute.

Weaver, Richard. 1970. "The Cultural Role of Rhetoric." In *Language is Sermonic: Richard M. Weaver on the Nature of Rhetoric*, edited by Richard L. Johannesen, Rennard Strickland, and Ralph T. Eubanks, 161–84. Baton Rouge: Louisiana State University Press.

12
DE PIE SOBRE LA VALLA Y MIRANDO POR LA VENTANA
Border Realities of the Immigrant Experience

Vanessa Cozza

INTRODUCTION: THE AERIAL VIEW OF BORDERS

When some of us think of borders within the Americas, we may imagine the southern states bordering Mexico.[1] Public, political discourse has partially influenced our association between the concept of borders and the image that represents them. Some of us may also visualize a fence if asked to produce an image of a physical barrier in our minds. A fence helps create visible and identifiable landmarks that separate landscapes, properties, and houses. Borders become most evident through aerial travel. Different types of fences—wooden, metal, pasture, and natural fences—appear from a plane's window, permitting us to see only a limited section of land. From this viewpoint, the borders become compartmentalized, fixed; they only allow us to observe what is immediately available within view while forcing us to dismiss our surroundings beyond that view. Different types of borders exist, not only affecting a person's physical surroundings but also influencing a person's cultural identity. For instance, Gloria Anzaldúa describes borders as "set up to define the places that are safe and unsafe, to distinguish *us* from *them* . . . a dividing line, a narrow strip along a steep edge" (Anzaldúa 1999, 25). She also refers to psychological, sexual, and spiritual borderlands, which become part of a person's culture (Anzaldúa 1999). While fences prevent people from sharing the same space, they also symbolize cultural isolation, a hierarchical segregation based on major social factors such as race, ethnicity, class, sexuality, gender, and education that affect our ability to ground ourselves on one or the other side of the fence. Thus, the land on either side of a fence becomes simply a territory occupied by people who do not or cannot easily look beyond their bordered land.

DOI: 10.7330/9781607324034.c012

Some of the messages delivered through political discourse metaphorically create a small aerial window that obstructs our ability to look beyond borders established by such discourse. Public, political messages through various mediums—print- and web-based news sources, television, film, politically charged organizations and groups, literature—continue to alter our perceptions of people who live on either side of the geographical boundaries. For instance, Arizona has received much attention since 2010 for its bill S.B. 1070 (Support our Law Enforcement and Safe Neighborhoods Act), which "make[s] the failure to carry immigration documents a crime and give[s] the police broad power to detain anyone suspected of being in the country illegally" (Archibold, *New York Times*, April 23, 2010). While S.B. 1070 maintains cultural borders, citizenship status, English fluency, and society's perceptions also impact how immigrants are perceived as "becom[ing] insiders" (Jones-Correa, *New York Times*, Nov. 15, 2012) or "becoming American" (Danquah 2000b), reinforcing cultural borders and labeling the immigrant experience as Other, if not criminal.

In this chapter, I challenge the different cultural borders that distort our understanding of the immigrant experience. I argue that we must pay particular attention to historical and personal accounts of writers who know what it is like to leave one's home and begin a new life in an unfamiliar place. Their narratives can expand our limited view, providing insight into the immigrant experience and offering a valuable perspective, which can destroy fences, erase borders, and allow readers to engage in a different kind of rhetoric, the rhetoric of acceptance and community. In the first section, "*Una nueva* retórica:[2] Acceptance and Community in Immigrant Literature," I introduce the theoretical framework for my analysis, including the significance of storytelling, self- and communal acceptance, solidarity, cultural sensitivity, and border consciousness.

Throughout the rest of the chapter, I focus on four women writers: Meri Nana-Ama Danquah, Nina Barragan, Julia Alvarez, and Jamaica Kincaid. I chose these women because their works have contributed to my own and many others' understanding of what it means to identify as a second-generation[3] Latina in the United States. In the second section, "*Narración de cuentos con un* propósito:[4] Self- and Communal Acceptance in Danquah's Recollection," I introduce Danquah's immigrant experience to show the significance of storytelling, which allows writers to represent their true selves. By representing their true selves, writers who attempt to capture the immigrant experience through storytelling also try to illuminate the effects of cultural borders. In the chapter's third section, "*Una comunidad de* escritores:[5] Solidarity in Immigrant Literature," I transition into Barragan's story to begin showing the effects of cultural borders, particularly their impact on the children of immigrant parents. The next section, "'*Mi nombre es Rocío*':[6] Sensitivity toward Cultural Differences," highlights the characteristics that become cultural markers of difference within the immigrant experience, and the fifth section, "*Encontrarse en la soledad*:[7] Geographical and Cultural Isolation," introduces Kincaid's experience to demonstrate how cultural borders, markers of difference, and mainstream expectations lead immigrants to feel culturally isolated from their surroundings, others, and themselves. In addition to presenting Danquah's, Barragan's, Alvarez's, and Kincaid's stories, I offer my own narrative in the chapter's sixth section, "*La historia de la hija* Americana:[8] Coming to a Border Consciousness," where I show how these writers have expanded my limited, aerial view and have led me toward border consciousness. Finally, in the last section, "Application and Conclusion: Border Realities in the Classroom," I conclude by emphasizing the importance and contribution of immigrant literature, stories, and voices for research and teaching in composition and rhetoric.

UNA NUEVA RETÓRICA: ACCEPTANCE AND COMMUNITY IN IMMIGRANT LITERATURE

Not only do Danquah, Barragan, Alvarez, and Kincaid make sense of their experiences, they also make social awareness about the immigrant experience possible through storytelling. Paul John Eakin, in *Living Autobiographically: How We Create Identity in Narrative*, points out that "narrative identity . . . is an essential part of our sense of who we are" (Eakin 2008, ix). He adds that "autobiography is not merely something we read in a book; rather, as a discourse of identity, delivered bit by bit in the stories we tell about ourselves day in and day out, autobiography structures our living" (4). Storytelling, then, allows writers to share their experiences with others not only to self-reflect and represent but also to create a new rhetoric. For immigrants, this new rhetoric highlights multiple aspects of the immigrant experience, including, but not limited to, immigrants' reasons for leaving the mother country, their desire to belong to the new country, and their struggle to maintain connections with the motherland. In relation to Latino/a literature, specifically, Harold Augenbraum and Ilan Stavans add that "a sense of self, place, and history pervades our literature" (Augenbraum and Stavans 1993, xix); they claim that narrative writing is "fueled by the individual writer's need to assimilate confusion and anger that often results from growing up and being ethnic in a country in which ethnicity is not always prized" (xx). Creating a new rhetoric of self- and communal acceptance becomes especially important for writers who have struggled to navigate through cultural and linguistic barriers and who have sought to understand their own experiences. Moreover, creating a new rhetoric of community involves solidarity and cultural sensitivity. Solidarity brings people who share similar experiences together, while cultural sensitivity inspires empathy in people whose experiences differ. Becky Thompson and Sangeeta Tyagi explain how "remembering one's history and heritage . . . enables [writers] to explore individual life history while tapping into communal memory and experience" (Thompson and Tyagi 1996, xii). Although Danquah's, Barragan's, Alvarez's, and Kincaid's cultural backgrounds differ, they share similar experiences, representing a community of writers who aim to reflect and represent themselves and their cultures through writing.

A border consciousness that challenges notions of assimilation, acculturation, and retroacculturation is also necessary to build a rhetoric of acceptance and community. For writers to attain self-acceptance, achieve solidarity, and promote cultural sensitivity, they require "a consciousness of Borderlands" (Anzaldúa 1999, 99). Anzaldúa describes "a consciousness of Borderlands" as one that reflects a "mixture of races, rather than resulting in an inferior being" (99). The border consciousness, or *mestiza* consciousness, reflects the hybrid identity of the navigator, the person balancing on the fence or navigating among different cultural borders. Anzaldúa's experience mirrors border consciousness; she calls herself "a border woman" because she grew up along the Texas-Mexican border (19). She has learned to embrace different cultures, languages, and dialects, referring to their place in society as "Borderlands." For readers to reach communal acceptance, recognize the importance of solidarity, and achieve cultural sensitivity, they also must adopt border consciousness. Unlike Anzaldúa's description of border consciousness, a reader's awareness of cultural borders—that is, the awareness of a person whose experience differs from a border woman or man—must extend beyond the limits of self-identification and their own cultural preservation. Border consciousness, rather, is empathetic; it expands the reader's aerial view, which encourages them to recognize hegemonic oppression and its effects on marginalized individuals or groups. Border consciousness—whether from the writer's perspective or reader's perspective—understands notions of assimilation, acculturation, and retroacculturation and challenges these ideologies as normal, expected processes that immigrants undergo.

Rosie Molinary defines the first concept, assimilation, as "a process in which people leave behind their native culture in order to adapt to the new culture" (Molinary 2007, 2). It is easy for people to neglect their cultures when feeling pressured to assimilate into the dominant culture. Pressures to assimilate, as Alma M. García adds, may encourage "immigrants [to] move toward an acceptance of an American culture," which becomes "a way of life in which immigrant ethnic loyalties and attachments are replaced with a belief in and a commitment to a common American culture" (García 2004, 13). For immigrants and their children alike, adapting to the dominant culture means more than just learning English, sending their children to American schools, attaining citizenship, paying taxes, and so on. It means accepting American beliefs and values, regardless of whether the dominant culture's expectations negatively affect a person's identity.

The second concept, acculturation, however, is "a gradual process in which people, without dismissing their native cultures, begin to adopt aspects of the dominant culture as a result of exposure" (Molinary 2007, 2). While acculturation allows people to avoid leaning more toward one side or the other, they must perform a balancing act by maintaining their home cultures and adding aspects of the dominant culture. Finally, the third concept, retroacculturation, is "a process that happens when people who have assimilated to their new cultures begin to search for elements of their ethnic identities to incorporate into their new lives" (Molinary 2007, 4). Assimilation, acculturation, and retroacculturation can occur in different stages of a person's life, particularly for children of immigrant parents. Some may assimilate as children, but as they get older they may choose to retroacculturate or desire to learn more about their ethnic backgrounds. Thus, border consciousness recognizes the effects of these complex processes—assimilation, acculturation, and retroacculturation—that first- and second-generation immigrants face regardless of their decisions to maintain, sustain, or ignore their home culture.

NARRACIÓN DE CUENTOS CON UN PROPÓSITO: SELF- AND COMMUNAL ACCEPTANCE IN DANQUAH'S RECOLLECTIONS

Self- and communal acceptance are clear objectives in Danquah's introduction to her edited collection *Becoming American: Personal Essays by First Generation Immigrant Women*. She explains her intentions for publishing *Becoming American*, noting her desire at an early age to read literature that captured the immigrants' cultural experiences. Storytelling allows Danquah and her contributors to reflect on their experiences and reach a broad audience. They deliberately use language for self-expression and self-exploration—an opportunity to represent their own identities. Rhetoric, or the use of expressive and persuasive communication, becomes a means to influence readers, leading them toward communal acceptance or recognition of the immigrant experience. While growing up, Danquah found self-reflection and self-representation to be essential as she strived to understand her own identity. At six years old, in 1973, Danquah and her parents immigrated to Washington, DC, from Ghana. She explains that although she has "lived in America for most of [her] life, it has always been difficult for [her] to think of [herself] as an American" (Danquah 2000a, xiii). She adds, "I learned to view America as a place, not an identity—at least, not for me" (xiii). For Danquah, America became a replacement of landscape, a geographical isolation, and not a replacement of culture, not cultural isolation. She describes how her family "brought as much of Ghana with them as they could. . . . Inside our apartment we spoke our languages—*Ga* and *Twi*; we ate gari and fufu with groundnut soup, using our fingers instead of utensils; we wore batakaris and dashikis; we called each other by our 'real' names, not those English names we answered to when we were out in public" (Danquah 2000a, xiv). Danquah and her family spent most of their lives trying to navigate between their home culture—a private culture—and the dominant culture, the American culture—a public culture, as it seemed to them. Balancing on the fence between two cultures became "patchwork" for Danquah (2000a, xviii)—an acculturative process, as she chose to maintain her family's culture. In this sense of patchworking, first- and second-generation immigrants weave in and out of various situations in which they face the dominant culture's expectations to assimilate or acculturate. Holding onto customs, particularly to native foods and languages, might seem like markers of resistance. However, sometimes tradition alleviates the pain of transition from leaving one's native country to live in an unfamiliar place.

UNA COMUNIDAD DE ESCRITORES: SOLIDARITY IN IMMIGRANT LITERATURE

The contributors in Danquah's *Becoming American* attempt to represent their true selves through storytelling by sharing their experiences of leaving their homelands. They make up a community of writers and achieve solidarity. The Argentinean writer, Barragan, is one of the contributors in *Becoming American*. In "Doing Archeology in My America," she traces her family's struggle to assimilate, which reveals the effects of cultural borders and expectations. In 1944, at nineteen months old, Barragan, along with her mother and five-year-old brother, emigrated from Buenos Aires to Miami. Her father, who through a Guggenheim Fellowship had been studying at the New School of Art, awaited their arrival (Barragan 2000, 1). Her father, she explains, did not want to stay in "the Argentina of Juan Peron" (3), the president of Argentina at the time. Barragan adds, "He left behind a difficult country, struggling under political dictatorship and economic uncertainty, and he left behind a difficult family" (5). Barragan's father wanted to leave Argentina due to its political state, one factor that influenced my own parents' desire to leave Buenos Aires as well. Barragan's father desired assimilation; he wanted to leave everything behind and begin a new life in the United States. Unlike Barragan's father, however, her mother did not want to leave her birthplace. Barragan notes, "I remember my mother telling me that the saddest day of her life was the morning she woke up in our first, rented home in Iowa City and suddenly realized that she was there to stay, that she would not return" to Argentina (4). Obligated to do so, Barragan's mother left Argentina to follow and stay with her husband.

While Danquah's family maintained their native customs, Barragan, her brothers, and her sister learned "little of [their] parents' past"; their father refrained from talking about "family events, customs, or religious traditions" (Danquah 2000a, 5). Instead, Barragan explains, he only shared with them stories about the "hard times of the depression and his family's poverty" (5). Her father's lack of interest in raising his children with Argentinean traditions and customs reflects his reasons for leaving the country and shows his desire for wanting his children to adopt US culture. Despite the fact that both of Barragan's parents distanced themselves from Argentina and their extended family, she became interested in her family's history and visited Argentina to explore her family's roots. Barragan's interest in her family's history, in my view, signifies her desire to retroacculturate.

"MI NOMBRE ES ROCÍO": SENSITIVITY TOWARD CULTURAL DIFFERENCES

Barragan's interest in her family's history gave her the opportunity to claim an important part of her cultural identity. Exposures to historical and personal accounts of immigrant experience like those of Barragan help writers promote cultural sensitivity when they interpret the immigrant experience. Being culturally sensitive requires one to adopt empathy toward people whose experiences differ and avoid making judgments, assumptions, and generalizations about an individual or group. It requires acknowledging, for instance, that customs from the immigrant's native land usually remain in the home—a private, intimate space. A person's physical appearance, name, and language become cultural markers outside of the home, in the public realm. Aside from Barragan's physical appearance, her birth name, Rocío Aitana Lasansky, became her public, cultural marker. After describing her physical appearance—"blond, with a fair complexion and light eyes" (Barragan 2000, 3)—she notes that a person "might easily assume that ... becoming an assimilated American could be as easy as apple pie" (3). She explains further, "Yet fate would have that plate [of apple pie] just slightly out of my reach, always. As I matured, I came to understand that the development of my identity in the process of 'becoming American' involved the instinctive act of pushing that plate away, as much as pulling it toward me" (3). As Barragan suggests, some people make judgments about appearance, associating physical characteristics with a person's cultural background. Public, political discourse additionally sends messages that may cause individuals to make assumptions and generalizations about certain groups of people. Assumptions and generalizations about a person's race, class, gender, sexuality, and so on complicate the struggle of that person to become a member of a particular group or society. Barragan describes her name as "one of [her] biggest barriers to assimilation" and explains that "in grade school [she] didn't look different from other kids, but her name said [she] was" (9). Because people always mispronounced her name, Barragan changed it to Nina—her "parents' nickname for [her]" (9). Correct pronunciation of a name is important because of its relationship with language. As a number of authors in this collection suggest (see Hernandez et al. and Schroeder), English as the dominant language can create a sense of entitlement along with exclusion within the United States. If a person's name poses pronunciation difficulties, it signals a threat to the dominant language because it is different from the dominant culture. Most importantly, the name itself challenges expectations of assimilation because it is not recognized by many as an American name.

Similarly, the ability to speak English is another significant public, cultural marker. In the United States, English proficiency is important. Whether or not parents expect their children to learn English, teachers expect their students to use standardized English, and Americans expect immigrants to speak English; these linguistic and cultural expectations affect everyone. Alvarez (1998) alludes to this in her book *Something to Declare: Essays*. Alvarez was born in the United States, and three months after her birth in New York City in 1950, she returned to the Dominican Republic with her parents. Alvarez (2013, 18) notes that her parents "[preferred] the dictatorship of Trujillo to the U.S.A. of the early 50s." In 1960, due to her father's involvement in the underground political movement, however, the family returned to the United States. In one of her book's chapters, she describes her relatives' stated reactions as they waited for the family's departure from the Dominican Republic: "Meanwhile, we girls better practice our English! We would get so tall and pale and pretty in the United States, and smart! Maybe we would marry Americans and have little blue-eyed babies that didn't know how to speak Spanish!" (18). Not only do Alvarez's relatives encourage the opportunity for her to learn English, but they also praise the possibility of the next generation's losing their family's native tongue or at least adopting a new one. In addition, they highlight physical and intellectual characteristics that some people value in American society. Alvarez's description of her relatives' reactions depicts the expectation for emigrants and immigrants to transform and change their identities, including their languages and cultures. In other words, her relatives' reactions demonstrate pressures to assimilate. The dominant culture is not the only influence; immigrants who have assimilated can also encourage others to follow suit. In this instance, to become an "American" means to talk a certain way (speak English), to look a certain way (stand tall, look white, appear pretty), and to act a certain way (have a family and children who fit all of these descriptions as well). At the same time, however, a person's language and culture, if not the "norm," can slowly diminish because of the pressures to assimilate or the expectations to adapt to the new culture. As Alvarez (1998) describes her relatives' praise for the transformation of "becoming American" (Danquah 2000a), she also notes that "the climate was not favorable for retaining [her] Spanish" in the United States (Alvarez 1998, 61). As Alvarez's example shows, insensitivity toward people's native languages and cultures can lead them to feel geographically and culturally isolated from those native experiences.

ENCONTRARSE EN LA SOLEDAD: GEOGRAPHICAL AND CULTURAL ISOLATION

As I have demonstrated through descriptions of the experiences of some immigrant writers, a dominant culture's expectations for immigrants to assimilate can lead them to experience both geographical and cultural isolation. While geographical isolation occurs through physical distance between families and friends, cultural isolation occurs when individuals are exposed to unfamiliar beliefs, values, languages, customs, and traditions. Geographical isolation encompasses more than the physical border, as Anzaldúa notes in *Borderlands/La Frontera: The New Mestiza*. Thousands of miles separate immigrants who settle in the United States from their families and friends who stay in the homeland. Oftentimes, an expensive flight is the only option available to unite them with their families and friends. Danquah, Barragan, and Alvarez all report experiencing geographical isolation. Danquah's family emigrated from Ghana. Barragan's family arrived in the United States from Argentina. Alvarez's parents came from the Dominican Republic. The border described by Anzaldúa, which aims to segregate individuals or groups based on race, ethnicity, class, sexuality, or gender, reinforces cultural isolation beyond this physical separation. For instance, Kincaid, born in 1949 in Antigua as Elaine Potter Richardson, experienced both geographical and cultural isolation when, in 1965, her mother sent her to Westchester, New York, to work as an *au pair* (Pupello 1997). In Kincaid's excerpt "Poor Visitor" from her novel *Lucy*—which mostly mirrors Kincaid's experiences (Pupello 1997)—she describes how her character, Lucy, faces expectations of assimilation and experiences cultural isolation. Kincaid describes Lucy's surroundings, focusing mostly on the climate Lucy is unaccustomed to because she comes from a place where "'the sun is shining, the air is warm'" (Kincaid 2003, 90). In the passage cited below, Kincaid's character, Lucy, notices how her new environment affects the people around her.

> Outside, always it was cold, and everyone said that it was the coldest winter they had ever experienced; but the way they said it made me think they said this every time winter came around. . . . When people walked on the streets they did it quickly, as if they were doing something behind someone's back, as if they didn't want to draw attention to themselves, as if being out in the cold too long would cause them to dissolve. How I longed to see someone lingering on a corner, trying to draw my attention to him, trying to engage me in conversation. (Kincaid 2003, 93)

Kincaid's character, Lucy, realizes that she is "no longer in a tropical zone and [she] [feels] cold inside and out, the first time such a sensation [has] come over [her]" (Kincaid 2003, 91). Lucy—as Kincaid did—feels culturally isolated from her family and friends in Antigua. She misses her home and longs for familiar surroundings and faces. However, Kincaid's character, Lucy, knows she cannot return home and instead must assimilate and accept the climate, the people, and the emptiness she feels.

Similar to Kincaid's character, Lucy, Alvarez describes feeling culturally isolated when thinking about her family and friends in the Dominican Republic. She explains, "For weeks that soon became months and years, I would think in this way. What was going on right this moment back home? . . . I would wonder if those papers[9] had set us free from everything we loved" (Alvarez 1998, 19). After living in the United States for so long, there are moments when Alvarez thinks about home and wonders if her family's freedom in the United States has kept them apart from familiar places and faces, "from everything [they] loved" (19). Feelings of cultural isolation can cause some immigrants to question their reasons for leaving their homeland. Kincaid's character, Lucy, constantly thinks about her home, Antigua: "In books I read— from time to time, when the plot called for it—someone would suffer from homesickness. A person would leave a not very nice situation and go somewhere else, somewhere a lot better, and then long to go back where it was not very nice. . . . I longed to be back in the place that I came from, . . . I longed to sleep in a bed I had outgrown, . . . I longed to be with people" (Kincaid 2003, 91). Alone in an unfamiliar place with unfamiliar faces, Kincaid's character feels culturally isolated from her surroundings and desires to return home despite her reasons for leaving the Dominican Republic. Barragan's mother feels similar emotions to those felt by Kincaid's character, Lucy, and by Alvarez. Barragan's mother realizes she will never return home to Argentina: "For my mother, it was different. During those winter months in Buenos Aires, she had slowly prepared herself for the reality of her departure, her emigration. Immigration was another matter. Her understanding was that this would be a year's visit, and I believe she fully intended to return to Argentina. Nowhere on her map did it say anything about staying away from her country and her family forever. In fact, she did, and the year became a lifetime" (Kincaid 2003, 3). Barragan's mother assimilates and becomes permanently geographically and culturally isolated from her native country. Experiencing geographical and cultural isolation in this way can strengthen border consciousness; immigrants' awareness heightens as they continue to navigate between different worlds.

LA HISTORIA DE LA HIJA AMERICANA: COMING TO A BORDER CONSCIOUSNESS

Danquah, Barragan, Alvarez, and Kincaid possess "a consciousness of Borderlands" (Anzaldúa 1999). Their experiences have made it possible for them to challenge cultural borders and see them for what they are.

From Danquah's, Barragan's, Alvarez's, and Kincaid's works, I have also come to a border consciousness—both as the navigator on the fence and as the observer looking out the window. My awareness regarding the complexities of the immigrant experience has led me toward self- and communal acceptance, solidarity, and cultural sensitivity. Because of my experiences as *la hija Americana* who navigated between two different cultures and learned two different languages, I have become interested in others' experiences similar to my own. Below I share my own story to highlight similarities between my own and Danquah's, Barragan's, Alvarez's, and Kincaid's experiences, connections that helped me understand the importance of border consciousness in my own experience.

I am a second-generation Argentinean American. My parents and two older brothers emigrated from Buenos Aires to Philadelphia in 1974. I have seen a few photos of their departure. From what I can recall, in one of those photos my *abuela*[10] wore a purple dress and dark sunglasses. I can tell by her facial expression, despite the sunglasses covering her eyes, that she was overwhelmed with sadness. Her daughter and son-in-law were leaving the mother country to live in another. But, most important, her grandsons, my two older brothers, were leaving, too. Similar to Barragan's father who wanted to leave Argentina due to its political state, my parents decided to leave the political Buenos Aires. Six years after their departure to the United States, I was born.

Maintaining tradition became important to my family after their arrival in the United States; we acculturated. I learned many Argentinean customs that were already familiar to my brothers. We drank *Yerba mate*[11] from an oval, metallic cup with a metal straw. In fact, I remember *Mamá* worrying that my brothers' friends would think we were drinking drogas.[12] We spoke Spanish at home, and my brothers, cousins, and I still speak Spanish with our parents today. We ate pounds of *asado*,[13] a diet I have restricted as an adult because I realize too much of it is unhealthy and because my parents' cooking skills far surpass my own abilities. These customs helped my family maintain, as Danquah describes, "the influences of our native culture" (Danquah 2000a, xiii).

During the 80s, however, my family did not receive praise for acculturating or trying to maintain our language as we learned about other ways and languages. Instead of praise, we were encouraged to compromise our home language to learn English or to ensure assimilation. I always recall a conversation I had with *Mamá*, which reminds me of a crucial moment when our linguistic backgrounds seemed to interfere with the dominant culture's expectations. *Mamá* told me that during a parent-teacher conference, my second-grade teacher, Mrs. Sweeny, cautioned my parents that I would never learn English if they kept speaking to me in Spanish. Although I struggled to learn English, it was not due to a lack of ambition that I struggled but rather because my first language was Spanish. According to Mrs. Sweeney, I would *always* mix Spanish and English and, therefore, would never do well in English classes. She advised my parents that they should avoid speaking Spanish at home. This was the same advice given to my older brothers when they were in elementary school. Our primary educators expected us to assimilate by forgetting or dismissing our family's native tongue. If my brothers and I had taken our teachers' advice, we would have experienced a linguistic barrier that separated us from our family. Similar to Barragan's experience, we likely would have been left to desire retroacculturation, eventually yearning to learn about our family's culture and language. Although we have maintained our family's culture, our home language and other customs have become markers of difference.

As immigrants such as my family members struggle to become members in multiple aspects of society, they encounter racism and discrimination because people might view their cultures and languages as unfamiliar or different. Recalling her learning experiences, Alvarez describes her literacy skills as a marker of difference. She exclaims, "I did pick up enough English to understand that some classmates were not very welcoming. *Spic!* a group of bullies yelled at me in the playground" (Alvarez 2013). I too heard that word many times from my classmates and eventually learned its meaning—an offensive term used to describe Spanish-speaking immigrants and their children. Similar to Danquah, Barragan, Alvarez, and Kincaid, I familiarized myself with my environment and its people, and I grew accustomed to the name-calling. As Alvarez's, Kincaid's and Barragan's mothers felt isolated, after graduating and moving on, I too have felt culturally isolated, often longing to return home, to my family's home. The house in Philadelphia where I grew up became a safe space for me. It became a place where I could freely speak my family's language without ridicule. In contrast, during my elementary and high-school years, I dreaded school because I hated how people treated me and because I could not use the language most familiar to me. I did not want to attend school. Instead, I desired to stay home with *Mamá*. Expectations for me to assimilate negatively affected my life—as they had for Barragan when she resorted to changing her name—making it difficult for me to make friends and learn English. These feelings sometimes emerged for me after leaving my family for the first time to attend graduate school. When I realized after high school that I could hide my identity, I did not tell my college classmates anything about myself. They did not know I could speak Spanish fluently, that my family and I drank *mate*, nor that we ate *asado*. I refrained from sharing these differences with anyone because I wanted to avoid markers of difference. My experiences led me toward "a consciousness of Borderlands" (Anzaldúa 1999, 99). Eventually, I learned how to maintain my balance on the fence.

APPLICATION AND CONCLUSION: BORDER REALITIES IN THE CLASSROOM

What can we learn from the experiences of immigrant writers such as those I have described? And can we, as teachers, apply this learning in our classrooms? For my own part, as I walk into the composition classroom on the first day, I find myself navigating my way through a maze of different cultural borders. I am aware that the classroom setting, where multiple rows of desks face the front of the room, creates a physical barrier between the students and me. The classroom setting reinforces a compartmentalized, fixed vantage point that forces us to observe what is immediately in front: the students focus on me and I focus on them. Because I am aware of these borders, I purposely make an effort to avoid standing at the front of the room; instead, I walk around. My movement allows me to pay attention to my surroundings and widens my aerial view. Emotional barriers, such as those raised when students stare anxiously at me, create borders. Whether they are seasoned or first-time students, fear of the unknown can seem to overwhelm them. The classroom environment can intensify unpleasant emotions, making it conducive to cultural isolation and segregation. For instance, some students choose to sit in the back of the classroom; they distance themselves from other students and the teacher. I am also aware of the unconscious (and sometimes conscious) decisions students make to sustain cultural borders. And I always wonder if students are aware of the barriers that manage to keep us distant from each other. To increase their awareness of such barriers, I ask students to arrange the desks in a circle or to occupy empty chairs that will bring them closer to others. Their movement around the classroom helps alleviate some of the unpleasant emotions and allows for an unobstructed view of their surroundings.

Once the classroom becomes a space where physical and emotional borders begin to dissipate, I commence introductions: "Tell us your name, and something about yourself that'll help us remember who you are. I'll go first." Introductions can help ease the fifty-minute or seventy-five-minute torment for some students. Then, I combine introductions with storytelling: "I became interested in communicative practices, especially in composition and rhetoric, because I struggled with literacy growing up." Storytelling creates a sense of communal familiarity within a short time, which helps students feel a sense of belonging, a sense of acceptance and community. By encouraging movement, introductions, and storytelling on the first day of class, I guide students through the first lesson: how to become border conscious and how to value others' experiences along with their own.

We, as teachers and scholars in such fields as composition and rhetoric, may have similar experiences or goals on the first day of class with respect to borders. As teachers we become aware of the effects of different cultural borders within our own classrooms. In some cases, students may segregate themselves by remaining silent or distance themselves by sitting alone. Therefore, we seek ways to destroy the fences by bringing students together and getting them to trust their peers and us. Writers such as Danquah, Barragan, Alvarez, and Kincaid share our concerns on a greater scale. Their historical and personal accounts of potential commonalities as well as distinctions among the immigrant experience portray a rhetoric that oftentimes is not publicly discussed nor made visible in public, political discourse. Jacqueline Royster notes that "the viewpoints of . . . writers [also] counter, question, or open new doors in the interpretation of experience—and engage readers provocatively in a consideration of other ways of seeing and understanding" (Royster 2000, 20). Similar to the introductions and storytelling we may encourage on the first day of class, immigrant stories allow writers to make their voices heard and their experiences known. Such writers choose to introduce themselves to the world and desire to tell their stories. In turn, such stories stimulate a response, sometimes forcing readers to reflect on their own and others' assumptions.

As our students get bombarded daily by public, political messages through television, film, and social networking sites like Facebook and Twitter, we can help change their perceptions of themselves and others. Aside from encouraging movement, introductions, and storytelling on the first day, I believe we also can help change perceptions by exposing students to immigrant stories. Literature that depicts accounts of leaving a homeland, desiring to belong to a new country, and struggling to maintain connections with family and friends can offer students a glimpse into others' lives as well as prompt them to reflect on their own lives. While some of our students can relate to the immigrant experience more so than others, it is important for us to point out that some of them may have faced similar situations. Danquah explains how "literature became the most immediate and effective way for [her] to ease [her] feelings of confusion and isolation" (Danquah 2000b, xv). While our students' experiences differ, they may share "feelings of confusion and isolation" (Danquah 2000b, xv), which is a commonality among all four women discussed in this piece.

As an illustration of how we can use such literature to help students overcome isolation, I recall one of my classroom experiences here. I assigned students to read Judith Ortiz Cofer's (1990) "Marina," a short, autobiographical essay in Cofer's memoir about her relationship with her Puerto Rican mother. In "Marina," cultural differences create tension and conflict between Cofer and her mother. Specifically, the story reveals their perceptions toward gender roles: Cofer's valuing a woman's independence and her mother's believing in a woman's responsibility to her children and spouse. To help students seek significance in Cofer's narrative, I asked them to write on one of the following topics: (1) a time when you chose to assimilate; (2) a time when your cultural beliefs interfered with someone else's views; (3) a time when you experienced a language barrier; or (4) a time when you discovered that something or someone was not what you expected. The writing topics furthered the students' understanding of Cofer's essay and enabled them to explore how the story related to their own experiences. Some students had experienced a language barrier or culture clash or class-related obstacle. Others had moved across the country to attend college, which forced them to leave their families and friends. Other students did feel like imposters; they had tried to belong to a community of learners and academics, but they had continuously found themselves struggling to fit in since the first day they arrived on campus. In addition to identifying with Cofer's story, the students explored the importance of cultural sensitivity by discussing social values and gender roles. By reading Cofer's essay, writing about their experiences in relation to the essay's themes, and sharing their own stories with the rest of the class, the students gained the opportunity to challenge the different cultural borders that oftentimes permeated their lives.

Reading immigrant literature can guide students toward communal acceptance. Writing can lead them toward self-acceptance. Reacting to Danquah's, Barragan's, Alvarez's, and Kincaid's narratives, for instance, can motivate students to discuss political debates surrounding immigration and public notions of the immigrant experience. Dialogue can help create solidarity among students and inspire sensitivity toward cultural differences. Finally, exposing our students to the immigrant experience can direct them toward border consciousness, whether they are the navigators on the fence or the observers looking out the window. As a result, they will benefit immeasurably as they learn to navigate different cultural borders that test the identity and adaptability of all of us in an increasingly diverse world.

To challenge cultural borders, particularly within institutional boundaries, students, teachers, and scholars must pay attention to historical and personal accounts of the immigrant experience. I purposefully focus on Danquah's, Barragan's, Alvarez's, and Kincaid's narratives because they provide insight into the complex processes—assimilation, acculturation, and retroacculturation—that many immigrants face. They also offer different perspectives on experiencing cultural isolation, and they engage readers in a dialogue, paving the way for self-discovery, self-expression, acceptance of the self and others, and moving readers toward border consciousness. Storytelling becomes a means of expressive and persuasive communication, which exposes the effects of cultural borders within the immigrant experience. After ignoring or rejecting my own cultural identity as a child and adolescent, I openly align myself with the writers presented throughout this chapter to participate in the dialogue they initiate and to invite readers to join the conversation with us.

Notes

1. *De pie sobre la valla y mirando por la ventana* means "standing on the fence and looking out the window."
2. "A new rhetoric"
3. I am adopting descriptions from the Pew Research Social and Demographic Trends (2013) report to define first-, second-, and third-generation immigrants. First-generation includes "immigrant adults [and children] who live in the United States but were born outside the United States or U.S. territories." Second-generation includes "U.S. born adults who have at least one immigrant parent," and third-generation includes "adults who are the children of U.S. born parents" (http://www.pewsocialtrends.org/2013/02/07/second-generation-americans/).
4. "Storytelling with a purpose"
5. "A community of writers"
6. "My name is Rocío."
7. "Finding oneself in solitude"
8. "The story of the American daughter"
9. In the context of Alvarez's piece, "those papers" refers to the necessary government documentation that allowed her family to travel and settle in the United States.
10. "Grandmother."
11. "Argentinean herbal tea."
12. "Drugs."
13. "Argentinean barbeque."

References

Alvarez, Julia. 1998. *Something to Declare: Essays*. New York: Plume.
Alvarez, Julia. 2013. "About Me." Julia Alvarez. http://www.juliaalvarez.com/about/.
Anzaldúa, Gloria. 1999. *Borderlands/La Frontera: The New Mestiza*. 2nd ed. San Francisco: Aunt Lute Books.
Augenbraum, Harold, and Ilan Stavans. 1993. Introduction to *Growing Up Latino Memoirs and Stories: Reflections on Life in the United States*, edited by Harold Augenbraum and Ilan Stavans, xv–xxix. Boston: Houghton Mifflin.
Barragan, Nina. 2000. "Doing Archaeology in My America." In *Becoming American: Personal Essays by First Generation Immigrant Women*, edited by Meri Nana-Ama Danquah, 1–11. New York: Hyperion.
Cofer, Judith Ortiz. 1990. "Marina." In *Silent Dancing: A Partial Remembrance of a Puerto Rican Childhood*, 151–60. Houston: Arte Publico Press.
Danquah, Meri Nana-Ama, ed. 2000a. *Becoming American: Personal Essays by First Generation Immigrant Women*. New York: Hyperion.
Danquah, Meri Nana-Ama. 2000b. Introduction to *Becoming American: Personal Essays by First Generation Immigrant Women*, edited by Meri Nana-Ama Danquah, xiii–xviii. New York: Hyperion.
Eakin, Paul John. 2008. *Living Autobiographically: How We Create Identity in Narrative*. Ithaca, NY: Cornell University Press.
García, Alma M. 2004. *Narratives of Mexican American Women: Emergent Identities of the Second Generation*. Walnut Creek, CA: AltaMira.
Kincaid, Jamaica. 2003. "Poor Visitor." In *Crossing into America: The New Literature of Immigration*, edited by Louis Mendoza and S. Shankar, 89–96. New York: New Press.
Molinary, Rosie. 2007. *Hijas Americanas: Beauty, Body Image, and Growing Up Latina*. Emeryville, CA: Seal.
Pew Research Center Social and Demographic Trends. 2013. "Second-Generation Americans: A Portrait of the Adult Children of Immigrants." pewsocialtrends.org. http://www.pewsocialtrends.org/2013/02/07/second-generation-americans/.
Pupello, Vanessa. 1997. "Jamaica Kincaid." *Emory University*, Fall. Accessed November 15, 2012. https://scholarblogs.emory.edu/postcolonialstudies/2014/06/10/kincaid-jamaica/.
Royster, Jacqueline Jones. 2000. *Traces of a Stream: Literacy and Social Change Among African American Women*. Pittsburgh: University of Pittsburgh Press.
Thompson, Becky, and Sangeeta Tyagi. 1996. "Storytelling as Social Conscience: The Power of Autobiography." In *Names We Call Home: Autobiography on Racial Identity*, edited by Becky Thompson and Sangeeta Tyagi, ix–xvii. New York: Routledge.

13
FOSTERING INCLUSIVE DIALOGUE IN EMERGENT UNIVERSITY-COMMUNITY PARTNERSHIPS

Setting the Stage for Intercultural Inquiry

Elenore Long, Jennifer Clifton, Andrea Alden, and Judy Holiday

University partnerships with surrounding communities are considered by many to be a good idea, and we agree.[1] But partnerships also bring to light borders that exist between universities and communities that may need to be acknowledged in order for universities to do their best work. In this chapter, we locate this volume's desire to improve conditions for inclusive deliberative democracy at the border between communities and universities. We are concerned with the tendency of the community-university boundary to limit local public imagination—to limit what constitutes engagement, what public life is good for, and how to relate to one another publicly. The model we take up grounds community-university partnerships in intercultural inquiry to transform the very ways local public life is manifest and experienced (Ackerman and Coogan 2010; Flower 1997, 2002; Grabill 2007; Higgins, Long and Flower 2006; Long 2008). This model is an alternative to partnerships cast as sites where services are delivered from the university (bestowed with resources) to the community (fraught with needs). However, in the work described in this chapter, we found ourselves heeding the call of intercultural inquiry in a more ill-defined context than the ones in which intercultural inquiry first emerged, where community-university partnerships were already relatively well formed and where the partnerships' issues of shared concern were largely already framed (Flower, Long and Higgins 2000; Peck, Flower and Higgins 1995). In contrast, in our work, we tested the capacity of intercultural inquiry to foster inclusive dialogue in the preliminary stages of partnership building. In this context, community-university partners were in the very throes of discovering the concerns that could call diverse stakeholders together for the purposes of dialogue, discovery, and change. Yet, despite the partnership's emergent qualities, the pervasive overriding script of service already held sway, bending the partnership toward the common tropes of volunteerism and service delivery. We asked, what practices could encourage and grow local public life under such conditions?

Intercultural inquiry, as we practiced it, brings local stakeholders from across university and community boundaries together to discover and to deliberate pressing open questions of shared concern—urgent felt difficulties in people's lives—such as responding to pending curfew-policy enforcement (Flower 2008), handling emergency-room healthcare communication about pressing needs (Young and Flower 2001), or overcoming biases in a high-school suspension policy (Peck, Flower, and Higgins 1995). According to this model of intercultural inquiry, everyday people's encounters with policies and practices are viewed as valuable and necessary components of public dialogue, illuminating, as these encounters do, the ways actual policies and practices play out in real people's lives (Flower 1997, 2002). Such inclusive dialogue reflects the limitations of Habermas-ian critical rational discourse in which propositional claims are valued but do little to sustain productive relations among strangers, to construct a more inclusive democracy, or to recast the work at hand (Benhabib 1992; Fraser 1993; Young 1997). Instead, these efforts require the distinct rhetorical work of productive knowledge building (Coogan 2002; Flower 2008; Higgins, Long, and Flower 2006). For Bent Flyvbjerg, this productive knowledge building contributes to daily life when it actively interrogates values and power and is oriented toward action (Flyvbjerg 2001, 3). Pragmatic, variable, and context dependent, such knowledge building bends wise action toward a desired outcome and works to invent tools and paths for transforming limits and barriers into opportunities for accomplishing shared goals (Atwill 2009, 141; Clifton 2013a). Intercultural inquiry, then, attempts to reconfigure social relations and expertise in pursuit of the more just distribution of social capital and what that capital can purchase and create.

This reconfiguration must include not only what partners talk about but also how partners engage in talk together across boundaries. Scholars concerned with the ways borders have been drawn—with how public and private identities enact and reinscribe those boundaries—warn of the potential for universities to do real harm when reaching out beyond their campus borders in the name of service. Institutional privilege tips the balance in favor of the university's interests (Goldblatt 2007; Grabill 2001; Himley 2004; Mathieu 2005). In fact, that warning is so familiar it circulates as a commonplace on university campuses and in nonprofit organizations. That everyday people have firsthand knowledge of this fact bears repeating (cf. Cushman 1998, 47). Despite these warnings, across our campus—and, we venture, likely yours—talk reinscribes literacy as one of the primary services for a university to provide. This talk tends to reflect and reinforce not only institutional power but also long-held notions of the Great Divide literacy myth and lingering faith in an autonomous literacy that renders those with "less literacy" as somehow more primitive and those with "more" as somehow superior (Street 1993, 4). Against this backdrop, then, in this chapter we hope to show that for all its local details, the situation we describe here is not unique to the people who populate it. Rather, the situation depicts a larger socioeconomic system fueled by such boundary drawing (Carter and Mutnick 2012, 4–10; Clifton 2014; Gee, Hull, and Lankshear 1996; Himley 2004; Long, Fye, and Jarvis 2012, 59–62; Welch 2012, 36–51).

This chapter ventures a framework for intercultural inquiry in emerging partnerships. As we developed this framework, we drew on available tools from community-literacy scholarship when the situation afforded such an approach (Clifton 2013b, 230–31); when necessary, we invented new ones. Five practices constitute this framework.

1. Listening deliberatively

2. Looking for alignments

3. Documenting, constructing, and testing critical incidents

4. Representing how people are located in systems

5. Calling for public response.

These practices are attentive to power differentials and competing social values. Through these practices, this framework decenters the university. Moreover, it distributes the work, values, and concerns of a partnership across alignments in which the university is just one networked site within a complex system.

THE CONTEXT

The partnership described here began as a response to an actual invitation. At the time, the four authors of this chapter were working and studying at the university where Emily,[2] an initial instigator for this partnership, worked as an undergraduate writing center tutor. Emily attended a presentation sponsored by a human-service organization, referred to here as the Sudanese Refugee Support Center (SRSC). At the presentation, Sudanese men showed the film *God Grew Tired of Us*

(2007) and told their stories of fleeing war-torn south Sudan, spending decades in refugee camps, and being relocated through a lottery system to the United States. At the conclusion of their presentation, the men asked those in attendance to volunteer at the SRSC, the organization that sponsored them and served the Sudanese diaspora in Phoenix. In particular, the men asked for people who could help with writing. This event set off a chain of e-mails and phone calls across campus to writing center directors, academic-success administrators, rhetoric and composition faculty, and graduate students in the department of English.

When we (Emily and the authors of this piece) contacted the executive director of the SRSC, he told us to "just show up" for a while. He was no stranger to white women coming to the SRSC to spend time with the Lost Boys of Sudan, hoping they could extend motherly care to young abandoned boys. However, the Lost Boys—so dubbed because of their childhood flight from their villages after the brutal torture, killing, and burning of their homes and adult kin—were actually women as well as men now ranging in age from their early twenties to late forties and often with families of their own. In following the executive director's direction to "show up," we met Tap Dak, the SRSC's outreach coordinator at the time. Over the next months, working with Dak as he wrote papers for his community college composition courses, we learned of his concerns about posttraumatic stress disorder, arranged marriages, teen pregnancy, and care of elders—all concerns that held different meanings, different complications, different consequences depending on the contexts in which members of the Sudanese diaspora found themselves in Phoenix or in South Sudan or scattered across the United States or across north and western Africa. As we heard Dak and other Sudanese leaders foreground these larger concerns over the writing assignments they worked on with us, our roles, relationships, and work shifted. With the help of the framework described below, what began as an organizational partnership with the SRSC became more fluid, networked and responsive as Dak connected us to the broader diaspora.[3]

As Dak connected us to men and women who were elected leaders of the Sudanese diaspora, we came to know many Sudanese who were engaging in sophisticated, creative work—such as designing and selling dresses marking hybridized identities, starting a small hair-braiding business, translating legal documents and court proceedings for tribal kin—creative, inventive work that does not often find an easy home in our schools or institutions. The contradictions among the multiple literacies they were using in their everyday lives, the ways those literacies were being shunned by educational institutions, and the ways the

Sudanese in Phoenix both invoked service (calling for writing tutors) and were cautious with service providers (asking us to "just show up") didn't add up. Without charting an alternative discursive landscape, it seemed to us that any literacy services we provided would continue to perpetuate the poignant if elusive institutional arrogance about which the Sudanese were so wary.

The practices described below comprise a framework for jointly constructing the work and relations of this emergent partnership. Although we treat each practice in turn and offer some sense of sequence, the work of engaging them was often far more fluid, shared, coconstructed, distributed, reflexive, and iterative than sequential.

1. LISTENING DELIBERATIVELY

To listen deliberatively—to listen in ways that foster deliberation—is to engage the call and response of public world making. Or, as Michael Warner puts it, "Run it up the flagpole and see who salutes" (Warner 2002, 114)—and, just as important, respond attentively when the flag and flagpole are the initiatives of others. In the venues available to the Sudanese refugees who had come to the United States as boys, in their public speeches and on their websites, the issues they were raising were complex transnational concerns well beyond the scope and reach of the SRSC, any of the Sudanese tribes, or any single American citizen or institution. And yet Sudanese representatives from the SRSC called for responses that paralleled what they, as refugees, had come to recognize as white ways of engaging: volunteering or donating— two calling cards of service. From the start, our currency was cast in terms of writing and literacy. We aimed to deliver in terms of writing support, but we also aimed to respond deliberatively—in the spirit of intercultural inquiry—primarily in two ways: (1) by engaging with the issues Dak and other Sudanese men were naming in their writing and (2) by rhetorically coconstructing issues of shared concern. At Dak's bidding, initially we did our best to register (literally, on big sheets of poster paper) the issues he and his colleagues named as most pressing across a range of stakeholders. Early on, these issues fell across genders and identified the challenges of four distinct generations of Sudanese refugees: elders, first generation, second generation, and teens. Later, this record revealed issues among the dynamic set of stakeholders displayed in the social-arenas map in Figure 13.1. Conversations that started between a writer and a writing mentor grew to include more people and to include issues and concerns related to but well beyond

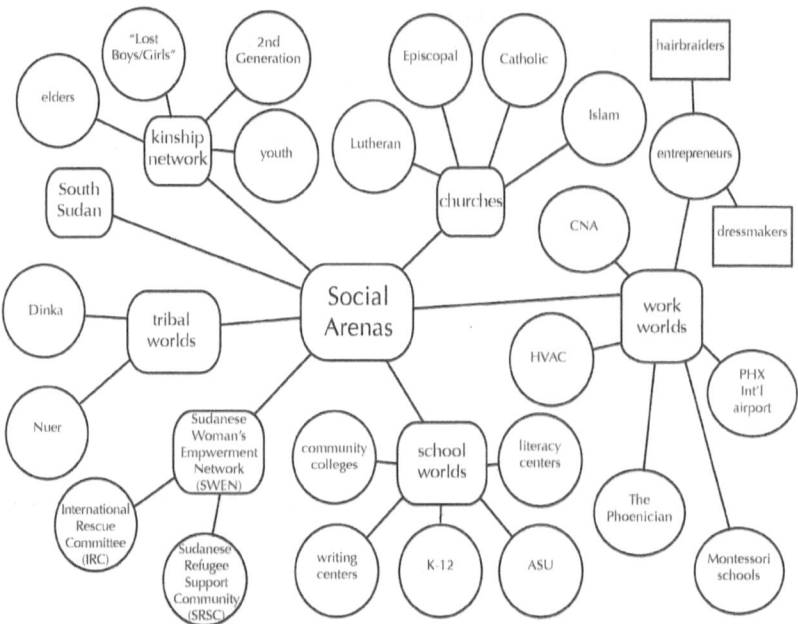

Figure 13.1. Social-arenas map.

those Dak and others initially named in the papers they wrote for their writing classes.

For us as writing mentors, responding deliberatively meant listening for concerns Dak and others were raising in their writing and in our conversations with them. Over the first several weeks that we responded as writing tutors, Dak, and later the current as well as the previous director of the SRSC, identified other shared goals for us to pursue collaboratively for the health of the Sudanese diaspora in Phoenix—specifically, aims of identity construction and creating intergenerational and cross-gendered deliberative spaces to consider the men's and women's changing roles across generations. Dak deemed these aims different versions of "community health" and described them to us in ways inextricable from concerns about writing and literacy. As such, these ideas of health called for different versions of our knowledge and abilities in the rhetorical arts, primarily around community building and democratic deliberation.

After a series of conversations, Dak and other Sudanese leaders invited us to attend a board meeting of the SRSC. In the meeting, we presented a tentative plan we had previously drawn up with Dak and vetted with the directors for a series of conversations across genders and generations. The board members endorsed the collaboration. For us, responding deliberatively meant continuing to show up as writing mentors, for that was the social contract we had entered into. But it also meant listening for ways to improve conditions for sponsoring more inclusive deliberation—possibilities that would invite everyone at the table to contribute to and learn from one another. Responding deliberatively in this way invoked a different "stranger sociability" (Warner 2002, 39). No longer were we entirely bound by service; instead, call and response invoked the alternative stance of wonder—the basis for Iris Marion Young's model of inclusive communicative democracy in which—in addition to argumentation—all kinds of discourse moves (markedly greeting and storytelling) are valued for their contributions when strangers come together around a shared concern (Young 1997, 56). Certainly, one of us still had a dissertation to write and Dak and others still needed to pass their community college courses, but we began to wonder about one another's lives, about other kinds of work we could be up to together, about our worlds being better than they are.

2. LOOKING FOR ALIGNMENTS

Looking for alignments is a dialogical practice. In an emergent partnership predicated on inquiry rather than service, it might be the case that alignments will form among those most sturdy, visible, and funded institutional entities. But maybe not. In the vignette that appears below, alignments are forged amidst partners' multiple identities and the attendant resources those identities are able to leverage. This vignette reflects findings in existing scholarship that speaks to the need for such institutional alignments to sustain community partnerships (Cushman 2002, 2006), to network working-class agitators (Parks and Pollard 2010), and to leverage groups' resources toward a shared vision (Goldblatt 2007). Moreover, this case study highlights the rhetorical efforts required to leverage such alignments toward the distinctly public work of local public deliberation.

Just weeks after we met with the SRSC board, Dak raised issues he had not previously named. Working on his own two-year degree at a local community college, Dak was frustrated that many of the younger Lost Boys and second-generation Sudanese youth who were finishing high school and attending universities and community colleges were not able to find meaningful work. Dak questioned these institutions' responsibilities to their graduates who couldn't find ways to leverage their degrees, either in Phoenix or in Sudan. In part, Dak's critique shifted the self-other relations undergirding the partnership we were forming. No longer were we either misguided Americans to keep at bay or university experts/visitors to be treated with deference. Now, Dak seemed to be signaling, we can get down to the work at hand. In addition, Dak's critique opened up possibilities for public dialogue; expanded the range of stakeholders involved; and invoked a version of public life that included everyday people speaking back to and shaping institutional policies, practices, and commitments.[4]

Dak shifted his own positionality as he moved in and among institutions to draw and redraw alignments among community partners affiliated with the SRSC; men and women leaders of the SCAA; and ourselves, coming from the university. By shifting alignments, Dak navigated not only among his own multiple I-positions[5] but also among ours and implicitly asked us to do the same. A few days after the board meeting described above, Dak arranged for two of us authoring this piece to meet with the president and vice president of the Sudanese Community Association in Arizona (SCAA), a geopolitical organization that oversees Sudanese tribal networks across the state. We hadn't known there was such a thing. While SRSC's mission at the time was to serve the Lost Boys in Phoenix,[6] the officials of this geopolitical organization were elected by the three thousand-plus Sudanese in Arizona to help care for and meet the needs of Sudanese scattered across the state.

Dak was moving us into a position in which Sudanese leaders would endorse us, allowing us to work in a more networked and relational way to extend beyond the reach of the SRSC. However, because of the contested nature of cross-gendered, cross-tribal, cross-generational relations within the Sudanese diaspora in Phoenix, endorsement from these male leaders would only take us so far. Our work, then, would become more grassroots as Dak connected us—in another act of redrawing boundaries—with young Sudanese mothers. At the time, the Sudanese women in Phoenix had a governing and organizational structure that coordinated with, but was intentionally distinct from, the male-governed SCAA. Dak's rhetorical work galvanized the work ahead. We didn't work with the SRSC in any official capacity again, although we continue to talk with the executive director as "a community leader who gets things done," a role he distinguishes from his administrative position. For those of us from the university engaged in this encounter, there could have been no better assurance that the collaborative venture was proving valuable to the Sudanese than Dak's gesture to enlist our participation within this extended network of people.[7]

Institutional locations aren't necessarily as fixed as the service paradigm might have us believe or perform. For example, in relating to us,

Dak might call on his position as outreach coordinator of the SRSC, but he might also flex and call more directly on his positions or resources as a Nuer leader; a Christian; husband to a Filipino woman; father of biracial daughters; former child soldier; the outreach coordinator at a local nonprofit; community college student; heating, ventilation, and air conditioning expert; stellar cross-country runner; adult Lost Boy; an elected leader of the SCAA. Understanding Dak and ourselves as dialogical selves expands the ways we understand the rhetorical means and rhetorical alignments available in forging emerging partnerships (Ellis and Stam 2010, 424; Hermans and Kempen 1993).[8]

3. DOCUMENTING, CONSTRUCTING, AND TESTING CRITICAL INCIDENTS

In our work with members of the university whose capacity to know other city residents depends on the documents we can prepare for meetings, we need additional practices to humanize representations of community partners and to invoke their situated expertise. The best method we have found for this work is storytelling—but telling a particular kind of story: the critical incident, a genre designed to foreground situated knowledge (Flanagan 1954, 328). In meetings with administrators on campus, we have found that documenting and constructing critical incidents in writing can shift the priorities and tenor of university discussions about potential partners. Fronting the experiences of community partners in writing has become a regular practice for shaping meetings and partnerships as spaces of intercultural inquiry and public deliberation.

The practice of documenting, constructing and testing critical incidents draws heavily from existing scholarship in community literacy that theorizes how texts produced in the context of critical incidents can contribute to intercultural dialogue. The critical incident is a resource for subsequent joint inquiry among people who otherwise have few occasions to talk.

> Personal stories alone don't necessarily support intercultural inquiry. . . . Narratives that elaborate on stakeholders' reasoning, social positioning, and life contexts generate new information and propel discussion that can move people beyond personal expression to public problem solving. When narrative is elaborated in this way and focused around the causes of and responses to problems, it can be used for case analysis. . . . In the context of community-based deliberative inquiry, critical incidents elicit carefully contextualized accounts of how people actually experience

problems involving, for instance, landlord-tenant relations, gang violence, school suspension policies, or welfare reform. (Higgins, Long, and Flower 2006, 21)

As a tool for intercultural inquiry, critical incidents bring our pet theories up short and can lead participants to seek out more information to enlarge their understanding. Consider, for instance, a critical incident in a college mentor's experience at Pittsburgh's Community Literacy Center (CLC) that spurred him to frame and to pursue a new open question: "When I first began to volunteer as a freshman, I thought of myself as male, college-bound role model to the boys I tutored. Now I see why African American men can be more important to them as *role models*. So how do they see *our* intercultural relationship working?" (Flower 2008, 235).

The critical incidents we documented emerged from the same principles for public listening theorized elsewhere (Clifton 2013b; Clifton, Long, and Roen 2013; Clifton and Sigoloff 2013; Higgins, Long, and Flower 2006, 21). In our day-to-day interactions, the Sudanese with whom we worked recounted situations they found particularly troubling, demanding, or otherwise challenging. Some were stories Dak recounted during our deliberations together. Others were narratives we had heard other people tell us: for example, Samra's experiences filling out a financial aid form, Ajak's experiences trying to employ his university credentials. Other incidents we experienced firsthand while working as writing mentors. As we documented and constructed critical incidents in writing, we tested them with those whose experiences were represented: is this how you see or hear you representing yourself or others?

Our practice of listening for critical incidents has led members of the Sudanese community to volunteer experiences in subsequent conversations with us.[9] Consider, for instance, a critical incident Roda produced in a video entitled *Figuring Out What to Write* (see Fig. 13.2). In the video, Roda narrates an assignment from her college writing course asking her to write a profile of a rich person and to use song lyrics to portray that person. A busy mother of three, she doesn't listen to much popular music as the assignment description assumed she would.

On video, Roda narrates a writing session during which she and her literacy mentor worked one morning at her apartment in search of connections as they tried to find a way into the assignment. Roda describes recounting a song her mother sang to her brother when they were children in Sudan. As Roda remembers, recounts the lyrics, and reads from her essay, she starts describing her mother as well.

Fostering Inclusive Dialogue in Emergent University-Community Partnerships   237

Figure 13.2. Critical incident: Figuring Out What to Write.

> She rented a canoe . . . to get the food from her farm. She traveled for two days and two nights in the sea. It was the rainy season. Sudan is a jungle. She had to push the canoe through the grassy water for two days. When she left us, she was fresh. But when she returned, she was very, very tired. When she got back, I remember my brother crying. He was nine years old. He cried, telling my mom he wanted to take the canoe back. She said, "No, you are a little boy. But one day you're going to grow up, and you will help me." At that time, my mom made up a song.

In the video, Roda first sings the song and then explicates its lyrics: "That song was telling my brother that one day he will grow up. 'You aren't growing smaller; you're growing bigger. One day you'll be able to help me for what I am doing now.'" Roda looks into the camera and continues:

> It's a sad song. It brought her husband to mind. Traveling in the sea for two days is a man's job. The song was a kind of prayer, asking God to part the grassy water that made it so hard to push the canoe. In the song, she told the blades of grass, "I told God to move you guys." She was saying, she is a widow, and the grass in the sea made it hard for her to go fast. If there were no grass, maybe the trip would only take one day. But because of the grassy water, it made the trip harder for her to go so fast. That's why she called on God to help her by making the grass in the water disappear.

Then it would be easier for a widow lady like her to do everything she needed to do for her children.

With this song and her mother clearly in mind—Roda explains on camera—she drafted an essay around this story, an essay featuring her mother, rich in character; the lyrics, testament to that strength.

On tape, Roda recounts learning several weeks later that the decisions she had made as a writer did not track with the instructor's intentions to teach proper citation methods by having students first work with textual sources more familiar to them than academic ones: the lyrics of popular songs that circulate online. Roda failed the assignment.

Over time, as we heard critical incidents like this one, we noticed themes. For instance, numerous critical incidents resisted or exposed myths of assimilation; others recounted specific experiences within educational settings where requirements for credentials created obstacles; still others sung of a desire for what Mary Belenky, Lynn Bond, and Jacqueline Weinstock have called "a public homeplace" (Belenky, Bond, and Weinstock 1991, 13; cf. Clifton 2013b). And as elaborated further below, many such incidents narrated storylines in which Sudanese women were endowed with special responsibility for the diaspora's ability to thrive—and, conversely, were blamed for particular struggles (Clifton 2012).

An important implication follows from listening for critical incidents. Always attentive to warnings of colonizing moves that mine communities for their stories and leverage them in ways that dehumanize, objectify, strip, or damage communities (e.g., Tuck 2009, 410), this practice acknowledges that community residents not only may have problem narratives to tell but also may be eager to go public with them in order to help shape responsive institutional and public practices.

4. REPRESENTING HOW PEOPLE ARE LOCATED IN SYSTEMS

To open up conversation about the choices people are making in relation to the systems they are navigating—what they're afforded and constrained by in relation to those systems—a necessary step is to represent people as "persons-in-systems" (Engeström 2001, 135) rather than isolated actors. Adele Clarke's situational analysis provides a technique for taking up this work. Situational analysis "address[es] head-on the inconsistencies, irregularities, and downright messiness of the empirical world" (Clarke 2005, 15). Such analysis responds to the questions "Who and what are in this situation? Who and what matters in this

Fostering Inclusive Dialogue in Emergent University-Community Partnerships 239

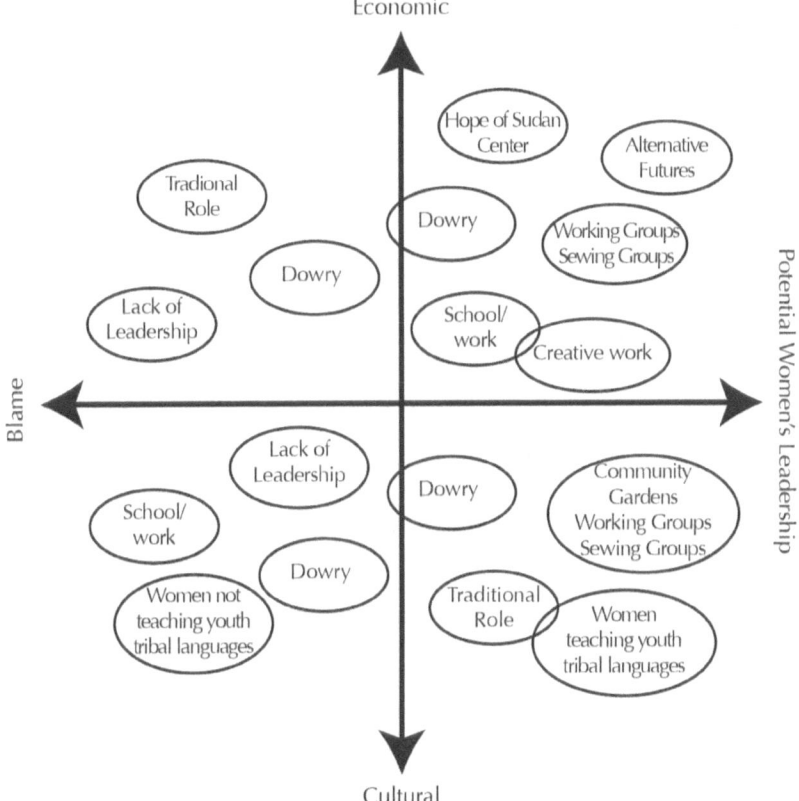

Figure 13.3. Themed map: Sudanese women's contributions in Phoenix.

situation? What elements 'make a difference' in this situation?" (87). Two kinds of situational maps—the social-arenas map shown in Figure 13.1 and the thematic map shown in Figure 13.3—were especially helpful for seeing individual people and particular critical incidents located among systems.

Mapping themes identifies a situation that merits attention, codes across four broad themes, labels these themes as continuums along x and y axes, and maps findings in quadrants along x and y axes (see Fig. 13.3). For instance, as we attended to themes emerging from our notes, we noticed incidents in which people—whether the women themselves or other people—were talking about women, and we coded claims from those incidents. Below are representative excerpts from various situations we observed.

- *Bearing Blame.* Ponte: "You see, you have done nothing." (meeting in which 14 Sudanese women resign in visible frustration with each other and with the male leaders of the SCAA)
- *Bearing Responsibility for Progress.* Ramsey: "Every woman should be at work or at school." (interview 4.16.2010)
- *Bearing Responsibility for Nation-building.* Ponte to second-generation girls who graduated from high school: "You are the hope of Sudan." (graduation party 6.10.2010)
- *Initiating Grassroots Leadership.* Samra, Amou, Ajak, and other local Sudanese women work with the Sudanese Women's Empowerment Network to hold a conference in Phoenix informing the Sudanese diaspora about voting in the referendum on the secession of southern Sudan. (meeting 6.26.2010)
- *Sustaining Culture.* Suzana teaches Dinka children Dinka language and songs at the Sudanese Episcopal Mission in Phoenix on Sundays.
- *Procuring and Circulating Social and Economic Capital.* Suzana: "The more children you have, the more you are respected." (field notes from a Chuck E. Cheese birthday party 11.10.2010)
- *Maintaining and Resisting Traditional Roles.* Samra described the traditional roles of women in her mother's village in the Nuba Mountains: "In the Muslim culture, the woman do not go to school. But my father, he made me go." (field notes 6.17.2010)
- *Caring for Others.* Samra, to her mother when Dalila talked about wanting to cook at her own restaurant but not wanting to teach other women domestic arts as she had in Sudan: "You don't want to help no one?!" Dalila responded: "I'm tired." (field notes 6.20.2011)
- *Creating Alternative Futures.* Saher about her hopes to sponsor a youth center, supported in part from proceeds from selling dresses: "If this thing works and I'm able to do the Center I want to do and like kids are learning, improving" (field notes 3.24.2012).

The map organizes these data along two axes: a blame-credit axis that indicates the valence of the responsibility attributed to women, and an economic-cultural axis that indicates the value ascribed to specific contributions attributed to the women.

Critical incidents portray felt difficulties. When people narrate critical incidents, they're theory building to account for what went wrong and what are potential sites of change at the intersection where lived lives meet institutional structures (such structures as family, education, healthcare). The logic of that theory building goes something like this: *Man, the systems we find ourselves in are not really working out for us all that well. Somehow we need to hang onto some agency in the midst of this. I know our difficulty must be due to actions or outcomes that seem to be affecting me and those I care about. The problem is. . . . The solution is. . . . What really matters is. . . . If only we (or they) would. . . .* Mapping the ways people's theory building shows up in critical incidents represents people's social locations as deeply personal and highly situated as well as systemic and structural.

The themed map above (Fig. 13.3) helps identify the structural conditions that contribute to the pressure many Sudanese women are under in Phoenix. The map shows that women were simultaneously blamed when they were not going to school or working outside the home and blamed for letting school or work interfere with home life. These contradictions and pressures put women in a tough space in large part because of the ways the multiple systems they are navigating demand and compete for their limited energy and resources with little promise of paying off. This representation lets us read critical incidents, which dramatize priorities and values in a given moment in light of other logics, values, and priorities that might be circulating across systems in practices, policies, or talk. This representation also lets us see patterns, showing that these values are not one-off outliers but are instead recognizable, predictable, repeated, and ongoing; that is to say, the map lets us see that there is something systemic/structural about the pressures and constraints Sudanese women face in Phoenix. Situational analysis helped us prepare for dialogue about the *choices* people are making in relation to the systems they're navigating. It is important to note that as we sought to expand deliberation to include stakeholders across social arenas (Fig. 13.1) in conversation with these Sudanese women, the themed maps (Fig. 13.3) opened up dialogue about the *priorities and practices of these systems* as potential sites for change.

5. CALLING FOR PUBLIC RESPONSE

Institutional affiliations are often so fixed it is easier to see walls rather than the thresholds of doorways, sprawl rather than roadways. To transform such limits, this next practice aims to create an alternative discourse for focused, intercultural public dialogue. This practice can resemble a community think tank (Flower 2002) or problem-solving dialogue (Coogan 2006; Higgins, Long, and Flower 2006), but in an emergent partnership, this practice also includes building anticipation for such dialogue and the literal work of beckoning people to deliberate as a public in this way. Calling for public response also asks stakeholders to coconstruct shared concerns and to take informed action.

Almost from the outset, the partnership described here had been building anticipation for public dialogue across institutions. Listening for and documenting critical incidents had illuminated for us specific ways Sudanese refugees in Phoenix were simultaneously navigating commitments of kinship, the city's service economy, and pressures of fast capitalism in attempts to thrive under conditions neither of their making nor under their control (Clifton 2013b, 231–32). When called to attend meetings across campus about what our research was yielding, we circulated critical incidents dramatizing such experiences—in which writing matters but not quite in the ways one would predict. As the lively complexity of those experiences revealed the limitations of what campus members often had in mind for outreach, these incidents also created the desire for more public dialogue to inform better responses. These critical incidents created expectations—"hunger," even, as some colleagues told us—for the opportunity to hear how people with different responsibilities and life experiences would make sense of the documented dynamics. It was in anticipation of such purposeful, intercultural dialogue that several colleagues told us they awaited the culminating event of a two-day public literacies symposium held on campus recently—the chance, as one colleague put it in an e-mail message, to "interact in depth" with "several people I don't necessarily know . . . about a subject I care about but not always for the same reason that it matters to others in the room."

Calling for public response also quite literally calls strangers together to deliberate as a public. Four critical incidents proved sufficient for this purpose at the community conversation held the second afternoon of our spring's public literacies symposium. These incidents were selected from a constellation of narratives recounted by Sudanese women navigating literacy organizations.[10] Including Roda's critical incident described under our framework's third practice, these incidents were entitled:

- "Figuring Out What to Write"
- "A Mentor Comes up Short"
- "'Chronic Plagiarizers'"
- "'That's Just the Way the World Works.'"

Forty-five in all, participants in the community conversation included the executive director of the county's largest adult-literacy center; the community-outreach officer for our region's United Way; writing center tutors and writing instructors from the regional community college system; several social workers; Dak and ten other members of the Sudanese Diaspora of Phoenix; a Sudanese psychologist specializing in refugee resettlement; a journalist; several graduate students in rhetoric and composition and other writing instructors from our university; and three nationally renowned community-literacy scholars and one coauthor, who had returned to Phoenix from the University of Missouri to cofacilitate the event. Critical incidents dramatizing specific sites of conflict indicate something of an impasse or challenge. But they are also sites of culture building; as such, they hold the potential to inform institutional critique and change (Porter et al. 2000, 601).

In several respects, these critical incidents were textual versions of the flag in Warner's directive for public world making on which so much of this chapter is predicated. According to Warner, public world making involves issuing invitations and waiting to see who replies. Public life, that is, is conjured in the call and response of discourse. "Public discourse says not only 'Let a public exist' but 'Let it have this character, speak this way, see the world in this way.'. . . Put on a show and see who shows up" (Warner 2002, 114). Consider, for instance, the Sudanese psychologist, John Kuek, who specializes in refugee resettlement. Kuek spoke at the symposium and participated actively in the culminating community conversation. Initially, he didn't return our repeated phone calls requesting to hire him as a consultant for the event. That is, our initial attempts to engage him in a public conversation about refugee resettlement in southern Arizona went unheeded. What stirred Kuek to respond was—upon suggestion from Roda—an invitation that foregrounded the critical incident entitled "Figuring Out What to Write," including excerpts from Roda's classroom essay explicating her mother's toil and song. In response to Roda's writing, Kuek accepted the invitation to the symposium, a gesture that communicated *To this, I will come. Of this, I will be a part.*

In addition, the set of four critical incidents elicited focused and purposeful dialogue. In small groups, participants considered one another's interpretations of each narrative: what actions and decisions transpired and why they mattered. Furthermore, participants were asked to network narratives—to listen for how commitments or values were connected, for instance, and how specific affordances or constraints (such as transportation or daycare) affected other decisions (Dingo 2012, 11). In articulating intersections among social-arena and themed maps (e.g., Fig. 13.1 and Fig. 13.3) and critical incidents (e.g., Fig. 13.2), such talk illustrated to actual stakeholders how lived experiences are in fact networked—indicating, for instance, *When we talk about "the chronic plagiarizer" in this way, here's how this charge travels.* Such dialogue makes visible the warrants underneath those claims, and it can expose contradictions or inconsistencies, putting them up for the kinds of interrogation and dialogue that can create alternatives.

In emerging partnerships, the call for public response also asks strangers to reconsider the work they are up to in relation to one another (Flyvbjerg, Bruzelius, and Rothengatter 2003). This practice elicits this broader coconstruction of shared concerns. As the social-arenas map indicates (Fig. 13.1), institutions operate in relation to one another because of the ways people move into, out of, and among them. This is true whether we recognize it or not. So this practice asks people to consider their work operating within this broader networked system. For instance, calling for public response drove home an insight that had otherwise remained for us at the university an abstraction. Our institution's influence may not be unidirectional or unilateral, but it shapes many of the attitudes and practices that circulate across the county at large—within community colleges, tutoring labs, literacy centers, boys and girls clubs, churches, synagogues, and universities. For instance, a graduate of our institution's master's program in rhetoric and composition directs the largest volunteer literacy agency in the region; others serve as tutors at these and other centers and work at community colleges as both instructors and writing center tutors. Whether by grants, funding cuts, legislative decisions, competition over students, admission standards, or specific institutional practices such as assignment descriptions, uses of content management software, even hiring practices, our university participates in policy and practices that create ripple effects. The call for public response calls attention to those ripples.

Calling for public response also invites the invention of new and distributed work. Some of this may be work people can do on their own; other work may require specific stakeholders to call others into dialogue in order to chart together a next step. For instance, from the above conversation emerged two current projects. One response is a collaborative initiative among the city, our university, and a human-service organization to produce an online digital resource of literacy services in Maricopa County. Another is a photovoice project with ten Sudanese women to explore competing claims of women's empowerment that currently circulate in local discourses promoting adult literacy learning.[11]

This fifth practice, calling for public response, spurs actions that can revise or reform how institutional practices are experienced. A couple of months after the community conversation described here, Roda's writing teacher told her not to use the first-person pronoun in the researched argument she was writing at the time. Prior to the symposium, such a declaration often caused Roda to scrap an entire idea for a paper and begin again—often drafting a far more formulaic response to the assignment, one requiring far less personal investment or sense of purpose. In this case, however, Roda told us she stayed after class one evening to take up with the teacher the comment, giving him the chance to explain his rationale. She explained to us that the teacher said he wanted readers to consider her evidence to be credible; readers could dismiss a personal anecdote but would likely accept a generalizable trend. Moreover, the teacher showed Roda how to mine her personal observation for evidence of such a trend. Certainly, many factors influenced Roda's decision to request this conversation. But to us she attributed her decision to the community conversation at which people related to her not only as a developing writer of English but also as a rhetor with ideas—a rhetor, that is, looking to public institutions to help her articulate and circulate those ideas on behalf of others in her community.

CONCLUSION AND IMPLICATIONS

In this chapter, we have pushed against well-guarded borders of community-university partnerships that demarcate distinct territories, especially as those borders become stabilized and normative—something all borders are bound to do. As Lewis Hyde reminds us, "Every group has its edge, its sense of in and out" (Hyde 2010, 7). In offering a framework of intercultural inquiry for emergent partnerships, we aim "to disturb the established categories" and "by so doing, open the road to possible new worlds" (13). Foremost, this framework takes up questions of inclusion, putting the borders themselves as well as the ways we mark and guard those borders up for deliberation among those in the borderlands.

This volume began with a discussion of democracy that positioned *Our Town* in relation to Derrida's grappling with a terror-ridden version of democracy based on insider-outsider notions of friendship. The analysis highlighted the precarious features of democratic life: effective participation, enlightened understanding, and control of the agenda. In this chapter, we have suggested an alternative tack toward theorizing a similar conundrum: that democracy is necessarily limited by the contingencies at hand as well as by the need to get something done (Flyvbjerg 1998, 156); by power relations (Cintron 2010, 99; Rai 2010, 39); by all of us as perhaps well-meaning but nonetheless fallible participants (West 1993, 140); and by the very nature of democracy's reliance on language that always navigates and constructs an uncertain interplay between the metaphorical and the material (Bruner 2010, 56) and between the ideal and the "is" (Branch 2007, 139). In this rhetorical space, none of us sees "the problem" the same way, and our agreement is always a negotiated symbolic construct. Rather than focusing on democracy as a function of the state or of a broad imaginary public, this chapter takes its cues from rhetorical models of public life (Flower 2008; Grabill 2010; Higgins,

Long, and Flower 2006; Warner 2002). We have focused on democratic discourse as situated rhetorical work of particular local publics. Members of a local public come together not because of an affinity they share but rather as people who are "stuck with one another" because of a shared concern and the need to pool limited resources to address that concern (Young 1997, 67). That means they are tangled across difference—differences in language, power, goals and desires—yet drawn to marshal available resources in the hope of making or building something together that somehow matters—albeit differently, provisionally—to those who share of their own accord in a rhetorically formed, perhaps loosely aligned, temporary collective We.

The "hospitality" we aim to invoke within and across public institutions is one that recognizes the self-other relations underneath models of deliberation invoking consensus or tolerance, as the editors discussed in the opening chapter; that values argumentation and dissensus as productive engines of collaborative rhetorical invention; and that, most of all, asserts that both the arguments themselves (perhaps over institutional practices, policies, or resources) and the self-other relations underneath those arguments need to be on the table for deliberation. That is to say, values of sociability need not be normative. For example, the social norms the editors invoke in their opening chapter or the values we invoke in ours may sometimes be the kinds of sociability a given polity needs. But it may also be the case that those deliberating in a particular time and place under particular constraints and navigating particular points of stases and particular borders (say, in negotiations among war-torn tribal leaders of South Sudan and Sudanese leaders in the north who have perpetrated genocide; or in deliberations about city and state police training in Ferguson, Missouri or campus police training at Arizona State University) may need to invent for themselves alternative ways of being together rather than to ascribe to normative stances determined a priori in some other place, in some other time, and by people outside of those who find themselves somehow "stuck with one another." This negotiation of an alternative discourse among strangers (Higgins, Long, and Flower 2006) recognizes that each public in each context has its own way of being, of caring, of deliberating; this is especially true if we are attentive to the dialogical nature of publics, seeing that each local public called together in a particular time and place is also somehow comprised of multiple networked publics—weak, strong, subaltern, counter—that rise up, fold under, and reconfigure themselves in response to new exigencies (Hauser 2008, 67). Rather than offering a normative rhetorical theory of democratic discourse, we suggest a different way of building and doing rhetorical theory. Normative theories grant us the means by which to critique specific instantiations and the means by which to understand the ways efforts at democracy fall short. This is important work with a long tradition. But normative theories alone are not necessarily responsive to particular conditions of contemporary public life that take the limitations of democratic discourse as a necessary starting point. It is not a fault of democracy that it is limited; being limited is simply a characteristic of democracy because it is a social and rhetorical practice among limited people navigating affordances and constraints of limited resources. Deliberative discourse, often seen as the hallmark of democracy, is a situated rhetorical practice for leveraging available means in (at its best) just ways among people who need to work together but otherwise have no rhetorical reason to listen and to learn from one another. The five practices we commend—listening deliberatively; looking for alignment; documenting, constructing, and testing critical incidents; representing how people are located in systems; and calling for public response—are but one set of situated practices with one ethic of "stranger sociability" (Warner 2002, 39) useful in one context of building an emergent transnational community-university partnership. We hope some readers might find the five practices we commend of some use. Even more, we hope the observation-based theorizing we seek to demonstrate will register as a useful version of rhetorical theory building in its own right. As Janet Atwill contends in *Rhetoric Reclaimed*, this version of rhetorical theory building is never static or normative (Atwill 2009, 2). Nor is such theorizing immediately transferrable from one context to another (3). So what is it that such rhetorical theory building has to offer? Why go to the trouble? Rhetorical theory building offers the promise of practical wisdom. As contemporary global citizens, we must get better at not only understanding rhetorics but also at doing rhetoric, at taking wise rhetorical action in the most uncertain and unpredictable of contexts in which public institutions matter most in or bear down most on people's lives. Quite simply, in this line of work, normative theory with its panoramic view only gets us so far. Each new situation we encounter—no matter how familiar—is somehow also quite new and unexpected and demands a response attuned to its own particular nuances. It is in the doing and embodied theorizing across contexts, in the dynamic space between the given and the new, that over time we develop *phronesis*, allowing us to respond to each new situation with some inkling of cumulative (and accumulating) wisdom. As rhetors, we must engage in the work of theorizing individual instances of rhetorical work, including (and perhaps especially) the rhetorical work of democratic deliberation, so that over time we can recognize the shades of variations in rhetorical situations and in available means and in the precise leveraging of available means. Recognizing these variations and markedly different ways of navigating them allows us to get better and faster at acting wisely when we encounter a new situation with its faint glimmers of the familiar (Dreyfus and Dreyfus 1986; Flyvbjerg, Bruzelius, and Rothengatter 2003). In these new encounters, we can call on past experiences—our own or someone else's—for what they have to offer as *technai*. The five practices we commend here suggest one starting point for this work.

Notes

1. This chapter reports scholarly activity made possible by seed funding from the College of Liberal Arts and Sciences and the Institute for Humanities Research at Arizona State University.
2. As a condition of approval from our institution's Internal Review Board, the name of the human-service organization has been changed as have been names of individuals except in the case of decidedly public figures or individuals who have chosen to be identified.
3. For details, see Jennifer Clifton (2013b), "Mastery, Failure, and Community Outreach as a Stochastic Art: Lessons Learned with the Sudanese Diaspora in Phoenix" and Jennifer Clifton (2012), "Imagination and Transformation Among the Sudanese Diaspora in Phoenix."
4. As narrated in the remaining sections of this chapter, these alignments came to include connections among stakeholders represented on the social-arenas map (Fig. 13.1) who, several months later, would heed a call for public response by participating in a community conversation.
5. Rather than a single "core" that does not change, Hubert Hermans and Harry Kempen suggest that the dialogical self includes the social and emerges from and resides in the continuous attempt to synthesize multiple, possibly conflicting, parts: "The Self can be seen as a synthesizing activity, that is, as a continuous attempt to make the self whole, despite the existence of parts that try to maintain or even to increase their autonomy" (Hermans and Kempen 1993, 93).
6. The organization's mission has since been revised to be more inclusive.
7. In pursuing community-university partnerships, readers affiliated with universities will inevitably find themselves navigating situations not of their making—venturing courses of action with consequences they can neither predict nor control. Whether learning new information, encountering additional or changed constraints, or bumping against unpredictable results that refine the ever-shifting rhetorical situation, attending to situational "backtalk" (hooks 1989, 5) allows us to "connive with reality" (Atwill 2009, 93) and chart alternative courses of action (Flower 2008, 98). At the same time, community partners will be taking initiative, listening for responses, and adjusting their steps. In moving us as he did, Dak revealed his own rhetorical shrewdness.
8. The dialogical self is apparent in the ways we navigate among our many real-world identities to construct a consistent sense of self. Our natural desire to maintain a consistent and coherent sense of self is what motivates us to create a dialogical space

where we can navigate among and keep in conversation our multiple I-positions (Akkerman and Meijer 2011, 312). The dialogical self is a conglomeration of live interactions among the "dynamic multiplicity of I-positions in the landscape of the mind, intertwined as this mind is with the minds of other people" (Hermans and Kempen 1993, 147). Further, the dialogical self is continually unfolding in space and time. The self, thus, emerges from a dialogue among multiple, spatially positioned I's that take on different voices in turn and create new meanings over time (Ellis and Stam 2010, 424). The dialogical self is, thus, a decentering of the I.

This decentering does not, however, make us all schizophrenic. Rather, the multiple self is still experienced as a single and permanent person (Hermans and Kempen 1993). We maintain our continuity of identity through narratives (Faber 2002), through routinized personal behavior, and by cultural and historical mediation (Akkerman and Meijer 2011, 313). We continuously, and in large part without awareness, rely on responses and solutions that have proven helpful in what (and whom) we previously encountered. These patterns can be valuable, helping us to work more efficiently and effectively and keeping us from starting over each day like Drew Barrymore's character in *Fifty First Dates*.

9. At a recent public event, for instance, Samra sought out one of us, Jennifer, to recount a disturbing incident of police intimidating family members during a traffic stop and then continued to recount the incident to others at the table where Samra and Jennifer were sitting. Similarly, in recounting to another one of us, Elenore, a recent medical crisis made more complicated because of insufficient provisions for daycare, Roda leveraged that crisis to draw more public attention to it.

10. Sponsored in part by ASU's writing programs on campus, this symposium represented a local effort to take up the activist work that Linda Adler-Kassner commends when she calls on writing program administrators to instigate deliberative dialogue with other invested stakeholders around contested claims of literacy and literacy learning. She writes, "As those of us who teach writing and/or run writing programs know, writing is everybody's business" (Adler-Kassner 2013, 157). We would like to thank Shirley Rose for her leadership organizing this event at ASU.

11. Transnational feminist scholarship echoes what critical incidents at the symposium documented and dramatized: contemporary women's empowerment narratives often leave women (especially those who must relocate under the pressures of forced migration) to carry an undue burden in the name of progress and community well-being (Giles 2008, 55; Matlou 1999, 128). To take up the lived experiences of women negotiating these competing narratives, the photovoice project will identify connections among three related themes:

- child care: specifically, concrete details for a daycare collaborative
- getting there: issues of education and service offerings, access, and scheduling
- opening up possibilities: the capacity of literacies and credentials to create new plans, new futures.

By making such connections visible as sites for inquiry at subsequent community conversations with other committed stakeholders, the situated details of lived lives can make for more dynamic, responsive institutions.

References

Ackerman, John, and David J. Coogan. 2010. *The Public Work of Rhetoric: Citizen-Scholars and Civic Engagement.* Columbia: University of Southern Carolina Press.

Adler-Kassner, Linda. 2013. "Agency, Identities, and Action: Stories and the Writing Classroom." In *Texts of Consequence: Composing Social Activism for the Classroom and Community*, edited by Christopher Wilkey and Nicholas Mauriello, 157–76. Cresskill, NJ: Hampton.

Akkerman, Sanne F., and Paulien C. Meijer. 2011. "A Dialogical Approach to Conceptualizing Teacher Identity." *Teaching and Teacher Education* 27 (2): 308–19. http://dx.doi.org/10.1016/j.tate.2010.08.013.

Atwill, Janet. 2009. *Rhetoric Reclaimed: Aristotle and the Liberal Arts Tradition*. 2nd ed. Ithaca, NY: Cornell University Press.

Belenky, Mary, Lynne Bond, and Jacqueline Weinstock. 1991. *A Tradition That Has No Name: Nurturing the Development of People, Families, and Communities*. New York: Basic.

Benhabib, Seyla. 1992. "Models of Public Space: Hannah Arendt, the Liberal Tradition, and Jurgen Habermas." In *Habermas and the Public Space*, edited by Craig Calhoun, 72–98. Cambridge, MA: MIT Press.

Branch, Kirk. 2007. *Eyes on the Ought to Be: What We Teach When We Teach About Literacy*. Cresskill, NJ: Hampton.

Bruner, M. Lane. 2010. "The Public Work of Critical Political Communication." In *The Public Work of Rhetoric: Citizen-Scholars and Civic Engagement*, edited by John Ackerman and David J. Coogan, 56–75. Columbia: University of Southern Carolina Press.

Carter, Shannon, and Deborah Mutnick. 2012. "Writing Democracy: Notes on a Federal Writers' Project for the 21st Century." Special issue, *Community Literacy Journal* 6 (1): 1–14.

Cintron, Ralph. 2010. "Democracy and Its Limitations." In *The Public Work of Rhetoric: Citizen-Scholars and Civic Engagement*, edited by John Ackerman and David J. Coogan, 98–118. Columbia: University of Southern Carolina Press.

Clarke, Adele E. 2005. *Situational Analysis: Grounded Theory After the Postmodern Turn*. Thousand Oaks, CA: Sage.

Clifton, Jennifer. 2012. "Imagination and Transformation as Stochastic Arts: Lessons Learned with the Sudanese Diaspora in Phoenix." PhD diss., Arizona State University, Tempe.

Clifton, Jennifer. 2013a. "Embracing a Productive Rhetorical Pragmatism: Teaching Writing as Democratic Deliberation." *Teaching/Writing: The Journal of Writing Teacher Education* 2 (1): Article 8, 62–76.

Clifton, Jennifer. 2013b. "Mastery, Failure and Community Outreach as a Stochastic Art: Lessons Learned with the Sudanese Diaspora in Phoenix." In *Unsustainable: Re-Imagining Community Literacy, Public Writing, Service-Learning, and the University*, edited by Jessica Restaino and Laurie JC Cella, 227–52. New York: Lexington Books.

Clifton, Jennifer. 2014. "Feminist Collaboratives and Intercultural Inquiry: Constructing an Alternative to the (Not-So) Hidden Logics and Practice of University Outreach and Micro-Lending." Special issue, *Feminist Teacher* 24 (2): 110–137. http://dx.doi.org/10.5406/femteacher.24.1-2.0110.

Clifton, Jennifer, Elenore Long, and Duane Roen. 2013. "Accessing Private Knowledge for Public Conversations: Attending to Shared, Yet-to-be-Public Concerns in the Deaf and Hard-of-Hearing DALN Interviews." In *Stories That Speak to Us: Exhibits from the Digital Archive of Literacy Narratives*, edited by Scott Lloyd Dewitt, Cindy Selfe, and H. Lewis Ulman. Logan, UT: Computers and Composition Digital Press; http://ccdigitalpress.org/stories/roenlongclifton.html.

Clifton, Jennifer, and Justin Sigoloff. 2013. Writing as Dialogue across Difference: Inventing Genres to Support Deliberative Democracy. Special issue, *English Journal* 103 (2): 73–84.

Coogan, David. 2002. "Public Rhetoric and Public Safety at the Chicago Transit Authority: Three Approaches to Accident Analysis." *Journal of Business and Technical Communication* 16 (3): 277–305. http://dx.doi.org/10.1177/1050651902016003002.

Coogan, David. 2006. "Community Literacy as Civic Dialogue." *Community Literacy Journal* 1 (1): 96–108.
Cushman, Ellen. 1998. *The Struggle and the Tools: Oral and Literate Strategies in an Inner City Community.* New York: SUNY Press.
Cushman, Ellen. 2002. "Sustainable Service Learning Programs." *College Composition and Communication* 54 (1): 40–65. http://dx.doi.org/10.2307/1512101.
Cushman, Ellen. 2006. "Toward a Praxis of New Media: The Allotment Period in Cherokee History." *Reflections: A Journal of Writing, Community Literacy, and Service Learning* 5: 111–32.
Dingo, Rebecca. 2012. *Networking Arguments: Rhetoric, Transnational Feminism, and Public Policy.* Pittsburgh: University of Pittsburgh Press.
Dreyfus, Hubert, and Stuart Dreyfus. 1986. *Mind over Machine: The Power of Human Intuition and Expertise in the Era of the Computer.* New York: Free Press.
Ellis, Basia D., and Henderikus J. Stam. 2010. "Addressing the Other in Dialogue: Ricoeur and the Ethical Dimensions." *Theory & Psychology* 20 (3): 420–35. http://dx.doi.org/10.1177/0959354310364280.
Engeström, Yrjö. 2001. "Expansive Learning at Work: Toward an Activity Theoretical Reconceptualization." *Journal of Education and Work* 14 (1): 133–56. http://dx.doi.org/10.1080/13639080020028747.
Faber, Brenton. 2002. *Community Action and Organizational Change: Image, Narrative, Identity.* Carbondale: Southern Illinois University Press.
Flanagan, John C. 1954. "The Critical Incident Technique." *Psychological Bulletin* 51 (4): 327–58. http://dx.doi.org/10.1037/h0061470.
Flower, Linda. 1997. "Partners in Inquiry: A Logic for Community Outreach." In *Writing the Community: Concepts and Models for Service Learning in Composition*, edited by Linda Adler-Kassner, Robert Crooks, and Ann Watters, 95–117. Washington, DC: American Association for Higher Education.
Flower, Linda. 2002. "Intercultural Knowledge Building: The Literate Action of a Community Think Tank." In *Writing Selves, Writing Societies: Research from Activity Perspectives*, edited by Charles Bazerman and David Russell, 239–70. Fort Collin, CO.: WAC Clearinghouse; http://wac.colostate.edu/books/selves_societies/flower/.
Flower, Linda. 2008. *Community Literacy and the Rhetoric of Public Engagement.* Carbondale: Southern Illinois University Press.
Flower, Linda, Elenore Long, and Lorraine Higgins. 2000. *Learning to Rival: A Literate Practice for Intercultural Inquiry.* Mahwah, NJ: Erlbaum.
Flyvbjerg, Bent. 1998. *Rationality & Power: Democracy in Practice.* Chicago, IL: University of Chicago Press.
Flyvbjerg, Bent. 2001. *Making Social Science Matter: Why Social Inquiry Fails and How It can Succeed Again.* Cambridge: Cambridge University Press. http://dx.doi.org/10.1017/CBO9780511810503.
Flyvbjerg, Bent, Nils Bruzelius, and Werner Rothengatter. 2003. *Megaprojects and Risk: An Anatomy of Ambition.* Cambridge: Cambridge University Press.
Fraser, Nancy. 1993. "Rethinking the Public Sphere: A Contribution to the Critique of Actually Existing Democracy." In *Habermas and the Public Sphere*, edited by Craig Calhoun, 109–42. Boston, MA: MIT Press.
Gee, James, Glynda Hull, and Colin Lankshear. 1996. *The New Work Order.* Boulder, CO: Westview.
Giles, Wenona. 2008. "The Gender Relations of Home, Security, and Transversal Feminism: Refugee Women Reclaiming their Identity." In *Not Born A Refugee Woman: Contesting Identities, Rethinking Practices*, edited by Maroussia Hajdukowski-Ahmed, Nazila Khanlou, and Helene Moussa, 55–66. New York: Berghahn Books.
God Grew Tired of Us. 2007. Directed by Christopher Dillon Quinn and Tommy Walker. National Geographic. Film.

Goldblatt, Eli. 2007. *Because We Live Here: Sponsoring Literacy Beyond the College Curriculum.* Cresskill, NJ: Hampton.
Grabill, Jeffrey T. 2001. *Community Literacy Programs and the Politics of Change.* Albany: SUNY Press.
Grabill, Jeffrey T. 2007. *Writing Community Change: Designing Technologies for Citizen Action.* Cresskill, NJ. Hampton.
Grabill, Jeffrey T. 2010. "On Being Useful: Rhetoric and the Work of Engagement." In *The Public Work of Rhetoric: Citizen-Scholars and Civic Engagement,* edited by John Ackerman and David J. Coogan, 193–210. Columbia: University of Southern Carolina Press.
Hauser, Gerard. 2008. *Vernacular Voices: The Rhetorics of Publics and Public Spheres.* Columbia: University of Southern Carolina Press.
Hermans, Hubert, and Harry J. G. Kempen. 1993. *The Dialogical Self: Meaning as Movement.* San Diego: Academic.
Higgins, Lorraine, Elenore Long, and Linda Flower. 2006. "Community Literacy: A Rhetorical Model for Personal and Public Inquiry." *Community Literacy Journal* 1 (1): 9–43.
Himley, Margaret. 2004. "Facing (Up to) 'the Stranger' in Community Service Learning." *College Composition and Communication* 55 (3): 416–38. http://dx.doi.org/10.2307/4140694.
hooks, bell. 1989. *Talking Back: Thinking Feminist, Thinking Black.* Brooklyn, NY: South End.
Hyde, Lewis. 2010. *Trickster Makes This World: Mischief, Myth, and Art.* New York: Farrar, Straus and Giroux.
Long, Elenore. 2008. *Community Literacy and the Rhetoric of Local Publics.* West LaFayette, IN: Parlor.
Long, Elenore, Nyillan Fye, and John Jarvis. 2012. "Gambian-American College Writers Flip the Script on Aid-to-Africa Discourse." Special issue, *Community Literacy Journal* 6 (1): 53–76. http://dx.doi.org/10.1353/clj.2012.0032.
Mathieu, Paula. 2005. *Tactics of Hope: The Public Turn in English Composition.* Portsmouth, NH: Boynton/Cook.
Matlou, Patrick. 1999. "Upsetting the Cart: Forced Migration and Gender Issues, the African Experience." In *Engendering Forced Migration: Theory and Practice,* edited by Doreen Indra, 128–43. New York: Berghahn Books.
Parks, Steve, and Nick Pollard. 2010. "Emergent Strategies for an Established Field: The Role of Worker-Writer Collectives in Composition and Rhetoric." *College Composition and Communication* 61 (3): 476–509.
Peck, Wayne, Linda Flower, and Lorraine Higgins. 1995. "Community Literacy." *College Composition and Communication* 46 (2): 199–222. http://dx.doi.org/10.2307/358428.
Porter, James E., Patricia Sullivan, Stuart Blythe, Jeffrey Grabill, and Libby Miles. 2000. "Institutional Critique: A Rhetorical Methodology for Change." *College Composition and Communication* 51 (4): 610–42. http://dx.doi.org/10.2307/358914.
Rai, Candice. 2010. "Power, Publics, and the Rhetorical Uses of Democracy." In *The Public Work of Rhetoric: Citizen-Scholars and Civic Engagement,* edited by John Ackerman and David J. Coogan, 39–56. Columbia: University of Southern Carolina Press.
Street, Brian. 1993. Introduction to *Cross-Cultural Approaches to Literacy,* edited by Brian Street, 1–21. Cambridge, UK: Cambridge University Press.
Tuck, Eve. 2009. "Suspending Damage: A Letter to Communities." *Harvard Educational Review* 79 (3): 409–27. http://dx.doi.org/10.17763/haer.79.3.n0016675661t3n15.
Warner, Michael. 2002. *Publics and Counterpublics.* New York: Zone Books.
Welch, Nancy. 2012. "Informed, Passionate, and Disorderly: Uncivil Rhetoric in a New Gilded Age." Special issue, *Community Literacy Journal* 6 (1): 33–51. http://dx.doi.org/10.1353/clj.2012.0028.

West, Cornel. 1993. *Keeping Faith: Philosophy and Race in America.* New York: Routledge.
Young, Amanda, and Linda Flower. 2001. "Patients as Partners: Patients as Problem-Solvers." *Health Communication* 14 (1): 68–97.
Young, Iris Marion. 1997. *Intersecting Voices: Dilemmas of Gender, Political Philosophy, and Policy.* Princeton, NJ: Princeton University Press.

14
RHETORICAL EDUCATION AT THE CITY'S EDGE
The Challenge of Public Rhetoric in Suburban America

Robert Brooke

At least since Paula Mathieu (2005) identified the "public turn in composition," college and secondary teachers have been interested in connecting student writing to public projects outside the academy's walls. Central to this work is our field's commitment to rhetoric and writing as a tool for civic engagement and reform. Many of us hope to engage young writers in rhetorical work that will improve the body politic and perhaps even help bring into being a world more just, more sustainable, and more peaceable than the one we inherited. Equally central to this work is our field's recognition that many forces in American society seemingly aim to limit public engagement to something narrower, perhaps individually careerist. As Nancy Welch puts it in her recent review essay of several public-rhetoric collections, the public turn locates itself in the conflicted space between these possibilities. She writes:

> These authors affirm the efficacy of public voice *at a time when actual public space and decision-making rights are being converted to private property and prerogatives.* They examine and debate the rhetorical training and expertise needed for public agency *at a moment when the future of public programs and institutions (including institutions of public higher education) is in question.* They urge academics toward deeper, more sustainable, and more reciprocal forms of community involvement *even as such community problems as under- and unemployment, rising debt, lost health care, and growing class stratification and racial exclusion are not only "out there" but "right here," within the academy as well.* (Welch 2012, 701; italics original)

Welch's (2008) longer treatment of these ideas argues for robust critique of neoliberal public policy and exhorts us to guide young rhetors in the creation of public spaces that speak back to policies that limit their lives (and ours). If neoliberal policy emphasizes our competitive individuality on the global market (with the narrow aim of individual

DOI: 10.7330/9781607324034.c014

success, leaving any public issues to official experts), then the work of public rhetoric means—in response—the critique of narrow individualism, the creation of communal opportunities for action, and the claiming of public policy as a citizen's issue, not merely something that belongs to experts.

Like many compositionists influenced by the public turn, I have been working with various rhetorical action projects in my writing classes for college undergraduates, for preservice secondary English teachers seeking certification, and for inservice school teachers active in our local Nebraska Writing Project. In general, I find many writers become enthralled by such projects and committed to their work, discovering an enhanced reason for their intellectual labor because of this public engagement. (Specifically, we study and engage in community dialogue and advocacy projects like those described in Flower [2008]; community history and education projects like those of Rethinking Schools's Linda Christensen [2009]; and place-conscious rural community advocacy, as I've documented in Brooke [2003].)

Yet I have also noticed a disconnect. For many, nay, most of the students I work with at my large Midwestern institution, something about the turn to public rhetoric seems foreign to them. The move to public rhetoric asks them to cross the boundaries between school and community, to claim local opportunities for open, democratic discourse as part of their role as student and citizen. Save for a particularly radicalized few who enter my classes already involved in some kind of community action, the majority of my students describe themselves as "struggling to relate" to the examples of public rhetoric we read in class: the working-class radicals in Welch's (2008) University of Vermont classes seem too "east coast," too "liberal," while the small-town Nebraska rural activists in my own collection seem "too political" (Brooke 2003). My students describe themselves as skeptical, not sure they "buy" the explicit and implied political critiques, not sure they've "ever experienced anything like this" in their lives.

In discussion with colleagues, I have tried out many explanations for this disconnect. I teach in a "red" state, so perhaps many of my students are fearful of the liberal education agenda they hear critiqued on talk radio. I teach in a predominately conservative Christian state, so perhaps many students are challenged by religious and intellectual diversity. The majority of my students are white, so perhaps it is a race thing. Depending on the day and the discussion, any of these explanations can seem compelling. At the same time, though, I am not finally compelled. There is a counter example to each. For race: Lincoln, Nebraska, is one of the Midwest's major refugee resettlement cities, with over forty distinct languages spoken in our public schools, and our university has a vibrant international student population. It is hard to live here and not be critically aware of race. For conservative Christianity: the majority of our Christian students have memorable service-mission experiences, where they have lived the social-justice mission of their faith communities and come in contact with good people very different from themselves. For red-state ideology: most of the college-aged young people in my classes are eager to try out ideas and ideologies that differ from their home communities, so they are likely to follow blogs and media across the political spectrum instead of only those approved by their community of origin.

What I want to suggest is a different explanation for this disconnect: geography. Specifically, the geography of suburbia, of the edge cities, relovilles, and suburbs proper that make up most of my students' experience. The local borders of civic geography create explicit—if often unacknowledged—boundaries for our lived experiences. Learning to see—and cross—those boundaries is, I suggest, a crucial act in the claiming of public discourse.

According to US Census (2010) demographics, the vast majority of American citizens are currently educated in suburban spaces. According to contemporary geographers' critiques of suburban spaces, suburbia is both designed and experienced as a "space apart" from the more complex social interactions of urban and rural locations. I want to suggest, thus, that suburban geography may well be a major compelling reason for the difficulties facing our field's turn to public rhetoric. If we public-turn compositionists are to succeed in guiding the next generation to more robust public engagement, we must understand the particular geography we are up against. In this essay, I hope to help us see suburbia as a clearly definable and problematic space for public rhetoric. And I hope to suggest some possible pedagogical moves toward public rhetoric in suburban space, drawn from the collective experience of Nebraska Writing Project teachers from the front lines of Midwestern suburbia.

SEEING SUBURBIA: STATING THE PROBLEM OF SUBURBAN PUBLIC SPACE

The specific plight of suburban public rhetoric emerges from three areas of public life.

1. Civic design for suburban spaces that emphasize isolation from the surrounding natural and cultural landscapes

2. Educational policy that emphasizes contextless, so-called universal skills and curricula, as in the national assessment programs of No Child Left Behind and the Common Core, as well as the current moves to extend such assessment into colleges
3. Economic policies of professional class geographic mobility that equate middle-class success with regular geographic migration.

The combination of these three factors makes it especially hard for suburban students to see their local communities as a place for any kind of public rhetoric.

CIVIC DESIGN

What exactly is a suburb, and what is it like to live there? According to contemporary geographers, suburbs are communities that surround a given urban center, and they come in at least three identified forms:

- traditional suburban housing developments, either inside or outside the official boundaries of a metropolis, primarily residential in character (Beauregard 2006)
- edge cities, or urban centers of recent design that now function as a "single end destination" for jobs, shopping, and entertainment, with a population that increases during workdays, such as the Tech Center area outside Denver or the Bloomington-Edina area outside Minneapolis-St. Paul (Garreau 1991)
- relovilles, or planned/gated communities for affluent, mobile workers of large corporations drawing annual incomes between $100,000 and $200,000, who expect to stay in any given community only two to four years and need new, resellable housing, such as Alphaville, Georgia, or Castle Rock, Colorado (Kilborn 2009).

While all three forms of suburbia are distinct at any specific moment in time, all share a common population history, and over time the forms blend into one another. Most of the people who live in these spaces now did not live there twenty years ago. Most of the buildings are new; most of the populace is even newer. As Joel Garreau puts it, "Edge City's problem is history. It has none" (Garreau 1991, 9).

Historically, as metropolitan scholars Robert Beauregard (2006) and Jon Teaford (2006) both explain, the development of suburbia has followed a relatively consistent path. The development of suburbia proper can be dated to the period 1945–1970. Prior to 1945, the downtown of any major city centered on urban life. While cities certainly were segregated into neighborhoods by race, class, and ethnicity, the primacy of the downtown area for jobs, shopping, and entertainment meant that daily life routinely involved contact with cultural and ethnic pluralism. Living in a city in the United States, thus, meant living with an awareness of the cultural, racial, and ethnic diversity of that region, with all the corresponding tensions brought about by living in such close quarters.

Teaford (2006) suggests that part of the motivation behind the explosion of suburbs after 1945 was a release from these tensions. Between 1945 and the 1970s, traditional suburbs allowed most urban workers to move their families into lives of greater homogeneity. The country's economic prosperity allowed individual workers to afford the main elements of "the American Dream" of the 1950s: a single-family dwelling and a car. In the new traditional suburbs, the urban population segregated itself by class, based on the cost of those houses in a given area. In a traditional suburb, shopping, schooling, and entertainment all were within biking distance of the new residence. Beauregard suggests that the rise of the suburbs meant that Americans "turned away from a robust and compassionate public culture" (Beauregard 2006, 196). He sees both the country's enduring political divisions during the civil rights era of the late 1960s–early 1970s and the urban crisis of the mid-1970s–early 1980s economic downturn as emerging from the "amnesia and chauvinism" of the rise to suburbia (196).

Of course, suburbanization has not ceased since the mid-1970s economic downturn. Instead, claim contemporary geographers, it has changed its form. As Garreau (1991) famously argued, since the late 1970s, suburbs have ceased to be subservient to any preexisting urban core. The very word *suburb* no longer captures the geographic reality: where a traditional suburb existed sub, or under the city it surrounded, in the metropolitan landscape post-1975 there is no actual center. Instead, our major metropolitan areas have evolved into "edge cities." People living in edge cities work, sleep, shop, and recreate wholly within that civic space, not needing the once-center city to which they are sometimes attached. Garreau's examples of edge cities included the Eastern Seaboard cities stretching from New Jersey to Boston, the Western Seaboard of southern California, and the conglomerates of new cities around Atlanta, Phoenix, Washington, DC, and Dallas/Fort Worth. By 1991 Garreau identified more than two hundred "edge cities" that fit under his now-famous five-part definition: a city with at least five million square feet of leasable office space; six hundred thousand square feet of retail space; a population that increases at nine o'clock in the morning on workdays; a clear local awareness of the city as a destination itself for jobs, shopping, and entertainment; and a recent history (the city didn't exist as an urban center thirty years ago).

Peter Kilborn (2009) provides an intriguing update of the edge-city idea. Up until (and perhaps past) the home mortgage crisis of 2007, the development of newer and more affluent edge cities has been a constant feature of the new globalization of American business. With the development of global technology and large multinational corporations that sustain it, a growing number of American professional workers have become "relos." Kilborn defines relos as "corporate relocatees or career transferees" who move every few years as they shift companies or positions within companies and are relocated to new parts of the United States or abroad (Kilborn 2009, 13). As an upwardly mobile professional class, relos are "economically homogenous, with midcareer incomes of $100,000 to $200,000," and are predominately white and Midwestern in origin (13). Relovilles, or edge cities that cater to the new confluence of corporation and mobile professionals, are built on the cheap land outside existing metropolitan centers. Kilborn lists the top twenty-five relovilles just after his title page, and his list includes several of the edge cities identified by Garreau (1991) and studied by Teaford (2006): Alpharetta, Georgia; Plano, Texas; Woodbury, Minnesota.

In short, the history of suburban development since 1945 suggests some enduring themes for suburban living, whether in the traditional suburbs that sprung up after World War II or in the edge cities and relovilles of today. Suburban living in all three forms is

- tied to mobility and our financial ability to migrate
- based in the American Dream of single-family housing, located in communities of others who are "like us"
- dominated by the "new"—new construction, new communities, and so forth
- historically naïve and disconnected, that is, not linked to the cultural history of the region's traditional urban centers, nor to the natural and agricultural history of the land on which the suburban development now rests.

EDUCATIONAL POLICY

If the physical geography of suburbia locates many college-bound American students apart from the cultural and natural histories (and issues) of their regions, the current emphasis on national standardization in educational testing also works against any connection to local public rhetoric. As many critics of No Child Left Behind (NCLB) and the Common Core have repeatedly pointed out, the very idea of nationwide standardized tests means educational attention is drawn away from regional, local, community, and individual distinctions. FairTest (2007), the National Center for Fair and Open Testing, offers a succinct five-point summary of the identified negative consequences of high-stakes tests.

1. High-stakes tests are unfair to many students.
2. High-stakes testing leads to grade retention and dropping out.
3. High-stakes testing produce teaching to the test.
4. High-stakes testing drives out good teachers.
5. High-stakes testing misinforms the public.

Three of these criticisms are directly connected to the opportunity for public rhetoric in suburban schools. Item 1 emphasizes the inability of high-stakes standardized tests to acknowledge individual differences (cultural, linguistic, ethnic, or regional) between students. Item 3 emphasizes the effect of testing on curriculum, as areas of study not directly linked to the tests (or, more crucially, not able to be tested well by the standardized processes) are increasingly dropped from the school day. Item 5 emphasizes the inability of test results to show the public what they are meant to show—so, for example, the achievement in writing score measures only success on the narrowly defined test writing as opposed to writing ability across a range of tasks and contexts. These problems (and others) have led organizations such as the Coalition of Essential Schools (2013) and the International Society for Technology in Education (2013) to propose robust and sensible alternative lists of standards for teaching that include many items unreachable by the current national high-stakes tests. Within writing studies, scholars such as Thomas Newkirk (2009, 2013), Chris Gallagher (2007), and Linda Adler-Kassner (2008) have emphasized the need for college writing educators to "speak back" to the discussion of NCLB and the Common Core and to offer "principle based alternative narratives" to them. These lines of critique are well known. For understanding the particular difficulties of suburban teaching of public rhetoric, however, the point to emphasize is that the dominance of nationally standardized testing reinforces the geographic insular character of suburban space. Nothing in the national-standards movement helps teachers focus attention on local issues, problems, and opportunities for public rhetoric.

ECONOMIC POLICY FOR WHITE-COLLAR MIGRATION

The final difficulty for suburban public rhetoric is a peculiar version of the "narrow careerism" Welch (2012) and others have identified as the potential dark side of service-learning programs. A striking feature of the career trajectories of suburban residents is their career-migration patterns. One of the key arguments in Kilborn's (2009) expose of relovilles, for instance, is that the "boundaryless professional class" that live in these new edge cities really have few economic options other than migration. To maintain their personal currency in an increasingly migratory professional market, the new suburban professional class must jump at the chance to relocate to higher salary positions or risk falling behind. Kilborn describes the typical relo career path:

> Paid $40,000 or $50,000 a year and handed a $3,000 moving expense check, [relos] mount the bottom rung of ladders, which the most agile among them will climb to Alpharetta, Plano, Denver, Singapore, and on up, to the six- and seven-digit wages of executive vice presidents and chief executive officers. As a slice of the American middle class, rookie Relos are neither their hometowns' transient poor nor the elite, endowed with connections and the infinite options that money can buy. They are kids who are told they can be president if they work hard enough and get out of town. (86–87)

Kilborn quotes Emory University anthropologist Bradd Shore, whose analysis of the class structure of today's metropolitan centers focuses on the plight of the suburban middle class. For Shore, a town's upper class and lower class both have cultural and career experiences that can tie them to local communities. The very wealthy have the means to integrate their ability to travel for recreation and business to their regional commitments. (I think here of my state's major philanthropic foundations, all funded by long-established regional families.) The working class is similarly tied to local place, both because of their lack of marketable professional skills and because of what Shore calls their "real wealth: their extended families, churches, ethnic ties, and shared interests and rituals" (quoted in Kilborn 2009, 87). In contrast to these two demographics, the 70 percent of the population in the middle class are "congenital itinerants whose families raise them to chase the American Dream wherever it leads" (quoted in Kilborn 2009, 87). For Shore, we define ourselves as middle class precisely through "various kinds of mobility" (quoted in Kilborn 2009, 87). In short, Kilborn's analysis suggests that many college-aged suburban students really have no option other than professional migration. Whatever the emotional and relational costs to individuals who may feel ties to their communities of origin, most members of the contemporary professional middle class are destined to migrate.

Taken together, then, civic design, educational policy, and economic policy create a curious cluster of geographic influences on the typical suburban young adult. When these young people arrive in my classes at my typical Midwestern university, they arrive with strong geographic tendencies toward homogenous isolation (from the civic design of suburbia since 1945), toward standardized, national skills and knowledge (from current educational policy), and toward migratory professional careerism (from current economic policy). These geographic tendencies help create the disconnect my students express about the tasks of public rhetoric.

TOWARD PUBLIC RHETORIC IN SUBURBAN SPACE (AND CONSCIOUSNESS)

If, as I suggest, the geographical location of suburbia (broadly understood) does help create the disconnect college students experience when they encounter public-rhetoric projects, how then might we respond as compositionists committed to the work of the public turn? If we see our work to be the scaffolding in school of the democratic discourses that allow all citizens an active say in the creation of the future, then we must guide writers in moving across the geographic boundaries that limit their visions of public space.

In the relatively scant pedagogical literature that identifies suburbia as a particularly interesting location for teaching writing, I have noticed three distinct approaches to this question. First, Thomas Hothem (2009) suggests making the representation of suburbia itself an organizing theme for student reading and writing. In his classes at Cornell, California-Davis, and California-Merced, his students read critics of suburbia, such as James Kunstler (1993); environmental representations of suburban space, such as presented by Barry Lopez (1998); and they watch a variety of films set in suburban spaces, such as *Clueless* (1995). Students then write in response to these readings, both analytically and with essays that represent their own take on suburbia. These literacy experiences guide his students to see their locales in a new light. He writes,

> Writings on suburbia often have pointed personal implications. So when it comes time to conclude the course, students often find themselves reflecting on the legacy of suburban history in their academic as well as personal lives. (53–54)

Second, Ed Nagelhout (2009) suggests compositionists draw on "hyperspace" writing to key into the "post-suburban" experience of multitasking connections to many places at once (virtual and real). Drawing on Michael Dear (2000) and Kling, Olin, and Poster (1995), Nagelhout draws attention to the "centerless" experience of postsuburban living and the corresponding mixing of genres and contexts that follows from this experience. In his classes, he asks students to "hyperwrite" in ways that blend genres from different locations in their daily lives, "to commute, if you will, into and through the genres of their lives, to find a voice, a conscious space, in an environment of rapidly changing print and electronic mediums" (155).

Third, the Keeping and Creating American Communities teacher-research team at Kennesaw State University outside Atlanta explored an American studies approach to suburban spaces (Robbins and Dyer 2005). This project immersed teachers in historical study of the greater-Atlanta metropolitan region, the identification of five "national themes" for the development of classroom units, and a praxis of linking classwork to "local applications" in the surrounding communities. One of the identified themes was Shifting Landscapes, Converging Peoples, with a local application of Re-Configuring 21st Century Suburbias. Sylvia Martinez (2005) describes a pedagogical unit she developed at Campbell High School in Smyrna, Georgia, from this work. This unit took students into the community to photograph, interview, and take notes about the intriguing features of this suburban space. The students then were guided to find their personal connections to place through considering their journeys.

Here in Nebraska, secondary and university teachers active in the Nebraska Writing Project network have been following the teacher-research-team approach suggested by Robbins and Dyer (2005). Since 2007, a growing team of teachers from the suburban corridor between Omaha and Lincoln have been reading about suburban experience and pondering how to engage suburban students more effectively in public-rhetoric projects. This team of teacher-researchers all share a common grounding in the Nebraska Writing Project's commitments to place-conscious education, as articulated in Brooke (2003) and explored in my biannual graduate seminar, Place-Conscious Teaching. For this group of teachers, the thinking problem has been how to adapt the direct local community-history-and-ecosystem pedagogies that have proved successful in rural Nebraska (Bishop 2004; English 1998) to the different contexts and challenges of the suburban Midwest. To respond to the suburban disconnect created by the civic design of suburban spaces, the current standardized educational policies, and the migratory professional careerism so widespread in suburban culture, our teacher-research team has been emphasizing a three-pronged approach.

1. To design projects that help suburban students see their local communities as entities historically connected to our region, environment, and metropolitan centers. (Local secondary teacher Mary Birky Collier, from Papillion-La Vista High School, has sensibly called such projects "pre-advocacy work")
2. To guide students in developing social-action projects (Berdan et al. 2006) that allow them to meet curricular goals through direct community engagement
3. To employ a rhetoric of "meets and exceeds standards" in describing and documenting these projects for administrators, school boards, local journalists, and concerned parents.

Members of our teacher-research team are currently preparing a book-length collection of some of these projects, which may help teachers in other regions imagine new ways to address the widespread challenges of suburban public rhetoric (Brooke 2015). In the space remaining, I'd like to offer small snapshots of three of these projects.

The Urban Justice League

One powerful way to help suburban students see their community as connected to the wider region is to establish direct connections to other schools. The Urban Justice League project, facilitated by Dan Boster from Ralston High School and Jeff Grinvalds from Omaha Westside High School, brought together teachers and students from six high schools in the greater Omaha metro area (three urban and three suburban). Each of the six participating teachers identified a group of four to eight students in their school to participate in the project. The collective interschool group read and discussed several published narratives on urban justice issues, participated in several movie nights on similar issues, and developed a public workshop open to all students at their schools at the end of the project. This project allowed participating students to connect across urban/suburban boundaries, to focus on social justice issues, and to earn English school credit for the experience. The project thus served as "pre-advocacy work" for the many students at each school who chose to attend the final workshop and learn about the array of social justice organizations and opportunities available in the greater metro area. It also served as direct social-action experience for the small groups of student organizers at each school.

Native American Literature for the Suburban Midwest

University teacher Bernice Olivas guided her students from preadvocacy to social action in her Native American Literature course, one of several courses that fulfill a general education diversity requirement at Nebraska. Her first unit asked students to explore their local communities to create a digital collage of Native American presence and representation in the community. In Pecha Kucha PowerPoint presentations, the students captured how Native Americans are represented in local art galleries, mall merchandizing, official tribal headquarter buildings, area casinos, and government buildings. These representations formed a backdrop for some initial reading of Native American literature and theory. Olivas's second unit asked students to take a character from one of the novels they read and imagine how that character's life would proceed if they lived in Whiteclay, Nebraska (the small town located just south of the Pine Ridge Reservation and the subject of several local documentaries and legal battles). Both of these preadvocacy projects guided students to notice direct connections between their experience and our region's ongoing history with Native peoples. The course's final project asked groups of students to create and conduct some social-action project of their own design.

SPUR Online Writing Exchange

For the past five years, I have been connecting my university junior-level course for the secondary-English education certification students to three secondary classes representing suburban, urban, and rural Nebraska through an online writing exchange. For my preservice education students, this experience is often their first contact with actual secondary-student writing. For all the students, the online writing exchange allows them to interact with writers from significantly different communities in the region. Throughout the years of this writing exchange, our rural and urban participating schools have remained constant, with Jennifer Troester and Katie Morrow's eighth-grade class at O'Neill Secondary School (far north-central Nebraska) representing the rural demographic and Jennifer Razor's sophomore and junior classes at Omaha Burke High School representing the urban. Depending on the year, we have worked with two different suburban classes: Kelly Honz's juniors at Ralston High and Sally Hunt's juniors at Lincoln East. We start the writing exchange with a common assignment: our own versions of George Ella Lyon's (1993) "Where I'm From" poem, a piece of writing that draws on careful descriptions of local place. To match the existing curricula in all participating schools, the other required writings are a persuasive piece and a descriptive narrative. Within these genres, the student writers often tend to focus local experiences—hunting and farming for the O'Neill students; race encounters, urban adult mentors, and ethnic music for the urban students. In this context, the suburban secondary writers—and most of the university preservice writers—notice that their topics gravitate to the very general (large social issues such as gun control) or the specifically personal (sports stories, homages to grandparents). The differences between the writing topics and abilities of the three groups becomes a common topic for class discussion in all the courses (and perhaps a particular form of educators' preadvocacy work for the university preservice teachers).

These three snapshots represent some of the range of projects our Nebraska Writing Project teacher-research team is currently developing. Behind each of these projects lies our growing commitment to open the possibility of public rhetoric for suburban students. If, as I have argued in this chapter, the particular geographic cluster of civic design, educational policy, and economic professional migration creates a disconnect between the work of public rhetoric and suburban experience, then projects like these—at both the secondary and college level—may help prepare our students for the work of the public turn.

Obviously, the kinds of projects undertaken by our research team have implications beyond suburban experience. The same issues of seeing the geographies that surround us affect young citizens in many different civic contexts (rural and urban communities, military migrants, immigrant populations in any context). No matter where we live, the same contemporary combination of civic design, educational practice, and economic policy makes it hard to see the boundaries we must cross to engage in public rhetoric. And lack of practice with public rhetoric makes it hard to engage in the full work of democratic citizenship.

Place-based community projects linking school work to the lived local experiences—and ongoing local public controversies—are in any context a way of cutting through the blinders so the possibility of public work can become visible. In any civic space in the wider United States, public rhetoric can emerge as a possibility once we draw attention to the borders between local civic action and narrowly individualizing educational practice. Crossing those borders can allow all writers—no matter their civic location—to see options they cannot see if the space of education remains inattentive to local place. Much of the current literature on place-based education describes projects in rural and urban contexts where the boundaries between a student's local home community and the seemingly placeless world of school are sharply drawn. For urban schools, places to start are McComiskey and Ryan's (2003) collection of secondary and college city-based projects, Linda Christensen's (2000, 2009) two volumes of home- and heritage-based projects from the most ethnically diverse areas of Portland, Oregon, and Linda Flower's (2008) rich account of the work of the Community Literacy Center in Pittsburgh. For rural schools, places to start are Donehower, Hogg, and Schell's (2007, 2012) two volumes on rural literacies and my own collection (Brooke 2003) on school/community partnerships in rural Nebraska.

Given the rich options described by place-based educators in rural and urban settings, the specific geographic context of suburbia remains vexing. If part of the entry to public rhetoric involves the identification of boundaries and borders that need to be crossed or blended in the quest for participatory citizenship, then the special problem of suburbia is one of visibility. Suburbia, in all its forms, makes the borders that surround us hard to see. The organization of civic space in suburbs, edge cities, and relovilles makes it difficult to see social classes different from one's own or the possible fracture lines between classes and ethnic diversity. As Teaford (2006) points out, many contemporary suburbs include ethnic diversity while still eliding class boundaries. Kilborn (2009) extends this insight to relovilles, where the new cultural class consciousness of the migratory middle class may include distinct international groups while also sectioning off contact with different classes. The real boundaries of civic space clearly matter, especially in the suburban realms. Since current national demographics tell us more citizens are now educated in suburban areas than any other location in civic design, the borders of suburbia loom as a central problem for education in the twenty-first century. Drawing attention to those borders, making them permeable, becomes a necessary move for educators committed to writing and rhetoric as a training ground for public engagement. This is the work that confronts us after composition's public turn.

References

Adler-Kassner, Linda. 2008. *The Activist WPA: Changing Stories about Writing and Writers.* Logan: Utah State University Press.

Beauregard, Robert. 2006. *When America Became Suburban.* Minneapolis: University of Minnesota Press.

Berdan, Kristina, Ian Boulton, Elyse Eidman-Aadahl, Jennie Fleming, Launie Gardner, Iana Rogers, and Asali Solomon. 2006. *Writing for a Change: Boosting Literacy and Learning Through Social Action.* San Francisco: Jossey-Bass.

Bishop, Sharon. 2004. "The Power of Place." *English Journal* 93 (6): 65–9. http://dx.doi.org/10.2307/4128896.

Brooke, Robert, ed. 2003. *Rural Voices: Place-Conscious Education and the Teaching of Writing.* New York: Teachers College.

Brooke, Robert. 2015. *Writing Suburban Citizenship: Place-Conscious Education and the Conundrum of Suburbia.* Syracus: Syracuse University Press.

Christensen, Linda. 2000. *Reading, Writing, and Rising Up: Teaching about Social Justice and the Power of the Written Word.* Madison, WI: Rethinking Schools.

Christensen, Linda. 2009. *Teaching for Joy and Justice: Reimagining the Language Arts Classroom.* Madison, WI: Rethinking Schools.

Clueless. 1995. Directed by Amy Heckerling. Los Angeles: Paramount.

Coalition of Essential Schools. 2013. "The CES Common Principles." http://www.essentialschools.org/items/4.

Dear, Michael. 2000. *The Postmodern Urban Condition.* Malden, MA: Blackwell.

Donehower, Kim, Charlotte Hogg, and Eileen Schell. 2007. *Rural Literacies.* Carbondale: Southern Illinois University Press.

Donehower, Kim, Charlotte Hogg, and Eileen Schell, eds. 2012. *Reclaiming the Rural: Essays on Literacy, Rhetoric and Pedagogy.* Carbondale: Southern Illinois University Press.

English, Cathie. 1998. "Do You Remember Me? Writing Oral Histories with Nursing Home Residents." National Writing Project. http://www.nwp.org/cs/public/print/resource/274.

FairTest. 2007. "The Dangerous Consequences of High-Stakes Standardized Tests." http://www.fairtest.org/dangerous-consequences-highstakes-standardized-tes.

Flower, Linda. 2008. *Community Literacy and the Rhetoric of Public Engagement.* Carbondale: Southern Illinois University Press.

Gallagher, Chris. 2007. *Reclaiming Assessment: A Better Alternative to the Accountability Agenda.* Portsmouth, NH: Heinemann.

Garreau, Joel. 1991. *Edge City: Life on the New Frontier.* New York: Doubleday.

Hothem, Thomas. 2009. "Suburban Studies and College Writing: Applying Ecocomposition." *Pedagogy* 9 (1): 35–59. http://dx.doi.org/10.1215/15314200-2008-016.

International Society for Technology in Education. 2013. "ISTE Standards for Teachers, Students, and Administrators." http://www.iste.org/standards/iste-standards.

Kilborn, Peter. 2009. *Next Stop, Reloville: Life inside America's New Rootless Professional Class.* New York: Times Books.

Kling, Rob, Spencer Olin, and Mark Poster, eds. 1995. *Postsuburban California: The Transformation of Orange County since World War II.* Berkeley: University of California Press.

Kunstler, James. 1993. *The Geography of Nowhere: The Rise and Decline of America's Man-Made Landscape.* New York: Simon and Schuster.

Lopez, Barry. 1998. "The American Geographies." In *About this Life: Journeys on the Threshold of Memory*, 130–43. New York: Vintage.

Lyon, George Ella. 1993. "Where I'm From." George Ella Lyon. http://www.georgeellalyon.com/where.html.

Martinez, Sylvia. 2005. "Discovering the Power of My Place: Personal Journeys to a Community Focus." In *Writing America: Classroom Literacy and Public Engagement*, edited by Sarah Robbins and Mimi Dyer, 27–38. New York: Teachers College.

Mathieu, Paula. 2005. *Tactics of Hope: The Public Turn in English Composition.* Portsmouth, NH: Boynton/Cook.

McComiskey, Bruce, and Cynthia Ryan, eds. 2003. *City Comp: Identities, Spaces, Practices.* Albany: SUNY Press.

Nagelhout, Ed. 2009. "Commuting Genre: First-Year Composition through a Postsuburban Lens." In *Composing Other Spaces*, edited by Douglas Reichert Powell and John Paul Tassoni, 145–59. Cresskill, NJ: Hampton.

Newkirk, Thomas. 2009. *Holding On to Good Ideas in a Time of Bad Ones: Six Literacy Principles Worth Fighting For.* Portsmouth, NH: Heinemann.

Newkirk, Thomas. 2013. "Postscript: Speaking Back to the Common Core." http://samplechapters.heinemann.com/speaking-back-to-the-common-core-by-thomas-newkirk.

Robbins, Sarah, and Mimi Dyer, eds. 2005. *Writing America: Classroom Literacy and Public Engagement.* New York: Teachers College.

Teaford, Jon. 2006. *The Metropolitan Revolution.* New York: Columbia University Press.

US Census. 2010. "Population Distribution and Change 2000 to 2010: 2010 Census Briefs." http://www.census.gov/prod/cen2010/briefs/c2010br-01.pdf.

Welch, Nancy. 2008. *Living Room: Teaching Public Writing in a Privatized World.* Portsmouth, NH: Heinemann.

Welch, Nancy. 2012. "The Point Is to Change It: Problems and Prospects for Public Rhetors." *College Composition and Communication* 63 (4): 699–714.

15
IN SUM AND REVIEW
The Rhetoric of Lines across Us

Barbara Couture and Patti Wojahn

> *Symbolic and material, affective and performative, the border is an omnipresent force in our everyday lives, materializing and shifting across registers of geography, history, politics, economics, citizenship, identity, and culture.*
>
> (DeChaine 2012, 1)

> *Humans draw lines that divide the world into specific places, territories and categories. We are "geographic beings" for whom the creation of places, and by consequence the process of bordering, seems natural. . . . [But] borders are not "natural" phenomena; they exist in the world only to the extent that humans regard them as meaningful.*
>
> (Diener and Hagen 2012, 1)

As readers who have either read this compilation from beginning to end or simply sampled a few chapters, you might be considering how the research and scholarship related to borders and bordering offered here could or even should affect the work of scholars or engage the general public today. In taking up the rhetorics of borders and bordering, the chapters in this collection offer a partial response to the gap in scholarship D. Robert DeChaine has found in studies across many disciplines, studies that have "included the symbolic study of borders within their purview" but have not specifically attended to the "rhetorical processes and practices of bordering" (DeChaine 2012, 5). In our opening chapter, we propose one primary way in which all authors in this collection can offer value not just to rhetoricians but also to compositionists and scholars in border studies, American studies, communication studies, and more: that is, by examining the concept of borders within the meaning and uses of *democratic discourse*. In that first chapter, we wrestle with democratic discourse and what that concept implies for and requires of those interacting in a society rife with lines that divide what some consider good and bad, appropriate and inappropriate, right and wrong, worthy and unworthy, us and them. In that first chapter, we also examine the ways in which current if not ongoing practices deny key criteria for democratic discourse, thereby drawing boundaries between certain people (including some presuming to embrace democracy) and those considered outside the bounds, for whatever reasons, of *belonging*.

Woven through each chapter in this collection, we see at play echoes of Alexander Diener and Joshua Hagan's argument that borders are not natural but created by humans who can use them for good or ill (Diener and Hagen 2012). Clearly, with its expansive reach across geographies of the material and the mind, the concept of *the border* calls for attention, and the authors in this collection respond, describing it, challenging it, confounding it, and, at times, erasing it. To explore additional and alternative considerations suggested by the authors in this collection, we briefly review here each chapter and suggest implications for further work that can build from the ideas shared with us. To that end, we offer some comments and questions of our own related to each chapter, placed in italics so researchers, teachers, students, and other readers can easily find topics that may warrant or launch further work or thought.

PART ONE—IMAGINING BOUNDARIES
Rhetoric Resisting/Defining Symbolic Borders

In his recent book historicizing the impact of border rhetorics on conceptions of identity and citizenship, Josue David Cisneros supports a view of borders as "*figurative* spaces of identity, culture, and community" (Cisneros 2014, 4; our emphasis). The various authors of "Imagining Boundaries" also treat the border figuratively, prompting us to consider the many ways in which language is used to shape, define, reflect, and delineate our world. These authors' exploration of border as *symbolic* in this first section of the book allows us, in turn, to consider the role rhetorical study and analysis can play in uncovering, if not resisting, symbolic constructions that limit and constrain not only our interactions and connections with others but also our visions of what our world and lives can be. Indeed, in describing *the border* as a "rhetorical mode of enactment," DeChaine explains it is always "produced, defined, managed, contested, and altered through human symbolic practices" (DeChaine 2012, 2), shaping our interactions and our visions.

Taken together, the "Imagining Boundaries" authors additionally allow us to explore roles each of us can play in supporting—or denying—the vision of a democratic discourse that emphasizes openness to all participants and transcends boundaries, however defined. They outline a variety of limiting restrictions on engagement, specifically the limiting that occurs through deemphasizing the critical role language plays in establishing borders among diverse people (Villanueva); devaluing code-switching as a means to bridge others' languages and experiences (Schroeder); ignoring the power of humor within serious discussions (Rossing); teaching about argumentative strategies without offering methods critical for civil discourse (Peirce); wholly banning languages other than English while missing opportunities to benefit all learners (Hernandez, Montelongo, and Herter); excluding holistic approaches to education if not life (Schiller); or side-stepping topics that can lead to discomfort (such as racial or cultural differentiation) (Torres and Valentine).

In the first chapter of "Imagining Boundaries," Victor Villanueva calls for rhetoricians to publicly use their expertise to show how language constructs "realities" about national borders that are potentially damaging to some citizens and not others. He asks that we reject constructs of metaphorical or national borders that "protect" some groups from others different from themselves. In the specific example he cites, language in documents and laws "protects" mainland Americans from Puerto Ricans by throwing doubt on the latters' claim to citizenship. As he explains, through a studied analysis of how language and rhetorical strategies shape perspectives, rhetoricians are uniquely qualified to shape democratic participation by revealing and teaching how language use can differently affect citizens within our national boundaries, and, in fact, all who are either included or excluded by metaphorical boundaries created by name or policy.

We left Villanueva's chapter with a number of immediate questions. As instructors who include assignments involving rhetorical analysis, we might ask how students can best learn about the rhetoric of borders and "bordering"—and the implications of these concepts. Teachers might ask students to explore personally the notions of nation and what it means to be "American." DeChaine tells us, for instance, that "rarely are values of respect, belonging, and tolerance for difference included" (DeChaine 2012, 2) in claims to national identity. Do our students—and can we—confirm this claim? In general, we might ask whether the social effects of language use should be defined as an instructional basic for students of rhetoric. We also wonder whether advocating such explorations in college classrooms could lead to charges of political advocacy for disenfranchised groups, along the lines of the charges made in Arizona House Bill 2281 (2010), which forbids schools from offering classes designed primarily for students from a particular ethnic group, that is, classes the law claims promote ethnic solidarity instead of treating people as individuals. We might also ask whether we are ethically bound to discuss these matters and how continuing standard practices affects the success of our students in the workplace or limits their role as engaged citizens.

Echoing the literal and figurative bounds of national identity, Christopher Schroeder addresses strategies some in the United States are using to overcome boundaries between those who use English and those who also speak other languages. Schroeder takes up code-switching, or code-mixing, which he describes as moving between languages, as a way to honor meanings best conveyed by all respective languages available to a communicator. He also illustrates how code-switching can be used both for *continuity* (to maintain aspects of cultural identities) and to make *contact* with those who might have one but not all languages in common. He argues that more research should explore the effects of code-switching on marginalization or acceptance of some multilingual speakers in the United States, along with other potential benefits or drawbacks for the speakers themselves; such research could help reveal how popular notions of language and literacy (especially with respect to English-only movements) create borders and boundaries within and even beyond the United States. Schroeder also suggests that increased use of code-switching within the media could change public discussions about individual rights and the rights of those whose first language is not English, discussions frequently exacerbated by legal claims to national identity associated with language use.

> To extend Schroeder's work, we ask whether his claims for the ameliorative effect of code-switching can be further explored and confirmed. In a recent Chronicle of Higher Education piece, English professor and linguist Ann Curzan demonstrates that these effects are already being popularly felt. She notes, for instance, that even humorist Weird Al Yankovich's new song "Word Crimes" set off a public debate between those disparaging "'abuses' in/to the language" and those who understand language as evolving and fluid, something we all in fact "change in relation to different cultural and linguistic spaces and in relation to different parts of our identity" (Curzan 2014). Putting popular instances of code-switching's effects aside, we might consider in our teaching and research the extent to which code-switching can disenfranchise readers who "don't get it" because they see English as a fixed rather than fluid, living language—or for other reasons that remain disguised. Such discussions might also extend to variations of these issues as spotted in other countries, such as France, where insistence on language purity is associated with national pride.

Also addressing *the border* with respect to national identity, Jonathan Rossing argues that using humor in serious public discourse opens the way to new perspectives and understandings; it humanizes "all stakeholders in a particular struggle" and "creates unique pathways for identification with marginalized perspectives." Rossing implies that not only can we teach students how to use humor to this effect, but we can also use humor in the classroom when discussing serious conflicts to help students understand the "paradoxical rigidity and fluidity of identity borders." Drawing from cases related to current US immigration policy, specifically the approaches employed by humorist Stephen Colbert in his popular satirical news show *The Colbert Report*, Rossing shows how humor can help even those who disagree with a stance see an issue in a new light and, perhaps, reconsider their own stance. He makes a clear plea for teachers and rhetoricians to study and teach using humor to this effect.

> *Rossing displays the value of humor in the hands of one some consider masterful in this regard—Stephen Colbert, who plays the satirical role of a conservative to highlight irony in the policies of lawmakers and the reporting of media—a feat not easy to achieve. To begin implementing Rossing's scheme, instructors might offer readings that illustrate the approaches Rossing highlights. Students could also try writing arguments employing satire or irony and then test these effects on others. In an attempt to introduce humor to problematize hardened positions, we may find that students, or other audiences for such attempts, strongly resist the changes such discourse challenges them to make in their thinking. To manage this response in the classroom or elsewhere, we might seek help from colleagues in disciplines that address social conflict more directly. Overall, we are drawn to the power of humor to reveal the absurdity of some popular perspectives; at the same time, we cannot dismiss the power of humor to obscure painfully serious issues, or worse, do damage to those affected by them. Nonetheless, we see great potential for researchers to take up questions of audience reception to arguments carried by humor in contrast to more straightforward and traditional approaches.*

Like Jonathan Rossing, Karen Peirce argues that we need to motivate students to more fully explore facets of and positions on controversial issues, but her approach is quite different. Peirce claims that composition textbooks do little to help students use rhetoric to negotiate difference; rather, as she demonstrates, textbooks assert the importance of winning an argument and maintaining an authoritative ethos that will help them to persuade others to take on their views. Citing support from other scholars, she calls for a pedagogy that will encourage students to write in ways that invite readers to see different points of view as a means to bridge the hardened lines of difference. In her concluding pages, Peirce asks why scholars and teachers persist in pushing authoritative argument in the classroom when researchers and theorists have for several decades advocated a rhetoric in which participants come to agreement through understanding.

A first response to Peirce might be, "This could be nice, if only the world would work this way." At the same time, teachers of writing or related subjects focused on controversy should not dismiss roles they might play in promoting contention as a singular discourse strategy. We might remind ourselves, as well, that the scholarly ethos advocated for many years, that of the lone writer/scholar creating a unique work that stands apart from others, also contributes to the support the academy gives for exclusively teaching persuasive argument. Argument is favored by most academic disciplines, which ask researchers to defend claims or conclusions with evidence. Nonetheless, we believe there is room within the curriculum to add projects, such as those Peirce advocates, that encourage students to practice discourse that invites readers to fully explore a position, and, as a consequence, asks the student authors to reexamine their own thinking about topics they are exploring. We might ask how often students are taught to write about controversial issues in ways that invite readers who hold divergent positions to consider and respect others' views. Examples of such practices in legal, medical, or other fields, for instance, could be sought and collected, a worthwhile research project in itself.

Also focusing on educational practice, Anita Hernández, José Montelongo, and Roberta Herter offer an alternative to English-only classrooms, an alternative they have shown can expand the linguistic repertoires of all students, not just those who are English-language learners. They call for an end to restrictions on bilingual education in public schools, citing the failure of English-only schools "to close the gap between [our country's many] Latino emergent bilinguals and their English-speaking peers." These authors provide substantial evidence that teaching Spanish-English cognates in public schools not only strengthens English-language learning for Spanish-speaking students but also enhances language learning among native speakers of English, particularly with respect to academic language. The authors overtly claim, contrary to the belief of some, that our evolving society is not experiencing a national identity crisis exacerbated by language differences, and they advocate teaching all students, native and nonnative speakers of English, to expand their academic vocabularies through exposure to other languages from which English draws.

Although Hernández, Montelongo, and Herter limit their study to public-school classrooms, we believe similar approaches to language learning could be introduced into college composition classes. For instance, instead of separating English-language learners from native speakers of English, we might create dual-language courses, particularly in Hispanic Serving Institutions (HSIs), where there are many Spanish-speaking students. Such a model has for some time been advocated by leaders in second language writing such as Matsuda and Silva (1999), who discuss the advantages for all students to learn from one another about linguistic as well as cultural variations. Helpful comparisons between languages—such as through teaching cognates and other linguistic similarities—might improve students' understanding of all languages they are using or learning. In institutions where multiple languages are spoken, inviting students who are English-language learners to draw comparisons between their first language and English also might give them ways to participate more comfortably in composition classes currently dominated by native speakers of English. Also, such approaches could make any "grammar lessons," as students often call them in the composition class, more rhetorically interesting for students who have experienced years of correction in primary and secondary schools.

While also addressing pedagogy, Susan A. Schiller explores another teaching strategy confronted by academic borders: spiritual or holistic education. Schiller asks rhetoricians and teachers of writing, well trained in the uses and purposes of written analysis and argument (as discussed in Peirce, this volume), to cross a border perhaps very difficult for most of us to pass: to move from analysis and argument to promoting a spiritual approach to the whole writing task. Schiller defines her spiritual approach by referring to research on holistic learning and creativity that describes experiences not easily connected to directly observable reality or to "evidence" as we might traditionally describe it. Yet her approach, if we accept it, appears to help students more fully engage their individual energy in the writing experience and produce works not only more interesting for the reader but also more memorable and meaningful for themselves. Offering the reader a wellspring of resources crossing established boundaries between academic analysis and spirituality, Schiller shows the value creative, holistic approaches can provide in the classroom, allowing students to expand their ways of thinking, learning, and knowing.

> We and others might ask whether teachers employing a spiritual approach could side-step the concern some may have about mixing religion with education by using a word other than spiritual to describe such holistic approaches. As part of international educational movements, promoting holistic learning is already widespread. Moreover, holistic approaches are akin to multidisciplinary approaches to problem solving, strategies academics more readily embrace. Yet we might ask whether investing classroom time and energy in evoking creative processes can successfully work for instructors who must cover a variety of analytic and argumentative strategies in their teaching of college writing. At the same time, it does seem worthwhile to us to explore the work of teachers such as Schiller and perhaps test for ourselves whether students can indeed engage with their college experience and academic writing more fully through exploring creativity and spirituality as Schiller describes them. We invite our colleagues who are provoked by this possibility to help demonstrate this possible result. We also propose that teachers consider drawing on the many dimensions of the whole learner—not just the cognitive—including the learner's creativity, sense of self, character, and so on—when helping students learn to write and engage with others.

Schiller is not alone in advocating divergent approaches to enrich our learning. As Mónica Torres and Kathryn Valentine defend with research, cross-racial interactions contribute to both intellectual and social growth. Yet, cross-racial interactions in many contexts in the United States remain fraught and "bordered." Recent events such as an uprising after the shooting of an unarmed black teenager by a white police officer in Ferguson, Missouri—followed a few months later by student protests at the University of Missouri, Yale University, and other schools—and the 2014 debates about what should be done about the hundreds of unaccompanied Central American children crossing into the United States have made clear our country is not in a "post-racial" era, as some people have argued. Torres and Valentine traverse the territory of race relations as reflected in focus-group conversational exchanges among college students. They conclude that Burke's dramatism, reinterpreted by other theorists and themselves to explain participants' identification and disidentification with others, can teach us how to uncover assumptions about difference students make when interacting in ethnically/racially mixed school settings. At the same time, Torres and Valentine explain, differences with respect to race are not easily addressed, and common practices such as denying, ignoring—or even attempting to bridge—difference can introduce new complications, further confounding presumably helpful strategies for improving cross-racial interactions.

> We believe study of the student exchanges analyzed in this chapter may help teachers tease out students' efforts to disguise difference and potentially stifle meaningful interchanges that could helpfully acknowledge ethnic/racial difference. Also relevant is the chapter's focus on the potential, detrimental role of instructors who, when managing such interchanges, discount the positions of students because of their own disguised positionality. We would like to see more studies like those conducted by Torres and Valentine as well as reports that clarify how interchanges can be successfully monitored and guided by instructors to help students—and their teacher guides—better address questions of difference in the classroom. Such exchanges may also help students question their positionality, which might otherwise be "naturalized" or transparent, when addressing such topics in their writing for the classroom or workplace.

PART TWO—LIVING BORDERS

Rhetoric Confronting/Erasing Physical Boundaries

While the authors in "Imagining Borders" explore the impacts we experience as a result of interactions, shaped as they are by language, the authors in "Living Borders" take us to specific experiences and places where lines across the Americas have literally impacted people and their quest for participation through a more democratic discourse. These authors bring to life DeChaine's claim that "the effects of rhetorical bordering are not 'merely' symbolic; they have real consequences for those toward whom their influence is directed" (DeChaine 2012, 14). It is these "real consequences" that we take up here: we go to the Occupy Wall Street encampment and its related online presence *We Are the 99 Percent* and examine discourse strategies such as scapegoating that established lines between "us" and "them" (Cauthen); to Latin America where rhetorical strategies employed by activist local women are "disappeared" just as their loved ones had been physically removed from their lives (Serviss); to a regional museum in the Pacific Northwest where local history with an aim to celebrate tolerance not only hides violence against diverse others, but also denies the presence of certain others (Brewster); to concrete negotiations of immigrants mindful of borders between their pre- and post-relocation lives, whose narratives expand our perception of immigrant Others (Cozza); to a university-community collaboration designed to achieve a range of understandings between scholars and Sudanese immigrants (Long, Clifton, Alden, and Holiday); and to the US suburbs, where students have been found to be markedly resistant to engaging with civic and societal issues (Brooke).

In the first chapter of "Living Borders," Randolph Cauthen takes up Burke's pentad to analyze the success or failure, depending on your viewpoint, of the Occupy Wall Street movement. Through careful analysis of both the extensive online record of participants who identified with the movement as well as extensive media coverage of both sympathizers and critics, Cauthen lets us see that rhetorical positioning through identification, in the case of the protestors, and through scapegoating, in the case of their critics, does indeed have a powerful effect on changing the tenor of discourse about important social issues. Cauthen asks us to examine whether protest movements that effectively employ the techniques of identification described so thoroughly by Burke can obtain any real success in a corporatized media environment. The "people-powered" Internet media offer some space for this kind of resistance, but Cauthen asks whether discourse in this public space can result in meaningful political influence in "real life." The scapegoating of protestors, he suggests, brings to mind the persistent scapegoating of racialized Others in our society, particularly of African Americans.

> *We agree with Cauthen that Burkean analysis remains a powerful tool for studying rhetorical practices that both encourage and stifle democratic discourse, and we believe more deliberate use of it and other such tools can draw attention to discourse that creates more open environments for democratic exchange. At the same time, we have more hope for the power of disruptive discourse to catalyze environments for change. For instance, the "I Am the 99 Percent" and Occupy Wall Street protests*

have now dispersed into other movements questioning—if not responding to—economic and other injustices. *The Rolling Jubilee project that grew from the Occupy movement is one example; in this project economic activists have purchased student-loan debt and reduced or eliminated that debt to draw attention to the need for policy change. In part, this has occurred because of the power of the Occupy discourse strategies themselves. More work is needed to help us understand not only the range of modern activist activity (whether event-based, social, violent, or civil disobedience protests) but also how such activity affects the environment for democratic discourse and the societal change it can bring about.*

Already taking up this call, Tricia Serviss examines local activism responding to societal violence. Serviss addresses rhetorical responses to physical realities that most of us will never personally experience and that would strike fear in our hearts if we should: the reality of the "forced disappearance" of individuals who are politically persecuted or victims of violent, and often sexually abusive, criminal activity. She describes how the rhetorics of Juarez activists who have taken on the decades-long issue of mass femicide and brought attention to the plight in their own voices and in their own ways have been overlooked in favor of simply ascribing their rhetorical moves to other agents, such as Amnesty International, working in this space. Serviss explains why conflating international and local efforts misses important aspects of the unique rhetorical strategies employed by local activists, marring rhetorical studies of such protest movements, and she shows how cursory interpretations dismiss important aspects of the victims' actual physical struggles. To assure that we are not interpreting local activists within cultural frameworks that don't and can't completely explain their realities, Serviss asks rhetoricians to adopt what she calls "translocal" as well as "transcontextual" perspectives. And she asks us as teachers to help students understand these distinctions as they attempt to rhetorically analyze such activity.

Our readers might question, along with us, whether most scholars and teachers are adequately prepared to do the work Serviss advocates—and how they might be better prepared to do such work. Within current environments of political conservatism, we might also ask whether they can do so without being accused of inapposite political advocacy themselves. We believe not only that we could benefit from study of more situations such as those Serviss investigated, in the ways she suggests, but also that, through bringing to light such situations, we could help those afflicted by such travesties be heard on their own terms and, ultimately, procure actual relief. The line between research and advocacy in research is blurred we think by the very act of choosing to engage with such difficult situations (for more on academics studying, if not advocating for, community causes, see Long et al., this volume). And this in itself is a matter for serious contemplation and conversation for academics working as much as is possible toward open, impartial inquiry.

Through study of rhetorical strategies employed to describe historical diversity within a community, Cori Brewster explores a regional museum's depiction of the multicultural history of a small town in Oregon and questions whether explanations of past discrimination, passed off as the aberrant behavior of certain individuals or isolated incidents of exclusion, actually hamper the modern-day community's efforts to deal with institutionalized, discriminatory practices. Brewster shows that even sincere attempts to describe a diverse community with the well-worn term *melting pot* can devalue and even eliminate some groups' actual histories from public depictions of them. Brewster calls for community organizers, teachers, and scholars to examine how communities have rendered their pasts to assure that these collective narratives are not interfering with efforts to address real problems in the present.

> *We agree that a groundswell of analyses of local histories as memorialized in museums and other exhibits may help to raise consciousness about how nostalgic or sanitized renderings of discrimination in the past can prevent us from addressing the realities, if not needs, of increasingly diverse populations throughout communities in the United States. At the same time, we should ask whether direct challenges to such renderings in public-school classrooms, for instance, might put teachers in conflict with the communities that support them—particularly if creators and supporters of museums and other displays of community history are still prominent in the leadership of those communities. To avert this, we ask that scholars and teachers work to devise methods of holding such conversations—not only in classrooms, but also in community forums—that are respectful of past efforts, however faulty, to address the reality of a history of discrimination while introducing realities of present abuse and encouraging efforts to address them. The exploration of culture as a combination of remembering and forgetting, selective or unintentional, should prove promising in future studies identifying the types of borders and boundaries we address in this collection.*

In drawing on literature of immigrants to the United States, Vanessa Cozza reminds us that divides between the majority and Others are not only present in histories or in depictions of those histories. Those of us living in the United States have surely experienced first-hand the divides that separate recent immigrants from those citizens whose families have been here for a generation or more. Cozza categorizes such divides as they are experienced by recent immigrants and shows us how learning about them, hearing these immigrants' stories, can lead to "border consciousness," a quality she claims allows writers—and more specifically student writers in a classroom—to develop cultural sensitivity. She calls on us to draw from immigrant stories as we address social and other issues in our classrooms, allowing new immigrants as well as children or even grandchildren of older immigrants to realize their diverse and sometimes divided notions of "home" are in fact shared by many others and not parts of themselves to keep hidden or, worse, to regard with derision.

> Although Cozza does not set out to prove that exposing student writers to the experiences of immigrants who have written about their own border crossing increases cultural sensitivity, we agree that using such texts in the classroom may indeed help students connect more meaningfully to others in that setting, including their teachers. To us, in the wake of recent challenges to introducing multicultural approaches in the classroom in the United States and beyond (see Vertovec and Wessendorf 2010) or even challenges to depicting the United States as multicultural, as reflected in the boycott of the Coca-Cola company after its 2014 Super Bowl ad in which people from around the country sang "America the Beautiful" in different languages, it seems the true challenge for teachers today is not only to find ways to use multicultural material in the classroom but also to defend the use of classroom time to do so. At the same time, the business world, as we know, has urged public educators to prepare students to succeed in diverse workplace settings where cultural sensitivity is paramount. We may need to do more to encourage partnerships with community and business leaders who can work with teachers to overcome the barriers to educational practices that overtly emphasize difference and the barriers to cultural acceptance experienced in many in US classrooms and communities today.

Addressing the lived experiences of immigrants in real time, Elenore Long, Jennifer Clifton, Andrea Alden, and Judy Holiday's contribution to our collection takes a close look at the collaboration between a university English department and recent immigrants from a local Sudanese community. This collaboration "tested the capacity of intercultural inquiry to foster inclusive dialogue in the preliminary stages of partnership-building." A large group of Sudanese refugees worked with the department faculty and students "to discover and to deliberate pressing open questions of shared concern" in the context of the academy's public turn. Rather than entering the site with an agenda, the authors and their colleagues strove to listen closely to the Sudanese so they might, as academics in unfamiliar territory, learn from them ultimately how to be truly "hospitable," in Derrida's terms (see chapter 1), and truly collaborative in the eyes of the Sudanese immigrants. The experience of crossing linguistic and cultural borders recounted by Long, Clifton, Alden, and Holiday should prove especially instructive to rhetoricians and college teachers. In the specific case addressed in this chapter, the authors explain how diligently they worked to resist the typical structure of many community-university collaborations in which the university "bestows" its resources onto a needy community. As Long, Clifton, Holiday, and Alden argue, the latter model limits "what constitutes engagement, what public life is good for, and how to relate to one another publicly."

> It strikes us that college and university instructors who encourage students to take on service-learning projects or who develop such projects themselves would do well to study the experiences Long and her colleagues have had when working with a Sudanese community to help them address problems through writing as well as through conversation among themselves and with outside agencies. The characteristics of inclusive dialogue these researchers define and illustrate might be mirrored in classroom conversations in which students role-play their potential interactions with those in a community where they would like to work. At the same time, we would like to see more studies like this to confirm the findings Long and colleagues have revealed here and perhaps add to a "playbook" of sorts for university/community partnerships. Such a playbook—characterizing and defining the nature and consequences of certain kinds of participant interaction—may help universities that engage in community efforts assure that the community and the university mutually benefit from the interchanges that define their partnership.

Along with other authors featured in the "Living Borders" section of our collection, Robert Brooke emphasizes the need for rhetoricians and compositionists to actively support the public turn in our fields. Brooke identifies geography as a particularly difficult barrier to overcome when encouraging students to become publicly engaged in local issues and problems. Specifically, he argues, when students have come from suburban environments, their home locations in themselves can create a cultural context that works against desire to engage in public issues, a context exacerbated by standardized approaches to education that ignore local realities. Given that more students are being educated from birth in suburban locations, Brooke calls on educators to draw attention to what lies beyond the borders of suburbia in order to help students engage more meaningfully in discussions of public controversies. In practical terms, his study of suburban isolation illustrates the near impossibility of encouraging within suburban environments the "hospitality" Derrida finds requisite for healthy social interchange (see chapter 1). Nevertheless, Brooke attempts to show how teachers might meet an obligation to mitigate those social effects in the classroom.

> We agree with Brooke that standardized educational approaches can mask or ignore how local context can inform us about issues affecting those whose lives cross physical, ethnic, and other societal borders. We wonder whether scholars and students who explore the border *as a social invention* could reveal the many ways in which a suburban boundary serves to "designate, produce, and/or regulate the space of difference," as DeChaine claims borders do (DeChaine 2009, 44), consequently impacting the "boundaries of civic identity" (DeChaine 2012, 3). The three classroom projects Brooke describes appear to demonstrate that overt interventions that show students how local context can illuminate the significance of civic problems can also increase student interest in civic engagement. At the same time, we wonder if the limitations of geography, that is, where students were raised, actually prohibit

such growth from taking hold beyond the classroom, particularly if such broadening classroom experiences are too few and far between.

FINAL REFLECTIONS
Border Crossing, Toward a More Democratic Discourse

Border crossings affect our civic life on a daily basis, from encounters between strangers who share public spaces to responses to governments that swing from one political party to another. In every case, we have an opportunity to assess meaning, and how we do so affects our future, whether immediate or long term. Becoming more attuned to border crossings can help us ferry them in more productive ways. As John Louis Lucaites has put it, we must enhance our "ability to *observe* and evaluate the borders and boundaries that constitute our civic life" and to consider this "*act of seeing* as a primary mode of civic behavior" (Lucaites 2012, 228; Lucaites's emphasis). Doing so can help us create the supportive environment for democratic discourse we projected in our opening chapter. Overall, this collection calls on us to question the dominant discourses that, as Kent A. Ono and John M. Sloop explain, tend to be considered "common sense . . . both at a civic level and at the level of the individual" (Ono and Sloop 2002, 14), dominant discourses that often ignore what DeChaine (2012) calls the "rhetoricity of borders" (3), symbolic or physical, and their power to erase or support the identities of those defined within or outside of them. We trust that readers of one or more of the chapters in this collection will see the value of, if not the real need for, questioning what is considered natural or naturalized, common sense or nonsensical, within our civic practice as reflected in public discourse.

In representing just some of the ways in which borders are configured, literally or figuratively, our authors have allowed us to see anew the rich potential of considering and studying borders, whether they serve to bridge or to separate individuals across the human enterprise. We hope that going forward, readers can examine for themselves the function of such lines across the Americas—real or imagined, implicit or explicit—and their impact on conversations we can and cannot have with others, in short, their impact on democratic discourse.

As we mention in the opening chapter, we can act to strengthen our public discourse and our democracy's promise of fair participation by building from requisite criteria eschewing what we refer to as the *lines between us*. Such an endeavor includes recognizing and engaging others with a charitable perspective; generously acknowledging and working with difference, whether corporeal or performative; and approaching dissent with openness and hospitality, moving beyond mere tolerance, as Derrida has argued. In short, we can find ways to talk about and negotiate individual experience in the societies we share, and, in so doing, allow the spaces where we live build our American democracy as a rich, yet unfinished, ongoing project. As Lucaites contends, "The resources needed to engage . . . challenges to civic life—whether they concern the boundaries between the United States and Mexico, or red and blue states, or urban and suburban residents, or rich and poor, or gay and straight—need to be seen anew" (Lucaites 2012, 230). We hope this collection motivates others to see anew and to deliberate the many lines that can simultaneously unite and divide—and define—us.

References

Cisneros, Josue David. 2014. *The Border Crossed Us: Rhetorics of Borders, Citizenship, and Latina/o Identity*. Tuscaloosa: University of Alabama Press.

Curzan, Anne. 2014. "'Switchin' It Up,' Lingua Franca: Language and Writing in Academe." *Chronicle of Higher Education*, July 21. http://chronicle.com/blogs/lingua franca/2014/07/21/switchin-it-up/.

DeChaine, D. Robert. 2009. "Bordering and the Civic Imaginary: Alienization, Fence Logic, and the Minuteman Civil Defense Corps." *Quarterly Journal of Speech* 95 (1): 43–65.

DeChaine, D. Robert. 2012. "Introduction: For Rhetorical Border Studies." In *Border Rhetorics: Citizenship and Identity on the US-Mexico Frontier*, edited by D. Robert DeChaine, 1–15. Tuscaloosa: University of Alabama Press.

Diener, Alexander C., and Joshua Hagen. 2012. *Borders: A Very Short Introduction*. New York: Oxford University Press.

Lucaites, John Louis. 2012. "Afterword: Border Optics." In *Border Rhetorics: Citizenship and Identity on the US-Mexico Frontier*, edited by D. Robert DeChaine, 227–30. Tuscaloosa: University of Alabama Press.

Matsuda, Paul K., and Tony Silva. 1999. "Cross-Cultural Composition: Mediated Integration of US and International Students." *Composition Studies* 27 (1): 15–30.

Ono, Kent A., and John M. Sloop. 2002. Introduction to *Shifting Borders: Rhetoric, Immigration, and California's Proposition 187*, edited by Kent A. Ono and John M. Sloop, 1–25. Philadelphia, PA: Temple University Press.

Vertovec, Steven, and Suzanne Wessendorf, eds. 2010. *The Multiculturalism Backlash: European Discourses, Policies, and Practices.* New York: Routledge.

ABOUT THE AUTHORS

BARBARA COUTURE has held university posts ranging from university professor to associate dean (Wayne State University), college dean (Washington State University), senior vice chancellor for academic affairs (University of Nebraska), and university president (New Mexico State University). She has consulted for the Collaborative Brain Trust and the Association of Public and Land-Grant Universities. Couture received the Outstanding Book Award at the 2000 Conference on College Composition and Communication for *Toward a Phenomenological Rhetoric: Writing, Profession and Altruism*. Her publications include six authored/edited books and numerous chapters and articles; she was awarded the distinction of Fellow of the Association of Teachers of Technical Writing in 2010.

PATTI WOJAHN, associate professor at New Mexico State University, researches borders challenging communication and growth in various contexts: within online technologies; within transitions among languages—academic, personal, professional, first, or additional; and within diverse disciplinary fields. A former writing program administrator and associate head of the English Department, she now serves as interim head of the Interdisciplinary Studies Department.

* * *

ANDREA ALDEN is part of the English faculty in the College of Humanities and Social Sciences at Grand Canyon University, where she teaches undergraduate writing. Her research examines the intersection of psychiatry and the law. Her forthcoming book, tentatively titled *Morality and Myth: A Rhetorical History of the Insanity Defense*, analyzes the rhetorical processes that undergird the struggle to develop legal standards adequately addressing needs of mentally ill criminal defendants.

CORI BREWSTER is an associate professor at Eastern Oregon University. Her publications include "Toward a Critical Agricultural Literacy" in *Reclaiming the Rural: Essays on Literacy, Rhetoric, and Pedagogy* and "Trading on the Exploited: Fanny Fern and the Marketplace Rhetoric of Social Justice" in *Popular Nineteenth-Century Women Writers and the Literary Marketplace*.

ROBERT BROOKE is John E. Weaver Professor of English at the University of Nebraska-Lincoln. His current work considers issues of public advocacy in suburban areas, as in his book *Writing Suburban Citizenship: Place-Conscious Education and the Conundrum of Suburbia*. He has also published a book on rural literacy issues: *Rural Voices: Place-Conscious Education and the Teaching of Writing*. He also won the 1988 Braddock Award for his article "Underlife and Writing Instruction" in *College Composition and Communication*.

RANDOLPH CAUTHEN is professor of English at California State University, Dominguez Hills. His publications include *Black Letters: An Ethnography of Legal Writing* and "The Breadth of Composition Studies: Professionalization and Disciplinarity" in *History, Reflection, and Narrative: The Professionalization of Composition, 1963–1983*.

JENNIFER CLIFTON is assistant professor of English at The University of Texas at El Paso. Her scholarship puts theories and rhetorics of public life, deliberative arts, and situated action to work in current contexts in which globalization and transnational movement complicate the conditions and consequences of public engagement. In addition to her forthcoming book, *Argument as Dialogue across Difference: Engaging Youth in Public Literacies*, her publications include "Writing as Dialogue across Difference: Inventing Genres to Support Deliberative Democracy" in the *English Journal* and "Mastery, Failure and Community Outreach as a Stochastic Art: Lessons Learned with the Sudanese Diaspora in Phoenix" in the edited collection *Unsustainable: Owning Our Best, Short-Lived Efforts at Community Writing Work*.

VANESSA COZZA is an assistant professor of English at Washington State University Tri-Cities. Her research interests include student enculturation and assimilation; cultural differences in communication styles and their impact on literacy learning; visual literacy and activist rhetoric; and writing studies. Her most recent publication "In Their Own Voices: Validating Multilingual Identities through Student Literacy Narratives" appears in the edited collection *Teaching US Educated Multilingual Writers: Practice from and for the Classroom*.

ANITA C. HERNÁNDEZ is associate professor and Don and Sarrah Kidd Endowed Chair in Literacy at New Mexico State University. Her research includes professional development, biliteracy, and vocabulary development. She is coauthor of two professional books for teachers: *Theme-Sets for Secondary Students: How to Scaffold Core Literature and Interactive Notebooks* and *English Language Learners: How to Scaffold Content for Academic Success*. Her articles also appear in *Bilingual Research Journal* and *Reading Teacher*. Her next book, *Using Cognates in K–4 Classrooms: A Guide for Teachers and a Resource for K–4 Students Learning Spanish and English*, with José Montelongo and Roberta Herter, is forthcoming.

ROBERTA J. HERTER is professor of education at California Polytechnic State University, San Luis Obispo. Her research and writing have appeared in the *Journal of Adolescent & Adult Literacy*, *Reading Research Quarterly*, *The Reading Teacher*, *The California Reader*, and *Innovative Higher Education*. Her current work includes evaluations of teacher professional-development programs, faculty development, and teacher education, and a forthcoming manuscript, *Using Cognates in K–4 Classrooms: A Guide for Teachers and a Resource for K–4 Students Learning Spanish and English* with Jose Montelongo and Anita Hernandez.

JUDY HOLIDAY is assistant professor of writing at the University of La Verne. Her research interests focus primarily on issues related to postmodern difference. She has also published in *Rhetoric Review* and *Composition Forum* and has contributed book chapters to *The WPA Outcomes Statement—A Decade Later* and *What We Wish We'd Known: Negotiating Graduate School*, which she coedited. Currently she is working on a monograph about violence as a socially constructed cross-cultural episteme.

ELENORE LONG is associate professor of English at Arizona State University. With Linda Flower and Lorraine Higgins, she published *Learning to Rival: A Literate Practice for Intercultural Inquiry*. They also wrote the lead article—a fifteen-year retrospective—for the inaugural issue of *Community Literacy Journal*. Her book *Community Literacy and the Rhetoric of Local Publics* offers a local-public framework for comparing diverse accounts of "ordinary people going public." Her article "Rhetorical Techne, Local Knowledge, and Challenges in Contemporary Activism" appeared in *Rhetorics, Literacies, and Narratives of Sustainability*. Her most recent publications interrogate public rhetorics in transnational contexts, and her current project features a rhetorical art responsive to the particular demands of contemporary public life.

JOSÉ A. MONTELONGO is senior program specialist for the Improving Instruction for Bilingual Learners in New Mexico project at New Mexico State University. He has written numerous articles on vocabulary and reading strategies that have appeared in journals such as *Bilingual Research Journal*, *Reading Teacher*, and *Teacher-Librarian*. Dr. Montelongo is currently writing a book with Anita C. Hernández and Roberta J. Herter: *Using Cognates in K–4 Classrooms: A Guide for Teachers and a Resource for K–4 Students Learning English and Spanish*.

About the Authors

KAREN P. PEIRCE is associate director of the Center for Writers at North Dakota State University. Her publications include "Teaching English at West Point: A Dialogic Narrative," coauthored with David Wood, in *Military Culture and Education*; "Building Intercultural Empathy through Writing: Reflections on Teaching Alternatives to Argumentation" in *CEA Forum*; and "Becoming the Learner: Collaborative Inquiry, Reflection, and Writing Program Assessment," coauthored with Erik Juergensmeyer, in the *WPA Journal*.

JONATHAN P. ROSSING is assistant professor of rhetoric and media in the IU school of Liberal Arts at Indiana University-Purdue University, Indianapolis. His scholarship focuses on the rhetoric of race and racism in US public and popular discourse, with a particular emphasis on the way people use humor as a critical public pedagogy. His work has appeared in a variety of journals including the *Howard Journal of Communications*, *Critical Studies in Media Communication*, *Journal of Communication Inquiry*, *Studies in American Humor*, and *Communication, Culture, and Critique*. He recently received a National Endowment for the Humanities Enduring Questions Grant for a course on the Purpose and Value of Play.

SUSAN A. SCHILLER is professor of English and director of the MA in humanities program at Central Michigan University. Her research interests focus on spirituality in education, composition studies, and criticism in Willa Cather. Relevant publications include *The Spiritual Side of Writing: Releasing the Learner's Whole Potential* and *Sustaining the Writing Spirit: Holistic Tools for School and Home*, 2nd edition.

CHRISTOPHER SCHROEDER is professor of English at Northeastern Illinois University. He won the 2012 CCCC Research Impact Award for *Diverse by Design: Literacy Education within Multicultural Institutions*; he coedited *ALT DIS: Alternative Discourses and the Academy* with Helen Fox and Patricia Bizzell; and he wrote *ReInventing the University: Literacies and Legitimacy in the Postmodern Academy*.

TRICIA SERVISS is assistant professor in the writing program within Santa Clara University's English department. Her research interests include research methods, writing program administration, transcontextual literary practices, feminist rhetorics, and teacher preparation. Her recent publications appear in *College English*, *Assessing Writing*, *Writing and Pedagogy*, and *Reflections: A Journal of Writing, Service-Learning, and Community Literacy*.

MÓNICA TORRES is vice president for academic affairs at Doña Ana Community College in Las Cruces, New Mexico. Her research and teaching interests include cultural theory and criticism. She is particularly interested in institutional discourses and the ways in which those discourses shape how we think about knowledge and identity. Her work has appeared in *The Velvet Light Trap*, *Revista casa de las Américas*, the *International Journal of Qualitative Studies in Education*, and the *Journal of Diversity in Higher Education*.

KATHRYN VALENTINE is associate professor and writing center director at San Diego State University. Her scholarship focuses on issues of identity and literacy within the teaching of writing, often in the context of writing centers, and she has published in a wide variety of journals including *College Composition and Communication*, the *Writing Center Journal*, the *International Journal of Qualitative Studies in Education*, and the *Journal of Diversity in Higher Education*.

VICTOR VILLANUEVA is Regents' Professor, Edward R. Meyer Distinguished Professor, director of the writing program at Washington State University, and the editor of the Conference on College Composition and Communication's *Studies in Writing and Rhetoric* series. He authored the award-winning *Bootstraps: From an American Academic of Color*, *Latino/a Discourses: On Language, Identity, and Literacy Education* and *Rhetorics of the Americas:*

3114 BCE to 2012 CE. He was designated as the 1999 Rhetorician of the Year, the 2008 Advancement of People of Color Leadership Award winner from the National Council of Teachers of English, and the CCCC 2009 Exemplar, among other awards and honors. All of his work has centered on the connections between language and racism.

NANCY WELCH is Professor of English at the University of Vermont where she helped lead the drive to unionize faculty and where she is active in regional labor solidarity. She is author of *Getting Restless: Rethinking Revision in Writing Instruction* (Boynton Cook 1997), *The Road from Prosperity: Stories* (Southern Methodist UP 2005), and *Living Room: Teaching Public Writing in a Privatized World* (Boynton Cook 2008) as well as co-editor of *The Dissertation and Discipline: Reinventing Composition Studies* (Boynton Cook 2002). Her articles have appeared in *College English, College Composition and Communication, JAC,* and *Pedagogy,* and her short stories have appeared in such journals as *Ploughshares* and *Prairie Schooner.* In 2010 she received *College English*'s Richard Ohmann Award for "'We're Here and We're Not Going Anywhere: Why Working-Class Rhetorical Practices *Still* Matter."

INDEX

Abu Graib images, 176
"Academic Jargon and Soul-Searching Drivel" (Corder), 85
Academic Word List, 101
academic words, as English-Spanish cognates, 101–2
acceptance, self- and communal, 213–14
acculturation, 213, 214, 215, 220
achievement, standards of, 121–22
activism: Argentine women, 179–81; Ciudad Juarez women, 171, 174–75, 182–85, 279; Internet, 166–67; Occupy movement, 153–62, 165–66; rhetorics of, 175–76; translocal, 177, 279
advocacy, humor and, 71
AEPL. *See* Assembly on the Expanded Perspectives of Learning
AERO. *See* Alternative Education Resource Organization
African Americans, 165; scapegoating of, 163, 167, 278
AgJOBS bill (H.R. 2414), 62, 63; Colbert's testimony on, 68–69, 72
agreement, as goal, 88–89
Ainsworth-Land, George, 122–23
Alabama, anti-immigrant laws, 12, 33–34
Albany Free schools, 114
alignments, 229; developing, 233–35
Alpharetta (Georgia), 259
Alternative Education Research Organization (AERO), 113–14
Alvarez, Julia, 210, 218, 219, 221; *Something to Declare: Essays*, 216–17
ambiguity, tolerance for, 145–46
ambulatory appeals, of Mothers of the Plaza, 180–81
American Dream, 5, 6, 152, 162, 163, 258
American Indians, 193; represented at Four Rivers Cultural Center, 192, 195, 196
American Right, demagoguery of, 161
Amnesty International, 172, 177, 188(n4), 279; epistolary appeals by, 181–82; and Juarez disappearances, 174–75, 185; Urgent Action campaigns, 178–79

analysis, 118–19
Ancient Rhetorics for Contemporary Students (Crowley and Hawhee), 82–83
Antigua, immigrants from, 218
anti-immigration laws, 12, 33–34
Anzaldúa, Gloria, 131, 209; on border spaces, 135–36, 212, 218; on context, 136–37; on cross-racial interactions, 142–44, 145–46
appropriation, of identity constructs, 63–64
Argentina, 188(n5), 188(n6); Amnesty International and, 181–82; immigrants from, 214–15, 218, 220; Mothers of the Plaza, 175, 179–81, 188(n3); rhetorics of activism in, 171, 172
argument, argumentation, 79, 86, 86, 118–19; in contemporary culture, 83, 84; humor as form of, 67–69, 71; practices of, 78, 81–82, 274
Argument Culture: Moving from Debate to Dialogue, The (Tannen), 84
Aristotle, *On Rhetoric*, 79
Arizona: English-only legislation, 96; SB 1070, 12, 33, 60, 66, 210; Sudanese diaspora in, 230–38
artist, as counterweight, 153
ASCD. *See* Association for Supervision and Curricular Development
Assembly on the Expanded Perspectives of Learning (AEPL), 114
assertiveness, 79, 85
assimilation, 38, 212, 213, 215, 220–21, 238; English language use, 52, 95, 96
Association for Supervision and Curricular Development (ASCD), 115, 116–17
Atwill, Janet, *Rhetoric Reclaimed*, 247
audience, persuasion of, 79
Australia, as terra nullius, 11
authority, ethos of, 85, 274

Babiuk, Gary, 115–16
Barragan, Nina (Rocio Aitana Lasansky), 210, 211, 214–15, 218, 219, 221
barriers, 10, 12, 32; in classrooms, 222–25; differences and, 13–14

Basques, at Four Rivers Cultural Center, 192, 195
Bazze, Dora de, 180
Becoming American: Personal Essays by First Generation Immigrant Women (Danquah), 213–15
Bellafante, Ginia, 153
Benenson, Peter, 178
Bhutan, holistic education in, 116
bidirectional linguistic resources, 105–6
bilingual education, 94; models for, 99–101; use of cognates in, 101–6
Bilingual Education Act, 94
bilingualism, 99, 100; and assimilation, 220–21; circumstantial vs. elective, 97–98; use of cognates in, 101–3
biliteracy, 99, 100, 102, 107
Bobbitt, David, 165
Bonilla-Silva, Eduardo, 196
border consciousness, 212, 219–20, 222, 280–81
borderlands, 212; bilingualism, 97, 99; cross-racial interactions, 138–44
Borderlands/La Frontera: The New Mestiza (Anzaldúa), 136, 143, 218
borders, 18, 34, 40, 71, 94, 156, 158, 209, 271, 283; Anzaldúa on, 135–36; classroom, 222–25; constructed, 65–67; figurative, 4–5; linguistic, 56–57; storytelling about, 210–11; US-Mexican, 32, 93
Bordertown (film), 185
Borradori, Giovanna, 19
Boster, Dan, 264
Boston Marathon bombings, 10
boundaries, 4, 5, 16, 54, 130, 228; linguistic, 56–57
Bray, Mark, 154
Brazil, Amnesty International appeal in, 179
Brookfield Properties, 152
Brown, Henry Billings, 37
Burke, Kenneth, 131, 137, 151, 153, 156, 160, 166, 167; "Definition of Man," 154–55; on dramatism, 140–41, 277; on identification, 132–33, 134; pentad, 30–31, 278; on scapegoating, 161–62
Bush, George H. W., 76
Bush, George W., 96

California, 32, 96, 97, 98
Callaghan, Patsy, 81–82
Campbell High School (Smyrna, Ga.), 263
capitalism, 32, 152
Carter administration, 94

Casa Amiga Rape and Crisis center, 182
Catholic discourse, in Juarez anti-femicide activism, 183, 184, 185
certitude, and dialogue, 87
charity, 8, 9, 10, 20; in public discourse, 283–84
Chavez Cano, Esther, 182
Cherokee, bilingual newspaper, 51
Chicago, 51; ethnic press in, 46–47; Spanglish culture, 53–54
children: bilingualism, 97–98; as English-language learners, 98–99; learning environment, 116–17
Chinese, in eastern Oregon, 201, 207(n10)
Christianity, service-mission experiences, 256
Chronicle of Higher Education (Ferguson), 32
Ciceronian invention, 84, 88–89
citizenship, 20, 37
Ciudad Juarez: feminist activism in, 8, 171, 172, 174–75, 182–86, 188(n8),188(n9), 279; growth of, 173–74
civic design, of suburbs, 257–59
civil discourse, 76–77, 272; communication for, 78–79; ethos of, 84–85
Civil Rights Act, 94
Clarke, Adele, on situational analysis, 238–39
classrooms: borders and barriers in, 222–25; critiques of suburbia in, 262–63; cross-racial interactions in, 144–46; immigrant literature in, 280–81; multiple language, 275–76
CLC. *See* Community Literacy Center
Clinton, Bill, 76, 164
Clueless (film), 262
Coalition of Essential Schools, 260
code-switching, 12, 272, 273; in EXTRA, 48–51, 53–54
Cofer, Judith Ortiz, "Marina," 224
cognates: English-Spanish, 101–3; for English speakers, 106–7; teaching and learning with, 102–6
Colbert, Stephen, 17, 274; congressional testimony by, 67–71, 72; satire of, 61–63; use of appropriation and defamiliarization, 63–65; use of racial-border constructs, 65–67
Colbert Report, The, 17, 274; satire on, 61–62
colonialism, and cultural activity, 172
Colorado, English-only legislation, 96
colors, and mood, 90–91
comedy, 17; Colbert's use of, 61–67

Common Core, 259, 260
communication, 5, 82; across borders, 78–79; ethos and, 83–84; in Occupy Wall Street, 155–56; in rhetoric, 8–9
community, communities, 20, 35, 44; historical diversity, 195–200, 280; partnerships with universities, 227, 229–38, 248(n7), 281–82; place-based writing projects, 263–67; public dialogue in, 242–43; as sociohistorical formation, 12–13
community colleges, cross-racial interactions, 138–44
Community Literacy Center (CLC), 236
complicity, recognition of, 143–44
composition, 118, 223, 254; suburban rhetoric in, 262–63
composition textbooks/courses, 30; practices of argument in, 78, 274–75; spirituality in, 118
confrontation, cross-racial issues, 136
consubstantiality, 134, 151, 155, 157, 159
consumerism, secular, 22
contact, with others, 273
contemplation, 111
context, cross-cultural interactions, 136–37
continuity, of cultural identity, 273
contracts, 114
conversation, charity in, 8, 9
Conyers, John, 72
Coordinadora de organismos no gubernamentales contra la violencia hacia las mujeres (Coordination of Non-Governmental Organizations), 182
Corder, Jim, 85, 86; on ethos, 83–84
corporeal differences, 21
corporeal generosity, 11, 12
Counter-Statement (Burke), 153
Courage to Teach, The (Palmer), 117–18
Crable, Bryan, 131, 132, 133, 136, 144
creativity, 118, 119, 120, 125, 126, 127(n8); and holistic worldview, 123–24; phases of, 121–22
credibility, Arisotelian ethos of, 79–80
criminality, 166
critical incidents: documenting and constructing, 235–38; public dialogue on, 243, 249(n11); situational analysis of, 240–41
critical race theory, 65
Cross Campaign, 182, 183–85
cross-cultural issues: context in, 136–37; identification as, 132–33
crosses, as femicide symbols, 183–85
cross-linguistic transfer, 100

cross-racial interactions, 129, 131, 133, 277; in college setting, 138–44; context in, 136–37
Crowley, Sharon, *Ancient Rhetorics for Contemporary Students*, 82
cultural change, teaching, 113
cultural continuity, 43, 56
cultural differences, response to, 129–30
cultural diversity, 44; and Four Rivers Cultural Center, 192–200
cultural production, 54
culture: public, 70, 72; Sudanese, 240
curanderos, in Juarez femicide activism, 183, 184
curiosity, 86; and inquiry, 90–91

Dahl, Robert A., *On Democracy*, 7
Dak, Tap, 230–31, 232, 235, 242; drawing alignments, 233–34
Danquah, Meri Nana-Ama, 210, 218; on immigrant literature, 223–24; self- and communal acceptance, 213–14
databases, in bilingual education, 107
Davidson, Donald, 8
decision making, 155; collective, 6, 7, 8, 15
defamiliarization, 63–64
Defining Memory: Local Museums and the Construction of History in America's Changing Communities (Levin), 193
democracy, 21, 233; foundation of, 7–8; and public discourse, 283–84; spreading, 5–6, 32
Democracy, On (Dahl), 7
Democratic Education Movement, 114
Derrida, Jacques, 22, 23; on hospitality, 19–20; *Politics of Friendship*, 9
Dewey Decimal System, English-Spanish cognates in, 101
dialectic, of irony, 31
dialogue, 19, 87; and argumentation, 81, 88, 274; inclusive, 227–28; public, 84, 234, 241–44
Dienst, Richard, 156
difference(s): as barriers, 13–14; focus on, 76, 274; responses to, 129–30
Diprose, Roslyn, 11
Direct Action campaigns, 178
Dirty War, 179, 188(n3), 188(n6)
disappearance(s), 182, 185; in Argentina, 179–81; forced, 173, 176, 279; rhetoric on, 171–72
discourse, 6, 12, 13, 17, 63; civil, 76–77; democratic, 5, 7, 8, 18–19, 21, 270–71, 272; humorous, 60–61; hybrid, 71–74; public, 14–15, 246–47, 281–82, 283–84

discrimination, 192, 221; in Ontario, Oregon, 201, 202–4
disengagements, 143
disidentification, 134, 135, 142, 277
disputes, persuasion in, 82
disruption, 62; of discourse, 17–18
dissent, vs. tolerance, 19
divergent thinking, 123
diversity, 13, 192
division, 151, 154–55
Dobyns, Ann, 81–82
Domestic Security Alliance Council, and Occupy movement, 165
Dominican Republic, immigrants from, 217, 218, 219
Downes v. Bidwill, 36
draft, Puerto Ricans, 37
dramatism, 30, 132, 140–41, 152, 277
dual immersion, 94
dual-language programs/models, 96, 97, 99–101, 275–76

Eakin, Paul John, 211
economic capital, 240
economic concerns, 161, 165
edge cities, 257, 258–59
education, 12, 37, 78, 94; alternative, 113–14; holistic, 114–19; multiple perspectives on, 89–90; public, 95–96; in suburbia, 257, 259–60
El Dorado Ditch, 201
Elements of Argument (Rottenberg), 80
Elizondo, Virgilio, *Guadalupe: Mother of the New Creation*, 186
Ellison, Ralph, 132, 133
El Paso, bilingualism in, 99
emotional intelligence, 119
empathy, 155
empire, U.S., 32
enemies, illegal immigrants as, 10
engagement, 143; in classroom, 144–45
English for the Immigrant Children campaign, 96
English language, 12, 44, 51, 52; proficiency in, 216–17
English-language learners, 93, 96, 276; bilingualism and, 220–21; children as, 98–99, 101–7
English-only policies, 12, 45, 56, 273; challenges to, 51–52; in public education, 95–96
English-plus resolutions, 97
epistolary appeals, Amnesty International's, 178–79, 181–82
equality, political, 43

Erickson, Erik, 161
Espionage, Sedition, and Trading with the Enemy Acts, 45
ethnicity: in Puerto Rico, 38; self-identity and, 138–40
ethnic press, 44–45; in Chicago, 46–47
ethnic-studies classes, in Tucson, 33, 34
ethno-nation, Puerto Rico as, 38
ethos: of civil discourse, 84–85; credible, 79–80, 81–83; of rhetoric, 87–88
European Americans, 11; represented at Four Rivers Cultural Center, 192, 195, 197–98
exclusion, 11, 38
EXTRA, 47; code-switching in, 48–51, 53–54; language use in, 52–53

farm workers, undocumented, 62
fear, 41
femicides, 177, 187–88(n2); campaigns against, 182–85; in Ciudad Juarez, 173, 174
feminist activists, rhetorical practices of, 8–9
Ferguson, Niall, 32
Figuring Out What to Write (Roda), 236–38, 243
Find-A-Cognate database, 105
Florida, second-language learners in, 98
Flower, Linda, "Talking across Difference," 89
Foehr, Regina Paxton, *The Spiritual Side of Writing*, 114
folding in, 55
forced disappearance, 173, 176
Ford administration, 94
Four Rivers Cultural Center, 192; cultural-historical presentations at, 195–98, 206(n6), 207(n8); historical themes missing from, 201–2; museum at, 193, 205(n2), 205(n3), 207(n11); race and tolerance themes in, 194, 199–200
Fox News, and Occupy Movement protest, 153
freedom, 6, 7
Friedman, Thomas L., *The World Is Flat*, 55–56
friendship, moral dangers of, 9–10
Fuss, Diana, 134, 134
Future is Mestizo (Elizondo), 186

Gallegos, Ramon, on holistic education, 114–15
Garcia Marquez, Gabriel, *One Hundred Years of Solitude*, 23–24

Garcia Maturey, Eulalia, 63–64
Gardner, Howard, 123; on learning intelligences, 119, 120–21, 127(n6)
Geisel Award winners, 107
General Service List, 101
generosity of intercorporeality, 14
Georgia, 40
Ghana, immigrants from, 214, 218
Giffords, Gabrielle, shooting of, 76
globalization, 55, 56, 176, 259
God Grew Tired of Us, 229–30
Gonzalez, Guillermina, 183, 184
Grammar of Motives, A (Burke), 31
Grinvalds, Jeff, 264
Great Wall of China, 32
Guadalupe: Mother of the New Creation (Elizondo), 186
Guatemala, femicides in, 177, 184
guilt, 162, 165
Gullifoyle, Kimberly, 153

Habermas, Jürgen, 19, 22
Hariman, Robert, 72–73
Hawai'i, as bilingual state, 97
Hawhee, Debra, *Ancient Rhetorics for Contemporary Students*, 82–83
Hayakawa, S. I., English Language Amendment, 95
HB 56 (Alabama), 12, 33
hegemony, 41
Hesford, Wendy, *Spectacular Rhetorics*, 176
heuristics, and Burke's pentad, 30–31
hierarchical psychosis, 156
Hispanics, 46, 48; in Malheur County, 192, 195
history, 13; local, 195–200, 280
Holistic Curriculum, The (Miller), 113
holistic education, 114–15; analysis and argumentation in, 118–19; international interest in, 116–17; learning strategies in, 120–21; spirit in, 117–18, 124–27
Holistic Education, Pedagogy of Universal Love (Gallegos), 115
Holistic Learning: Breaking New Ground, 115
holistic worldview, 123–24
homogeneity, of suburbia, 258
Honduras, 184
Honz, Kelly, 265
Horne, Tom, "Open Letter to the Citizens of Tucson," 34, 38
hospitality, 21, 246; Derrida on, 19–20
Hothem, Thomas, 262
housing developments, 257

human rights, 21, 176, 178; basic, 10–11; inter-American infrastructures, 186–87
humor, 17, 273–74; as form of argument, 67–69; immigration discourse, 60–61; as pedagogical resource, 73–74; polysemy in, 64–65; public culture and, 70, 72; Stephen Colbert's use of, 62–64, 66, 71
Hunt, Sally, 265
Huntington, Samuel P., 34; *Who Are We?*, 39
hybridity, 55, 61
hyperspace, 262–63

Idaho, Ku Klux Klan in, 201–2
IDEC. *See* International Democratic Education Conference
IDEN. *See* International Democratic Education Network
identification, 156, 157, 165; Burke's views of, 132–33, 151, 155, 277; in cross-racial interactions, 139–40, 141–43, 144; and place, 135–36; Ratcliffe's views of, 134–35
identity, 43, 44, 45, 73, 133, 214, 228, 235, 248–49(n8); bodily recognition of, 12–13; cultural, 52, 215–16, 273; cultural markers, 216–17; humorous constructs of, 63–64, 273–74; linguistic, 55–56; national, 38, 40, 272–73; and place, 4, 282–83; self-, 138–40
Illinois: nativism in, 51; second language learners in, 98
immigrants, 10, 45, 93, 97, 235; acculturation and assimilation of, 214–15, 220–21; cultural markers of, 216–17; geographical and cultural isolation of, 217–19; identity, 45, 215–16; literature, 223–25, 280–81; multiple literacies of, 230–31; storytelling by, 210–11
immigration, 17; Colbert's discourse on, 63–65; humorous discourse on, 60–61
inclusive dialogue, intercultural inquiry, 227–28
indexing, 54
individuals, 3, 5, 7, 8, 21
inefficiency, political, 153
inquiry, 79, 81, 86, 89; intercultural, 227–28, 229; openness of, 90–91
Inquiry and Genre (Joliffe), 80–81
Insular Cases, 36
intelligence(s), 123–24, 127(n6); learning, 120–21; spiritual, 111–12, 119
Inter-American Human Rights Council, 187

intercorporeality, 14
intercultural inquiry, 229; and inclusive dialogue, 227–28
International Convention for the Protection of All Persons from Forced Disappearance, 172
International Democratic Education Conference (IDEC), 114
International Democratic Education Network (IDEN), 114
International Foundation for Holistic Education, 114
International Reading Association's Teachers' Choices, 107
International Society for Technology in Education, 260
irony, 31
Islam, and terrorism, 19
isolation, 20, 221, 221; geographical and cultural, 217–19

Japanese Americans, and Four Rivers Cultural Center, 192, 193, 195–96, 198, 205(n1), 207(n11)
Johnson, Lyndon, 94
Johnstone, Barbara, 54
Joliffe, David, *Inquiry and Genre*, 80–81
Jones-Shafroth Act, 37
Juan Diego, 186
Juarez. *See* Ciudad Juarez
judgment, considered, 86
Justicia para nuestra hijas (Justice for Our Daughters), 182, 188(n8)

Kennesaw State University, Keeping and Creating American Communities, 263
Kilborn, Peter, 260–61
Kincaid, Jamaica (Elaine Potter Richardson), 210, 211; *Lucy*, 218
King, Martin Luther, Jr., 34; "I Have a Dream" speech, 165
Klein, Naomi, 157–58
Knoblauch, A. Abby, 78
knowledge, 15, 16
Konczal, Mike, 164
Kratz, Corinne, 204
Kuek, John, 243
Ku Klux Klan, in Oregon and Idaho, 201–2
Kuntsler, James, 262

laborers, day, 64
language, 5, 12, 17, 45, 46, 52, 132, 224, 273; as bidirectional linguistic resources, 105–6; and boundaries, 54, 272; and identity, 55–56; multiple, 275–76; policies on, 93–94
language brokers, children as, 97
language policy, 93–94
Lantieri, Linda, on spiritual experience, 113, 116
Latin America, forced disappearance in, 176. *See also* Argentina; Guatemala; Mexico
Latina/os, 38, 40; stereotypes of, 29–30
Lau v. Nichols, 94
leadership: democratic, 138; grassroots, 240
learner-centered schools, 114
learning, 123; environments, 116–17, 129; holistic, 120–21, 124–27; spiritual approach to, 111, 112–13, 117–18
Levin, Amy, *Defining Memory*, 193
liberty, preserving, 44
Limbaugh, Rush, 161
Lincoln (Nebr.), refugee resettlement in, 255–56
Lincoln East High School (Nebr.), 265
listening, deliberative, 229, 231–33
literacy, literacies, 56, 102, 244; multiple, 230–31; transcontextualized, 54–55, 177
literature: as equipment for living, 131–32; immigrant, 223–25, 280–81
Living Autobiographically: How We Create Identity in Narrative (Eakin), 211
local-global encounters, 55
localizing moves, 55
Lofgren, Zoe, 70
Lopez, Barry, 262
Lopez, Jennifer, 185
Lost Boys of Sudan, 230, 233
Lucy (Kincaid), 218
Lyotard, Jean Francois: on disruption, 17–18; on postmodernism, 15; on sublime, 16–17

Maine, USS, as metonymy, 35
Malheur County, Ore.: demography of, 192–93, 207(n12); racial issues in, 201–2
Malheur Reservation, 197
Manifest Destiny, 40
mapping, thematic, 239, 240–41, 244
maquiladoras, 173
March of the Weeping Women, 182
marginalized people, rights of, 12
Maricopa County, literary services, 244
"Marina" (Cofer), 224
Marom, Yotam, 152–53
Marshall, Ian, 123–24

Martinez, Sylvia, 263
Massachusetts, dual-language programs in, 97; English-only legislation, 96
master tropes, Burke's, 31
media, 47; code-switching in, 273; response to Colbert's testimony, 69–70
meditation, 111, 114
Meeting of Minds, A (Callaghan and Dobyns), 81
mentors, writing, 231–32
mestizos, rhetoric of, 186
metaphor, 31
metonymy, 31–32, 34, 40
Mexican Americans, 38, 46
Mexicans, 10, 46, 48
Mexico, 40; holistic education in, 114–15
migration, Puerto Rican, 37–38
Miller, John (Jack) P., 115, 116; *The Holistic Curriculum*, 113
Miller, Ron, 113
minorities, ethnic, 44
Molinary, Rosie, 213
Montessori schools, 114
mood, colors and, 90–91
Morrow, Katie, 265
Mothers of the Plaza, 175, 188(n3); origins of, 179–80; strategies of, 180–81
multiculturalism, 193, 281
multilingualism, 52
multiple perspectives, 138, 235
murders, in Ciudad Juarez, 171, 173, 174
museums, 278; cultural narratives in, 193–94, 195–98, 204–5; race and tolerance themes in, 199–200
mutual understanding, 83, 85, 86, 89, 91
Myceneans, 32

Nagelhout, Ed, on hyperspace, 262–63
naming, power of, 11
nation: Anglo-American, 39–40; US as, 34–35
National Center for Fair and Open Testing, 260
National Council of Teachers of English (NCTE), 114
National Institute for Civil Discourse (NICD), objectives of, 76–77, 78–79, 84, 91
nationalism, 11–12, 273
nation-building, 240
Native Americans, representation of, 265
nativism, in Illinois, 51
NCLB. *See* No Child Left Behind Act
NCTE. *See* National Council of Teachers of English

Nebraska, refugee resettlement in, 255–56
Nebraska Writing Project, 255, 263; programs in, 264–66
neo-Aristotelianism, 31
neoliberal policy, 254–55
New Mexico, dual-language programs, 97
newspapers, 182; bilingual, 52–53; Spanish language, 47–51
New York: Occupy Wall Street protest in, 151, 152–53; second language learners, 98
NICD. *See* National Institute for Civil Discourse
Nichols, John, 157
Nietzsche, Friedrich, 11; concept of community, 12–13
99 percent trope, 157, 278; use of, 159–61
Noche de los Lápices, La (The Night of the Pencils), 179, 188(n5)
No Child Left Behind (NCLB) Act, 96, 259, 260
nonconfrontation, 130
nonidentification, 134, 142; and place, 135–36
Nuestras hijas de regreso a casa (May Our Daughters Return Home), 182, 188(n9)

Obama, Barack, 43, 94, 165; response to Occupy Movement, 163–64
Occupy Press Relations Working Group, 154
Occupy Wall Street movement, 16, 151, 158, 168(n3), 168(n4), 278, 278–79; communication in, 155–56; demands of, 153–54; impacts of, 165–66; scapegoating of, 161–62, 163, 164, 167; self-definition, 156–57
Olivas, Bernice, 265
Omaha, Urban Justice League project in, 264
Omaha Burke High School, 265
One Hundred Years of Solitude (Garcia Marquez), 23–24
O'Neill Secondary School (Nebr.), 265
Ontario (Ore.): demography of, 192–93; racial issues in, 201–4, 205(n1)
"Open Letter to the Citizens of Tucson" (Horne), 34, 38
openness: ethos of, 78, 79, 88; of inquiry, 90–91
Operation Gatekeeper, 32
Oregon: English-plus resolutions, 97; racial issues in, 201–2
origin stories, of Juarez activists, 174–75

Other(s), 18, 22, 32, 39, 61; immigrant, 278, 280
Our Town (Wilder), 3–4, 23–24

Paiutes, Northern, represented at Four Rivers Cultural Center, 196, 197, 207(n8)
Palmer, Parker, *The Courage to Teach*, 117–18
participation, and toleration, 21–22
partnerships: alignments in, 233–35; critical incidents in, 235–38; listening deliberatively, 231–33; public dialogue in, 241–44; situational analysis in, 238–41; university-community, 227, 229–31, 248(n7), 281–82
patriotism, American, 44
Payette, Idaho, Ku Klux Klan in, 201–2
Pecha Kucha PowerPoint presentations, 265
pentad, Burke's, 30–31, 278
people's mic, 155–56
Perez, Irma, 183, 188(n8)
persuasion, 79–80, 86, 132; through argumentation, 81–82; rhetoric based on, 82–83
Phoenix: public dialogue in, 241–43; Sudanese diaspora in, 230–41
photovoice projects, 244
phronesis, 247
picture books, vocabulary in, 102–3
Pittsburgh, Community Literacy Center, 236
Pittsburghese, 54
place, 261; identity and, 4, 214, 216, 282–83; in public rhetoric, 265–67; teaching, 263–64
planned/gated communities, 257, 259
Plano (Texas), 259
Pledge of Allegiance, 7
political debate, satire in, 70–71
political discourse, 72
Politics of Friendship (Derrida), 9, 23
politics of generosity, 11, 13–14
polysemy, in humor, 64–65
Postcard Campaign, 182
Postmodern Condition: A Report on Knowledge, The (Lyotard), 15
postmodernism, 15, 18
postracial ideology, 62
postsuburban experience, 262–63
presidential election, Latino/as in, 40
press, ethnic, 44–45
privilege, 62, 228
professional class, suburban, 261

Professional Interest Community (PIC) for Holistic Learning and Spirituality in Education, 115–16
property rights, European concepts of, 11
public life, rhetorical models of, 245–46
Puerto Ricans, 46, 48
Puerto Rico, 272; mass migration of, 37–38; and racial exclusion, 11–12; and Spanish American War, 35–36; as US territory, 36–37
pure persuasion, 156
Putnam, Robert, 43

Quakers, consensus-building, 155
questioning, 86, 89

race, 131, 132, 205(n1), 207(n12); discourse on, 14, 205–6(n5); hierarchies of, 141, 207(n12); as museum theme, 194, 199–200; and self-identity, 138–40; symbolicity of, 133–34
racialization, 38, 161
racism, 30, 40, 34, 131, 163, 193, 205–6(n5), 221; in anti-immigration laws, 12, 33; as museum theme, 199–200, 201–2; in national identity, 11–12
Ralston High School (Nebr.), 265; Urban Justice League project, 264
ranching, Four Rivers Cultural Center exhibit, 197–98
Ratcliffe, Krista, 131, 132–33, 137, 142; on identification, 134–35, 144
Raza studies, in Tucson, 33, 34, 38
Razor, Jennifer, 265
Reagan, Ronald, on English language instruction, 95–96
realities, 17, 272; "correct" vs. other, 15–16
"Realizing a World of Sustainable Wellbeing and Happiness," 116
reasoning from facts, 7–8
recognition: bodily, 12; of individuals, 21; and rights, 10–11
refugee resettlement, in Nebraska, 255–56
relationship building, 143
relaxation, 111
relovilles, 257, 259, 261
repetitive form, 160
Republican Party, and Latino/as, 40
resistance, 180, 184
responsibility, in Sudanese community groups, 240
retroacculturation, 221
rhetoric(s), 16, 154, 223, 248, 271, 274; Amnesty International's, 181–82; communication in, 8–9; in community-

university partnerships, 233–34; of Juarez activists, 171, 175, 176, 185–86; persuasion based on, 82–83; in public space, 254–55, 281–82; suburban public, 260–61, 262–63; teaching, 87–88
Rhetoric, On (Aristotle), 79
Rhetorical Listening: Identification, Gender, Whiteness (Ratcliffe), 134
rhetorical theory, 245–46; building, 247–48; and cross-racial interactions, 138
Rhetoric of Motives (Burke), 133
Rhetoric Reclaimed (Atwill), 247
Rhode Island, English-plus resolution, 97
rights, and recognition, 10–11
Robinson, Ken, 123, 124
Roda, 242; institutional practices, 244–45; *Figuring Out What to Write*, 236–38, 243
Romero, Oscar, 185, 188(n10)
Romney, Mitt, 161
Roosevelt, Theodore, 95
Rossi, Luiz Basilio, 179, 188(n4)
Rottenberg, Annette, *Elements of Argument*, 80
Royal Society of the Arts (RSA), 113
Royster, Jacqueline, 223
RSA. *See* Royal Society of the Arts

sacred, 117, 118
Sandell, Richard, 204
Santa Fe Bridge (Juarez-El Paso), altar and crucifix at, 184–85
satire, 17; Stephen Colbert's, 61–63
SB 1070 (Arizona), 12, 33, 60, 65, 66, 210
SCAA. *See* Sudanese Community Association in Arizona
scapegoating, 141, 278; of Occupy movement, 161–62, 163, 164, 167
Schiller, Susan A., *Spiritual Side of Writing*, 114
Schmidt, Ronald, 44
schools, alternative, 113–14; public, 44, 45, 51, 93
science, subordination to technology, 16
screenplays, writing exercise, 121–23
Selective Service Act (1917), 37
self-acceptance, 224
self-definition, Occupy movement's, 156–57
self-representation, 214
service: community, 256; university outreach, 228–30
Shore, Bradd, 261
silence, practicing, 111
situational analysis, 238–39; of critical incidents, 240–41

Sloane, Thomas O., Ciceronian invention, 84, 88–89
Smyrna (Ga.), Campbell High School in, 263
sociability, 246
social-assistance programs, racialization of, 161
social capital, in Sudanese diaspora, 240
social class/hierarchy, 141, 261
social networks, 46
social status, and Spanish language, 93
solidarity, of Occupy movement, 155
Something to Declare: Essays (Alvarez), 216–17
Soto, Hernándo de, 40
sovereignty, of Puerto Rico, 36
space, public, 254–55, 256–57, 262–67
Spanglish culture, 53–54
Spanish American War, 35–36
Spanish language, 93, 95; ethnic press, 46–47
Spectacular Rhetorics: Human Rights Visions, Recognitions, Feminisms (Hesford), 176
spirituality, 17, 22, 111, 123; in education, 115, 117–18, 276; in teaching and learning, 112–13, 124–27
Spiritual Side of Writing: Releasing the Learner's Whole Potential, The (Foehr and Schiller), 114
SPUR online writing exchange, 265–66
SRSC. *See* Sudanese Refugee Support Center
stakeholders, in inclusive dialogue, 227–28, 234
standardization, of education, 259–60
standards, academic, 121–22
stereotypes: immigrant, 63–64; Latina, 29–30
Stiglitz, Joseph, 157
storytelling: classroom, 223; of critical incidents, 235–38; of immigrant experience, 210–11; narrative writing as, 211–12
Strauss, Valerie, 34
students, 94; cross-racial interactions, 138–44; as language learners, 98–99; resistance from, 125–26; suburban-focused projects, 264–66
Suarez, Aida de, 180
sublime, Lyotard on, 16–17
suburbia, 20, 262; civic design of, 257–59; cultural context of, 282–83; education in, 259–60; narrow careerism in, 260–61; place-based projects in, 263–67; public space in, 256–57

Sudanese diaspora, 278; and community dialogue, 241–43; and institutional practices, 244–45; in Phoenix, 229–33, 234–41; public rhetoric on, 281–82; and work opportunities, 233–34
Sudanese Community Association in Arizona (SCAA), 234, 240
Sudanese Refugee Support Center (SRSC), 229–30; university partnership with, 229–31, 232–38
Sudanese Women's Empowerment Network, 240
Sudbury schools, 114
Support Our Law Enforcement and Safe Neighborhoods Act. *See* SB 1070
symbolicity, race in, 133–34
symbols, symbolism, 31; Juarez femicides, 183–85; of Mothers of the Plaza, 180; in Occupy Wall Street protest, 152–53
synecdoche, 31
systems, locating people in, 229, 238–41

Taino, 38
Take Our Jobs campaign (UFW), 62, 67, 70
"Talking across Difference: Rhetoric and the Search for Situated Knowledge" (Flower), 89
Tannen, Deborah, on argumentation, 83, 84
taste, 16, 17, 18
Taxpayer and Citizen Protection Act (Alabama), 33
teacher-research-team approach, 263
teaching, 126, 263; and national identity, 272–73; spiritual, 112–13
technoscience, 16
terministic screens, 64
terror, 18, 22
terrorism, and Islam, 19
tests, standardized, 259–60
Texas, second language learners, 98
"Textbook Argument: Definitions of Argument in Leading Composition Textbooks, A" (Knoblauch), 78
textbooks, composition, 78, 274–75
theory building, 240–41
Thompson, Becky, 212
tolerance, 19, 194, 205(n1); for ambiguity, 145–46; and participation, 21–22
traditional roles, 240
Trainor, Jennifer Seibel, 163
transcendence, 123, 124, 126, 141
transcontextualization, 177
translocalizm, 177

Treaty of Paris, 36
tres abuelitas: code-switching by, 48–51; Spanglish culture and, 53–54
Troester, Jennifer, 265
Troy, 32
Tsarnaev, Dzhokar, friends of, 10
Tucson: Gabrielle Giffords shooting, 76; Raza studies, 33, 34, 38
Tyagi, Sangeeta, 212

United Farm Workers (UFW), Take Our Jobs campaign, 62, 67, 70
United Nations, on holistic education, 116
United Nations Convention against Torture, 172
United States, 32; acquisition of Puerto Rico, 35–36; as Anglo-American nation, 39–40
US Congress, Colbert's testimony at, 67–71, 72
US Supreme Court, 43, 94; on Puerto Rico, 36, 37
unity, of Other, 39
universities: community partnerships, 227, 229–45, 248(n7), 281–82; service outreach, 228–29
University of Arizona, National Institute for Civil Discourse, 76–77
Unz, Ron, 96
Urban Justice League project, 264
Urgent Action campaigns, 174, 178–79

Vélez, Carmen, 33–34
videos, of critical incidents, 236–38
violence, 176
Virgin of Guadalupe, 185, 186
"Vision of Schools with Spirit, A" (Lantieri), 116
visions, "correct" vs. other, 15–16
Voces sin eco (Voices without Echo), 183–85, 188(n11)

Waldorf schools, 114
walls, 32
Washington, English-plus resolution in, 97
We Are the 53% blog, 161, 166, 168(n9), 168(n10); scapegoating in, 162, 163, 164
We Are the 99 Percent blog, 159, 278–79; posts on, 160–61; response to, 164–65
Westside High School (Omaha), Urban Justice League project, 264
West Side Story, stereotypes in, 29–30
whiny-baby topos, 163
White, Edward Douglas, 36, 37

Whiteclay (Nebr.), 265
Who Are We? The Challenges to America's National Identity (Huntington), 39
Wilder, Thornton, *Our Town*, 3–4, 23–24
Winterowd, Ross, 31
women, 249(n11); activism of, 8, 171, 172, 174–75, 179–81, 182–86, 188(n3), 188(n8), 188(n9), 279; in Sudanese diaspora, 239, 240, 244–45
Woodbury (Minn.), 259
World Holistic Education Forum, 114, 115
World Is Flat, The (Friedman), 55–56
worldview, and language, 132
World War I, 37, 45

writers: and cultural borders, 223; and mentors, 231–32
writing: achievement, 122–23; narrative, 211–12; online exchange, 265–66; phases of creativity, 121–22; spiritual pedagogy of, 124–27

Young, Iris Marion, 233
Young, Richard E., 84, 85–86; on teaching rhetorical ethos, 87–88

Zohar, Danah, 123–24
Zuccotti Park, 16, 151, 158; symbolism of, 152–53

www.ingramcontent.com/pod-product-compliance
Lightning Source LLC
Chambersburg PA
CBHW020355080526
44584CB00014B/1027